Out Since 14

A History of the 1/2nd Battalion
The Monmouthshire Regiment 1914-19

by John Dixon

Foreword by
Colonel John Chaston CBE, MC, TD, DL.

Old Bakehouse Publications

ISBN 1 874538 09 3

Published in the U.K. by
Old Bakehouse Publications
Church Street,
Abertillery, Gwent NP13 1EA
Telephone: 01495 212600 Fax: 01495 216222
http:/www.mediamaster.co.uk/oldbakebooks

Made and printed in the UK
by J.R. Davies (Printers) Ltd.

Contents

List of Photographs

BLACK AND WHITE

COLOUR PHOTOGRAPHS

I.   No Man's Land of Christmas, 1914

II. Mouse Trap Farm as it is today.

III. Trenches at Newfoundland Park. This trench may be one of those constructed by the Monmouths following the initial attack on Beaumont Hamel and Y-Ravine

IV. The junction of 88 Trench and 2nd Avenue on the outskirts of Auchonvillers.

V.   The St. Quentin Canal near Marcoing.

VI. Four unidentified casualties of the Monmouthshire Regiment in Gouzeaucourt New British Cemetery.

VII. The area defended by the battalion on 12th April, 1918.

VIII. The view the battalion had of the battlefield from La Crèche on 13th April, 1918.

IX. Outtersteene Ridge, the scene of the attack on 18th August, 1918.

List of Maps

Foreword

by

Colonel John Chaston CBE, MC, TD, DL.
Commanding Officer, 2nd Battalion, The Monmouthshire Regiment
(1950 - 1953)

My association with the 2nd Battalion, The Monmouthshire Regiment began in 1937. I served with it during the campaign through North West Europe in 1944 until I was wounded and evacuated in the attack on Goch in the Reichswald in February, 1945. I was later to command the Battalion as a Territorial after the Second World War. Later I was asked to become its Honorary Colonel. As someone who was very closely connected with the Battalion for over 30 years, it gives me much pleasure to write this foreword for Dr. John Dixon's new history of the 2nd Monmouths during the First World War.

The record of service of the 2nd Monmouths during the Great War was second to none. It landed in Le Havre on 7th November, 1914, and was one of only ten Territorial Battalions whose soldiers gained the 1914 Star. The Battalion was soon in the trenches and was the first Territorial Battalion to be entrusted with holding a battalion sector of the line. It recovered from difficult times following the Second Battle of Ypres in May, 1915 and became a remarkable Pioneer Battalion, often carrying out difficult and dangerous tasks under heavy fire, in support of the famous 29th Division. At the end of the Great War, it was the only Territorial Battalion to march into Germany.

In this book John Dixon has been able to describe what the life in the trenches was really like using soldiers' letters and personal accounts interwoven with the official diaries. It has taken much study, research and *'walking the ground'* in France and Belgium. The result is an invaluable record for those relatives who had young men serving with the 2nd Monmouths and for students of military history. Sadly, the 2nd Monmouths is no more, but this book should help us not to forget the courage, determination, and fine spirit shown by members of the Battalion during two World Wars and later in peacetime.

GWELL ANGAU NA GWARTH

A.J. CHASTON
Colonel

Newport,
Pembrokeshire,
August 2000

John Chaston

ix

Acknowledgements

It has been over fifteen years since I started researching the service of the Monmouthshire Regiment in the Great War. During this time I have co-authored two books on the regiment and this book represents the final chapter in this research. It is the product of the research undertaken over all those years though sometimes the research has been somewhat non-specific. Since that is the case, there are many people who have both influenced the research directly and indirectly and I have been very fortunate to have met some very interesting people who have helped to formulate the ideas this book contains. Of course, one of the earliest influences in my research into the Great War was Les Hughes with whom I completed the volume on the 1st Battalion the Monmouthshire Regiment. It was at Les' insistence that I began the research on the present work which has taken me to a new understanding of the conflict. Les is no longer with us but he is remembered fondly by those who knew him and I will always be grateful to him for being a patient and understanding mentor.

The completion of this work would have been very difficult without the help of many people. In the first instance Martin Everett, of the South Wales Borderers and Monmouthshire Regiment Museum, and his staff are to be thanked for placing the resources of the Museum at my disposal and I am particularly grateful to him for allowing me to use extracts from Lieut. Col. Bowen's notebooks and for access to the photographs taken by Captain Byrde in the trenches of 1915. These photographs were donated to the museum by Mr. Roger Byrde of Colyton in Devon and thanks are due to him for his generosity to the museum.

A very special thank-you goes to Patricia Gilbert-Chappell for proof reading the manuscript and for making observations and suggestions to improve the text.

Throughout the many years of research, my friends at the South Wales Branch of the Western Front Association have provided a sounding board for my ideas and I would especially like to say thanks to Peter Gorman, Gwyn Prescott, Viv John and Pam and Gareth Scourfield who are all probably thoroughly fed up of hearing about the Monmouthshire Regiment.

Thanks, also, to the many people over the years who have fed bits of information and photographs to me such as the Rev. A. Nunnerly, Gordon Hill, Simon Williams, Ian Griffiths and many others. Simon Williams also designed the dust jacket.

Thanks to the Imperial War Museum for allowing me to reproduce the photographs of the Monmouths repairing roads in 1918.

I owe a big thank-you to Ray Westlake for his encouragement over the years and for always doing his level best to help out with information or hunting down an unusual book for me when all other sources have failed.

Last, but by no means least, thanks to Francesca who has happily given up holidays in more exotic places to spend time tramping around the often wet and cold battlefields and has never complained - her navigation skills are second to none and have taken us, when needed, to some of the more obscure corners of France and Flanders.

John Dixon
October 2000

Chapter One

The Volunteer Movement

The history of the Monmouthshire Regiment as a whole can be traced back to 1859 when the first Volunteer Corps was founded with the blessings of the Government of the day. The history of volunteer service in the county goes back much further than that with various references to the men of Monmouth fighting for king and country way back into the days of the longbow. Indeed, Monmouthshire can boast the oldest Regiment of the British Army in the Royal Monmouthshire Royal Engineers (Militia) which was founded in 1539 and has been in continuous existence since that date. However, the foundations for the Volunteer Corps from which the Monmouthshire Regiment grew can be found around the turn of the 19th Century. At that time there was a continuous threat of invasion by the French and the first volunteer units were raised to combat that threat and offer some level of home defence. Throughout the country some 150,000 men were enrolled as volunteers but after the defeat of Napoleon at Waterloo in 1815 all the volunteers were stood down. That seemed to be the end of the 'irregulars' as far as the Government were concerned. However, there was a certain enthusiasm for a part time military life which went unrecognized by the Government of the day. Many of the volunteers remained together as unofficial Rifle Clubs and maintained a fairly high level of drill and musketry although they never attracted any support or financial help from the Government.

Early in the 1850s one such Rifle Club in Exeter offered its services to the Government and were accepted as the South Devon Rifle Corps. The seeds of the volunteer movement had been sown and more volunteer units became accepted by the Government during the next few years. However, it was several years before the Government completely changed its stance on the irregular volunteer soldiers. The reason behind this very cautious approach lay in the fact that many people in Government circles saw the volunteers as a positive danger to national security. These people were those who believed that the defence and strength of the realm could rest only with the Regular soldier because they were largely controlled by the landed gentry officer class. In the eyes of this group of people to place weapons in the hands of the volunteers and to actively encourage their training, was inviting a national catastrophe and the overthrow of the accepted order.

However, attitudes changed in 1859 with a further threat from France. There had been an attempt on the life of Emperor Napoleon III and the French believed that there was British involvement. Anti-British feeling ran so high that it was believed that an invasion of Britain was imminent. In fact, things went as far as some French generals boasting that they would cross the Channel and raise the Imperial flag above the Tower of London and then proceed to sack the city. Although this was little more than a boast, the sentiment it contained was not taken lightly by the British government. In May 1859 positive action was taken in the form of a letter to the Lords Lieutenant of the Counties instructing them to raise rifle corps within their counties thereby, once again, providing additional resources in the event of an invasion. In Monmouthshire, as in other counties, the order served merely to give existing rifle corps official recognition.

Monmouthshire had succeeded in raising two units in 1858, prior to any invasion threat, one at Chepstow and one at Pontypool. Once they had been officially accepted by the government of 1859 arguments over seniority were soon raised between the two corps; in fact the corps at Chepstow was the senior by just one day. Thus, following the order of May 1859, these corps became the first of the county's official volunteers and from them stems the history of the Monmouthshire Regiment. These two units became known as the 1st and 2nd Monmouthshire Rifle Volunteer Corps respectively. In the seniority of counties recorded as part of the Army List for that year, Monmouthshire was in 36th place.

Within a very short time of the issue of the order many companies (corps) were formed up and down the land. Each company was to be not less than 60 and no more than 100 strong. A company was to be commanded by a captain together with a lieutenant and an ensign. Where there were sufficient numbers a battalion was to be formed, the requirement being for eight companies or not less than five hundred men total strength. Each battalion would have a lieutenant-colonel, a major and the services of an adjutant. In Monmouthshire companies were raised at Monmouth, Newport, Abergavenny, Abertillery, Ebbw Vale, Pontypool and most of the other centres throughout the county. At this stage the companies were largely autonomous and it was soon realized that something would have to be done to rationalize the organization of the Volunteers. To simplify matters it was agreed that companies should be gathered together as battalions. Where the companies were from small areas, often densely populated industrial areas, they were to be collected together and a 'consolidated' battalion was to be formed. In the more rural areas where the companies may be spread over large areas the companies were to be collected together as 'administrative' battalions. In Monmouthshire both types of battalion were present; for example the companies of Ebbw Vale and Pontypool became part of the 2nd Consolidated Battalion Monmouthshire Rifle Volunteer Corps commanded by Colonel R.B. Roden, while the units from Blaenavon and Monmouth became part of the 2nd Administrative Battalion Monmouthshire Rifle Volunteer Corps. The reorganization was completed fairly rapidly and by 1861 the first rules of the Monmouthshire Volunteer Corps were set down. (For an example see Appendix 9). The first parade of the 2nd Consolidated Battalion took place on Whit Monday, 1861.

Although the battalions of the Volunteer Corps had gained official recognition, they had not been able to gain any official financial help at the same time. It was left to each county to organize its own finances. Initially, the financial situation was made easier by the threat of invasion by the French. Landowners and gentlefolk made generous donations and a variety of fund-raising events were held to support local volunteers. This method of providing for the volunteers often led to different companies having widely differing uniforms and accoutrements since this was dictated by local tastes and requirements. In some cases even the rifles were not standardized. From the outset the riflemen were expected to provide their own uniforms which often led to very 'irregular' dress within companies. Whilst the threat of invasion persisted money flowed into the volunteer units. As the threat of invasion receded the money gradually dried up as their sponsors took less and less interest and the very existence of the volunteer movement was threatened. However, all was not lost for in 1862, when the force numbered 162,681 members, a Royal Commission was appointed to examine the situation. On its findings the volunteer battalions received their first direct Government help in the form of a Capitation Grant. This award was not simply based on the establishment of a battalion but on the number of proficient riflemen in that battalion. To be classed as proficient it was necessary for a rifleman to be able to perform nine types of drill, thirty if a new recruit, so that a signed certificate could be issued by the commanding officer. It was also a requirement that a rifleman needed to complete a week in camp to be considered proficient. An example of the rules governing proficiency is given in Appendix 9. For each man in any unit being classed as proficient the battalion was allowed to claim the Capitation Grant of £1. This Grant could be increased by the sum of ten shillings (50p) providing a certain amount of ball shot could be fired as laid down by the regulations. There were variations in the Grant for sergeants, 35 shillings (£1.75), and officers, 50 shillings (£2.50). Therefore, the volunteers were placed on a reasonably firm financial footing which, in turn, allowed them to develop. Subsequent to this, on the 1st March, 1863, the parade strength quoted for the 2nd Consolidated Battalion the Monmouthshire Rifle Volunteer Corps during the celebrations for the wedding of the Prince of Wales and Princess Alexandra was given as 17 officers, 24 sergeants and 325 other ranks. With the establishment of the Capitation Grant it became possible throughout the rest of the county to make all battalions consolidated battalions by 1880. This necessitated a change of name for the battalions since the home base of two battalions was Pontypool, that is, one company of the Consolidated Battalion and one company of the Administrative Battalion. These two units of the town then formed part of the 2nd Battalion the Monmouthshire Rifle Volunteers. That name was relatively short lived because of the Army reforms that were introduced in that year. Under these reforms the regiments of the Regular Army lost their old regimental numbers and were given names, many of which are familiar today, which indicated some kind of territorial identity. Thus the 24th Regiment of Foot or 2nd Warwicks became known as the South Wales Borderers and its depot was moved to Brecon. In 1885 the three volunteer battalions of Monmouthshire became affiliated to the South Wales Borderers and, together with the Brecknockshire Volunteer Battalion, became known as the 1st,

2nd, 3rd, 4th Volunteer Battalions the South Wales Borderers. In 1887 the 2nd Volunteer Battalion of the South Wales Borderers suffered a serious blow when Col. Roden was assassinated whilst he was travelling in Corsica during March of that year. The command of the battalion was taken over by Col. T. Mitchell who proved to be a fitting replacement.

The organization put in place in 1885 was to continue for over 20 years. Before any further major reform was undertaken the country was plunged into the South African War of 1899 to 1902. The volunteer battalions throughout the country were eager to get involved for many saw it as a chance of proving themselves. At first the Government of the day was very reluctant to use the volunteers. The Government's standpoint was that it would cost as much to send a volunteer to South Africa as it would a Regular but the former would be nowhere near as efficient. This attitude changed in December 1899 after the Regular Army had suffered three heavy defeats in the space of one week. Reinforcements were needed for the Regular Regiments and where better to look than in the volunteer battalions affiliated to the Regular Regiments serving in the field. At this point orders were issued to the effect that a company should be raised from the Volunteer Battalions to reinforce their parent regiments in South Africa. There was, however, one problem with the system. The Government had no power to order the volunteers overseas because of the manner in which they had been raised, that is, they had been raised on the understanding that they were for home defence in the event of the threat of invasion. To overcome this problem the companies raised by the Volunteer Battalions were embodied in their parent regiments for the duration of one year, their place being taken by another similarly raised company on their return. In this way the volunteers of Monmouthshire became involved in the Boer War by providing a company to reinforce the 2nd South Wales Borderers in South Africa and, therefore, strictly speaking, the Monmouthshire Volunteers did not serve in South Africa as a unit at all since all the personnel were attached to the South Wales Borderers for their period of service overseas. In some areas in the country it was not easy to raise a company, and it has been said that the overall response of the Volunteers did little to improve themselves in the eyes of their critics. Be that as it may, there was no shortage of volunteers in the Volunteer Battalions of Monmouthshire and there the quota of one company was raised no fewer than three times during the conflict. The first Volunteer Company comprised men from the three Monmouthshire volunteer battalions of the South Wales Borderers. It arrived in South Africa to join the 2nd South Wales Borderers on 8th May, 1900 and two days later was in action when that battalion crossed the Zand River. During this action the only casualty was a man serving with the Volunteer Company. Among this first company of volunteers was Sgt. A. Search, of the 3rd VB South Wales Borderers, who was later mentioned in despatches for his conduct in the field. This company was replaced by a second which arrived in South Africa on 16th April, 1901. This company was commanded by Capt. H.L. Rosser and contained no less than 70 men from the 3rd VB South Wales Borderers since it had been difficult for the other battalions to provide sufficient volunteers to make up the quota at that time. However, when a third company was formed only 14 men from this battalion were attached as volunteers. The final company reached South Africa on 15th May, 1902 as the war was coming to a close. In all 131 men of the 3rd Volunteer Battalion the South Wales Borderers served in South Africa and although there had been a number of minor casualties only Sgt. R. Francis, who died of enteric fever, did not return.

The efforts of the men of the Volunteer Battalions of the South Wales Borderers did not go unrewarded for when the Battle Honour 'South Africa 1900 - 1902' was awarded to the Regular Army the Volunteer Battalions, quite justifiably, were also awarded the distinction, though at that stage they possessed no colours on which to bear such a reward.

Although the South African war had shown the value of the volunteer movement, it had also shown its weaknesses. The masses of men within the movement were recognized at last as a valuable resource, but a resource that was unwieldy and difficult to control. This was mainly because the highest level of organization within the volunteer movement was that of a brigade. A further problem was that of voluntary overseas service. Essentially the volunteers traditionally saw themselves as a home defence force and the rules governing their organization meant that no government could insist on their service overseas. These matters were tackled in the Army reforms of the Rt. Hon. R.W (later Lord) Haldane which were brought into effect in 1908.

The initial effect of the reorganization of the Volunteer Force was the setting up of fourteen infantry divisions each containing three brigades of four battalions. Further Volunteer units were attached to Regular Divisions as Army troops. Once again there was a reorganization at county level. In most cases the volunteer battalions maintained their associations with their parent regiments, the volunteer battalion taking on the next available number and carrying the suffix 'Territorial'. This was the birth of the Territorial Force. In some cases during the reform old affiliations were broken and new regiments of territorials were formed that had no Regular parent regiment. One of these 'new' regiments was the Monmouthshire Regiment formed from the four Volunteer Battalions of the South Wales Borderers and which contained three battalions itself. The new name gave the volunteers a much stronger county identity than had been possible under the old scheme. As might be expected such a change required internal reorganization. There was a considerable mixing of companies from within the Volunteer battalions before the Monmouthshire Regiment emerged in a form that was to be recognizable for over thirty years. This mixing of the companies is best shown by the following table which indicates the origins of the 2nd Battalion The Monmouthshire Regiment which came to be placed under the command of Colonel Joseph Bradney who had previously commanded the 3rd Volunteer Battalion the South Wales Borderers.

COMPANIES	PRE-1908 AFFILIATION	1908
Pontypool Garndiffaith Abercarn	3rd V.B. S.W.B.	
Pontypool Monmouth Blaenavon	4th V.B. S.W.B.	2nd Battalion the Monmouthshire Regt.
Llanhilleth Crumlin	New Companies	

5

For the ordinary volunteer in these new units there was still a set number of drills which needed to be performed though these were increased from nine to twenty with the advent of the Territorial Force. Also, Summer Camps were extended to fifteen days. The new Force seemed to be popular in Monmouthshire and in the years before the Great War the establishment of the 2nd Battalion the Monmouthshire Regiment never fell below 900 other ranks.

In the early part of 1909 the Territorials began to take on the trappings of Regulars. Following the successful formation of the Territorial Force an Army Order was issued which allowed the Territorial Regiments to carry Colours. However, the same Army Order stated that the cost of the Colours was not to be funded out of public monies. It fell to the commanding officers to cast around to find a benefactor who was willing to provide one or both of the Colours that were to be carried by the Regiments. The Colours were duly financed and were presented to the battalion by HM King Edward VII at Windsor Castle on the 19th June, 1909. On that auspicious day for the Battalion, the Colour Party consisted of the Lieutenants H.W.E. Bailey and E.D.T. Jenkins and Colour Sergeants Humphreys, Yew and Edwards. In 1911 Lieut. Col. Bradney retired and his position was taken by Lieut. Col. E.B. Cuthbertson a retired regular officer who had seen action with the Argyll and Sutherland Highlanders in the the South African War at the turn of the century.

Although the reorganization of the Territorials had been completed without too much difficulty, the question of overseas service remained a problem in these early days. This was simply because many of the men did not see their role as the Government would have wished. Essentially, the Territorials still saw their role as one of home defence. The Government, and Haldane in particular, wanted room for greater flexibility to allow themselves greater potential control over the masses of men enrolled in the Territorials. To attempt to gain this control the idea of Imperial Service was introduced. It was, strictly speaking, a compromise. It meant that Territorial soldiers were required to sign up for overseas service, those who did not want to sign up did not have to. Once a soldier had signed for Imperial Service his movements could be, in theory, controlled by the Government and he could   be directed anywhere in the world where a crisis threatening the Empire had developed. It was hoped that this system of two stage voluntary service would solve any problems in the event of a crisis. Initially the response was not good, for instance, in 1913 only 10% of the total Territorial Force had taken the 'pledge' as the obligation for Imperial Service was called by the soldiers of the Force. Perhaps, in a peace time Britain, that should have been expected but the poor response was fastened upon by the opponents of the Territorial Force to give them ammunition against Haldane's reforms. The Government needed the Territorials to provide men to release Regulars from outlying parts of the Empire and to provide reinforcements for the Regulars in the field should that become necessary. It seems that Haldane had had some awful premonition of the fate that was to befall Europe in the second decade of the 20th Century. However, the response to his call was not encouraging, though Haldane was satisfied with the Country's response to the Territorial Force.

Inevitably, there were criticisms from various factions of the political and military world. Some considered that a conscript army was the only way to provide a second line of trained men whilst others seemed to have been against any real second line believing that the Navy could handle just about anything. In

1914 one of the greatest critics of the Territorial Force was Lord Kitchener. He treated the Force with the utmost contempt, after all, had he not seen the performance of the French Territorials during the Franco-Prussian War of 1870? He did not understand, or, more likely, did not want to understand, the fundamental differences between the territorial systems of France and Britain. In France the Territorials were usually middle aged men who had already served as Regulars and Reservists before being relegated to the status of Territorials. Consequently, they did not provide the best material for warfare. The contempt shown to the British Territorial Force was unjustified on these grounds but, nonetheless it persisted and dominated much of the early thinking in the Great War. To some extent, this attitude aided the wanton wastage of the Territorial Force during 1914 and 1915. By the time the thinking had changed it was too late for many Territorial units - not least among these being the 1st and 3rd Battalions of the Monmouthshire Regiment.

It had not been an easy birth for the Territorial Force. Initially recruitment was good and during 1909 and 1910 the size of the Force swelled. Before the end of 1910 recruitment had fallen and the Force began to shrink by thousands allowing its opponents another chance to do all they could to see it abolished. However, the Territorial Force maintained its identity, even if sometimes there were problems in the numbers of men that could be officially classified as experienced. The political wrangling that surrounded the inception of the Territorial Force meant little to the soldiers. In many industrial areas, including the areas of north Monmouthshire, recruits were raised fairly readily as young men were drawn away from their workaday drudgery by a promise of Summer Camps. In this way by August 1914 there was a solid body of Territorial soldiers all over the country with a reasonably high level of training and discipline. By this time the 2nd Monmouths had companies at Pontypool, Abercarn, Blaenavon, Llanhilleth, Crumlin and Coleford with drill stations at Garndiffaith and Usk. Later developments were to prove the value of the training these men received as the British Regular Army fought itself to almost complete destruction in France and Flanders while Kitchener raised his 'New Armies'. Many Territorials were sent overseas before the end of 1914 and early 1915, to fill the gap while the New Armies were trained.

The fact that so many units had been welded into any sort of fighting force was a credit to both officers and men. There developed a spirit of comradeship which was unrivalled, since in civilian life these soldiers worked and lived together having common aims and ambitions and an understanding of their duty to both their Country and their County. Of course, compared to Regulars they were inexperienced and not highly trained but there was a strong regimental pride and that helped them to take their place alongside the Regulars in 1914 and 1915 as if they had always been meant to do just that. For four years the men of the Territorial Force went on proving this point and the men of Monmouthshire were not found wanting in their task.

Chapter Two

'We Are Soldiers Now'
(August to October 1914)

The Bank Holiday of August 1914 was very different to any that had gone before. Events in Europe following the assassination, on the 28th June, of the Archduke Ferdinand and his wife, Sophie the Duchess of Hohenberg, in Sarajevo had brought about growing tensions between the powers of the continent. One after another the countries of Europe began to take sides as old alliances were called upon and old differences were remembered. As the sabre rattling continued into July these countries started to mobilize their military machines - some more efficiently than others. By the end of July, Austria was at war with Serbia and one by one the powers of Europe were dragged into the conflict from which none escaped unscathed. On the 4th August, 1914, the Germans invaded Belgium and put their plan to conquer France, the 'Schlieffen Plan', into operation. Belgium's sovereignty had been guaranteed by Germany, France and Great Britain and although the Germans tried to mask their invasion with talk of pre-empting a French attack on them, it was not an acceptable excuse for the British government of the day. The British acted immediately and asked Germany for assurances of Belgium's neutrality. This was not forthcoming and as of 11 pm on the 4th August, 1914, a state of war existed between Great Britain and Germany. Finally, the power struggle that had been expected by many, and sought by some, was about to begin. It was to change the face of the continent for ever as the youth of the nations involved were thrown at each other with ever increasing ferocity that almost, but not quite, wore all the belligerents to a standstill.

The effects of this action on the people of the continent was much the same in all the nations ranged against each other. Everywhere people were excited at the prospect of going to war. There was enthusiasm for the conflict on a vast scale the like of which has never been seen in Europe before or since. In Britain, as soon as the news broke, young men rushed to enlist with the colours while the Regulars, Reservists and the Territorials were put on a war footing. The war fever was summed up by one member of the 2nd Battalion the Monmouthshire Regiment who was to comment later that:

> *A party of us coming home from Weston on (4th) August, 1914, (Tuesday) night, excitement everywhere in the train from Newport to Pontypool, people cheering on stations. We ask 'What's the noise?' Told the Territorials are called up, mobilized. England had declared war on Germany. A few of us are in the 'Terriers' and get excited. We went straight to the Drill Hall. Regimental Sergeant Major Askew says 'Come back at six in the morning'.*

and C.S.M. C.E. Edwards comments on the events of that day were in similar vein:

> *I was warned by the local police sergeant on Bank Holiday Tuesday to proceed at once to my Drill Hall, Crumlin, for embodiment. Most of the men of my company turned up, the few absentees being men away on holiday. I had no company officer, he being away on his honeymoon, having been married on the previous Saturday. The men were kept in the Drill Hall until about 11.30 pm when Col. Cuthbertson arrived and gave permission for all to return to their homes for the night, but to parade again at six next morning.*

Not everyone in the Battalion greeted the news with quite as much enthusiasm and L/Cpl. Cornelius Love even doubted the truth of the order to mobilize:

> *I was too busy and nearly thought it was leg pulling and did not report the first day and I had an extra night at home. But, next morning I had a very severe notice to present my body and full kit at Headquarters, Pontypool. I was there in quick time, knowing the penalty, and my old pals had been locked in and under guard all the previous night, so I stole one little march on them.*

At 36 years of age perhaps L/Cpl Love's attitude is more readily understood, but it is worth bearing in mind also that Love's company commander at this time was Capt. A.J.II. Bowen whom Love himself had commented upon by saying:

> *I often think that Capt. Bowen knew there was a World War near as he was very serious in everything he took part in, especially the training of men....*

Love was almost certainly taking a big chance by ignoring the order to report on the previous day!

Overall, throughout the county, there was an immediate response to the mobilization order and in very quick time all three battalions of the Monmouthshire Regiment were organized and ready for posting. In fact the men were 'All looking forward to a grand holiday, and hope it will last a month or two.' In 1914 the organization of the Territorial Force was such that the 2nd Monmouth, indeed all three battalions of the Regiment, formed part of the Welsh Border Brigade which in turn, together with the North and South Wales Brigades, formed the Welsh Division. Initially the 2nd Monmouths were ordered to their war station at Pembroke Dock. Today this may appear to be an odd military posting in times of war but it should be remembered that the main purpose of the Territorial Force was for home defence and in 1914 Pembroke Dock still had some considerable importance as a Royal Navy dockyard. Pte. C.P. Heare was to comment as follows on the move:

> At last we move off, marched to Crane St. station, some women crying but we are happy. One said, 'Good old Uncle Kaiser Bill, giving us a holiday'. Left Pontypool at 8 pm arrive Pembroke Dock into a field under canvas near Barracks of the South Wales Borderers about twenty to a tent but too tired to worry. Slept well.

Thus the majority of the battalion found itself in south west Wales but the conditions they encountered when they arrived in their camp were not as they would have hoped. It did not come as a surprise to any of them that they would have to live under canvas but it is fair to say that most of them expected to be fed. The rations were little more than Army biscuits ('like a large dog biscuit') and jam. To make matters worse, the morning after their arrival it rained heavily and not all the tents were as water tight as they might have been. To give the men some exercise on their first proper day on active service, the battalion was marched into adjacent fields, which were still to be harvested, and ordered to dig trenches amongst the potatoes and swedes. It seems that hunger got the better of many of the men before the day was over and the vegetables were chewed on raw to satisfy the appetite. To add to their discomfort the men's kit bags did not arrive and that meant that they could not wash or shave. One soldier remarked:

> No wash, no shave, no grub, nowhere to go and no one to look after us - we are soldiers now!

The soldiers were paid shortly after getting to Pembroke Dock but they were not allowed out to look for food or equipment. However, the coming of soldiers to the town had attracted many of the children to the camp and this seemed to present a possible solution to the men in need of food:

> We put ten shilling together in our tent, gave a boy at the gate half a sovereign for himself and a list for food - he never came back. People in a field near charging sixpence (2¹/2p) for a bucket of water, soap and a towel. A good thing happened for Pembroke Dock!

This sort of thing was not good for the morale of the men and after a few days there was a feeling amongst some that they wanted to get into town to settle a few scores. Fortunately, it did not come to that, for after four uncomfortable days the battalion was marched to the station where they entrained for Oswestry where it joined the rest of the Welsh Border Brigade. At Oswestry the serious training commenced. Considering that the date was still only the 10th August, a little over five full days since war had been declared, a remarkable job had been done in gathering together the units of the battalion that had been spread throughout the county. By the end of the 10th August after 'a wash and brush up' they were all feeling much better and eager to resume the roles as soldiers once again.

The absence of the kit bags in Pembroke Dock should have come as no surprise. For some reason the Transport Section, together with the kit bags, had set out from Pontypool on the 6th August but had been instructed to proceed to Oswestry in a series of relatively easy stages. By some chance L/Cpl. Love found himself in the Transport Section though he had little experience in the kind of work and even less knowledge of horses. He was to comment on his early days in the Transport Section as follows:

> I had never handled a horse before and most of our crew were the same so we had to pretend we did or get the officer loving us. After two days we had 45 horses etc. including 'Finns' big funeral horses and W.G. Bailey's heavy cart horses. Just imagine me getting these camels in trim for Transport work. And then, a move by road to Abergavenny, first bivouac and sleep under G.S. wagons. Early next morning to Hereford, after lassoo-ing several broncos. I complained several times on the trail that I knew nothing about horses and to cure me they put me with the worse pair we had in a G.S. and (I) had to walk every yard to see as no one stole the brake which was attached to the rear of the wagon.

As the Transport Section moved via Hereford and Ludlow it gathered more horses as it went. At Ludlow there was a chance for a bit of relaxation when the men were billeted in a pub and 'of course, we had to swill the dust down'. The journey was completed by the 11th August, 1914, a total of 110 miles in four days. For L/Cpl. Love, however, his stay with the Transport was short lived:

> First morning doctoring 'Finns' 17 hands funeral pair I hold one hoof up while the other was syringed and it only lasted a short while because the hoof I was trying to hold came down in a hurry and took the skin off my own leg from knee to ankle. I took a very severe dislike to horses and made an appeal to be returned to duty which, thank heaven, was granted and I commenced soldiering in earnest in a few days.

Whilst at Oswestry the training of the battalion took on a much more serious approach. It was the start of the period of preparation that would see the battalion fit to be sent overseas and no one escaped the rigours of route marches and battalion and company drills. It was in Oswestry, also, that:

> Col. Cuthbertson gave us a lecture and asks us to sign for foreign service, as Territorials are for home service only. One fellow asks our Colonel if we go would he come with us. The Colonel says certainly so we all sign for foreign service.

Shortly after the soldiers had signed what they knew as the 'pledge' the stay in Oswestry came to an end. On the 20th August when they entrained it was a very different battalion that left the town. Ten days of intensive training had started to turn the battalion of enthusiastic amateurs along the route of the professional soldier. They still had a lot to learn but they were all eager and willing and were improving very quickly under the experienced command of Colonel Cuthbertson.

After leaving Oswestry the battalion ended up in Northampton which, to many, was considered a second home. The people of the town were friendly and helpful and it was not wasted on the young men from Monmouthshire. Many of the men made life long friendships during this stay and a few who survived the war married sweethearts they had met in Northampton in 1914. The battalion, like many others, were billeted on the townsfolk, an arrangement which appears to have worked well. The soldiers were issued with their own rations but in many cases chose to add this to that of the household on which they were billeted and so everyone shared what was available. Pte. C.P. Heare states:

> We are billeted two or three to a house, two of us - the battalion tailor and I - are in W.F Wyman, 100, Greenwood Road, James End, Northampton. The language seems strange to us but the people are good ....The people put our food with theirs so we feed as at home.

During the stay in Northampton the military life became even tighter for the Territorials and the rules and regulations were adhered to or the consequences suffered. There were frequent attempts by some of the men to bend the rules especially to enjoy the pleasure of the local public houses but, on the whole, the message was received and the men accepted the discipline realising that they were now part of the preparation for war and there was no dampening of their enthusiasm to get to the war:

> We were still worrying that we may not get across the water in time to take part in the great game and to wear a medal showing we had done something to help our side.

The training continued and to some of the men it was a relatively enjoyable experience, after all they were comfortably billeted, well fed and getting plenty of exercise in the fresh air. This was echoed by one soldier who commented:

> What a great holiday, all the boys say it's the best war we ever been in - let's hope it lasts for forty (years).

At this stage of their service perhaps this comment is understandable, it would not take long for the real war in France to disillusion them and the officers realized that if the men were enjoying themselves at least morale was good and that was as important as any of the training for what was in store for them.

On the 29th September their stay in Northampton ended unceremoniously when they were ordered to move to East Anglia, to Grundisburgh a small village a few miles north east of Ipswich. In the months since the war had started there had been substantial rumour, and expectation, that the Germans would attempt to invade the British Isles by way of the east coast. To prepare for what seemed to be an eventuality, a system of defences was prepared in East Anglia and it was to take part in this defensive work that the 2nd Monmouths had been moved. There was but little time for the battalion to become involved in trench digging for on the night of the 30th September:

> We are all down to sleep that night when a telegram arrives. Our Sgt. opens it: 'Congratulations, your battalion are accepted for active service, orders following'. Down came our Col. and Adjutant Rolls, laughing - how excited we all are.

After a very brief stay in East Anglia it was back to Northampton but no one really minded since now the preparations were for the real thing. The battalion history comments as follows:

To be selected as one of the first Territorial battalions to reinforce the hard tried remnants of the original Expeditionary Force was a signal honour, which is eloquent of the high state of efficiency to which Colonel Cuthbertson had brought to the 2nd Monmouthshires.

It was, indeed, an honour, since many other Territorial units had months of training in front of them before they would be accepted to take their place in the front line in France.

The journey to the front line did not start immediately for the battalion was to spend a month in Northampton finalizing their training and getting used to the new kit issued to them in the run up to embarkation. The return to Northampton was an unexpected pleasure to the Monmouths and :

How pleased the people are to see us again, back to our same billets, no parading only fitting for France. Webbing, equipment, what a game trying to put it together. Short rifles and long bayonets, one hundred rounds of ammunition.

and another was to say:

After getting back to our training Depot, it was all hurry and scurry, new equipment new this new everything. We had no idea if they were upside down or not.

Now that the battalion was getting ready for overseas service some of the men were allowed home to see their families - in some cases for the last time - some men took it upon themselves to go anyway and although their actions may be understandable, they were inexcusable and these men suffered appropriate battalion punishment on thier return - Col. Cuthbertson was going to maintain discipline and his attention to the details of their preparation undoubtedly made the battalion stronger. It was, also, an emotional time for the new friends in Northampton and L/Cpl. Love was to write:

We started paying visits and saying goodbye to people we hadn't met before because everyone in Northampton were our friends and we still think of them.

But, soon enough it was time to leave, all equipment had been issued, all home leave finished and all the goodbyes in Northampton said:

.... a happier lot of men and boys never left England and the people of Northampton gave us a new life with their good wishes and kind thoughts to everyone..... On Friday 5th November we left Northampton, women crying, some fainting, a real parting this time, all Northampton turned out to see us off.

The first part of the 2nd Monmouths involvement in the Great War had ended. No one concerned can have had any idea of what the future held for them and they left for the battlefields of France in good spirits to take part in what one soldier described as 'the game across the water'.

Chapter Three

'How Strange to Sleep on Straw'
(November 1914 to March 1915)

The battalion embarked for its overseas adventure on the troop ship Manchester Importer from Southampton on the evening of 5th November 1914 - it was not the last of the fireworks for them, in the following four years of warfare few of those who climbed the gangway and stowed their kit were to return with the battalion. But in the darkness of the autumn evening of 1914 the adventure was still keen in the breasts of the young men making up the battalion. Few, if any, had been far outside the boundaries of their own county and yet here they were, like thousands of young men up and down the country, starting out on a task that was bigger than had been set any generation of soldiers before them - and probably since. In all 30 officers and 984 other ranks departed for France and in the words of L/Cpl. Cornelius Love:

> We arrived at Southampton and had to wait for the Manchester Importer a good time before the order was given to trot up the gangway and get aboard. The water was like a skating rink, hardly a move on it, and in what time we had learnt to fit our equipment and felt more comfortable afterwards.

In November, 1914, the war was but three months old and, although there had been heavy casualties, it was still thought to be a new and exciting experience in which so many of the young men wanted to be part. There can be no denying that the men of the 2nd Monmouths were no different and the general feeling was a hope that the war would not be finished before they got off at Le Havre. This kind of enthusiasm possibly showed great faith in their own ability as soldiers but more likely it showed, in a general sense, the complete lack of understanding amongst both the military and civilian population at home. The training that the battalion had undergone in the last three months had prepared them for something but it can scarcely have prepared them for the rigours of the Western Front. However, the commanders had prepared them as best they could, the rest would need to be learned as they went along, lessons would need to be learned quickly where survival depended on them.

Like many before, and many more after them, the 2nd Monmouths spent their first night in France under canvas in a camp on the hills above Le Havre. The camp was probably at St. Adresse and was used by successive units passing to the Western Front through Le Havre. L/Cpl. Love was to comment:

> We were not sorry when we stepped off at Le Havre next day and to know we had got there before the game finished. Up the hill to a camp where many others had been before and everything pointed to a war going on for all (to see). We had very little rest, we found time to adjourn to an estaminet and sample the wine.

Pte. Heare was to comment on his arrival in a similar vein:

> The battalion march off, no great welcome like the earlier troops, very quiet. The strange thing is we have to march on the right hand side of the road. We go up a steep hill, then under canvas. One fellow wants to know if the Germans could see our camp. Tea is ready which is very welcome. Too excited to rest, all go down to Le Havre, got lost but arrived back safe at last.

It was an exciting time and the soldiers took advantage of their first evening in France for visits to *estaminets* and so forth - they knew it would be a short halt before moving towards more serious things - they knew, also, that no matter how much fun they had or how excited they became that ultimately they were not in France for a holiday. The following morning the battalion was paraded before leaving St. Adresse. Each member of the battalion was issued with a tin of corned beef, six large biscuits and tea and sugar in a tin. The men were told that this was their 'iron rations'. Lieut. Col. Cuthbertson explained to the battalion that these rations could only be used with the specific orders from an officer and then only after two days without food. To hammer home the importance of the iron rations the Colonel explained that use of the ration under any other circumstances was punishable by court martial and field punishment which would include the loss of pay. That made the soldiers realize the importance of the meagre 'iron rations' and one was to comment: 'We all looked upon this ration as a precious thing.'

The next step for the 2nd Monmouths was their first train ride in France when they were introduced to the *'Hommes 40, Chevaux 8'* type of transport and were herded into the trucks like so much cattle. It was an uncomfortable form of transport, barely room to move, no room to sit down or anything to sit on, no hope of stretching aching muscles and it was expected that the men of the battalion would endure this as the train moved slowly northwards from Le Havre and ever nearer the front line. Not all were so uncomfortable, however, and Pte. Heare was to report, with some pleasure:

> I got in a truck with bicycles and horse rugs. I have my longest sleep on record in this truck, about fifteen hours. Considering the excitement of the last week no wonder I slept.

As they passed through the French countryside at little more than a walking pace the truth of their situation slowly dawned upon them, perhaps reinforced by the several hospital trains they saw in the area of Calais carrying the wounded away from the front. There was no doubt in their minds now that 'the game' had started and it made the party more pensive and some sources suggest that this sight stopped some of the joking amongst the men. Perhaps, two days in a cattle truck helped to dampen the mood further for that was the length of time it took them to travel from Le Havre to St. Omer, a short distance quickly covered in peacetime. L/Cpl. Love commented:

> We got near St. Omer and detrained or rather fell out because when the final stage was reached they always gave an extra brake and bump so that all hands by the door would fall out. The others would easily stir thinking it was a collision.

Whether or not that was a deliberate action the men were grateful to get out and stretch their legs and the march to billets in Wizerne was something of a relief. Even then things were not completely trouble free. Colonel Cuthbertson had sent on a billeting party to sort out accommodation for the battalion on its arrival in town. It was not successful for the reason best explained by Pte. Heare:

> An officer picks four of us with bicycles to go with him to get billets. We move off, get lost, by luck got to Wizerne. Not one of us able to speak French. When the battalion arrives we got no billets, the Colonel is wild. At last billets are found. I sleep in a barn with the signallers and cyclists. How strange to sleep in straw, rats and straw sticking in your everywhere.

It was their first experience of makeshift billets and not all the battalion found quarters the same as Pte. Heare. Some were billeted in a local school and, where possible, some were billeted upon the local people. The locals were familiar with soldiers by that stage of the war and some of the Monmouths noted that their billets had been used by many others passing through the area to the line. Probably it did not occur to them at this stage of their experience to wonder how many had passed through on their way back from the line. Whilst at Wizerne military discipline was tightened further as Colonel Cuthbertson left no one in any doubt how his wishes were to be carried out and how the battalion would be run. As a regular officer he understood, perhaps more than many in the battalion, the rigours that may be facing his men and his approach was to be direct and no nonsense to ensure his men were as ready as they could be. This was made more immediate for at Wizerne the guns could be heard regularly and for the first time the 2nd Monmouths probably felt they were truly on active service. During their week long stay in Wizerne there was strenuous training in preparation for their removal to the line. The training was of great importance and the battalion was placed under the direct control of Colonel A. A. Chichester who was C.O. Reserve Troops and no one was ready for the front without his say so. Of course, the pressures of the time meant that new battalions arriving in France were considered more or less ready for action and the training under the experienced Col. Chichester was to finish off the process started at home months before.

Whilst the battalion was finishing its training, the news arrived that Lord Roberts VC, known as 'Bobs' to the soldiers, had died whilst on active service. A party of the 2nd Monmouths were chosen to accompany the coffin to London - or so they thought. There was in this honour an indication of the readiness of the battalion for general duty but the honour was not great enough to carry the small party to London. In spite of the expectation of a short trip home the men chosen, accompanied 'Bobs' remains to the railway station at St. Omer and there their escort duties ended.

The training continued and in an old quarry near Wizerne some of the battalion were to get to fire their Short, Magazine, Lee Enfield (SMLE) rifle for the first time. There had been little time to practice musketry since the issue of these rifles shortly before their departure from England and now, with front line duty imminent, it can be easily imagined that the training was taken very seriously indeed. The targets on these practise ranges were described as 'old tins and jam pots' but it helped everyone, particularly those who had been with the battalion a short time, familiarize themselves with their rifle. After a week at Wizerne the battalion was considered ready for moving up towards the line and their move took them through Hazebrouck and Bailleul.

On the way to Hazebrouck the battalion met a battery of the Royal Field Artillery coming out of the line for a rest. It was clear to all that the battery had been in action but with the cockiness that often accompanied new arrivals to the front some of the battalion questioned the artillery men eagerly:

> *We were lucky to get them to answer as they were jogging along, one good chap promised, through pulling his leg, about what time the teams would kick off (and) that we would get all the information we required when we got on to the field and there would be no entry fee, and not a smile, a good reason why; he had been there and a very small percentage of his battery accompanied him back.*

At this time the British army had been engaged in a bitter struggle which had halted the Germans' advance through Belgium but had so depleted their own ranks that the Territorials, such as the 2nd Monmouths, were rushed to France to fill the gaps. This battle was to be known as the 1st Battle of Ypres and during the month that it was fought the pre-war Regular army all but ceased to exist. There was little enough reason for the artillery man to smile but the men of the battalion were not aware of the terrible things that had been happening or that they were heading in the general direction of that awfulness. They were also unaware of the importance of the part they were to play in the coming months as they filled the gap caused by the loss of the Regulars until such a time as the new volunteer army could be raised.

Pte. Heare was to be one of the billeting party for the second time as the battalion moved to Bailleul and was to comment:

> *French seems a hard language. On billeting party again. Six of us and an officer arrive at Bailleul, the prettiest town I ever saw. The civilians were good to us here and give the billeting party chips, eggs and coffee.*

The people of Bailleul had little chance to be good to the 2nd Monmouths for the following day they were off again. The marching between towns and the short rests were beginning to have an effect on the soldiers. One soldier was to comment on the march from Hazebrouck to Bailleul as follows:

> *I will say it was the hardest march we had done up to that date, the stone setts on the main roads were worn down on the corners and into these (we slipped) and me and Caffrey found the deepest ones, poor Caffrey.... his feet were raw and bleeding and a few others, we left them behind and went to Bailleul.*

The soldier was describing the effect of the *pavé* roads of France upon the feet of the British soldier. The *pavé* plagued the newcomers to France but like many more severe hardships it was something that the troops got used to. After two or three days marching under these conditions there can be little doubt that arriving at billets near Le Bizet, in the Armentieres sector of the front, was greeted with some relief although the billets were not very good. But tired soldiers sleep anywhere and the Monmouths were no different as they settled down on the night of the 20th November in a factory in Le Bizet which has been described as 'not very appetizing'.

On their arrival in Le Bizet they came under the command of the G.O.C. 12th Infantry Brigade, Brigadier General F. G. Anley, of the 4th Division. On the following morning the battalion was addressed by Brig. Gen. Anley who set out the ground rules for the battalion by saying that they should all feel very proud to be joining the 12th Brigade and also letting them know that none of them would let him down. Then the battalion began preparation for trench duty. Training of new battalions in the line was usually achieved on a company by company basis with the company concerned being attached to an experienced front line unit for a couple of days or so to get some kind of feel for trench life and its duties and rigours. In the case of the 2nd Monmouths, C Company was attached to the 2nd Lancashire Fusiliers and D Company were attached to the 2nd Essex Regiment on the night of the 21st November and were relieved by A and B companies on the 23rd November. It is by virtue of the two companies in the line on the 21st and 22nd November that the Monmouths were amongst that select band of Territorials who were entitled to wear the bar (sometimes known as the Mons Clasp) on their 1914 Stars when they were issued at a much later date. (See Appendix 7 for details). That was all for the future for the men going into the line on that November night. As can be imagined the news of the trench training was greeted with some excitement - at last the Mons were to get a crack at the Germans. For Pte. Heare there was only disappointment for he was ordered to the orderly room only minutes before departing to the trenches:

> *RSM Noble, a soldier of discipline but a good sort, told me to take off my kit, put belt and bayonet on and get on my bicycle and take a message at once to Division Headquarters at Nieppe. To say I am disappointed is putting it mild. I want to go in the trenches and be a soldier but have to go to Nieppe.*

Cornelius Love, recently promoted to corporal, gave an account of the Monmouths' first visit to the trenches:

> *As there was no communication trenches we had to get to our bit of cover over ploughed fields and we lost our first chum, named Crowley. Well we met some real soldiers in the 2nd Lancashire Fusiliers who gave us a fine welcome and began to learn us what we needed, such as building a bit of cover if only to keep the frost from biting the toes off us.*

The last comment is important since it should be remembered that this was now a winter campaign and that all soldiers of the warring nations were out in the open in the harsh weather of a northern European winter and keeping warm and dry was to take on as great an importance as defeating the enemy for the front line units. Two days later when the companies were relieved Pte. Heare witnessed their return:

> *When the companies come out they look terrible. No shave or wash, all mud up to their waist - an awful sight - all dead beat. Our first casualty, named Crowley. It sent a shiver through all of us, it seems war now. I feel ashamed to look at the boys in this state and I am clean.*

The alternation of the companies continued every two or three days allowing the men to adjust to their new environment. The companies out of the line were kept busy, though the army liked to call it rest, by forming work details for trench construction and repair during the night. One such work party came under the command of 2nd Lieut. Christopher Comely who described the work carried out:

> *We were guided to our work on the 21st November by a captain of the Essex Regiment. The bit of trench allotted to my platoon, No.8, was just behind our front line and about 100 yards from the Boche. We arrive just before dark and on being told we were not in view climbed over the top. After setting out two or three pairs of men to dig, our officer guide received a bullet in the elbow and had to leave us. Fairly active sniping was kept up by the enemy, so we waited till darkness hid us. This was our first time under fire, although new to the game the men behaved like old soldiers. The work was completed to the tune of bullets hitting the pollard withies under which the trench was made.*

The introduction to trench warfare was relatively gentle as the battle to the north, around the town of Ypres came to a halt. Gradually they became aware of the rules of survival, the need for cover, the need to keep movement to a minimum and the way to get on with their allotted tasks without coming into undue danger. The Lancashire Fusiliers took good care of the 2nd Monmouths showing them how to prepare their meals under trench conditions and by helping out with such duties as sentry duty to give the new men a better chance to acclimatize - presumably the Essex Regiment looked after their contingent of Monmouths in much the same way. It was a sobering thought to many of the Monmouths to realize that, as the light covering of snow in front of the trenches melted, the many low mounds in front of them were the last resting places of the comrades of their instructors who had fallen in the earlier fighting. The eagerness to learn nearly got the better of Cpl. Love in these early days in the trenches:

> *Whilst talking my head went a bit high for safety and a sniper took the skin off the bridge of my nose, I had not fired a shot at the enemy before this and thought there was no need to before the attack came off.... After the sniper nearly got me my blood was up and I spent the whole of my spare time at the same game trying to spot the fellow that aimed at me.*

At least he had been lucky enough to survive to tell the tale. Some of his comrades were less fortunate during the initial trench training period and the battalion had several casualties.

The training period came to an end quite quickly and on the 2nd December, 1914, the battalion relieved the 2nd Essex Regiment and took over 1100 yards (1000 metres) in front of Le Gheer in trenches between the railway and the Warnave stream some three miles to the north east of Armentieres near the border of France and Belgium. The routine of trench life was arranged with four days in the front line and four days at rest at Le Bizet from where working parties were sent out at night. The Monmouths soon became used to their duties as the days and nights of the early winter passed by. The trenches were in a fairly poor condition with mud and slush resulting from the recent thaw and large parts of the day were spent in keeping the trenches maintained. Wiring parties, usually sent out at night, soon learned to stay still when the Germans put up flares to light No Man's Land and they soon became used to the bursts of machine gun and rifle fire that accompanied these flares. During the first tour of the line Cpl. A.E. Pinchin won the D.C.M. for attempting to rescue one of his comrades whilst under fire and in so doing is reputed to be the first Territorial soldier to win the decoration in the field. His gallantry was emulated shortly afterwards by Pte. E. Jones who was also to be awarded the D.C.M.. It was an auspicious start for the battalion and the deeds of these two soldiers shows that the general morale in the battalion was good in spite of the bad weather they were experiencing in that winter of 1914. Indeed the weather had been so severe in their first month of trench duty that it had hospitalized more of the battalion than had the Germans. However, the battalion stuck to their tasks and began to earn the respect of the Regulars of the 12th Brigade. There was even the regular joke between themselves and the Essex Regiment:

> When the 2nd Essex come out of the trenches and the 2nd Mons are going up to relieve them the Essex men shout 'Last time in Mons?' The 2nd Mons answer 'Last time in Essex - war over before we come out'.

Banter of this type was probably a good thing as it helped to cement the camaraderie between the units. At this time it was perhaps of greater significance since the cry of 'Over by Christmas' was unlikely to be fulfilled and most of those who were involved in the conflict had been aware of that for some months at least. As Christmas 1914 approached the men in the front line were under no illusions. They were, in many cases, thinking of their homes and loved ones and this was more likely to have been the case for the Territorials most of whom had never been away from home at this time of year. Many of the veterans of the battalion would not have been expecting to see overseas service when they joined the battalion in the years before the war and so to be away for Christmas was quite an event. Of course, the families at home did all they could to make things easier for their soldier at the front line and there was no shortage of Christmas cards and parcels of food sent to the front. In a letter, dated the 20th December, 1914 Captain Bowen was to write his thanks to his parents at home in Usk:

> I have just received the parcels from Stevens containing the cakes and chocolate for which I am very much obliged. We are just going back to the

*trenches this evening for our turn which finishes on Xmas night. The last
one finished on the 15th so that the letters and gifts gave me a decent
present on coming out.*

Of course, for this the first Christmas of the war, there was an official Christmas
present made possible when Princess Mary sent a box containing cigarettes or
tobacco and chocolate to each and every serving soldier. These boxes were to
become treasured possessions for many of the men, some were even sent home,
unopened, to the care of relatives. The gift was much appreciated but in some
cases it was likely to have stirred longings for home at this special time of the
year. At a more local level a lady by the name of Maud Graham of Hilston Park,
Monmouth, was responsible for organizing the despatch of 'comforts' to the
2nd Monmouths for that first Christmas of the War. These included chocolates,
cigarettes, playing cards and an assortment of clothing. For the 2nd Monmouths
Christmas Day was to be spent in the front line. Their tour had been extended and
by that order the battalion was to take part in one of the most extraordinary events
of the entire war. Of course, the news of their extended tour of duty was greeted
with some disappointment as Cpl. Love was to comment:

> *.....some arrangement was made so that we should hold on for six days in the
> front line so that those that were out may have a good beano or a little extra
> to celebrate the work they had done and the hardships they had been through.
> Well, you should have heard what we called them - it was not fit for print or
> to go on their programme.*

Whilst the judgement may be harsh the sentiment is understandable. The
Regulars of the Brigade had certainly seen plenty of action leading up to
Christmas and although the 2nd Monmouths could feel aggrieved at having
their tour extended they were amongst the freshest troops in the Division and as
such there was probably some method in the decision to rest some battalions for
longer over the Christmas period than may otherwise have been possible.

As Christmas Day dawned there was a silence across the trenches. At first the
soldiers on both sides of No Man's Land were glad that there was a stillness and
no sound of artillery and rifle fire along the front. With that stillness began a day
that was described by one Monmouth as 'one of the greatest experiences of my
life'. The occasion was not lost on the men and there are many records of the
following hours. The records show that the Germans began showing themselves
and in various parts of the line soldiers remember them singing Christmas carols
including one known to all - Silent Night or *Stille Nacht* as it was known to the
Germans. Pte. Philip Morgan recorded the following:

> *Early morning Christmas Day I heard the Germans singing carols. There
> was no firing for a while and then Colonel Cuthbertson shouted across to
> them and a truce was agreed for one day but we were advised to keep our
> heads down. Eventually we went out and met the Germans in the middle of
> No Man's Land.*

Pte. Marcus Baldwin, who was later commissioned, was to comment on the event
in a letter to his sister in Ross-on-Wye:

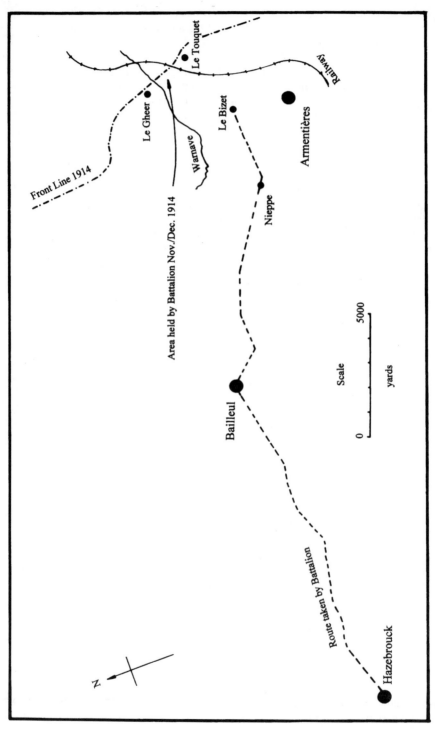

The First Winter in France.

The German fire stopped and in the silence a voice came to our ears. It was one of the 2nd Monmouthshires singing 'Has anyone seen a German band?' Through Christmas Day our firing was very quiet and I think every one of the boys thought of the loved ones at home.

Pte. B. Way was to write as follows of his experiences:

The Germans and ourselves sat in full view of each other, and we threw packets of tobacco etc. into their trenches but we did not get together generally.

It would appear that this last comment was especially for the home market since accounts by other members of the battalion tend not to support this. Pte. C. Hunter met a German who was able to speak English and so he was able to have a long conversation with him:

He told me he wished it was all over as he had had enough of it. He was a medical student who had been in England for two years and in France, and was coming to England last year only for the war. He asked me what we were at war for, and I told him he had better ask 'Willum'. He told me he had as many friends in England and France as he had in Germany and asked why should he be fighting his friends and his friends fighting him. He would much rather be having a game of football than this. He was only 20 years of age, but there was a lot of old men with them, and they were asking him too many questions to ask me. The first man I came to was an old man, and when we shook hands I thought he was not going to let my hand go. The tears came rolling down his cheeks and I felt sorry for him as he was old and wanted to go home.

Further evidence of contact with the enemy is given, though somewhat tersely, by Pte. Heare:

The Germans came out to fraternize. The 2nd Mons do the same, exchanging souvenirs of all sorts.

The account of Cpl. Love is fuller and perhaps as an older man he was a little cautious over the Germans' motives when he reported:

While we were in the line over Xmas we had a strange experience. The enemy and our men commenced shouting to one another across No Man's Land which was about 150 yards between the trenches. It came to offering cigarettes and bully to one another as souvenirs, then all heads were showing above the parapet, then a couple of bold ones went out and met the enemy to exchange any small present. There were several dead lying about and we took it as a kind of armistice to clear the dead away or bury (them) and enough time was given for this but it was not carried out. Instead the enemy was collecting rifles and bayonets from the dead and carrying them to the front line. Of course it was some time before our officer realized what was happening and orders were that all NCO's stand to in the line.

It appears that at one stage during the day there was a feeling amongst some of the men in the trenches that there was to be a 'big surrender' and this would have been fuelled, at least in part, by the conversations that men such as Pte. Hunter had with genuinely unhappy German troops. Perhaps the Germans had taken similar stories back to their own front line and likewise believed that some kind of major cease fire was imminent. However, this was not to be and before the afternoon of Christmas Day had passed any trust or belief that the 2nd Monmouths had in the Germans disappeared after two incidents which had very sad consequences for the battalion.

The informal truce had lasted a number of hours and there had been, without question, some contact between the opposing sides. Sergeant Frank Collins was returning to his own line when a shot rang out from the German side and broke the peace of Christmas Day. Cpl. Love recorded the events follows:

> One of our Company sergeants was spotted in No Man's Land. I honestly think it was a maniac in the enemy reserve trench who fired at and hit him in the breast. I could see he was hit bad as he staggered to where I was standing and just managed to reach our wire, I helped him in and commenced to bandage and treat the wound where the bullet entered but when I turned him over it was hopeless as the bullet had done all the damage, possibly to his lung, we did our best and sent him on a stretcher to the MO. He did not live long and we did not see him again.

It was a sad end to the truce and managed to change attitudes in an instant. Sgt. Jones who had been one of the first men to go to meet the Germans waving a newspaper as a flag of truce from the top of his rifle was report to his local newspaper that:

> I took some tobacco and jam to the Germans. But never no more. Another sergeant, a pal of mine from Pontypool, did the same, but when he was coming back to the trench they shot him through the back and killed him. He fell down and said 'My God, I'm done.' They are dirty cowards, after giving them tobacco.

The sentiment was echoed by others who recorded the day and it is a fact that the death of the 39 year old postman from Monmouth, not Pontypool as Sgt. Jones thought, was seized upon by the press of the day as an example of the dastardly behaviour of the enemy. It is recorded that Sgt. Collins was killed in action but that action was the taking of a Christmas present to the enemy! Whilst it may seem a wilful act to have shot the sergeant in that manner it must be remembered that there was a war on and perhaps of greater relevance to the incident is the story that Sgt. Collins had made an off the cuff comment on the parentage of a particular German soldier. Perhaps that soldier had taken offence and had exacted his own form of justice and in so doing had ended the Christmas truce for the Monmouths. As if this incident was not bad enough the battalion had another casualty shortly after the death of Sgt. Collins. Pte. Ernest Palfry, aged 21, had been engaged on a burial detail during the truce and as he was returning to his line he was shot in the back of the head and died instantly. All along this part of the line the Germans waved the Monmouths back into their trenches and the truce came to an abrupt end. The incidents had clearly caused the German command some embarrassment for later in the day an apology was sent to Colonel Cuthbertson. The official line adopted in the battalion War Diary was vague to say the least:

> *On Xmas Day practically nothing took place on either side by mutual arrangement. The opportunity was made use of to ascertain what German regiment opposed us.*

Of course, it would seem that the last comment is a clear reference to the fraternization that took place during the day.

The informal truce was condemned in no uncertain terms by senior officers who saw any form of fraternization with the enemy as tantamount to treason. Brig. Gen. Anley was 'wild' about it and his attitude was not dissimilar to those senior staff officers throughout the British army sector of the front. General Smith-Dorrien was to record his disappointment at the event describing what he saw as apathy and even went as far as calling for the names of the officers involved in the truce with a view to taking disciplinary action. The truce was not seen as the way to win the war and a continued offensive spirit was called for. Whilst this may have been true the short break in the fighting did little long term harm to the prosecution of the war and the events that occurred to the 2nd Monmouths served only to banish any general feeling of friendliness towards the Germans. The two Monmouths killed during the truce were buried later that day at Calvaire Military Cemetery, Ploegsteert where they lie today amongst their comrades from both the Monmouth and Essex Regiments. It is of some interest to note that Cpl. Love who had attended to Sgt. Collins immediately after he was wounded was promoted to sergeant immediately and that night took over the duties of a 'full blown sergeant'.

During the spell out of the line at the end of December, 1914 the battalion was treated to a bath at the Divisional baths which were in a local brewery. The men bathed in large beer vats a dozen at a time whilst their clothes were cleaned and disinfected to get rid of lice and so forth. Men bathed first and the NCO's after the men had finished.

> *Being a full blown sergeant I had to bathe last to see the men catered for first and while in the vat the order came to stand to immediately. It was no wonder a few of us were on parade with no more than Adam had on in the Garden of Eden but luck came my way and I scrabbled into my clothes without a shirt as they had to be drawn from a different part of the brewery. I should think they ought to be able to brew good beer there since the war! When we got outside the order was to line the street and who went by but His Majesty the King. I hope he thought well of the Mons because it was the best we could do straight from our bath, several of us had to go back to swill the soap off and get a shirt on.*

Sgt. F. E. Weller of Talywain, was to comment in a similar vein:

> *Whilst they were in every stage of dressing and undressing the word to stand to attention was passed along and directly afterwards the King walked by and acknowledged the men's greetings.*

Neither point out that the King was accompanied by the Prince of Wales and Field Marshal Sir John French. It was without doubt the most impromptu inspection of his troops the King had carried out and by far the least formal that the embarrassed men of the 2nd Mons had ever to endure.

There was one more spell in the trenches before the end of 1914 and that was to be over the New Year period. There was no cessation of hostilities to usher in 1915 for:

> On New Years Eve the Germans marked the arrival of the New Year by firing several volleys over our heads.

Again the tour was not a happy one and once again a sniper struck at the battalion and caused the death of 2nd Lieut. John Paton the first officer casualty the battalion received. He was just 19 years of age and although his military career had only begun a short time previously he had already been mentioned in dispatches. One of his men was to say of him:

> He wouldn't ask you to take a risk that he wouldn't take himself. If there was anything to be done he'd do it. He was a champion officer.

The battalion was to continue with their share of trench duty and was to see more than its fair share of mud and cold weather. Early January, 1915 saw them on the move to the area in front of Le Touquet where they set about making their trenches 'more comfortable'. They spent much of their time in the line improving the trenches during the day, digging new ones and revetting old ones as necessary. During the night wiring parties were out creating entanglements to slow down any rush the Germans may have been tempted to make. It was a relatively quiet time but casualties mounted as the tours of the line continued and more and more of the battalion were laid to rest in the cemeteries around the area. In the middle of the month the battalion lost another officer when Captain V. H. Watkins was wounded while the battalion was in the front line. Captain Watkins had gone to warn some of his men not to place themselves in danger when he was hit in the head by a bullet. The officer lay in an exposed position and a rescue was attempted by the stretcher bearers assisted by other men of his company. Cpl. Samuel Vaughan and Pte. William King were shot dead in the first efforts but L/Cpl Stanton and Sgt. C. Pritchard reached him with the help of Pte. John Price and discovered the officer in a very bad condition. They attempted to keep him warm with their great coats and get him back to the trench. In this they were successful though Pte. Price was killed and Sgt. Pritchard wounded. Captain Watkins was taken to No. 2 Casualty Clearing Station in Bailleul and then to the Empire Hospital in Westminster where he died on the 20th February, 1915. Sgt. Love was to comment:

> .....the Capt. lived until they got him practically home and then died, which was hard lines after a big sacrifice of our men, also his servant did some good work under fire giving his captain a drink and encouragement.

It was indeed a sad occasion for the battalion and for the Watkins family particularly since his brother, 2nd Lieut. Horace Watkins, had been killed while serving with the South Wales Borderers in the fighting around Ypres in the October of 1914.

The day to day duty in the trenches continued unabated and each tour saw more casualties. Sgt. Wallis was wounded while in command of a party digging a communication trench as a German machine gun swept backwards and forwards across the ground in which the Monmouths were digging. It was lucky that the casualties were not greater. Even out of the line the battalion was given very little peace as Pte. Heare was to report:

> Our battalion are out at rest at Le Bizet. All orderlies have Stand By for General Anley. After a while he gives us all a message to rush to our battalion. To the Colonel, off we dashed. It is an immediate order to Stand To. Being first back the General says 'Orderly, come around the battalions with me'. We all thought the Germans had broke through. Capt. Miers in charge of my company was shouting and firing a revolver in the air, in a fabric, lucky no one gets hurt. Another company we get to, the men are in a barn in the dark, no lights allowed. Men shouting and cursing, 'Who got my shoes?' 'Who got my equipment?' 'Where's my rifle?' One fellow rushed out with one leg in his trousers - General Anley smiled to himself but said to Colonel Cuthbertson 'You must have more practice at Stand To'.

Pte. Heare does not record what his comrades in the battalion thought of this as a training exercise, it can only be imagined that they grumbled as soldiers would. It can also be imagined that Col. Cuthbertson followed the General's hint and made sure the men got the practice they needed at Stand To.

Trench warfare required skills that were not readily learned in any environment other than the trenches themselves. It was a frequent concern of the British soldier of the winter of 1914/1915 that the Germans were better prepared for such warfare than themselves. In some aspects this would appear to have been true. The use of such weapons by the Germans as the rifle grenade was a continual worry to the 2nd Monmouths working in the forward areas and Sgt Love records that RSM Noble devised a response to the German weapon:

> Well, our RSM. to pay them back got a catapult and slung a few jam tins over filled with stone, black powder and a time fuse. If they did not kill anyone they put the wind up because they made a burst like a 'coal-box'.

It was this kind of adaptation that British soldiers along the line needed so that they did not lose the initiative totally, indeed the 'jam tin bomb' was used for many months in the line until regular supplies of mass produced hand grenades of a reliable type became available.

The winter passed slowly and casualties and sick mounted though the latter decreased as the winter weather improved towards spring. The routine of trench life and work brought further casualties amongst the officers with 2nd Lieut. C. A. Hillier being killed in mid February and Lieut. J.W. Taylor in early March. A few days later 2nd Lieut. R. B. Comely was badly wounded. At this stage of the war, however, there were sufficient replacements to keep the battalion up to strength now that it was receiving regular drafts from home and as the men of 1914 were slowly replaced the battalion tended to take on a slightly different aspect. At this time they were still a true Territorial unit with men taken largely from their old recruiting areas around Pontypool and Monmouth. Things were to change as the war progressed. None the less the wear and tear on the battalion after some five months in the trenches was considerable. In April 1915 the division was relieved to rest. The rest was cut short since the Germans were not ready to leave Ypres in the hands of the British and were intent on capturing the last Belgian town of significant size. The fighting for this town became known as the 2nd Battle of Ypres and is of particular importance to the Monmouthshire Regiment as a whole. The story of the events of this battle is told in the following chapter.

The Monmouths were not only involved in the ordinary trench warfare throughout this first winter. It is worth noting that a small party of Monmouths under Captain A.H. Edwards consisting of two NCO's and twelve men were detached from the battalion to form a small unit which was known as the 4th Division Mining Party. From early December until the formation of specific tunnelling units in the early spring of 1915 this small unit was responsible for the defensive mining of the 4th Division sector. As noted above, there was a feeling that the Germans were better prepared for trench warfare and this was certainly true of mining, where they had taken the initiative very early in the war as the front line tended to stagnate. It was in response to this threat that Captain Edwards had been given the task of forming the small mining unit. The miners' task, on both sides, was to tunnel under the opposing line, set a charge and take the enemy trenches, and as many men as possible, with it. Mining in Flanders was not an easy task because of the high water table, which frequently made the ground waterlogged, and the generally poor ground conditions in soft clays and loose sands. The first effort made by the Monmouths was abandoned for just this reason. A second attempt which commenced in the cellar of a house behind the line at Le Touquet was more successful. The object of the mine was a group of houses behind the German line which it was believed was used for billeting. After digging a gallery of about 500 feet (152 metres) the Germans were heard countermining. To deceive the Germans a secondary gallery was constructed and men posted in it to simulate work by banging rocks and tools together whilst the main gallery was continued in its original direction. Eventually it was possible to place a charge of 34 bags of gunpowder and 24 boxes of guncotton. When this was detonated half a dozen of the group of houses that had been the original target disappeared in the explosion. This was reputed to have been the first successful British mine of the war.

The danger involved in this sort of work is highlighted by an incident on the 28th February in which the mining party were involved. A mine was being extended towards the German line when the enemy's counter mine broke into the gallery. In the ensuing hand to hand struggle one man of the party, believed to have been Pte. William Varo of the 1st Hants, was killed before the enemy were beaten off and their mine destroyed. Towards the end of February the Tunnelling Companies of the Royal Engineers came into existence and it was not long after this incident that Captain Edwards and his party were returned to their battalion.

Chapter Four

'Life is Cheap'
(April and May 1915)

Though the first winter in action in Flanders had been hard on the men of the battalion none could have had any idea how bad things could get on the Western Front as the Spring of 1915 approached and the awfulness of trench warfare continued and developed. The rest out of the line was short lived and when the 4th Division returned to front line duty the battalion was to be introduced to a new sector which, for many of those men who fought there, came to symbolize the war - that place was Ypres. Ypres was already, by the Spring of 1915, the graveyard of the pre-war Regular Army since so many of its men had defended the town in October, 1914. With the passing of the Regulars the inevitability of the use of the Territorial Force overseas was finally confirmed and that was, indirectly, one of the main reasons for the 2nd Monmouths being in Flanders.

Prior to 1914 Ypres had been a busy market town with over 30,000 inhabitants. It was then, as it is now, a prosperous town though basking somewhat in an even more prosperous mediaeval past. The town had been a centre for the wool trade and had grown wealthy on the back of that trade - wealthy enough to build some magnificent public buildings including St. Martin's Cathedral and the enormous Cloth Hall (Les Halles) where the woollen cloth had been stored ready for sale in times gone by. In the first exchanges of the war, as the Germans swept almost unhindered through Belgium, Ypres had been occupied briefly by a small party of Germans who had not stayed long, probably expecting a superior force of French or British who were known to be close at hand. That was the only time that the Germans were in Ypres during the war years and, judging by the expenditure in life both attacking and defending the town over the next four years probably both sides would have been happier if the Germans had succeeded in getting a large force into the town before the allies reached it. By October, 1914, the Germans had made one attempt to wrest the town from the British and failed during a series of battles that came to be known as the 1st Battle of Ypres. Ypres was the only Belgian town of any real size that did not fall to the Germans in their rush to the sea, though in October, 1914, it was a close run thing as the British line was thinly manned but had held everything the Germans could throw at it. Seeing their prize elude them the Germans withdrew to the higher ground to the east of Ypres. In the context of the Flanders Plain the term 'higher ground' can be misleading to anyone unfamiliar with the countryside. The Flanders Plain is very flat and any rise can be of great importance during war for observation purposes if nothing else. East of Ypres there is a succession of low ridges each slightly higher than the surrounding countryside and becoming higher eastwards towards the Passchendaele Ridge which was to gain its own notoriety some years later. Although these hills are low and gentle they dominate the surrounding flat country and, in a military sense, provide very good positions which can be readily defended. The ridges tend to curve around Ypres such that the town lies in a shallow half saucer shaped depression. The Germans chose their ground well in 1914 and were able to hold the outer rim of this half saucer surrounding the Allied soldiers on three sides. In the Spring of 1915, as more troops arrived from Britain and its Empire the British began extending their line taking over sections of the line from the French wherever possible as they took on a greater responsibility for the conduct of the war. By April, 1915, almost all of the line in front of Ypres was held by the British with the French holding a sector to the north and east of the curved front line between the Yser Canal and Poelcappelle. The British held the line from here through Gravenstafel and Zonnebeke and thence south westwards through Hill 60 to the Ypres-Commines Canal. The area enclosed in this broad semicircular front protruded into the German lines with a maximum depth of five miles and it became known as the Ypres Salient or, simply, as the Salient. It was not a good place to defend since the Germans could fire on the unfortunate Tommy from three sides and in some places it was possible for the defenders of Ypres to be fired on from behind. However, the British, and to a lesser extent the French, saw the defence of Ypres as important since, on the face of it, the allies had come to the aid of Belgium and there was precious little of that country left to defend. Apart from this there was the more obvious reason that no army really likes to give up ground unless it is compelled to do so - it is more preferable to meet the enemy in a chosen field and to defeat him where he stands. For all that, the defence of Ypres for four years was to prove costly though in 1915 no one would have guessed just how costly. The great cost of defending Ypres would seem to question the wisdom of any philosophy that recommends it but the defence of the town and the Salient was as important to the prosecution of the war as any other aspect of the fighting of those years.

In spite of their failure in 1914 the Germans had decided that Ypres must fall and on the 22nd April, 1915 they launched an attack against the town. The day has been described as a beautiful spring day though there had been considerable shelling of Ypres by the German heavy howitzers. That gradually ceased by about mid day and all was quiet. It was the calm before the storm. At 5 p.m. that day the Germans opened up a terrific bombardment which was unusual if only for its ferocity. More significantly, perhaps, at the same time the Germans released two clouds of gas. These actions are taken as the opening moves in a series of battles over the next month that later became known as the 2nd Battle of Ypres.

This was the first use of poisonous gas during the war but it should not have come as a complete surprise to the British or French armies. On the 14th April, eight days before the attack, the French had taken a prisoner from the German 234th Regiment near Langemark in the north east of the Salient. This prisoner was interrogated and the French discovered the purpose of a simple kind of respirator that the German was carrying. This was thought to be some kind of trick and although the French were quick to pass on this information, it was largely ignored by the commands of the allied armies concerned. Both the French and the British refused to believe that such a weapon could be used, since it had been banned by the 1899 Hague Declaration and the 1907 Hague Convention to which all belligerents were signatories. Besides, they argued, it was too wind dependant to be very effective. Thus, the information was dismissed and precautions against its use were not taken. The outcome of ignoring the prisoner's information was the loss of thousands of men through gas poisoning during the closing days of April, 1915. It could easily have resulted in the fall of Ypres which could have had far reaching repercussions on the conduct of the war itself. The fact that Ypres did not fall during the coming days had far more to do with the tenacity of the infantry than in great leadership as will be recounted in the following pages.

The effect of the gas, in this instance chlorine, was immediate and, unfortunately for the allies, it was used against some of the poorest troops in the Salient. These were the French Territorial and Colonial troops holding the line north of Ypres between Steenstraat and Poelcapelle. It should be pointed out here that the French system of 'Territorials' was very different from that adopted in the United Kingdom. The French had a system of national service, much as it has today, and every able-bodied man was expected to serve for a number of years. Following this period the status of the men would be down graded to that of Reservists who were still expected to put in a specified period of training every year. After this period the men would be further down graded to Territorials and were then expected to complete rather more limited periods of training. Of course this meant that the French Territorials were mostly in their late thirties and early forties and would not be considered the best material for waging a war. Even Lord Kitchener had failed to realise the difference between the Territorial system in the two countries and that was, partly, how he came to treat the Territorial Force with some contempt and called for the raising of the aptly named 'New Armies'. Kitchener saw the Territorials as little more than useless but his beliefs were proven to be misguided time and time again throughout the early years of the war and especially in the fighting around Ypres in the Spring of 1915. At Ypres the French 87th Territorial Division was to bear the brunt of the first gas attack together with the 45th Algerian Division. Although some colonial troops had worthy reputations many of those units from north Africa were out of their depth in Flanders amidst the cold, the rain and the mud and soon became dispirited, the 45th Algerian Division were not the best suited troops to this kind of warfare.

As the gas cloud came towards them there was, initially, little panic since no one had seen anything like it and it seemed from a distance to be harmless. Within minutes, however, the two divisions mentioned above were overcome by the gas and they deserted their trenches as fast as their choking lungs would allow. In fairness to these soldiers they were totally unprepared for this new form of attack and their quality, or even their lack of it, is probably irrelevant since if they had even tried to stay in their trenches they would have succumbed to the gas - and dead soldiers provide little defence. Their withdrawal was, however, rapid and in no time at all a gap in the defences in front of Ypres some 8,000 yards (7,300 metres) had been opened which needed to be acted upon, and acted upon swiftly, by the British command. During the next few hours the 1st Canadian Division which was holding the line next to the French, was pressed in to service to extend their line to their left in an effort to fill the gap into which the Germans were pouring and thereby make contact with such French units that had remained. In this instance there were remnants of the 1/1st Tirailleurs and the 1/2nd bis Zouaves and they fought alongside the Canadians during the coming hours. This portion of the fighting of the 2nd Battle of Ypres which started with the release of the gas and which lasted for two days is known as the Battle of Gravenstafel Ridge during which time the initial advantage the Germans had achieved by the release of gas was halted but at some considerable expense to both the Canadian and British forces. The early defence of the north east part of the Salient relied not only on the Canadians filling the gap but actually carrying out localized attacks. Sir John French ordered these attacks, over unprepared and unfamiliar ground, in an effort to buy time for his French allies to reorganize and counter attack to win the ground they had lost. As the Battle of Gravenstafel Ridge closed on the night of 23rd April, 1915, the battlefield was strewn with the corpses of Canadian soldiers who had carried out their duty - the French, however, had not moved to retake any of the ground they had lost or even to come to the aid of the seriously overstretched Canadians.

The 2nd Monmouths were not involved in this phase of the fighting but the negative response of the French to the fighting had seen the 10th and 11th Brigades of the 4th Division sent up before this stage was over. The 2nd Monmouths were, together with the rest of 12th Brigade, forming the Divisional reserve and were stationed in the area of Elverdinge some miles away from the fighting. As the fighting increased this Brigade was moved up and the Monmouths took up positions in the area of La Brique a little to the north of the town centre of Ypres on the 24th April. Here the battalion was to stand in readiness for a move at a moment's notice for the next six days before they were called upon to take part in the action. It was as well that there were some troops available to act as reserves for there can have been little to indicate the determined attacks that the Germans were to make during the following days. The Salient had changed its shape as a result of the gas attack since this had produced a withdrawal from the north eastern portion to produce a large re-entrant in the northern flank but the pressure on the line was to come from other directions as well. To make matters worse the Salient was undermanned and the losses from two days of heavy fighting had exacerbated the problem and hence all available troops were rushed into the area as quickly as possible. A further problem for the defenders was that there was little in the way of artillery support. There was a lack of guns in the area and a shortage of ammunition for those guns that were available. In effect the infantry in the Salient was almost fighting without artillery support though it is recorded that the available artillery did magnificent work under the most difficult conditions doing everything in their power to keep old and worn guns firing and give some support to the embattled infantry. None the less the next few days were to prove to be a very trying time for all concerned.

All of these factors were adding pressure to the hard pressed defenders all around the Salient and it seemed clear to the commander of the 2nd Army, Gen. Sir Horace Smith-Dorrien, that a withdrawal from the extremities of the Salient to a prepared line nearer to the ramparts of the old town of Ypres was called for. This made sense if only because it made for a shorter line to defend with the diminishing number of men. The General put forward this idea at an early stage of the fighting. There can be no disguising the fact that Smith-Dorrien and Sir John French seldom saw eye to eye and this latest idea was greeted with some displeasure though probably French saw the wisdom of it. He had promised the French he would stand firm to give them time, but even when they made no move Sir John French was reluctant to give in to an idea of one of his senior commanders. Before the next phase of the battle, the Battle of St. Julien, had been completed Smith-Dorrien had been dismissed from his command and his place had been taken by Gen. Sir Herbert Plumer. This military in-fighting occurred at the height of the Battle of St. Julien and can have done little to improve the situation of the front line soldier manning the forward trenches and subject to the shelling and gas attacks as the battle gathered momentum. In spite of Sir John French's apparent disapproval of the idea he had issued orders for the preparation of a line closer to Ypres on the 27th April to allow for the withdrawal should conditions in the Salient worsen.

Whilst the 2nd Monmouths were held in reserve at La Brique there was time for its men to see the effects of the battle and Pte. Heare was to note:

> This is the real sight of war, houses all smashed, food on table as if people run
> off having a meal, shells screaming all the time. One pitched in a party
> behind us, what an awful mess..... the soldiers are lying about in the road
> screaming, groaning and swearing with wounds and gas..... The wounded
> on the road scream every time a shell lands. It seems no one can live in this
> for long.

This was penned while the battalion was some miles from the front but it is clear that they had seen nothing like this in their stay in the trenches thus far. Before the battle was over they would know that this was little more than an introduction to the intense fighting of the Ypres Salient.

The battalion was to remain in reserve throughout the next few days. Fighting all along the front intensified and the French remained resolutely stationary within their trenches making no attempt to regain lost ground and claiming, probably quite correctly, that their troops were too tired for an assault to stand any chance of success. Inevitably this led Sir John French to wonder about his ally's intentions as the battle progressed and their lack of action was undoubtedly causing him some disquiet. By the 1st May, with all the efforts of the British and Canadian forces achieving very little but costing very much, it would appear that the French commanders saw fit to act. The action was not what had been hoped for by the Commander-in-Chief. He received a letter from General Foch which clearly set out the position of the French and in part this letter read:

> In the present situation the principal object which the Command of the
> Allied armies has in view is the preparation of operations on the front Arras
> - Neuve Chapelle. The intention is to attack on that front and act on the
> defensive about Ypres.

Thus, the French were of the opinion that all offensive action around Ypres should stop and the energies of the armies should be directed elsewhere, particularly in the actions planned for Aubers Ridge and Festubert which eventually took place at the height of the Ypres fighting. This letter can have done little to comfort Sir John French, but he was able to see the truth of the situation. Further, since his resources in the Salient were diminishing, he was not really in a position to argue with the French on this matter. However, he had been trying to buy the French time at their request and now they had changed their mind. A letter of this type a week earlier could have saved thousands of lives for Sir John French would have been forced into the decision he was now to make. He had little or no choice and immediately ordered the withdrawal, proposed by Smith-Dorrien and organized some days earlier by General Plumer. Whilst, in principle, it would appear that the Commander-in-Chief agreed with the French that their efforts should be directed elsewhere he was not slow to realize that the French still had a commitment to him and to the defence of the Salient and that action was necessary by the French to ensure the enemy were kept busy and that they did not divert troops to the bat-tlefields in the south. In a response to the letter quoted above the Commander-in-Chief asked that the troops used for that particular duty:

> ...should be of the best quality, in sufficient strength, and that adequate measures of defence should be taken.

This comment could possibly reflect his disappointment in the French units to this point of the battle and in particular the hasty withdrawal of two low quality divisions under the first gas attack of the 22nd April. It may also reflect his disappointment in the fact that he had squandered his limited resources in an attempt to achieve something that was probably impossible.

Now the British army was faced with a sizeable military problem. This was to disengage the enemy and withdraw to prepared positions effectively undetected by the enemy so that a rout could be avoided. Gen. Plumer's plan was for a staged withdrawal from the Zonnebeke portion of the Salient to a line some three miles west and much closer to Ypres. The first of the stages began at 8 p.m. on the 1st May. The first troops to be taken out of the Salient were the Lahore Division who were in reserve and which enabled Plumer to keep his front line intact. Whilst this was taking place the artillery was moved closer to the Yser Canal which formed the diameter of the semicircle at the rear of the Salient. This was in preparation for their final removal to the west of the town in due course. For the time being they were in easy reach should they be called on to give support. That same day Plumer issued a preparatory order indicating that the final withdrawal from the present positions in the east of the Salient would be vacated by the night of the 3rd/4th May.

At this stage the Salient was held by the 5th Division in the extreme south; the 27th and 28th Divisions in the central portion most affected by the withdrawal and by the 4th Division in the extreme north where the attacks of April had already brought the front line significantly nearer to Ypres. The 2nd Monmouths were serving as part of the 4th Division whilst its sister battalions of the 1st and 3rd Monmouths were serving with the 84th and 83rd Brigades respectively of the 28th Division. This fact alone makes the 2nd Battle of Ypres very special in the history of the Monmouthshire Regiment since it was the only time in the course of the war that they fought in such close proximity to one another. It was on these divisions, some of which had been in action since the battle had started, that the responsibility of holding the line rested as the other forces within the Salient were gradually withdrawn.

On the 2nd May the Germans began the day by a thorough and heavy bombardment of the British positions. It was so intense that some considered it to have been the most ferocious of the war to that date. This was followed by a gas attack in the area of the 12th Brigade. The 2nd Essex and the 2nd Lancashire Fusiliers came under heavy fire and the lack of suitable protection against gas caused the Essex to evacuate part of their line. At this point the 2nd Monmouths were called to provide support and orders were issued to B and C Companies to move forward. Unfortunately, B Company did not receive the order in the confusion of the battle, but C Company under Captain A.J.H. Bowen moved forward immediately. As they moved to the aid of the Essex they came under heavy shrapnel fire but succeeded in making contact with the Essex men who had already regained their trench. C Company moved into the support trench ready to give assistance to the Essex as necessary. Later the same day two platoons of B Company went forward to reinforce the Royal Irish Regiment. During the heavy shelling that day the acting adjutant, Lieut. Alexander Fraser was killed by a direct hit whilst on duty at La Brique. He was a much respected officer well thought of by fellow officers and men alike and it has been recorded that Lieut. Col. Cuthbertson took his death particularly hard. Pte. Heare who was acting as a battalion orderly had his own story of this officer:

> *Up the trench one morning, just breaking day. I gave Col. Cuthbertson a message, while waiting for an answer or receipt I must have fallen asleep standing against the door frame of the dugout. The Colonel says it is a serious crime to fall asleep on duty. He terrified me but Lieut. Fraser our adjutant saves me and says, 'When did you sleep last Heare?' 'Not for two days and a night for sure, Sir.' 'All right, try and keep awake and keep going we are all so short handed'.*

To the south and east of the 12th Brigade the battle raged every bit as fiercely with the 28th Division bearing the brunt of the German storm. This must have caused great uneasiness in Gen. Plumer who was hoping to remove more men and equipment from the Salient on the night of the 2nd May. Fortunately, by 8 p.m. all the fighting had died down and at 9.45 p.m. the general issued instructions for the next stage of the withdrawal. This was completed safely during the hours of darkness leaving only the front line soldiers to be withdrawn to the original plan on the night of the 3rd/4th May.

It was going to be a long day for those men for on the 3rd May the Germans started where they had left off the day before and continued in their attempts to break the line by shelling it methodically and later by a determined attack. By this stage of the battle the semicircular front line was manned by almost unsupported infantry and there was little they could do but face the onslaught of the German forces. This was, perhaps, one of the most critical days of the whole of the battle since the British had begun a withdrawal and a break in the line at this stage would have had disastrous effects. As the German infantry assault took shape a number of guns were rushed back into positions to give some support to the beleaguered defenders of the Salient and it is recorded that those guns of the 39th Battery, 14th Brigade RFA were particularly effective in their use of shrapnel against the oncoming Germans. It was scant support and the infantrymen rose to their task with rapid small arms fire as the German advance neared their front line. Eventually the rattle of small arms fire died away as the attack faltered and then stopped and once again the Germans had been thwarted by the defenders. The effectiveness of the British defence should not be underestimated for one German account of the fighting states that:

> Again the attack had come to a standstill, the troops, whose strength had not been kept up were at the end of their powers. The Companies of the 51st Reserve Division average barely 90 men.

This is a clear indication of the lack of success of the German assault since companies in their army at that time should have averaged between 180 and 230 men. The Germans had suffered heavily in their attacks and, in spite of thorough artillery preparation, it demonstrates clearly the effect of determined defence - a point which the British and French commands failed to realize and which was to prove costly in many engagements during the coming years.

The relief with which the British front line soldiers greeted the evening of the 3rd May can only be imagined. It was now to be their turn to pull out of the eastern extremity of the Salient. For the 12th Brigade, and the 2nd Monmouths, it was to make very little difference since their position on the north side of the Salient was to remain unchanged as the line rotated about their right flank to bring it closer to Ypres. The line held by the 12th Brigade had been formed as a result of the fighting early on in the battle and had been caused by the use of the gas cloud - there was no desire in the command to bring this line closer to Ypres. The final evacuation of the line to the east of Ypres was piecemeal. Two companies of each of the front line battalions were withdrawn at 9 p.m. and the rest at 10.30 p.m. leaving small parties to cover the evacuation and to maintain a pretence of normal trench activity. These remaining groups were withdrawn by midnight. The withdrawal was a complete success and was completed without loss to any of the units involved. The 27th and 28th Divisions in particular had completed one of the most difficult manoeuvres possible and undoubtedly this pleased both Gen. Plumer and Sir John French. However, this success should be tempered by the losses of earlier days, a point graphically described by Pte. Heare:

> Going up to the battalion one night (I) saw the worst sight of the war. A man of our Regiment crying 'Shoot me'. When I looked he had his two legs and right hand blown off. He said 'Shoot me out of it'. 'Shoot me you coward', he said. My God I ran from him to the battalion, I told RSM Noble about him (and asked for stretcher bearers) but at present they were all away, worked to death. Going back the same way the man was still alive, when I got near him he said 'I know what I got, shoot me out of the way'. Once daylight comes he is here for a day for sure. He cries 'Shoot me' and swears at me, at last I got behind him but my courage fails me, but I look again at him - he is dead. I drop my rifle and run to Irish Farm.
> Sgt. Shaw is there, 'Hello, Taff, saw a ghost?' I tell him of it I am trembling and sweating.

The shock of the effects of the German assault were being felt by many young men like Pte. Heare all along the front and there are many similar records of the horrors produced by the German shelling during the battle. None the less the line had held throughout the attack but the Germans were not ready to give up just yet for their goal was still the town of Ypres.

On the morning of the 4th May the Germans began by methodically shelling the evacuated positions indicating just how successful the withdrawal had been. The Germans had been given no indication that the line was empty and expended a large number of shells before they realised that the trenches had been evacuated. In some ways the Germans must have seen the preceding days as a great success for their repeated assaults had, after all, resulted in a British withdrawal. The Germans followed up after a couple of hours of fruitless shelling and although the new British line was shorter to defend, it did not mean that it was going to be easier to defend. The smaller Salient resulting from shortening the line was little more than a large artillery target for the Germans and with all the problems of supply to the front line through the bottleneck of Ypres the defenders were hardly likely to have it easy. The new line ran from Hooge along the low Frezenberg Ridge to Mouse Trap Farm and thence towards the Yser Canal via Turco Farm. The 4th Division still held the northern portion with the 28th and 27th Divisions successively to the south.

The Germans quickly made contact with this new line as they followed up on the morning of the 4th May but, possibly feeling flushed with their success, mistakenly believed that the new position to be a rearguard position and not the forward defensive line. Although they tried to press home the advantage, the men of the 80th and 83rd Brigades stood their ground and by the end of the day the Germans realized:

> that the new position could not be taken without a thorough artillery preparation.

For the next few days that is exactly what they did as they shelled the British positions with everything at their disposal.

With the German advance of the 4th May the Battle of St. Julien officially ended and the three days in which the Germans 'prepared' the line are not given an official title. This could not have meant anything to the men in the front line for they still knew they were in the middle of a large battle, for whilst there may not have been the large scale infantry assaults of the previous days, there was plenty of shelling and localized assaults against points recognized by the Germans as being of importance. It would not have felt like a pause in the operation to the front line soldier. The next phase of the battle has been called the Battle of Frezenberg Ridge which officially began on the 8th May. Some historians, including the author of the Official History, consider the preparatory shelling of the lines as part of this battle.

On the night of the 4th/5th May the 2nd Monmouths relieved the 5th South Lancashires in the Brigade sector to the north of Ypres. They were in position in time to receive the full effect of a German gas attack. The gas attacks had begun but a short time earlier, but already rudimentary protection for the troops had started to appear:

Then a gas attack, our bit of flannelette is useless, it burns the eyes, the throat and terrible on the chest. Gas shells come over, we thought they were duds they burst so quiet, we are coughing and swearing. Black has made a drink of tea, very sweet, we gulp it down and both of us vomit all green, no doubt saves us.

The soldiers would appear to have had their own beliefs as to the remedies against gas but the flannelette face mask, to cover mouth and nose would have been of little use unless it was thoroughly moistened and many soldiers undoubtedly owed their lives to this basic protection and some to even more basic protection in the form of a urine soaked sock! The source of the flannelette used by the Monmouths was close to home and their issue as gas protection owed much to the resourcefulness of Lieut. Col. Cuthbertson as Capt. E.H. Byrde was to recall many years later:

That freezing winter the ladies of Pontypool had sent the battalion 800 body belts they had made out of flannel. The Colonel had them issued to each man with instructions always to carry then and keep them damp so that they could be wound round their heads to cover mouth and nose in the event of a gas attack. Even a safety pin was provided.

The events of the day were recorded by Sgt. Love as follows:

I saw the first green cloud of poison gas come over our front line troops, and in a short time we felt the effects of it. But the worst of the poison had gone to the ground before it reached our trench. Even so we had to protect our mouths and breathing with body belts that we carried with us. Unfortunately the men in the front line had no time to consider what to do before the poison gas had done its deadly work. Many fell on the way back and those I witnessed left this world in agony.

Fortunately for the 2nd Monmouths the gas attack of the 4th May was not followed up and it would appear that the Germans were squandering what little tactical advantage the use of gas had given them. If they had expected it to succeed then an infantry assault should have followed.

The position that the 2nd Monmouths were holding at that time included Mouse Trap Farm which was a moated group of farm buildings and which was seen as a point of some importance by the German commanders opposing them. The following is taken from a German account of the situation on the front in early May:

On the front of the XXVI Reserve Corps, Wieltje Chateau (Mouse Trap Farm) surrounded by its 3 metre (10 feet) moat, was recognized as an important strong point. Heavy howitzer fire was concentrated on it, yet surprise attacks attempted against it on the 6th and 7th failed.

During the attacks mentioned by the Germans above the strong point was defended by the 2nd Monmouths and on the attack of the 7th May the battalion were caught in the process of a company relief and the relieved company had to return immediately to the trenches they had vacated to give support to their comrades. The attack made by the Germans was a determined effort to capture

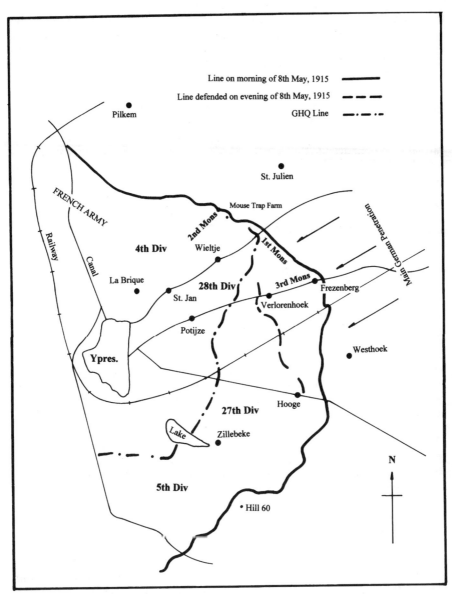

Legend:
- Line on morning of 8th May, 1915
- Line defended on evening of 8th May, 1915
- GHQ Line

Pilkem

St. Julien

FRENCH ARMY

Mouse Trap Farm

2nd Mons

1st Mons

Main German Penetration

Railway

Canal

4th Div

Wieltje

La Brique

28th Div

St. Jan

3rd Mons

Frezenberg

Verlorenhoek

Potijze

Ypres.

Westhoek

27th Div

Hooge

Lake

Zillebeke

N

5th Div

Hill 60

The Battle of Frezenberg Ridge 8th May, 1915.

the strong point and as their account states it was accompanied by heavy shelling. One of the shells made a direct hit on the farm house and most of the garrison, including the two officers and all the NCO's became casualties. Of the survivors Drummer (later A/Sgt) Danny White was first to react and he immediately swam across the moat returned to battalion headquarters under heavy fire to report the situation and ask for orders. He was told that he should get back to the farm and instruct the remaining men to hold on at all costs. Fortunately, and somewhat against the odds, White managed to complete the return journey unscathed and took charge of the situation at Mouse Trap Farm and his small garrison held out despite the best efforts of the enemy. Later Drummer White was awarded the DCM and the French Croix de Guerre. (The citation for his award can be found in the appropriate Appendix to this volume.)

At the same time C Company, under Captain Bowen, were in action in support of the Mouse Trap Farm garrison. As they reached the forward trenches Sgt. Love was to record that:

> The first thing that caught my eye was our commanding officer with his jacket off firing like hell from a 'buckshee' rifle to let Jerry know there were still a few left to fill the gap they had made by shelling during the day. The work of our commanding officer was an inspiration and encouragement to us. It gave us the bit of devil needed at the time.

Captain Bowen was wounded in the head early in the day but he remained on duty with his company continuing to control its work throughout the day. For Sgt. Love the day had become very difficult since he had lost contact with Bowen and his platoon was almost leaderless. Love made every effort to make contact with Bowen and, as luck would have it chanced upon him making the best of the available cover:

> He was cut about the head and face, and he was covered with blood and dirt of which he was not aware. He was badly wounded in the back. He was holding his shirt away from the skin as it was sticking and causing added pain. I really thought he was 'going on'. I suggested to him that it would be better to get his wounds dressed, as he was bleeding badly, but he had no intention of leaving the line because we were so short of officers. He was sick and becoming weaker, and the commanding officer gave him instructions to go that evening.

When the German assault had finally subsided C Company were relieved as they were in the process of doing when the attack took place. When the company reached La Brique it was realized that Captain Bowen had been wounded twice in the head and twice in the body. It was not until his men were safe at La Brique that this officer allowed himself to be sent to hospital for treatment. This was on the 8th May and was reported to his family in Usk by telegram in a very terse military style:

> Reference my wire record 1043: Alfred John Hamilton Bowen was admitted 1 British Red Cross Hospital Le Touquet eleventh May, bullet wound in head.

40

This must have done much to alarm his family but Capt. Bowen recovered from his wound and was awarded the DSO for his gallantry and leadership during the day's fighting around Mouse Trap Farm.

The battalion were to suffer further casualties amongst the officers as a result of the fighting on that day as every effort was made to hold Mouse Trap Farm. Capt. Illtyd Watkins and Lieut. H.J. Walters were killed in action while Capt. Byrde and Lieut. S. R. Hockaday were wounded. Capt. Byrde lost his leg as a result of the fighting and his active service was finished. Lieut. Hockaday recovered from his wound and returned to serve with the battalion until his death in action in 1916.

The six days between the 8th May and the 13th May, designated the Battle of Frezenberg Ridge, were to be a testing time for the British soldiers defending Ypres. The 8th May, in particular, is of great importance to the Monmouthshire Regiment since its 1st and 3rd Battalions were heavily involved in the fighting at the tip of the Salient and by the end of the day these battalions had all but ceased to exist as the Germans blasted the 83rd and 84th Brigades of the 28th Division off the Frezenberg Ridge. Although the line wavered, somehow it held but the cost to the divisions bearing the brunt of the attack was enormous. For the 2nd Battalion, however, things were different and the battalion historian records that normal routine was maintained and on the night of the 8th/9th May they were relieved by the Royal Irish Regiment and returned to their reserve line in La Brique.

During the confused fighting along the Frezenberg Ridge the 83rd Brigade received an ambiguous order which brought about the withdrawal of that brigade and consequently a breach in the line which the Germans exploited. Many casualties resulted from this action which may have been avoided, however, the brigade was so weakened by days of heavy fighting and shelling that it may not have held on for long in any case. By night fall on the 8th May the fighting had stopped and the German advance had been halted. This had been brought about by two counter attacks by the British forces during the day that had sufficiently worried the Germans for them to accept what they had won for the day. The first of these attacks, by the 85th Brigade, had begun during the afternoon and was followed up by an advance of the 10th Brigade of the 4th Division. The Germans were to record the latter attack as follows:

> A great counter attack that was only stopped at Frezenberg, threw the Fourth Army on the defensive and compelled the XXVI Corps to abandon the position captured. Only the XXV Corps held its ground.

The Germans had over estimated the strength of the counter attack since the 10th Brigade was itself under strength as it had been in action more or less continuously since the early days of the battle. Further, the Germans over stated the extent of the advance since it did not reach as far as Frezenberg running out of momentum some distance in front of that village. However, the counter attack was enough to stop the Germans and enough to give the British Staff the hope that they could regain the lost ground of Frezenberg Ridge. To this effect an order was issued to the 28th Division to counter attack to do just that. Fortunately for the survivors of the day's fighting the situation was explained more thoroughly and the order was cancelled. No doubt some one had pointed out that, for instance, the 83rd Brigade had been reduced to about 600 men and had been collected together to form a composite battalion under the command of Lieut.Col. H.W. Worsely Gough of the 3rd Monmouths. Not the ideal situation in which to be considering a counter attack! The position the Germans reached at the end of the fighting of the 8th May was about as far as they got during this phase of the battle. Fresh troops in the form of the 1st Cavalry Division were brought up and helped to maintain the line though a number of localized counter attacks were required to do this.

The 2nd Monmouths were held in reserve during most of the fighting for Frezenberg Ridge and were thus spared the heavy casualties suffered by the other battalions of the Regiment who were withdrawn from their brigades and amalgamated into one battalion with the strength of about one company. As the fighting died down on the 9th May the battalion was ordered to the reserve trenches at La Brique where it was to remain until it was relieved on the 20th May and proceeded for four days respite at Vlamertinge. At this time Lieut. Col. Cuthbertson was injured while on duty and left the battalion for hospital. Capt. S.P.A. Rolls, a Regular from the Dorset Regiment who had been adjutant since 1912 but had recently been acting as the commander to A Company, took over the Colonel's battalion duties. Sgt. Love was to record this as follows:

> On the way down I came across our C.O. with a junior officer. He was resting on the side of a sunken road and no officer was more pleased than he when I told him I had brought back 26 men after having consolidated the front line and other work. I could see that the Commanding Officer was beaten. When I looked back I saw him hobbling away on two sticks.

Although the battalion had been removed from the forward area their knowledge of the conditions was sought after. This was particularly true of the battalion orderlies whose work in the forward areas carrying messages to and from the front gave them a particularly detailed knowledge of the trench system. There were regular missions for these men to guide new officers to their units or, as in the case of Pte. Heare, to show artillery officers the whereabouts of such things as machine gun posts and ammunition dumps. On one such excursion Pte. Heare and an artillery officer were in a forward area as dawn began to break. Pte. Heare records the following and the account, though long, gives some idea of the prevailing conditions.

> The officer says, 'That's good, now we go back.' I say, 'It is breaking day, Sir, so we must go back the St. Jean way'. We are in the centre of the horseshoe though it is a bit straighter now. 'Who the hell are you giving orders to' says the officer, 'We go back this way.' I say again, 'It's not safe, Sir, although it is rather quiet now we must crawl back from St. Jean.' 'Damn you', he says, 'I will have you put under arrest when we get back, this way back, damn you'. So I jumped up and ran and fell into a shell hole about ten yards away. He came after me, 'What the hell is the game?' he said, but a burst of machine gun fire whistled across the hole, he soon ducked down, but got one in the arm. After a few bursts of fire he soon got civil. I dressed his arm, a nice one. He says, 'We are seen, what can we do now'..... 'When do you think we can get away?' 'Tonight, Sir,' I said. Timing the machine gun, 'Perhaps you had better go, but no stop with me', he says. The Germans are only fifty

yards away, I wasn't challenging a machine gun at that range..... His name is Dane and (he is) just out from England. 'Have a drink', he says. I take a good one, I could do with a meal, didn't I cough and splutter, raw whisky he had. The next I know the officer is shaking me, they are shelling close, I am muddled, it must be about mid day, as the sun is dead overhead. Then the clouds come over and it rains and it keeps on all day. Every now and again a few rounds of fire. We get away at dusk going shell hole to shell hole, cross ways, the machine gun is busy. When we got back to Brigade another officer is there thinking Dane was dead.

The officer in question here is believed to be Major (later Lieut. Col) James Auchinleck Dane of the Royal Artillery who was awarded the DSO in 1917 for his gallantry in manning the guns when under heavy fire and who had been on active service in France since 1914 - a lot longer than Heare had thought during their adventure.

The battalion were to spend the next four days at Vlamertinge and like many of the units engaged in the battle to that date they were able to spend some time resting and re-equiping though during the period the battalion provided a number of working parties to provide labour for the new defensive line being constructed either side of the St. Jean - Weiltje road. It was but a short respite from the fighting for on the 24th May the Germans launched a further fierce attack on the British line. This opened the final phase of the 2nd Battle of Ypres and became known as the Battle of Bellewaarde Ridge. The Official History records that the opening of the attack was accompanied over much of the front by the largest release of cloud gas seen to that date. The wind was light and the gas hung around the trenches for a considerable time and reached a height of some 40 feet above the trenches. Improved gas drill and the issue of the first gas helmets reduced the effectiveness of the gas though in the north of the Salient where the lines were close together, the Germans were able to make some headway and succeeded in wresting Mouse Trap Farm from the 4th Division. It was in to this area that the 2nd Monmouths were rushed expecting a break through at any time. Later in the day, when the break through had not transpired, the 2nd Monmouths were busy digging trenches behind the 10th Brigade ready for their use in the event of a withdrawal becoming necessary. Plans were being made for a counter attack to recover the lost ground. The plan initially received the backing of the French commanders to the left of the 4th Division and they offered three of their own divisions. Later the French clarified their position somewhat by saying that their divisions were to be used for support only and not for attacking purposes. That being the case the commanders of the 4th Division had little choice but to abandon the plan and eventually the Division was withdrawn from the trenches made untenable by the Germans' capture of Mouse Trap Farm and occupied the new line that the 2nd Monmouths had dug during the afternoon. Early on the morning of the 25th May the German High Command issued orders that operations in front of Ypres were to cease since the German units were now almost as tired as the defenders of the town. With that order the fighting that was to become known as the 2nd Battle of Ypres came to an end.

The 2nd Monmouths were withdrawn from the line and marched back to Vlamertinge where on the 27th May they received orders that they were to leave their brigade and join the remnants of the 1st and 3rd battalions to form one, under strength, battalion that was to be styled the Monmouthshire Regiment. This action demonstrates quite clearly the effects of 2nd Ypres on the British army which had suffered nearly 60,000 casualties in the fighting. The front line divisions had fought well but had, to some extent, been let down by a leadership that had squandered resources during the opening phases of the battle. The Official Historian recognized the major part the Territorial Force played in the defence of the Salient when he wrote:

> The Territorials fought more than well, but unfortunately with ever diminishing numbers; for as a result of the intensive recruiting for the New Armies and the failure to foresee that the Territorial Army might be employed overseas and suffer serious wastage, few Territorial reinforcements were forthcoming.

The latter point had probably hastened the amalgamation of the Monmouthshire battalions and it was a problem that was to remain with the Regiment throughout the remainder of the war. Sir John French also recognized the contribution of the Territorials when, some years later, he was to comment:

> I say without the slighest hesitation that, without the assistance which the Territorials afforded between October, 1914 and June, 1915, it would have been impossible to have held the line in France and Belgium, or to have prevented the enemy from reaching his goal of the Channel seaboard.

The 2nd Battle of Ypres has been seen as epitomizing the Great War with its poor planning and ill-conceived ideas together with the great bravery and fortitude of the soldiers in the trenches. Even the increased use of artillery as displayed throughout the battle became synonymous with the war. But perhaps the last words on the battle should be left to Pte. Heare who had served throughout the the month of fighting:

> Of Ypres a volume could be wrote. If Hell is worse then that is bad. Life is cheap, where you fell you stop unless someone passing would push your body into a shell hole.

The first colours of the 2nd Battalion the Monmouthshire Regiment were presented at Windsor Great Park, by H.M. King Edward VII on 19th June, 1909. The Regimental Colour bore the single Battle Honour 'South Africa 1900-1902'. These Colours are now in Trevethin Church. At the same parade Colours were presented to the 3rd Battalion and the Brecknock Battalion.

(Photo: SWB Museum)

Officers of the battalion at Ammanford during the camp of August, 1909. Back row: Capt. H. Charles, Capt. J. Evans, Capt. J. Williams, Capt. J.G. Broackes, Capt. G.B.C. Ward, Maj. Sillery, Surg. Lt. Griffiths, Lt. A.J.H. Bowen, Lt. A.W. Bowen. Middle row: Maj. E.J. Morris, Maj. R.H. Spencer, The Bishop of Llandaff Colonel J. Bradney, Brig. Banfield, Lt. Col. H.D. Griffiths, Maj. P.G. Pennymore. Front row: Lt. J.G. Thomas, Lt. A.H. Edwards, Lt. J.W. Sproule, Lt. H.W. Bailey, Lt. R.A. Hobbs.

(Photo: SWB Museum)

Officers of the battalion on 1st March 1910 after presentation to King Edward VII. Back row from left: Capt. J.C. Jenkins, Capt. C. Ward (adj), Lieut. A.J. Bowen, Lieut. J.W. Sproule, Lieut. A.J.H. Bowen. Centre: Lieut. A.H. Edwards, Lieut. M. Watkins, Capt. J.C. Broakes, Capt. J. Evans, Capt. J. Williams, Major A. Sale, Lieut. H. Bailey, 2nd Lieut. E.D. Jenkins. Front: Major P.G. Pennymore, Lieut. Col. H.D. Griffiths, Col. J.A. Bradney, Major R.H. Spencer, Major E.J. Morris.

(Photo: SWB Museum)

Above Men of the 2nd Mons. at Camp in 1911 and below a group at camp in 1912.
(Photo: SWB Museum)

Brig. Gen E.B. Cuthbertson commanding officer of the battalion 1912 - 1915.

(Photo: SWB Museum)

Lieut. Col. A.J.H. Bowen commanding officer from September, 1915 to March, 1917.

(Photo: SWB Museum)

Pte. Ivor John Griffiths in September, 1914. (Photo: Ian Griffiths)

Trench near Le Bizet in April 1915 - note the breastworks and the pump in the foreground.
(Photo: SWB Museum)

Breastworks near Le Bizet in April 1915.

(Photo: SWB Museum)

Chapter Five

'Over Kemmel Hill'

(June and July 1915)

The battles for Ypres were over. The battered, but not broken, divisions that had held the line were rested - they had earned it, but for all too many of their comrades there was only the rest that could be found out on the shell scarred battlefield. For the battalions of the Monmouthshire Regiment there was to be a considerable change in routine. The fighting of early May had left the 1st and 3rd Battalions sorely undermanned and they had been joined together, barely 400 strong, before the fighting around Ypres had subsided and were at rest at Vlamertinge Woods on the 27th May when the 2nd Monmouths, fresh from the line, joined them. The strengths of the battalions at that time was:

> 1st Battalion: 11 officers; 218 other ranks
>
> 2nd Battalion: 19 officers; 580 other ranks
>
> 3rd Battalion: 11 officers; 250 other ranks

The figures here indicate the level of involvement of the battalions in the fighting. Whilst the 1st and 3rd Battalions, serving in the 28th Division, had felt the full ferocity of the German storm of steel the 2nd Battalion had been on the edge of the main fighting serving with the 4th Division. That is not to say that they had seen little of the action, by most standards the battalion had suffered heavily during the fighting. The casualty list for the month of the battles for Ypres for the 2nd Battalion indicates 82 officers and men were killed, mostly during the fighting of early May. It can be assumed that something like three times this figure were wounded during the same period making the total number of casualties in excess of 300 for the month. They had certainly been involved in a battle and it was only the escalation in the use of artillery that had released such fury on the brigades of the 28th Division that makes the numbers appear small when compared to the other battalions of the Regiment. An indication of the ferocity of the fighting is that when the 2nd Battalion joined the other battalions to finish the formation of a composite unit, styled The Monmouthshire Regiment, it was to be commanded by Major W.S. Bridge the most senior surviving officer. As the battle had progressed all three battalions had lost their commanding officers; Lieut. Col. Charles Robinson of the 1st Battalion had been killed in action whilst Lieut. Col. Cuthbertson of the 2nd and Lieut. Col. Worsley Gough of the 3rd Battalion had been wounded and had returned to England. The Monmouthshire Regiment was assigned to the 84th Brigade of the 28th Division and on the 28th May the battalion was marched to Herzeele in the rear area some 15 miles (25 km) west of Ypres, for a period of rest and re-equipping.

The first step in making the unit ready for action was the reorganization of the companies. It had been decided that there was to be no separation of the original battalions and the men serving in A Company of their own battalion would serve in A Company of the combined battalion, and so on for the other companies. The four company commanders were Captains O.W.D. Steele, K.F.D. Gattie and E. Edwards and Lieut, D. Evans. This approach to the amalgamation was considered to be for the best and it has been described in the histories of the Regiment as a success:

> Brought about by the vicissitudes and calamities of war, the amalgamation had the happiest results in cementing friendships between the three units.

and also

> This amalgamation of the three Battalions under stress of war had the happiest results, and this service together as one unit immensely strengthened the cordial relations between the three battalions.

Perhaps this was the effect in the long term but at the time many of the ordinary soldiers seemed to have been less than pleased with the arrangement as they fiercely defended their battalion honour in the weeks to come:

> But what a mistake to put us together. The three battalions quarrelling amongst themselves all the time. The three battalions number about 500 (sic) all together. The Firsts would say 'You Seconds came out by mistake in '14, and when you did you were only resting out here. You lot haven't seen a war yet'. Then the Seconds would say 'You Firsts all go to Geissen, your battalion are the Kaiser's bodyguard, some of your battalion have gone to their country and the army put us with you to stop the rest of you going.' Then the Thirds would chime in 'You lousy lot, the two of your battalions should have been at Zonnebeke to know there was a war on. None of you have woke up yet'.

The comment about the Kaiser's bodyguard reflects the fact that a large number of the 1st Monmouths had been taken prisoner during the fighting of the 8th May as their flanks collapsed and most of these men ended up in the prisoner of war camp at Geissen in Germany. Perhaps such sentiments are understandable and rivalry can be healthy to keep the mind of the men on the job at hand. Just how far this rivalry went can only be guessed at, but the losses sustained by all the battalions during the heavy fighting of the previous month or so probably made the survivors all the more protective of their own identity. The difficulties of the merger of the three battalions was further remarked upon by Sgt. Love but as a senior NCO he appears to have been somewhat more understanding:

> *But anyone with half an eye could see they were not going to 'soldier' together because two were infantry and one a portion of a Rifle Battalion. To 'put the fat in the fire', I was posted to B Company as Platoon Sergeant and all my men were riflemen. When I gave them the order to 'slope arms' they nearly dropped dead with fright! I kept cool and got the Captain to talk to the men. They did their best while I was with them and we got along very well together.*

At Herzeele the battalion was gradually pulled together to form something like a useful unit again. The effects of the fighting was shattering on officers and men alike and a period away from the front line and the sound of the shells and stench of gas was absolutely essential. Within days of arriving at Herzeele the battalion was called upon to provide the men to be used in tests of equipment for protection against gas. It is not recorded which company, or companies, provided the men for the tests but since the battalions were now so thoroughly mixed it is probably fair to say that representatives of all three original battalions were present. The gas used during the opening phases of the Ypres fighting had been recognized as chlorine and the rudimentary protection issued during the latter phases of the fighting were a direct result of this knowledge and it undoubtedly saved lives. However, the use of a rag soaked in water was recognized as being an inadequate long term solution. The Monmouths were involved in testing new forms of protection including gas helmets. It is interesting to note that while the Germans had produced large quantities of chlorine to launch the attack the gas was, reportedly, in such short supply to the British Army that the tests undertaken by the Monmouths were held in sealed 'motor omnibuses'. As a result of such tests new gas helmets were developed which were able to combat the worst effects of the gas. Of course, initially the gas helmets were in short supply and when issued to the fighting troops they were issued first to the most 'valuable' members of the battalions such as the machine gunners. Perhaps this was somewhat harsh on the rest of the battalion but it was recognized that well trained machine gun crews could do much to hold up, or halt, any attack that may accompany the use of gas.

It was at about the same time that the men of the battalion began to hear disturbing stories from home. Many of the men had come from the heavily industrialized valleys of the county and many had been miners in civilian life. To read in letters and newspapers of their friends in the mines back home going on strike for more pay caused some consternation. The men amongst them who had been miners undoubtedly understood the feelings at home and it would be true to say that coal-owners were making money as a result of the war, but to some it still seemed wrong. After all, the men at the front were in considerably more danger than the miners though the conditions in the mines were recognized to be dangerous. Numerous letters from the soldiers were published in local newspapers such as the *South Wales Argus* and the *Western Mail*, many expressing the disgust of the soldiers which can be summed up by the short statement of one soldier:

We can combat gas, shells and bullets but indifference and selfishness we can never stand.

This comment had probably been published to show a kind of support for the coal-owners and it was, perhaps, overstating the case somewhat especially since the people of Monmouthshire were very supportive of their Territorials. In Tredegar, for instance, there was a call, made in the council chamber, for the Monmouths to be allowed to come home for a period of rest and recovery. This was brought about after the horrifying casualty lists from the fighting of May had reached the town. Of course, it was soon realized that the council had no sway with the military authorities and the motion was dropped. However, it serves to illustrate the fact that there was much support for the work of the Monmouthshire battalions in France and Flanders. As far as the soldiers were concerned there was little enough that they could do about the events unfolding at home and whilst it may have rankled with them they had been on active service long enough to realize they had work to be getting on with and for the next couple of months they did exactly that as an amalgamated battalion whilst the industrial unrest at home rumbled on through the summer of 1915.

The stay at Herzeele was short, about two weeks, but during that time the battalion had been brought up to strength and was marched back towards the front under the command of the newly promoted Lieut. Col. Bridge. They were bivouacked for the night on the Rozenhillbeek near Reninghelst while the commanding officer and a party of officers visited the front line between Bois Carré and Bois Quarante to the south of Ypres. The battalion was to defend this area in the coming weeks and compared to their experiences of April and May it was considered to be a quiet sector, described in the battalion histories as 'a pleasant change'. After the shelling they had suffered on Frezenberg Ridge this must be seen as a fairly typical piece of understatement.

On the 12th June, 1915, the amalgamated battalion was back in the trenches taking over the line from the 7th King's Royal Rifle Corps, a New Army unit and the first with which they had been in contact, in the area that the officers had visited the night before. As an indication of the shortage of men along this section of line it is interesting to note that the tours of duty in the front line had been increased from four days to seven days - perhaps in a quiet part of the line there was considerably less wear and tear on the units concerned but the main reason would seem to have been to make the limited resources available go just that bit further. The soldiers of the battalion were now all experienced in the ways of the front line and wasted no time in making themselves comfortable upon their arrival to face the enemy once again. The trenches in this area have been described as being very wet and uncomfortable and much work was needed to keep them in a reasonably good state. This was partly because the line of trenches followed a low point in the very gentle countryside and the trenches themselves were acting as drainage channels for the surrounding country. Rifleman D.C. Brooke, originally a member of the 1st Battalion, was to comment on this first tour of the trenches as a combined battalion as follows:

> We got into the trenches on Saturday night without anyone being hit. It was a fairly quiet part of the line, and I was sharing rather a decent dugout with a platoon sergeant so we were able to be fairly comfortable during the day. Of course, we were always awake at night. After we had been there three days

our platoon were moved to another part of the trench in which we had to do a lot of work. Naturally we weren't quite pleased we had to work like niggers to make things safe. Anyhow, the next day one or two of us were jolly thankful we had moved when we heard a shell had dropped plum on top of our old dugout, killing the occupants and wounding several who were near.

The casualties of this small incident included three men of the 2nd Monmouths who would appear to have been the occupants of the dugout and who had been serving with B Company of the combined unit. During this return spell in the trenches lasting no more than seven days and in a quiet sector, the battalion suffered seven killed and thirty-two wounded mostly as a result of the shelling of B Company's part of the line. This gives some idea just how 'quiet' the line was. The battalion was relieved by the 1st Welsh and the 2nd Cheshires on the night of the 17th/18th June and this was to establish the pattern for the next couple of weeks as these battalions took turns in the line. During the next two tours in the front line the battalion was shelled and the casualties were accepted as 'part of the daily routine'. Subsequent tours were not as unfortunate as the first in this area but after three tours the battalion had suffered forty-nine casualties from shelling and sniping.

At the start of July the battalion was withdrawn from this area to a rest camp known as Canada Huts near Ouderdoum some four miles (6 km) behind the firing line. At this time the senior officers of the battalion were consulted by Brigadier General L.J. Bols to discuss the possibility of reforming the original battalions. These were little more than preliminary moves since it had been barely five weeks since they had been amalgamated - it did, however, signal the intent of the commanders of the army that the present situation would not be allowed to continue for long and that the three battalions would resume their separate existence as soon as possible. For some of the men of the battalion this area proved to be of some interest since they had found a way of supplementing their army rations. The nearby Dikkebus Lake still had a population of wild ducks and some of the men were happy to shoot them and then throw off their clothes to swim out to collect their food - probably not sanctioned by the officers, but what they didn't know about couldn't hurt them!

The stay in Canada Huts was short, lasting about a week, before the battalion was moved to another camp, Badajos Huts, near Locre (Loker) where they remained until the 19th July. Whilst out at rest the officers of the battalion organized a sports day on the 9th July as a means to boosting the morale amongst the men. To ensure its success cash prizes were offered and the soldiers competed willingly in the hope of winning a few francs extra to boost their pay. As usual the period out at rest came to an end all too quickly and the battalion was assigned a new portion of the line in the area of Lindenhoek, in front of Kemmel. The battalion headquarters were established at Lindenhoek Chalet which was, in mid 1915, more or less untouched by the effects of war and was surrounded by woodland. At this time the 84th Brigade headquarters were in Kemmel Chateau some distance behind the lines on the flanks of Mount Kemmel. Those lucky enough to be engaged on Brigade duties had a relatively easy time of it at the Chateau though it was still dangerous to be seen at the front of the Chateau, for watchful German snipers were quite capable of adding to their tally even at what must have been the extreme range of their weapons:

49

We all have a swim in the moat at the back of the Chateau. No one allowed in the front. If you show a light in the front at night you get a bullet as it is in sight of the Germans. No one allowed over Kemmel Hill by day, orderlies and motorcyclists only. We have to push our bicycles near the hedge over the top, so far, although not allowed to stop what a wonderful view from the top of the Hill. We lie in the hedge and have a good look around from the top of the hill. You can see the trenches, two lots of barb wire, the soldiers - English and German - in their trenches, people working in their fields behind the German lines and German aeroplanes flying low behind their lines towards Ypres. A wonderful sight!

The battalion's status as old soldiers was clearly established whilst in this sector. As they had learned the skills of trench warfare from the Regulars some months before so they were to pass on their knowledge to the 6th Welsh, a Territorial unit newly arrived from England. Their commander was Lieut. Col. Lord Ninian Crichton Stewart who was later to fall in his battalion's attack at Loos. The fortunes of the Monmouth men had changed greatly since they had been given their trench instruction. They filled the role of instructors for but a short time. The battalion was withdrawn on the night of the 22nd July so that the process of separating its various elements could begin. The 2nd Monmouths were considered to be strong enough to recommence their duties on an individual basis though this cannot have been on the basis of the number of men available which was given as follows:

> 1st Battalion: 7 officers; 193 other ranks
>
> 2nd Battalion: 12 officers, 476 other ranks
>
> 3rd Battalion: 8 officers; 273 other ranks

These figures show that the 1st and 2nd Battalions were numerically weaker than when the amalgamation had taken place whilst the 3rd Battalion was only slightly stronger. If the reasons for the re-establishment of the 2nd Battalion were not numerical then they have not been recorded. It would appear to make no sense to break up a weakened unit in this manner, but perhaps it was felt that with the redistribution of the divisions in the summer of 1915 it was time for the 2nd Battalion to rejoin the 4th Division. In any event the men of the 2nd Battalion were removed from the combined unit and on the 23rd July they paraded at Locre, under the command of Capt. E. Edwards, where they later entrained for a journey that was to rejoin them with their division and take them on their first visit to a part of the front line in France with which they were to become very familiar in the next year or so. But even on that parting, if some reports are to be believed, some of the old rivalries re-emerged and they were wished farewell with swearing and oaths from the members of the other battalions.

The other two battalions were clearly way below their effective strength and were to remain together until the 11th August when the 1st Battalion, commanded by Major C.A. Evill, was finally separated from the 3rd Battalion, commanded by Lieut. Col. W.S. Bridge. It had been an unusual experience for all concerned and was certainly one which was remembered by everyone. Each battalion went on to different things and wherever they went, the three battalions added credit to the name the Monmouthshire Regiment had gained at the time of the 2nd Battle of Ypres.

Chapter Six

'A Rifle Shot Makes Us Jump'
(August 1915 - January 1916)

As the 2nd Monmouths climbed aboard their train at Locre there can have been no one amongst them who was fully aware of the reason for their rapid departure from the Ypres area. They were an under strength battalion commanded by a captain but were still part of a major move within the British Army. It had been agreed, at the highest level within the allied command, that the British Army should begin extending its line and take a greater responsibility for the prosecution of the war. This, of course, was only possible as Britain mobilized her resources and more and more units became available to the army commanders and allowed them to redistribute their forces accordingly. In July, 1915, the first units of the British Army took over a section of line near the town of Albert, in the Picardy region of northern France, and throughout the following month or so new units arrived to enable the line to be manned by the British from Curlu in the south to Hébuterne in the north. This fifteen miles (25 km) length of front came under the command of the Third Army which was made up of the VIII Corps and the X Corps. It was to join the former of these Corps that the 4th Division, including the 2nd Monmouths, had been sent south. To the north of Hébuterne was the French Tenth Army and to the south of Curlu was the French Sixth Army. The south, or right, of the British line was against the River Somme, a name which was to become familiar to all the units of the British Army before the war was over and which has come to typify the slaughter of the Western Front to generations of Britons. However, in 1915 this sector was very quiet. The French had here, as in other parts of the line, tended to allow a kind of peaceful coexistence with the Germans to develop and there are records of French and German troops using the same front line village for billets at the same time without fighting breaking out between them.

The 2nd Monmouths moved via Godewaersvelde, where they changed trains, to Doullens where they arrived on the morning of the 25th July, 1915. From Doullens they were marched to Louvencourt, a distance of 8 miles (13 km). This march was almost relaxation for some of the men. They were now away from the stresses of the defence of the Salient and in a part of the country which had escaped the effects of the war to a large extent. To the men who two months earlier were fighting in the mud and gas of the Salient, it was a very green and pleasant countryside and as the battalion marched it sang almost in memory of the long route marches in England, now a lifetime behind them. At Louvencourt there was a short pause of one day while the battalion put its internal organization in order. The following day the battalion was marched to Forceville where it rejoined the 12th Brigade of the 4th Division. It had been two months since they had parted company and during the day spent at Forceville many friendships were resumed. The following day the battalion moved to its position on the front at the village of Auchonvillers facing the Germans holding the line in front of Beaumont Hamel. It is recorded, rather incredulously, by the battalion historian, that a number of civilians were still living in Auchonvillers although much of the village had been smashed by shelling throughout the recent months. This further served to indicate to the Monmouths that this was a quiet area since civilians within some 800 yards (738 m) of the enemy would have been unthinkable at Ypres. The Monmouths, however, considered that, for their safety, the remaining villagers should be cleared out before they could settle down to their duty. Battalion headquarters was set up in one of the undamaged houses and the junior officers mess was organized in a house near the cross-roads in the village. For the next few weeks it was to be the duty of the battalion to turn Auchonvillers in to a strong point. It was ideally situated for just such a use since the village offered good views of the front line and good fields of fire which would assist its defence in the event of an enemy breakthrough. At Auchonvillers Capt. A.J.H. Bowen rejoined the battalion and, fully recovered from his wounds received during the 2nd Battle of Ypres, took over the command of the Battalion from Capt. Edwards as a temporary measure.

The trenches in this area are described as 'flimsy' and served to underscore the almost casual approach of the French to the defence of this part of the line. Conditions for trench digging were, overall, much better in this area of chalk down-land than they were in the muddy low lying Flanders Plain and there can be no doubt that the Monmouths took to their task with a measure of confidence in their ability to dig trenches in good ground. Pte. C.P. Heare was to report on the conditions as follows:

> The battalion goes in the trenches, but what a picnic, communication trench dry, all brick bottom, the weather is grand. The front line is dry and straight so our boys have to alter it and dig (fire bays) in case of shell fire, dugouts, dry and beds in some. The French officers have done well here. It is so quiet, it is getting on our nerves, so quiet. At night we almost whisper. To go up the line and not meet a soul either way, it's lonely, a rifle shot makes us jump.

There was little interference from the enemy at this time but some shelling occurred at the same time every day and, since everyone was expecting it, casualties were very light. There was little that the British Army could do to respond. The artillery shortage so keenly felt during the fighting at Ypres, was still a problem leaving the British gunners with little with which to reply. It is said that shells were rationed to as little as four per gun per day at this period - hardly sufficient to trouble the Germans in this sector. For the 2nd Mons there was, however, much work to be done to ensure the defence of Auchonvillers for besides the trench digging, houses, ruins and cellars were fortified against attack. In this kind of situation where there was much less danger of battle fatigue or injury than earlier in the year, it was possible for the battalion officers to experiment with methods of working in an attempt to achieve even greater efficiency. Up to this time the work had been allotted to the men in fixed time periods, that is the men worked for a fixed number of hours every day until the task was completed. However by experimentation it was demonstrated, at least to the satisfaction of the battalion officers, that the best method of working was to set the task and allow the men to stop working when the task was completed, that is, 'job and finish' as it was known to many of the men in their civilian lives. In most cases the work could be finished more quickly since the stronger or more capable men would help their comrades so that all could finish. It is suggested that this was the beginning of the reputation which the 2nd Monmouths were to build for themselves for their work in rapid trench digging and similar works later in the war. Perhaps, the experiments did demonstrate this fact quite effectively but it was not a time to accept it as a once and for all idea for as the war progressed various experiments in the use of manpower were conducted. For the men it was work and no matter what they did there was, generally, a will to see the job done well, no matter what the conditions. This was to become particularly relevant following their conversion to a pioneer battalion in 1916.

No sooner had the battalion arrived in Auchonvillers when there was reason to believe that the enemy were actively mining in the area. Capt. A.H. Edwards, whose mining party had been so successful in the winter of 1914, was called upon to do something about it. Capt. Edwards and a party of forty men were detached from the battalion to be attached to one of the newly formed Tunnelling Companies of the Royal Engineers. It is not recorded which company they joined but the 178th and the 179th Tunnelling Companies were formed in July, 1915 and assigned to the Third Army. It is possible that the mining party was attached to one of these units though their main work areas were farther south in the X Corps sector from La Boiselle southwards. Later in 1915 it is known that the battalion was attached to the 252nd Tunnelling Company for work in the Redan area. At this time the British mining effort was growing to meet a large demand, so large, in fact, that in part of this area recently occupied by the British infantry French engineers were kept on to assist with the mining works. In this context the 12th Brigade probably felt very pleased to have many experienced miners in the Monmouthshire Regiment and were able to offer assistance to the hard pressed Royal Engineers. The enemy had taken the upper hand in military mining early in the war and it was taking time for the allies to get on even terms so every success, no matter how small, was considered important. In July, 1915, it was known that the enemy were mining towards an area known as the Redan and it was to be the job of Capt. Edwards and his party to do what they could to dissuade him. In this instance it was a very close run thing. All through August Capt. Edwards' party dug galleries in the chalk of the area keeping an ear to the sound of the working of the enemy miners. On the 30th August the enemy could be clearly heard tamping their explosives. Quickly Capt. Edwards organized his counter move in the form of a small charge, or camouflet, which he exploded on the 31st August. He had succeeded in taking the enemy completely by surprise. So complete was the surprise and such was the damage done to the enemy's fighting galleries that the action of the Monmouthshires had effectively put an end to the offensive mining on the part of the enemy in this sector for some time to come.

It would appear that the Germans were aware of the changes that had been taking place in front of them during the summer of 1915. When the 12th Brigade arrived in the sector they organized raids on the enemy and succeeded in bringing back prisoners from Bavarian units which were not, by consensus, considered to be of the best fighting material. Soon after their arrival, however, it was discovered that the Prussians had taken up residence in Beaumont-Hamel and that additional guns of all sizes had been bought into the area. Clearly the Germans were anticipating more problems from the British than they had received at the hands of the French. It was, in effect, a kind of arms race in which the two sides tried to establish themselves as the strongest force in the area. This was to culminate, a year later, in one of the largest battles of the war and one in which the 2nd Monmouths would be involved.

On the 13th August, Lieut. Col. J.C. Jenkins arrived from home to take over the command of the battalion from Capt. A.J.H. Bowen. Lieut. Col. Jenkins had served in the volunteer forces in two spells since 1899 and was an experienced officer. Possibly of greater interest to the ordinary soldier was the fact that he had a formidable reputation as a rugby player and had been capped by Wales in 1906. The men anticipated sound leadership from Jenkins who was, apparently, a man after their own hearts. Unfortunately, his stay with the battalion was short. Possibly as a result of his age, he was 35 years old when he went to France, it would appear that he was not as fit as his sporting career would tend to suggest and he was sent home sick after commanding the battalion for a little over three weeks. It was a disappointment to many of the men and raised a few eyebrows amongst some of the other battalions in the Brigade. On the departure of Jenkins on the 5th September, Capt. Bowen was promoted to Lieut. Col. and given the command of the battalion. This was, perhaps, a rapid elevation for the young Captain, but he had shown his worth at Ypres and was generally respected, if not liked, by the men in his command:

Capt. Bowen has one idea only; duty always, first and last.

was the way one soldier summed up the appointment and in general terms the appointment of someone who had been through the things the ordinary soldier had was to make a good choice for a commanding officer.

For the last week of August the battalion were relieved from the front line in front of Beaumont Hamel and returned to tented billets in Mailly-Maillet. Here, after a month in the area, they were to receive their first real bombardment, probably reflecting the build up of German artillery that almost everyone was aware of:

The Germans shell a small wood at Mailly-Maillet and kill and wound over a hundred horses and a large number of artillery horsemen. The Germans must have brought a heavy gun up on a railway as we have never had this do before. They shell us for half an hour, it's very uncomfortable. The Signal Sergeant says, 'All you infantry with rifles and ammunition go at once to the artillery officer at Mailly Wood.' The officer says 'Shoot all the horses which are not dead, hit them between the eyes.' I had cold sweats, 'Don't stand about', says the officer, 'in case they shell us again'. It's awful to see the horses some standing on three legs and some with large wounds and all whining like babies, but I am surprised how easy it is to shoot a horse. Only a dozen were got away and twenty men were killed and a large number wounded.

Shortly after that the battalion was moved from Brigade reserve to Divisional reserve at Beaussart which was followed by a further spell in the trenches in front of Beaumont Hamel. After a seven week period in and around the front line the battalion was rested in Varennes, to the south of Forceville, during the third week of September. It was pleasant to be away from the line though it had been fairly quiet and there had been but few casualties. All knew, however, they were close enough to the line to be called back at very short notice and could be in action in a very short time. The soldiers made the most of their time of relaxation and one officer was to write of the stay in Varennes as follows:

At the end of the first day the men grouped themselves round the village square with its old church in one corner, and as the brilliant autumn sun slowly sank below the broken line of trees and roof-tops, they commenced to sing, and continued for an hour or more, old Welsh airs and songs in that beautiful untutored harmony of which Welshmen are masters.

No doubt, also, that these tunes were in the minor key and were of longing for home and the remembrance of times gone by, and as they sang they would have remembered the comrades they had lost since their arrival in France a little over ten months earlier - it was but a short time during which the battalion had seen much and their experiences would stand them in good stead for the things that were yet to come.

At this time the expansion of the British Army was proceeding at a rapid pace as units continued to arrive from home in preparation for the attacks planned for the autumn. It was now a quite common sight to see the units raised since the start of the war taking their place with both Regulars and Territorials but as one soldier of the Monmouths commented:

Kitchener's Army are out in number now. New Army, so they call themselves, but it's all one to the Germans.

Many of these 'new', untried units were to find this out at Loos before the month of September had finished. As the autumn progressed the battalion continued its work in and around the front line near Auchonvillers, and there were times when a tour of the line was completed without a single casualty which was unusual even for this relatively quiet portion of the line. The British energies were directed elsewhere as the fighting around Loos continued with heavy casualties on both sides and the Germans, for their part, were looking to their plans for 1916 to bring an end to the siege warfare of the Western Front. As the weather grew steadily worse through the autumn so did the condition of the trenches. Where there had been good dry trenches there were now streams and waterlogged ditches, communication trenches carefully constructed during the summer months became impassable as they filled with mud and water and the front line was little better. The chalk may have provided better ground for trench digging and, as such, required less work for revetment but when it rained they still flowed with water as the soon to be infamous mud of the Picardy fields was washed into them by the rains of autumn and early winter. The maintenance of the trenches under the worsening weather was labour intensive and during this period the battalion was to lose more of its number through the effects of these conditions than through the direct effects of the enemy's action. Even when, supposedly, at rest, the battalion like others of the Brigade, was expected to produce working parties to carry on work under the direction of the Royal Engineers. Sometimes the stresses of continual work made it difficult for individual companies called upon to produce the required numbers of men for working parties. This always produced the displeasure of the hierarchy with the implication, perhaps, that the battalion was not pulling its weight. It is recorded that the Company Sergeant Major of C Company got around this problem by instructing those men already counted into a trench by the RE officer to crawl out of the trench and back to the line of men entering the trench to be counted by him again. In this way C Company always produced the required number of workers for any task that the Engineers may throw at them. What is not recorded, however, is whether or not this action was sanctioned by the company officers, never mind the commanding officer. Bearing in mind that Lieut. Col. Bowen was to become known as something of a disciplinarian it is highly unlikely that he ever got to know about the Sergeant Major's little trick. Presumably the tasks set to the company were always completed and no one complained and the sergeant was able to keep his stripes!

Although it was quiet in this area it was not without incident. Shortly before the arrival of the British in the area the village of Mailly-Maillet had been in German hands but had been retaken by the French. Consequently the discovery of a civilian with a German rifle and bayonet by sentries of the Monmouths was taken very seriously. The Monmouths had been providing guards along roads in the area where pits were being prepared in readiness for heavy guns which made the area somewhat sensitive. The discovery of an armed civilian raised some suspicion and there were immediate thoughts of spying. It was discovered that the civilian had been living in the cellar of a deserted house which, although piled with furniture, gave access to a window that was in clear view of the German lines. It was considered that this could provide the means to allow the civilian to contact the Germans either by the use of a light or by releasing carrier pigeons and thereby impart the information of the distribution and size of the guns to the enemy. However, no direct evidence for either activity was found in the cellar and thus the civilian could not be proved to be a spy which was fortunate for him, at least, since his punishment would have been severe and, more or less, immediate. The 'spy' was taken away by the French authorities for internment and the 2nd Monmouths got to keep the German style bayonet as a souvenir of the incident.

The work in this area continued without a break as winter deepened. On the 14th November, 1915 the Battalion War Diary records that:

During the battalion's tour of 7 days in the trenches the men's behaviour under such adverse conditions was admirable. The work carried out was chiefly the rebuilding of parapets and dug-outs and the keeping of the trenches clear. Four men were sent to hospital with frostbitten feet

The battalion had served overseas for a year and had seen plenty of what the war could offer. All thought of adventure that the ordinary young soldiers had carried with them as they boarded the Manchester Importer in Southampton a year ago was now gone - blown away by the shelling and slaughter of May, 1915. As Christmas 1915 approached there must have been those who thought back to the first Christmas in the line and of the unusual events that took place. This year there was to be no repeat of the informal truce - the military hierarchy had made that perfectly clear. Pte. Arthur Nunnerly, who had landed in France as a replacement in October, 1915, was to write to his brother William as follows:

I received your Christmas cards and thank you. We shall be in the trenches Christmas Day, there is to be no truce this year. They told us we have got to shoot them if they come out..... Don't come out here if you can help it, we are up to our necks in mud.

However, Pte. Nunnerly was mistaken for, apart from a party of 150 men supplied to the 252nd Tunnelling Company for work on the Redan, the 2nd Monmouths were spared the front line duty this time and spent Christmas near the front line at Mailly-Maillet where there was opportunity for a good feed for the men during the day. Some of the men were later entertained by the 4th Division 'Follies', a concert party who did everything to lift the spirits of the soldiers. Those who had been out a year were used to things but Christmas was always considered a bad time to be away from family and friends. None the less throughout Christmas, where possible, everything was done to give the men a good time with cafés and *estaminets* doing a roaring trade amongst certain elements of the troops. It was not the sort of Christmas that any one of them would have wished for but veterans of the front made the most of it - there was no way of telling when they would be called upon to take part in a bold attack or a stubborn defence or even if they would make it to the end of the next week never mind live to the next Christmas.

Chapter Seven

'Three Months Great Holiday'
(February to April 1916)

At the end of January, 1916, with the battalion stationed in the Somme sector at Mailly-Mallet, it was ordered to leave the 12th Brigade of the 4th Division and proceed to rear areas where it was to undertake work on the Lines of Communication. This work was a relief from the 'hardships of the trenches' as the Battalion Historian was to comment years later. For a short time, at least, the battalion was to be split up into companies to provide the manpower for guarding of ammunition dumps and crucial points behind the lines of the Somme sector as well as, on occasion, providing the muscle power for the Army Service Corps when it needed help in the unloading of equipment at rail-heads and docks in north France. Initially the distribution of the companies was:

> Headquarters and C Company to Etaples
> A Company to Doullens
> B Company to Boulogne
> D Company to Calais.

This basic distribution was further complicated since each company was split further into groups of about 20 men and scattered all over the *départements* of the Pas de Calais and the Somme. The work was largely the guarding of ports, rail-heads and ammunition dumps and it can be imagined that the men, some of whom had been in the trenches for over a year, thought it was a 'cushy' number. There were regular baths, clean clothes and plenty of food and none of the dangers associated with the rigours of living in the front line.

At this time it was necessary for the companies to act almost independently whilst staying within the structure of the battalion commanded by Lieut. Col. A.J.H. Bowen. For the Colonel it presented a number of problems not least the maintenance of discipline in his far flung battalion. But Bowen managed this and one of the entries in his notebook shows exactly how he managed this task:

> *Inspected detachment at DESVRES under Sergeant Wallis. Rode on horse-*
> *back to SAMER then DESVRES and back (42 kilometres). 4 men short of iron*
> *rations. Sentry (off duty?) sitting down away from rifle, buttons undone.*

But, for all the spread of the battalion, the time was one of relaxation by comparison to the previous months. Bowen's accounts of the period indicate the detail which he paid to all things and to the various problems he addressed as part of his daily routine as commanding officer.

> *Inspected MONTREUIL detachment. Exchange Kembrey for a man from*
> *HQ. K(embrey) now in hospital. 1209 Pte. Phipps wants a pair of boots*
> *(No.8). 2263 Pte. Francis wants another pair of trousers: at present he has*
> *only one pair of pantaloons, also wants to exchange his tunic, present one*
> *too short. Phipps claims time expired. Rooms in billet clean and tidy, latrines*
> *clean but smell in yard from old refuse pit trench. Cookhouse clean - one*
> *canteen top lying out...*

and the following day at Longpre, he records:

> *Sgt. Pike guardroom dirty and smoky, arranged that hut should be*
> *provided for the guard. Billet, latrines and cookhouse clean and tidy. Two*
> *men recently down with (gonorrhoea), warned men against indulgence.*
> *Turner recently in hospital with scabies, returned. Room and blankets have*
> *been disinfected. 303 SAA deficient. Rifles clean.*

The work of the Colonel was not diminished by the change of duty and the type of notes made by Bowen indicate the problems. Nonetheless the last entry mentioned above indicates quite clearly that some men, at least, were doing their very best to have a good time and unfortunately at some cost.

In early April, Headquarters and C Company moved from Etaples to Boulogne where they joined B Company. This was the only major change in the disposition of the troops of the 2nd Mons during their stay on the Lines of Communication. Undoubtedly, Bowen saw this as an opportunity to do some much needed training as he insisted the company should move by march route the nineteen miles between Etaples and the new camp in the St. Martin's district of Boulogne. The War Diary for the 11th April, 1916, records an extract from Routine Orders which states that:

> *Commanding Officer congratulates ETAPLES Detachment on their very*
> *creditable performance of marching to Boulogne, a distance of 30 kilometres,*
> *and particularly compliments all ranks on that fact there was not a single*
> *case of anyone falling out.*

Bowen may have been a man who paid strict attention to detail but he also appears to have been happy to give credit where he considered it was deserved.

The work away from the front line would have been thought of as being relatively free from danger but working in an industrialized area, such as much of north west France had become, was not without its risks. Whilst on duty in Calais, Pte. Fred Jones was to discover just this but at the same time he was to earn

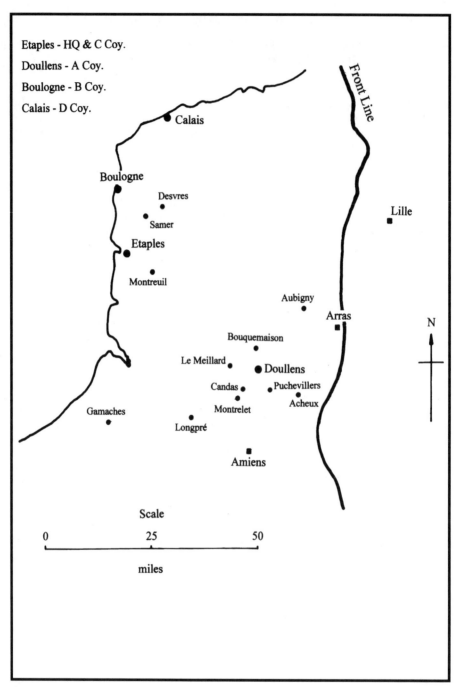

Etaples - HQ & C Coy.
Doullens - A Coy.
Boulogne - B Coy.
Calais - D Coy.

Front Line

Calais

Boulogne

Desvres

Samer

Etaples

Montreuil

Aubigny

Arras

Lille

N

Bouquemaison

Le Meillard

Doullens

Candas

Puchevillers

Montrelet

Acheux

Gamaches

Longpré

Amiens

Scale

0   25   50

miles

Lines of Communication. Sketch showing dispersal of the battalion.

himself a little praise from the Inspector General Commanding the Lines of Communication, Lieut. Gen. F. T. Clayton, who was to write, as part of Orders, that:

> The I.G.C. wishes to express his appreciation of the plucky conduct of No. 3328 Private F. Jones, 1/2nd Monmouthshire Regiment. On the 7th April, 1916, at Calais, Private Jones was crossing a bridge when he heard someone in the water shouting for help. It was dark at the time and the depth of the quayside was at least 12 feet. Private Jones jumped in, caught hold and supported the man until a rope was thrown to them and both rescued.

Pte. Fred Jones was killed in action later the same year. The facilities enjoyed by the battalion at this time varied greatly depending on where each party was billeted. At Puchevillers, for instance, Sgt. Jackson and his group of 17 men were living in tents since there were no houses nearby which could be used. However, they were well organized with separate bathing and dining tents. Sgt. Jackson's party was engaged on 'police work by day and sentry work by night'. At Acheux, where the 'civilians were not very clean', Sgt. Webb's party was billeted in a barn whilst at Aubigny 2nd Lieut. Sankey and his men were billeted in cottages that were considered to be 'very comfortable'. Bowen commented also:

> SAVY BERLETT. Sgt. Walters and 15 men. Billeted close to station in red French huts. Comfortable wire beds, each man had three blankets but only 1 tunic, 1 pr trousers and boots each. The Sgt. stated he had indented 3 days ago to complete clothing to 2 per man. Cooking and dining hut very clean and tidy. Baths in hut nearby. Cooks provide hot water. No sick lately. Men wash their own clothes.

Of course, the conditions for some were not without problems and there were requests to Bowen for all manner of things from packs of playing cards to promotion. Where possible the needs of the men were authorized by Bowen. This helped to keep the morale of the battalion high particularly since it was so widely spread out there was no opportunity for it to be gathered together for such things as company drill or even the sporting events for which some of the battalion officers were justly famed. Sometimes it appears that the soldiers of the small units took things into their own hands. At one of the guarded ammunition dumps in A Company's area, a young and enthusiastic officer of Royal Artillery came in for a particular kind of rough soldier's justice. The officer concerned was in the habit of turning up, unannounced, at dusk in the effort to surprise the guard and then berating the unfortunate soldier for lack of attention to duty. One Private Green decided it was time to do something about this officer's annoying habit. Pte. Heare recorded that:

> About a week later Green and I were on sentry. Almost dark, Green says to me 'There is that officer watching us'. Green put up his rifle and let go 'Say I shouted halt three times' says Green 'It'll stop his game'. A bit later down came the officer, white as death, Green had missed him 'What the hell do you mean firing like that? I will have you under arrest' Green said, 'I shouted halt three times and receiving no answer I fired as you told us to' All the other sentries and the Corporal in charge were out by now. The officer questioned me, I stood by Green, then he asked the Corporal, he said, 'I was in the tent with the other sentries off duty and heard Green, heard him Sir'

'Oh' says the officer, 'when did you land in France?' '1914' says the Corporal smiling, off goes the officer and we never hardly saw him again and never after dark.

The soldiers of one little group felt that they had sorted out one small irritation for themselves but it was not without some considerable risk when it is remembered how they all lied to support Private Green. Perhaps, morale was better than may have been expected and sticking together as they had done demonstrated this. There was, also, a touch of pride in the comment that they had arrived in 1914 - something that tended to set the battalion apart by the spring of 1916.

All good things must come to an end and there had been changes under way in the organization of the British Army throughout the latter part of 1915 and early 1916 which were about to catch up with the 2nd Monmouths. It had been recognized from the early part of 1915 that there would be a need for specialist units to carry out the more mundane work of trench warfare. Things, which we may consider as ordinary, such as the digging of fire trenches or communication trenches required special knowledge and skills but was far too labour intensive to be left to the Royal Engineers all the time. Early in the war labour units had been created by the Royal Engineers and the Army Service Corps to lessen the load on the more highly trained front line soldiers. However, these men were usually those who were too unfit or too old for service in the front line and as such were used far behind the firing line. It was clear to the military hierarchy that similar units were required by the infantry and that such units would need to be fit and trained in infantry methods but still be of sufficient skill, and strength, to carry out the labour of trench warfare. The result of this thinking was the formation of the pioneer battalions in the last quarter of 1915. These battalions were often drawn from the mining areas of Britain where soldiers were commonly skilled in the use of pick and shovel and so it became almost natural that the men of the South Wales valleys would become involved in this work. In September 1915, the 3rd Mons, a sister battalion, became attached to the 49th (West Riding) Division as pioneers. Later the 1st Mons were attached to the 46th (North Midland) Division. It must have seemed inevitable to the officers of the 2nd Mons that the battalion would eventually end up as a pioneer unit and it could have been that the transfer to the Lines of Communication was the first step in this process. However, it was not until the 23rd April, 1916, that it was recorded in the War Diary that:

> *Secret orders were received that the battalion would be converted into a pioneer battalion and would join the 29th Division by the end of the month. Indents for conversion from Infantry establishment to Pioneer were prepared and sent into the G.O.C Boulogne. These were subsequently amended as the old table in possession of the Battalion was not the latest issue. Warning orders were sent out to the various Detachments it being arranged that the concentration of the Battalion would be in the 4th Army area at Doullens. Preliminary concentrations of B, C, and D companies at Boulogne. A Coy. and Lewis Gun Section at Doullens.*

Thus the wheels had been set in motion and for the next couple of days the battalion was busy reorganizing itself in line with the instruction in the above extract. There is no comment on the Division it was to join but there must have been some feeling of pride amongst the officers since the 29th Division was a Regular division that had seen sterling service in Gallipoli and had only recently reached France where it was to continue its reputation of magnificent service. One of the first tasks to be dealt with as part of the reorganization to pioneers was that the Transport Officer, Lieut. J.E. Dunn, together with a small party, left for Abbeville where he was to collect additional transport allotted to the battalion as part of its conversion. His instructions were to collect 32 light draught horses and eight pack ponies together with eight general service wagons and to join the battalion as it concentrated in Doullens. These horses were recorded later as being Australian and not in very good condition. At about the same time Pte. Heare was to comment as follows:

> *After three months of great holiday, football, nights in Doullens - when we had money - we form up for a short arms inspection, how many we do have. Then we all join our companies and the battalion reforms at Doullens. Capt. Edwards, a short man, is our company officer - a good sort.*

B and C companies, at Boulogne, were relieved by the 1st Royal Munster Fusiliers whilst the outlying guards in areas such as Bassin and Petit Port were relieved by members of the Black Watch. These two companies left the Gare Central, Boulogne at 8.30 am on the 28th April though their transport had gone on ahead some two hours earlier. The journey for this portion of the battalion was typical of those endured during the war and was slow and they arrived in Doullens, after covering a distance of 50 miles, at 3.45 pm where their transport awaited them. It had not been possible for D Company to get to Boulogne and so it had been decided that they would make their way to Doullens independently. They fared even worse in that it took them almost twenty four hours of travelling to reach Doullens where they arrived at mid-day on the 29th April. The battalion strength on concentration in Doullens was 29 officers and 735 other ranks.

Immediately work started on getting the companies organized as they had been before they had taken on their work on Lines of Communication. The men were given a short route march of some four and a half miles and 'the men were very soft on the feet and shoulders owing to their having no practice while on Lines of Communication' reports the War Diary. The following day a similar route march in the heat of a warm spring day was said to be found trying. Perhaps this was not the best start for the men who were soon to be in some very difficult conditions. However, the next route march in the cool of the evening of the next day found the 'men much better'. This was the 29th April. A day earlier the Commanding Officer had issued an instruction to the Adjutant

> *Please instruct Lieut. Braddeley and CQMS + 1 man of each company and 1 man for Transport and 1 man for HQ to proceed to BEAUSSART tomorrow 29.4.16 as an advance party to arrange billets. They will proceed by train for ACHEUX leaving Doullens at 7.28 am and march from ACHEUX to BEAUSSART. They will take rations up to and for the 30 inst. Bathing in the River AUTHIE is forbidden.*

With this order Bowen identified the area to which the battalion was moving to officially start its job as a pioneer battalion and where it became attached to the 29th Division. The battalion marched to Beaussart on the 1st May, 1916 which was described as a warm day. During the march of fifteen and a half miles only seven men were to fall out. The battalion was inspected on this march by Lieut. Gen. Hunter-Weston who, apparently, spoke to the officers of the battalion concerning the need for drill and good march discipline. Whether anything was considered to be amiss with the battalion's discipline at the inspection is not recorded but one can only assume that the general felt it his duty to at least remind the officers of the battalion of their's. Good discipline was needed later on the march when enemy observation balloons were spotted. Initially the march was continued with a gap on 300 yards between the companies but as their destination was reached the battalion was strung out further by a spacing of 100 yards between the platoons. On arrival in Beaussart there was some disappointment since the War Diary records the billets as 'very poor and dirty' whilst one of the soldiers goes even further and describes it as 'a god forsaken hole'. Nonetheless the battalion was now back in the rear of a fighting zone, something they had not seen since they left the 4th Division in January of the same year.

From that moment on the battalion ceased to have a strictly infantry rôle as it was now to provide the manpower for the labouring tasks of the three brigades of the 29th Division. In future months, and eventually years, they were to face the rigours of trench warfare more or less continuously. It was to be hard, often dangerous, but necessary work and something that the battalion seem to have excelled in, as will be seen in the coming pages.

Chapter Eight

'And there was No Element of Surprise'
(May to July 1916)

For many the attack at 7.30 a.m. on 1st July was the first experience of going over the top. For too many it was the last. (The Story of the 29th Division)

In joining the 29th Division, the 2nd Battalion the Monmouthshire Regiment was becoming part of a division that had already built up a reputation in the Gallipoli campaign as the 'incomparable 29th'. The division was, in spite of its high identification number, a regular division composed of units who had been serving overseas when the events of August 1914 changed their peacetime Empire duty to active service. Its three brigades contained battalions of regiments as famous as any in the British army amongst whom were the 2nd Battalion the South Wales Borderers, the regular regiment to which the Monmouthshires were always closely affiliated. The division had gained substantial honour during the Gallipoli campaign, but in doing so had suffered heavy casualties that threatened to change the character of the units involved in much the same way that the regular divisions in France and Flanders had changed to some extent following the fighting of late 1914 and early 1915. Nevertheless, the character of the regular battalions in the division was not completely lost as a result of the Gallipoli fighting since there remained a core of regular officers and NCO's who were able to instill in the newcomers a sense of identity and duty that may have been absent in less famous divisions. The reputation it had gained in Gallipoli had been expensively won and it was not to be surrendered lightly. Thus the Monmouths, with their somewhat lesser reputation, had a lot to live up to and there can be little doubt that a lot was expected of them by both divisional and brigade commanders. However, by May, 1916, the 2nd Monmouths were veterans of the Western Front and although they may have preferred to have remained as an

65

infantry unit, decisions at high level had assigned them the task of pioneers to the 29th Division. Part of the problem, as with the other battalions of the Monmouthshire Regiment, was that the losses that had occurred throughout 1915 had never been fully replaced. This meant that divisional commanders had a measure of reluctance to accept them in place of a full strength battalion that may have been earmarked for pioneer duty. The 2nd Monmouths, along with its sister battalions, had shown its mettle as infantry in 1915 - no one disputed this - but it made sense to convert a numerically weak unit from an industrial area into pioneers when the divisional reorganizations occurred during 1915 and 1916. In the 29th Division the addition of the 2nd Monmouths as pioneers was accompanied by the addition of the 16th Middlesex and the loss of the 1st Munster Fusiliers who had relieved the Monmouths from their Lines of Communication duties in Boulogne. Whilst the War Diary makes little comment on the change to pioneers it is probably fair to say that there was a measure of disappointment at not being able to continue as infantry. However, the change was accepted and they got on with adopting their new identity. One of the soldiers of the battalion was to comment:

> It looks like war now. All the men of the 29th Division have a triangle piece of cloth, scarlet, sewn on each sleeve near the shoulder and regiments have their own colours sewn on the back of the coat near the collar. The 2nd Mons is a green piece with a red stripe through it. The thin red line the boys call it.

Thus the battalion became the pioneers to the 29th Division. Of course, battalions raised in the heavily industrialized areas of Great Britain were an obvious choice as pioneer battalions since many contained manual labourers and miners - ideal material for the works of trench digging and road repair and so forth. The Welsh valleys produced a rich source of such men. All three battalions of the Monmouthshire Regiment were converted to pioneers in 1915 and 1916 whilst two battalions of the South Wales Borderers and three of the Welsh Regiment were also to become pioneers. As mentioned above, the losses sustained by the Monmouthshire Regiment had, somewhat perversely, made their conversion to pioneers an inevitability in the eyes of the divisional commanders they were eventually to serve. Sadly, perhaps, no objection to this was offered by higher echelons as the Regiment received scant recognition for its service as infantry. However, many of the officers recognized the worth of the men in their command and sought the same level of excellence from them as pioneers as they would have as pure infantrymen. In this manner the 2nd Battalion the Monmouthshire Regiment was able to gain recognition from those with whom it served.

The end of the fighting in Gallipoli had released troops for service in France, where most of the senior Staff believed the war would be won or lost. Amongst these troops were the 29th Division. Its presence in France was part of a general build up of forces on the Western Front in early 1916 for what was to be a major joint offensive with full co-operation between the French and the British being fundamental to the scheme. At a conference in Chantilly in December, 1915, both nation's military commanders had considered that the joint offensive was necessary to break the deadlock that was the warfare of the Western Front. The policy of both nations' commanders was one of attack to drive the Germans off French soil and, perhaps logically, the best place for this joint action to occur was along the junction between the two armies, that is, along both sides of the River Somme. The French were to attack to the south of the river while the British forces were to attack the Germans to the north of the river. There was no particular military reason for the siting of the attack - there was no reason to believe the Germans were any less prepared for attack here than at any other point in the line. In fact the Somme had been a quiet sector for most of the war and as such the Germans had had a long time to prepare their defences. It is, however, worth remembering that to make a joint attack anywhere else was likely to have created logistical problems bearing in mind the large quantities of both men and equipment that would be needed to move to the front on a transport system that was already stretched almost to breaking point. It was, in all probability, easier to accomplish the attack with the minimum re-arrangement of the front line forces and consequently this was achieved by the British extending their right flank as the French moved troops from their left.

Whilst the plan may have had sufficient merit for there to have been considerable hope of success one factor was to play a major role in the strategic planning for the offensive. That factor was that in February, 1916, the Germans launched an enormous offensive against the French at Verdun - a name that was soon to represent the dogged determination of the French nation and the slaughter that was the Western Front. In a matter of months the casualties at Verdun meant that the commitment of the French to the fighting about the Somme was reduced as more and more of her soldiers were sucked into the fighting. Further, it was becoming increasingly difficult for the British to watch the suffering of her ally. Such was the pressure on the French that it became clear that firm action was needed on the part of the British to allow the attention of the Germans to be diverted away from Verdun and give the French a measure of breathing space. There was a problem for the British in that the plans had been for a joint action - but as Verdun continued it became clear to the British commanders that the planned joint attack would now need a different character. That is, the British would need to take the bulk of the fighting upon themselves while the French effort was reduced proportionally by those divisions withdrawn from the Somme front for the defence of Verdun. The responsibility was onerous since it was necessary to alleviate both the pressure on the French and to deliver a blow to the Germans that could be considered a victory and could, perhaps, lead to the end of the war. It was in to this situation that the 29th Division was placed upon its arrival in France along with many other divisions from Great Britain and the the colonies of the Empire. The build up of troops was the biggest that had ever been attempted by the British army in an effort to deal the enemy a knock out blow. By the time the 2nd Battalion the Monmouthshire Regiment had joined the ranks of the 29th Division detailed planning for what was to be known as the Battle of the Somme was well under way.

The immediate task of the battalion was that ordered by the CRE of the 29th Division on the 2nd May, 1916 and compared to the grand schemes being worked out it was rather mundane. This was for the construction of a new road leading form Acheux to Engelbelmer. This order was issued to the troops by Lieut. Col. Bowen who is precise about the arrangements:

Parade for work on FAIRWEATHER RD. tomorrow at 7.45 a.m. Order of companies work from left, B,A,C,D. Companies will march to the left of the sector with 1 pick and 1 shovel per man and commence work as already directed.

Hours of work daily	*9 - 12*
Interval for dinner	*12 - 13.30*
Hours of work	*13.30 - 16.30*

Men must be started on their work by 9 a.m. and 13.30 punctually.

Travelling kitchen will bring out dinners.

Dress: Marching order without packs.

Tea on return to billets.

Breakfast at 6.30.

The work was to construct a 20 feet (6.5 m) wide un-metalled road with a drainage ditch at each side. It was further instructed that all the earth was to be thrown to the centre of the road to allow a camber to be formed. It is clear why this road was to be known as Fairweather Road since a compacted earth road in the Somme area would soon become impassable in any period of wet weather. This name did not last long, for by the end of the first week of May it had been renamed Rotten Row though whether this was the result of experience is unclear but conditions in the woodland through which the road passed were described as 'very wet and muddy'. The line of the road took it through both Acheux Wood and Mailly Wood where conditions were made even more difficult by the heavy undergrowth and an extensive root system - the War Diary records that the men working in this area used ammonal to blow out particularly difficult obstacles. Nonetheless the work progressed well and after a few days work had taken sufficient shape for the new divisional commander, Major General de Lisle, to show his satisfaction of the work carried out by the battalion.

Whilst this work was in progress the battalion had moved from its unsatisfactory billets in Beaussart to a camp in Acheux Woods where the men were accommodated in 78 tents which worked out as roughly ten men per tent. The camp, at one end of Rotten Row, was to be maintained in a clean condition and the men were ordered to clean their tents thoroughly before they left for work each morning. Bowen was mindful of the need to maintain discipline and, since his force was often likely to be split up or separated from the camp, he issued the following order on the day the camp was first occupied, the 6th May 1916:

While engaged with the present work the Battalion will be prepared to move into action on 2 hours notice, every man fully equipped and with 1st line transport. Owing to working parties some difficulty may be experienced in getting men concentrated in Camp. Coy. Commanders will ensure that communications with their Coys is kept open and for the rapid transmission of orders and concentration of men. As soon as a Coy is concentrated, the Commanders will report position and numbers to Cmdg Officer.

Normally concentration will take place in Coy lines but if a Coy is out working an orderly should be sent out at once to report to HQ. To ensure the rapid concentration of their Coys Commanders should warn men what to do in case of the alarm being sounded. Rifles and equipment may be left at the place of concentration but men must always have their smoke helmets by them.

This order reinforced the fact that whilst the battalion was now a pioneer unit it was still expected to fight and Bowen's order gives a clear message to company commanders of what was expected of them apart from ensuring that the work proceeded according to plan.

Three days after this order was issued the battalion was split into two with A and B Companies continuing to work on Rotten Row whilst C and D Companies were moved to Mailly Wood where they came under the control of the West Riding Field Company R.E. and were put to work constructing a communication trench running to the south side of Auchonvillers. The object of this work was to provide a safe link to 2nd Avenue, itself a communication trench, and thereby a relatively safe route to the front line opposite Hawthorn Ridge. The following day Headquarters and A and B Companies were moved to Mailly Wood and pitched camp. This was to be the battalion's billet for the run up to the Battle of the Somme and although the men were often attached to various units over the next six weeks the bulk of the battalion remained at Mailly Wood.

This new billet placed the battalion much closer to the firing line and in direct observation from the enemy balloons along the line and all ranks were advised by Bowen to keep all movement to a minimum. Not only was it possible for the enemy to observe the battalion it was also possible for him to shell it and Bowen was to order his company commanders that:

In the event of the wood being shelled all ranks with arms and equipment will take shelter in the trench by the hedge. O.C. Coys will practice this movement. Platoons must keep together so that the battalion can move rapidly if ordered to do so.

This was the closest the battalion had been to the front line for some time and it was appropriate that Bowen should be reminding his command of the dangers that were now facing them.

During the next six weeks, whilst billeted in Mailly Wood, the battalion was to be involved in all manner of pioneering works. Rotten Row, their first job was finished by mid May and the standard of work they achieved met with the approval of the divisional commander. At about the same time as this work was drawing to a close, Major Edwards of A Company was informed that:

Your Company will work tomorrow, 11.5.16, for the Kent Field Coy. R.E. Work will be (a) Making tunnel dugouts; for this work 80 men with underground and mining experience should be detailed. (b) Sinking a well. (c) other work as detailed by the Field Coy. (b) will require men with mining or pit experience.

It was appropriate that Major Edwards was given these instructions for, oddly enough for a battalion with its roots in the coalfields of South Wales, he was the only officer with mining experience. His company was known to contain 56 experienced miners so it may be assumed that the deficit required for the work

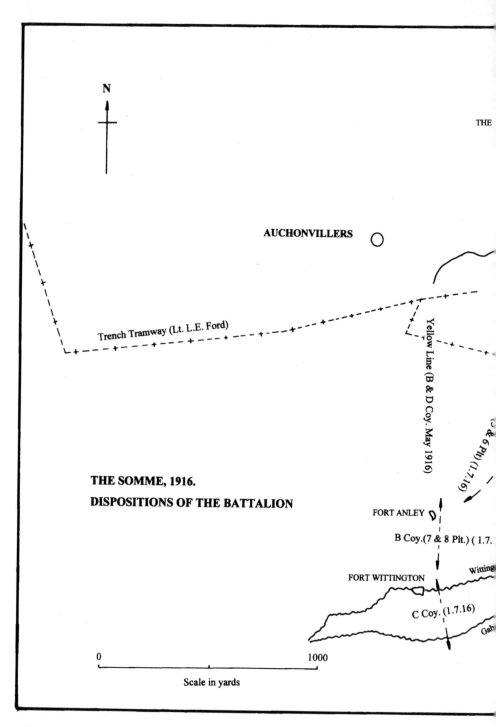

THE

N

AUCHONVILLERS

Trench Tramway (Lt. L.E. Ford)

Yellow Line (B & D Coy. May 1916)

THE SOMME, 1916.

DISPOSITIONS OF THE BATTALION

FORT ANLEY

B Coy.(7 & 8 Plt.) (1.7.

FORT WITTINGTON

Wittin

C Coy. (1.7.16)

Gal

0   1000

Scale in yards

The Somme 1916. Dispositions of the battalion.

70

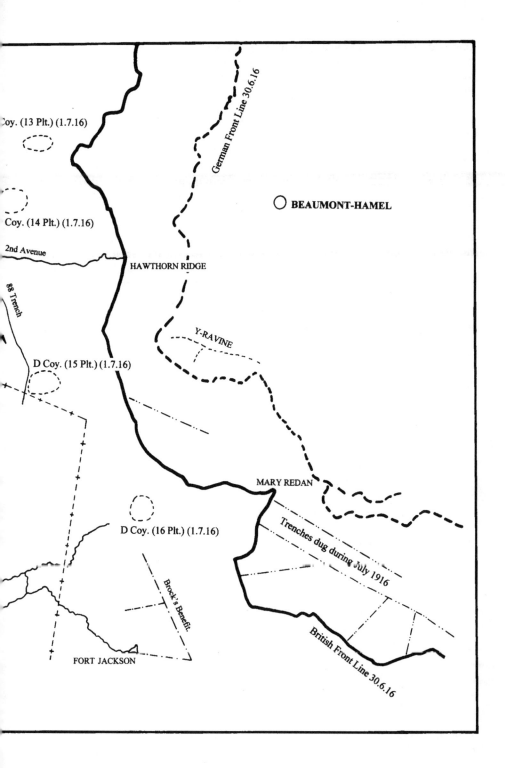

Coy. (13 Plt.) (1.7.16)

Coy. (14 Plt.) (1.7.16)

2nd Avenue

German Front Line 30.6.16

○ BEAUMONT-HAMEL

HAWTHORN RIDGE

88 Trench

Y-RAVINE

D Coy. (15 Plt.) (1.7.16)

MARY REDAN

D Coy. (16 Plt.) (1.7.16)

Trenches dug during July 1916

Brock's Benefit

FORT JACKSON

British Front Line 30.6.16

outlined by Bowen was made up from the other 167 experienced miners known to be present in the battalion. Work on the well was to continue until early June when it was handed over to the CRE having reached 'a depth of 60 feet with an estimated supply of 300 gallons per hour of excellent water'. Work on the Tunnel Dugouts lasted well into June and gradually used up more men as the urgency for their completion grew in the run up to the coming offensive which by that stage much have been obvious to all concerned.

The remaining companies were also required to bend their backs in the toil of trench warfare. B Company was employed on constructing dugouts in the trenches immediately behind the front line. C Company were employed building redoubts near Auchonvillers between the communication trenches known as 2nd and 3rd Avenues; D Company was digging the communication trench linking 2nd Avenue to the south of Auchonvillers with the rear areas. All of this work should be seen as preparatory work for the Battle of the Somme: the well to supply large numbers of men; the communication trench to protect the men from shell fire and the redoubts to improve the defence of the line immediately behind the front line. Further evidence, if any were needed, of the intentions of the Staff came on the 18th May when the battalion with the exceptions of those men involved in tunnelling and the well party were all assigned to various tasks in the preparation of the Yellow Line. The Yellow Line, worked on by the 2nd Monmouths, ran from the south east edge of Auchonvillers in the general direction of Fort Anley some 2,000 yards (1830m) to the south. The Yellow Line was essentially to serve as a reserve line and assembly trench for the coming battle, but that does not mean that any less care was taken over it or that it was constructed to a lesser standard. This was made perfectly clear in Bowen's order of 19th May which ran:

Order of work tonight on Yellow Line 19.5.16

B Coy from 2nd AVENUE to TIPPERARY AVENUE inc.(lusive) wiring a new line about 20 yards from trench between trench and pre-set wire. Height of wire about 3 (feet) and with trip. Remainder of men deepening trench and providing fire step.

A Coy (less 3 platoons) and D Coy from TIPPERARY AVENUE to bridge at FORT ANLEY. Work deepening trench, making fire step out of filled sand bags and building traverses. Earth must not be thrown on the parapet. This now will be concealed from the enemy as fresh earth would be seen. Wiring will be done later.

C Coy (with 1 platoon from A Coy) will dig a new fire trench from the end of present trench south of FORT WITHINGTON on the side of the road to GABION AVENUE where the trench runs on to FORT MOULIN. Depth of the trench 4'6". Bays 8 yards long, traverses 3 yards deep by 4 yards wide, width of trench 3', fire step to be left out of natural earth. Leave a berm for sand revetment. Cover all work up with grass etc.

Work will be started at 8.30 p.m. and finished by 2 a.m. Haversack Ration to be taken. Officers are reminded that they are responsible for the protection of their command against surprise.

Thus, the battalion was employed for the following week. Work was divided into two shifts to keep the pace going; much of the digging was done at night while the revetting and sandbagging was done by day since the men had rather more cover for these tasks. With all this work going on it is to be expected that more would be found to keep the battalion fully employed. On the 26th May the order was received that some of the men would be taken off the Yellow Line to construct a trench on the ridge in front of Fort Jackson at the southern edge of the 29th Division sector. The purpose of the trench was to link up a number of observation posts and make the movement between them easier. The trench was to be known as Brock's Benefit and the work carried out by the battalion was to include two communication trenches, one to the north of Fort Jackson and the other to the south. The War Diary records that Brock's Benefit was:

> an emergency fire trench with a continuous natural fire step of 18" and 18" sandbag front parapet with elbow rest, deepening from 6' to 7'.

Throughout all this work which must have been observed, at least in part, by the Germans, the battalion did not suffer any casualties and apart from admissions to hospital for sickness the battalion was left to get on with its work more or less unmolested. At the beginning of June, 1916, the nearness of the battle was becoming apparent as the battalion was not now continually involved in the labour for trench work. The War Diary records that:

> In accordance with Divisional orders that Thursdays should be devoted to drill and training the battalion, less the working parties employed on the Tunnel dug-outs in course of construction and which were not to be delayed, devoted the day to drill and training. At 8 a.m. all the day men paraded under Co. Commanders for a route march FORCEVILLE to HEDAUVILLE and back, distance 6 miles. Night men did the same march parading at 2 p.m. The day men also paraded at 2 p.m. and practised Extended order, Bayonet fighting and bombing up to 4.30 p.m. The men much appreciated the break in the continuous round of trench work, it was evident to they were in need of such training and continuance of the system will be of great advantage to all ranks.

The one day of training every week was designed to allow the battalion to brush up on its infantry skills which had not really been used since its days with the 4th Division before being posted to the Lines of Communications. It is difficult to judge how successful this exercise was since it was still only a small portion of their time. Probably the greatest benefit was that it gave a break from the continual round of trench work and that in turn helped to boost and maintain morale - essential when a big offensive was about to take place and a point not wasted on the divisional commanders. For the next three weeks the battalion maintained work on the schemes they had begun previously and with one or two new ones such as the preparation of trench mortar pits for the divisional Trench Mortar Battery. In all twelve pits were constructed near the front line opposite Beaumont Hamel. Each pit was to be 8 feet by 8 feet (2.5m x 2.5m) and 13 feet (4m) deep but each was to be provided with a dugout and an ammunition dugout. The pits were dug in groups of four and each group was further provided with an ammunition trench and a large bomb store. This work was to keep a substantial portion of the battalion busy for ten days. There was an urgency about the work at this time. As the War Diary pointed out the men working on the Tunnel Dug outs were not allowed to break for training since their completion was considered to be of some importance. However, there was to be one short stop in this work on the 7th June when as recorded by Bowen in his notebook:

> *The men working in deep dugouts BUCKINGHAM PALACE ROAD reported today that they heard sounds of digging at about the same level i.e. 15' underground. Work was stopped in both dugouts but the digging continued. It was as if a man was working with a pick, slow strokes, and working in the German manner according to the men who have had experience of German mining in other parts of the line. The digging was heard on the eastern side of No.2 dugout. The Sergeant i/c reported the matter to a Lieutenant of the 1st Inniskillings. Two men were left on guard on the dugout.*

This was disconcerting to say the least, particularly to those men of the battalion who had been involved in mining in Flanders in the winter of 1914-15. However, it appears that this incident caused little problem - the War Diary does not even record it - and what the Germans were up to can only be guessed. They may have been involved in the preparation of a mine but if they were it was never fired and the following day the miners of the battalion continued their work which was completed about a week in advance of the original date earmarked for the commencement of the offensive.

It was a busy time and there were few men to spare for additional duties but nonetheless in the middle of June, with all the preparations proceeding at a pace, an order was issued from division requiring the battalion to improve a road and make it 'Motorable'. This road was to link up the Mailly - Hedauville road and the Mailly - Auchonvillers road by way of Mailly Convent and, by virtue of the last point, was to be known as Convent Road. The battalion was so heavily involved in works throughout the 29th Division sector that the only men available to construct this road were the officers' servants who were put to work at once. Some assistance was provided by other units of the division in the early stage though it would be fair to say that the response to requests for help to get the road started was poor. However, progress was made and as men became available from completed tasks elsewhere they were put on the work of finishing Convent Road which was achieved in only four days for which the battalion received the thanks of the senior divisional officers for a job well done. While all this was going on the battalion was to lose one officer, Lieut. L.E. Ford, who was assigned the task of 'management' of the 29th Division Trench Tramway System with lines running from the station in Mailly-Maillet to Essex Dump opposite Beaumont Hamel and Knightsbridge Barracks a little way to the south. His command was small consisting of two lance corporals, one supplied by the battalion, and six privates who appear to have been Royal Engineers. The purpose of the tramway was to assist in keeping the front line supplied with all manner of 'trench stores' and this was done by supplying dumps such as Essex Dump and Thurles Dump from which carrying parties could supply the relevant front line units. The tramway approached to as little as 400 yards of the front line and in that respect should be considered of some considerable value for making the work of the carrying parties that much less.

The 23rd June, 1916, saw the bulk of the preparation work completed and the battalion was ordered to move to the rear and back to their billets of six weeks earlier at Acheux Wood. Consequently the camp at Mailly Wood was broken and all was packed to move by 9 a.m. By 1 p.m. the camp had been re-pitched in Acheux Wood where the battalion was to spend the run up to the start of the battle. For the next week the battalion was engaged in training though it was remarked that 'the training ground (was) very limited'. Training comprised bayonet fighting, bombing and practice at extended order. Perhaps if more had been known, or understood, of what was to happen in a few days time the training would have been different and many lives that were lost could have been saved. However, for most of those involved in the build up to the attack everything was as ready as it could be, all the soldiers were trained and knew what to do, all the preparatory work had been completed to give what was considered to have been the best possible chance of success and the artillery preparation was considered to have been thorough enough to allow the British army the opportunity to stroll across No Man's Land and claim the enemy line for its own.

The task of the 29th Division for the 1st July, known as 'Z Day' to those involved, was a stern one but perhaps no worse than many that day. They were expected to capture Beaumont Hamel, lying as it did behind Hawthorn Ridge and Y Ravine (*Leiling Schluct* to the Germans) it was to be no easy task. To assist the attack a number of mines had been prepared by the Tunnelling Companies of the Royal Engineers along the German front line. The plan had originally been that these mines would be detonated at the same time, namely, zero hour on Z Day and that the craters so formed would be rushed and captured by the attacking troops whilst the Germans were still reeling from the detonations. In the 29th Division sector of some 2,000 yards it was organised that the 87th Brigade would attack the right portion, that is Y Ravine, whilst the 86th Brigade would attack the left portion, namely Hawthorn Ridge. To the north, or left, of the 29th Division was the 4th Division; to the south or right, was the 36th (Ulster) Division. Thus the scene was set for the beginning of the largest offensive the British army had ever undertaken and there seems to have been every reason for optimism.

Into this scheme of things the 2nd Battalion the Monmouthshire Regiment was fitted as considered necessary. It was to be a piecemeal involvement and the details of the arrangements were quite complex as the orders for D Company's attachments shows:

No.13 Platoon Sections 1 & 2 (Lieut. T.E.R. Williams) C Coy 1st Lanc Fus.
No.13 Platoon Sections 3 & 4 (2012 Sgt. Jones) B Coy 16th Middlesex
No.14 Platoon Sections 5 & 6 (Lieut. J.D. Simpson) 2nd Royal Fusiliers
No.14 Platoon Sections 7 & 8 (Sergt. Stockham) 1st Dublin Fusiliers
No 15 Platoon Captain A.C. Sale 1st Border Reg.
No.16 Platoon 2nd Lieut. H.B. Davies 1st K.O.S.B.

Thus, one company was split amongst six battalions and two brigades for the forthcoming attack. Their rôle was essentially one of support and consolidation and although they were to come under the command of the respective battalions the task for Lieut. Col. Bowen to keep himself informed of what his men were doing was a very difficult one indeed. The remainder of the battalion was sent to forming up areas about 1,000 yards behind the front line, A Company in the north opposite Hawthorn Ridge, B Company to the south of them and C Company from the southern divisional boundary to Fort Withington. The tasks of these companies was similar to that of D Company but they were to go over the top with the second wave of the attack and were to await further orders before they could commence their consolidation works in the captured ground. A full disposition of the battalion is given in the War Diary together with matters relating to dress and equipment and arrangements for communication. This is reproduced in full in Appendix 5. It is interesting to note at this point that there were very clear instructions for all concerned and an Operational Order (Battalion) issued by Bowen a week before the attack clarifies one such point:

> 4 underground galleries have been constructed leaving MARY REDAN (Q17a 4.3), 1st AVENUE (Q10d 0.75), HAWTHORN RIDGE (Q10b 0.7), and SAP 7 (Q4d 5.7). The 252nd Tunnelling Coy. have arranged to break through these tunnels on the morning of 'Z' day. The tunnel will only be used for runners and for getting telephone wires and water pipes forward. They will not be used as communication trenches. The forward Bdes will be responsible for policing the entrances and exits of the tunnels of their sub-section.

and as a part of the same Operational Order Bowen was to stress that:

> The Coy SB's (stretcher bearers) will not dig but will attend the wounded only. No other men will cease work to attend the wounded.

Everything had been spelled out quite clearly, nothing was to be left to chance. Amongst the men there was a feeling of anticipation on the evening of the 30th June. Pte. Heare notes the anticipation with more than a touch of black humour:

> Sgt. Mason, or Mike as he is to us all, one of the best, our orderly room Sergeant says 'Charlie, we are up to our eyes in this advance. It will cost some men but we have to go on. Our headquarters will be in Beaumont Hamel Cemetery after the breakthrough.' Our adjutant, Ibbs, says 'Heare you know where to find us tomorrow'. 'Yes Sir! In the corner of Beaumont Hamel Cemetery' 'It may be', he said smiling. Perhaps he is the only one who has doubts about us advancing.

The men of the forward units, including the 2nd Monmouths, had even been issued with details of underground workings in Beaumont Hamel. In the event of its capture it was expected that these would be used by the Germans for 'secreting' large numbers of men. This is a further indication of the optimism of the soldiers and the expectation with which the attack for the 1st July, 1916 was opened. Thus, everything was ready for the big push which everyone, perhaps including the Germans, had been expecting for some time. For a variety of reasons the mine prepared under Hawthorn Ridge, to the left of the 29th Division sector, was fired ten minutes before zero which had been set for 7.30 a.m. on the 1st July. Lieut. Gen. Hunter-Weston, Commander of VIII Corps, to which the 29th Division belonged, had wanted to fire the mine even earlier but had been refused permission. After some discussion the time of 7.20 a.m. was offered to the General as 'a kind of compromise'. It has been suggested that his reason for firing the mine early was to protect his advancing troops from the falling debris. The Official History states that although dust from the explosion may remain in the air for some time after the detonation, debris likely to have caused injury would all have fallen back to earth within 20 seconds. Thus the Hawthorn Ridge mine was fired at least 9¹/2 minutes too early. On this matter the historian of the 29th Division was to write:

> *The Germans took the broad hint that something was going to happen and there was no element of surprise.*

The events of the 1st July are well documented and the tragic circumstances that befell the British army on that day still resound through the regimental histories of those units involved. During the day's fighting the 29th Division did not manage to gain any ground though not through the lack of effort or sacrifice. The Newfoundland Regiment sustained over 700 casualties as they were thrown into the attack on Y Ravine in support of the South Wales Borderers. In about half an hour of that morning the Newfoundland Regiment had all but ceased to exist and it was not on its own. In all thirty two battalions suffered over 500 casualties on that day and six of those were from the 29th Division who were in the thick of things as they pressed home the attack on Beaumont Hamel. The 2nd Monmouths, as pioneers, had a much smaller involvement in the events of this the opening day of an offensive which it had been hoped would produce a breakthrough. By nature of the distribution of the battalion their involvement was piecemeal and episodic and is a story best relayed by the War Diary, the full entry for the 1st July being reproduced here:

> *'Z' day. The attack started at 7.20 a.m. At 7.30 a.m. A Co. moved up to the front line along the Old Beaumont Road. The Bombers under Lt. W.M. Sankey proceeded up the SUNKEN ROAD to clear the way for three Platoons of the Coy. who were to carry bombs into BEAUMONT. They were held up by machine gun fire at a distance of 100 yards from their objective. Attempts were again made to get into BEAUMONT but the infantry had not cleared the enemy trenches and at 9 a.m. it was still strongly held. Casualties: Killed O.R. 3. Wounded Officers 1 (Lt.Hunt) O.R. 10*

> *B Co. At 7.50 a.m, No. 5 & 6 Platoons proceeded to 1st AVENUE TUNNEL via YELLOW LINE, TIPPERARY and 1st AVENUES. At the same time No. 7 & 8 Platoons proceeded to MARY TUNNEL via WITHINGTON AVENUE. The work of the Co. was to dig communication trenches from this position (to) ends of 1st AVENUE and MARY TUNNELS respectively. Great difficulty was experienced in trying to get to their respective positions owing to the congested state of the trenches and the enemy's barrage. 5 & 6 Platoons were unable to get to the (bastion) end of the TUNNEL at 1st AVENUE it being full of wounded and signallers and orderlies trying to get through. This party remained in the support trenches all day and suffered considerably from the enemy's barrage. 7 & 8 Platoons, after two attempts, found it impossible to get out to NO MAN'S LAND to start digging as the enemy's trenches had not been taken. Later in the day the party did manage to get out and do a little sapping - 10 yards - towards the*

enemy's trenches but suffered considerably from the enemy's barrage.
Casualties: Killed 3 O.R. (including Co. S.Maj.) Wounded 21.

C Co. on YELLOW LINE. This company was intended for consolidating the
3rd Objective when captured by the 88th Brigade, owing to the failure of the
attack on the 1st Objective the Co. remained standing by in the position of
readiness until 7 p.m. when it was ordered to rejoin the Battalion.
Casualties: nil

D Co. No 13 Platoon Sections 1 and 2 attached to C. Co. LANCASHIRE
FUSILIERS (the consolidating company) laden with stakes and wire. These
sections went over the parapet in rear of the Co. and turned up the
SUNKEN ROAD. There they were ordered to dump all material and
advance across the open. They got to within 50 or 60 yards of the enemy's
front line and lay there under cover of a slight ridge and 'dug in'. The Co.
had Stokes guns and two Lewis guns, these were used, but orders were given
to cease fire as it was thought that hostile fire would be drawn and position
rushed by the enemy. The party consisted of about 150. They withdrew about
10 p.m. into TENDERLOIN leaving a bombing party behind to cover them.
Casualties: Killed O.R. 2. Wounded Off. 1 (Lt. T.E.R. Williams) O.R. 8
Missing O.R. 2.

Sections 3 and 4 attached to B Co. 16th MIDDLESEX REGT. and went
over the parapet in rear of Co. carrying coils of tench wire and two
BANGALORE TORPEDOES. They advanced in the rear of the Co. towards
the enemy's front line and laid down. In the meantime some of the
Middlesex had got into the enemy's front line. The enemy bombed them out
and they retired. Our two sections retired into our front line.
Casualties: Killed O.R. 1. Wounded O.R. 12.

No 14 Platoon. Sections 5 and 6 attached to ROYAL FUSILIERS were split
up amongst the different sections of the Co they were attached to and there
does not appear to be a clear account of what happened other than the attack
was a failure and when the RF withdrew our men were collected and placed
in a deep 'dugout' and remained there until ordered to rejoin the Battalion.
Casualties: Killed O.R. 1. Wounded O.R. 2. Missing O.R. 3.

Sections 7 & 8 attached to the DUBLIN FUSILIERS and carried
material up to our front line. They were ordered into 'deep dug-outs' in
rear of our front line when it was found the enemy's front line had not
been taken. They carried wounded back during the day and bombs and
ammunition to our front line from the reserve dump in AUCHONVILLERS.
They also acted as ration party during the early hours of the 2nd.
Casualties: Wounded O.R. 1.

No 15 Platoon. Attached to 1st BORDER REGT. This platoon got over the
parapet from FETHARD ST. each man carrying 8 full water bottles in a
sand bag and also signalling material. They filed over the parapet through
our wire, then got into extended order. To cross our front line they again got
into file until clear of our wire. They then lay down as the advance was
checked. After being in this position about 2 hours a withdrawal into our

front line was made. This Platoon after assisting the wounded retired into dug-outs in JOHN ST.
Casualties: Wounded Off. 1 (CAPT. A.C. SALE) O.R. 7. Missing O.R. 3.

No 16 Platoon. Attached to A Coy. KOSB (1st Bn). They advanced in rear of the Coy. over the open from JAMES STREET to our front line near the MARY REDAN. By the time our front line was reached the companies in front had got mixed up and the Platoon could get no information about A Coy movements and no orders having been given they joined CAPT. COX, B Co. of this Battalion and assisted on work in MARY TUNNEL. About 8.30 p.m. orders were given for this sap to be closed.
Casualties: Killed O.R. 2. Wounded O.R. 13. Missing O.R.1.
6 p.m. Orders received from 29th Div. that the battalion was to be collected and reformed in Mailly Wood and a small working party under an officer detailed to clear and keep clear each of the main communication trenches. The Battalion reserve of 10% was used for this purpose and divided into 3 parties of 9 and 3 of 10 each under an officer and were sent to 1,2 and 3rd AVENUES, BROADWAY, WITHINGTON and GABION. The trenches were found to be comparatively little damaged and the work of clearing was done without incident, enabling to return to camp between the hours of 3 and 5 on the 2nd. Reformation of the Battalion at MAILLY WOOD was completed by midnight.

This lengthy account from the War Diary illustrates clearly the fragmentation of the battalion and the tasks set it during the day. It also illustrates the lack of success along the entire 29th Division front as the German machine gunners completed their day's work with relative ease while the casualties of the division reached around 5,300. The 2nd Monmouths had been attached to the battalions who had suffered some of the heaviest casualties of the day and although they had little direct involvement in the fighting they had still sustained 98 casualties and had achieved little of what they had set out to do. As stated in the War Diary the Monmouths did good work in caring for the wounded - none more so, perhaps, than Pte. G. Burnett of A Company of whom Lieut. Col. Bowen was to write to divisional Headquarters and say:

I beg to bring to your notice the gallant conduct of 2097 BURNETT, G. 2nd Monmouth Regiment. On the 1st July (yesterday) after the attack on BEAUMONT, Lt. T.E.R. WILLIAMS was left severely wounded in NO MAN'S LAND. Pte Burnett crawled out under continuous machine gun fire and shell fire over 100 yds, pulled him into a shell hole and finally brought him back to our line. He undoubtedly saved Lt. Williams' life.

For this act of bravery amongst the carnage that was the first day of the Battle of the Somme, Pte. Burnett was awarded the Military Medal and thanks to his gallantry Lt. Williams recovered to finish the war as a captain in the battalion. This was not the only award during the slaughter of that day and both Sergeant J. Jones and L/Cpl. S. Woodland received the Military Medal for their parts in the action.

Immediately following the events of the 1st July, 1916, plans were drawn up for successive attacks on the Germans to attempt to wrest the front line from them and make progress all along the line. The ultimate failure of the 36th (Ulster) Division, in spite of its intitial successes, in the area of the Schwaben Redoubt, south of the Ancre, was, in part, seen as a direct result of the failure of the 29th Division to make progress against such strong holds as Y Ravine north of the Ancre and ultimately the failure to capture Beaumont Hamel. By the early morning of the 2nd July, before the full cost of the fighting on the 1st July could possibly have been known, this fact was clear. In an effort to provide such a flank the VIII Corps staff were making plans for a further assault on the German lines. The 2nd Monmouths War Diary records at 6.15 a.m. that they received orders to join the 88th Brigade who were to be attached to the 48th Division (in Corps reserve) ready for an attack on Y Ravine planned for 3.15 a.m. on the 3rd July. It was decided that the 4th Worcesters and the 2nd Hampshires who had seen little action on the 1st July would be thrown into the fighting. The objective of this attack was the same as the first attack, that was to take the first three lines of the enemy trenches and the 2nd Monmouths were to be used for consolidation works if it was a success. If, however, the attack did not reach all objectives Bowen had been ordered that his men were to be used as infantry. This element of the plan was different from that of the opening day and a change that was likely to have been viewed with some concern particularly when it is remembered that the battalion had already suffered almost 100 casualties and had not really been involved in the fighting. Nonetheless the battalion moved into its position in Fethard Street in the evening of the 2nd July. Even the move into position proved to be difficult as the enemy bombarded the approaches with lachrymatory gas and goggles had to be worn which in the failing light did little to aid their progress along the communication trenches. By midnight most of the battalion was in position but had been somewhat concerned to see the assaulting infantry withdrawing from their positions. It was probably with some measure of relief that they received the orders that the attack was cancelled. The Germans shelled Fethard Street heavily for the next two hours and the battalion was forced to remain in deep dugouts since they could not withdraw. Fortunately the deep dugouts prevented any further casualties and the battalion withdrew safely a little after 6 a.m. on the 3rd July and reformed in Mailly Wood. It had been a stressful night which had resulted in the expenditure of effort for absolutely no return - though, thankfully, all the men returned to their billets in one piece.

For the next couple of days, as far as the 2nd Monmouths were concerned, it was back to the old routine as they were out on work parties repairing trenches along the 29th Division sector. Things were soon to change since part of the failure of the attack on the 29th Division front was put down to the depth of No Man's Land - here over 400 yards - and it was decided that a new front line would have to be dug closer to the Germans. Pte. Heare was to put it almost ironically:

> Now, after two years of war it was found that the trenches, 400 yards, are too wide apart for an advance. The 2nd Mons are all collected together, every man, at Mailly Wood under canvas and huts. All of us are to go up at night and dig a new line near to the German line and run communication trenches back to our front line. How comfortable we all feel. We shall be like the Newfoundlands by tomorrow says the boys but Black and I are sent to advance Division Headquarters at Mailly so we don't go to dig and not sorry.

This comment on the state of things indicates quite clearly that the front line soldier had a good idea of what had happened in his sector on the 1st July and Heare perhaps more than others since he was an orderly. It shows also that there was an element of fatalism developing; perhaps two years of war had produced this in Heare but fortunately the expectation of high casualties as they carried out this new work was somewhat off the mark.

The battalion began digging the trenches in No Man's Land on the 5th July. They began on the southern part of the divisional sector and extended northwards in front of Beaumont Hamel. There can be little doubt that the Germans were aware of what was going on and it was expected that efforts would be made to disrupt the work by shelling and aggressive patrolling of No Man's Land. In an effort to alleviate the problem the battalion was marched from billets in Mailly Wood every evening so as to be able to begin work as soon as it was dark. This minimised their time in the front line and kept them out of harm's way during the day. The line they were to dig was marked for them and initially the front line troops of the division provided covering parties so that the Monmouths could carry on the digging without the fear of German patrols. After a day or two the Monmouths had to provide their own covering parties, each party consisting of one NCO and three or four bombers. These men were required to lie out in No Man's Land all night in front of the trench diggers listening for the approach of the Germans. These parties became trusted very quickly and it is said that the Monmouths got on with their task as if they were doing it in daylight way behind the lines. The battalion was involved in this work for two weeks and in that time they were never bothered by German patrols. That however, does not mean that they carried on the work without casualties. All through this period there were a number of casualties every night from German shelling and the battalion suffered a further 116 casualties during this period of the Somme offensive.

Pte. Heare was to comment on this digging still further for although he was not involved he still had to get to the front to deliver messages.

> *The first night's digging goes well......I go up once to Colonel Bowen. All is quiet only the ordinary sniping and firing. The second night the Germans saw the chalk turned over......didn't they lay it on, everything they had.... To get up and back now is a trying time, run, crawl, drop in shell holes crawling amongst the dead men, some not too fresh, but with Colonel Bowen it is 'Get on!'*

As might be expected on a battleground where so many had perished the men of the battalion worked with the ever present feeling of death all around them, sometimes the digging parties unearthed bodies buried by the terrific bombardment and these were reburied behind the lines whenever possible. Lieut. Col. Bowen was to send a message to the 86th Brigade on the 12th July which gave details of one such discovery:

> *I found the body of the officer (2nd Lieut. J. Hollywood, Royal Irish Rifles) and enclose herewith his identity disc and small articles which were all I could find on him. I was informed that the stretcher bearers of D Company 5th R. Sussex (Pioneers) Regt. had just previously searched his body which is now lying in a shell hole 20 yards in rear of the fire trench and about 120*

yards N of the junction of the fire trench and communication trench dug tonight. The badge of rank is on his shoulder straps.

The 12th Royal Irish Rifles had suffered heavily on the opening day of the attack on the left of the 36th (Ulster) Division fighting on the right of the 1st Inniskilling Fusiliers of the 29th Division. Repeated assaults had resulted in the battalion suffering heavy casualties. 2nd Lieut. James Hollywood was one of the casualties of these assaults and although Bowen had reported the location of the body it appears that it was never recovered since his name can now be found amongst the thousands on the Thiepval Memorial to the Missing.

By the 18th July the trench had been completed along its entire length fully served by communication trenches. The new front line was then taken over by Brigade and the battalion was ordered to dig a new line some 100 yards in front of the one they had just handed over to Brigade. The purpose was to close the distance with the German front line which would then be some 100 yards distant. This trench was to be provided with communication trenches linking it with the old front line and provided the battalion with another few days work in the front line in more or less continuous view of the Germans who periodically shelled the work. As can be imagined this work was hazardous and the comments of Sgt. Love demonstrate the kind of problem encountered:

> *We were digging an advanced trench as a jumping off place for the new attack. Jerry disputed it and pummelled us flat while we were sinking it. We were practically under his very nose and he shared between us all his spare ammunition. We lost heavily in this work but it had to be done. I had a narrow escape. A trench mortar dropped one where three of us were working and we were buried alive. Captain Comley got me out. I told him that two others were buried with me. When (we) got (them) out one was dead and the other in a bad state. This continued night after night until the trench was completed.*

The War Diary of the 21st July gives details of the work in a similar vein:

> *Enemy shelled heavily from 11.45 pm to midnight on the RAVINE, NEW SUPPORT and FIRE TRENCH. This intense shelling was continued without a break up to 12.45 am but only interfered with the section of trench started on the night of the 19/20th where a bay and a traverse were knocked in, killing 3 men and wounding 10. Getting the wounded out delayed the work in this trench and also in the communication trench. Two stretcher bearers (B Coy) were killed in CONSTITUTION HILL, presumably on return journey from dressing station..... In addition to the provided covering party, 2 of D Coy bombers were posted in front of this section, on of whom was killed.*

By the 23rd July their work was more or less completed and the battalion was ordered to 'move with the Division to another part of the line'. Their work was to be taken over by the 6th South Wales Borderers who were pioneers of the 25th Division.

The 2nd Monmouths had completed their tour of duty on the Somme. Compared with many of the units they had got off lightly. Casualties for the month of July amounted to 278 all ranks. It had been a difficult time for all concerned and was remarked upon by Pte. Heare when he wrote:

The 29th Division all move to Proven; to see a battalion march past - it's more transport than men, the Newfoundland seem the smallest number.

For the battalion it must have felt that little had been achieved for the loss of so many of their comrades. However, it must have come as some satisfaction to them when they learned that when Y Ravine and its accompanying trenches fell in November, 1916, it did so from an assault by the 51st (Highland) Division made from the trenches the battalion had prepared in No Man's Land in July.

Chapter Nine

'A Loss to the Whole Army'
(July 1916 to March 1917)

The move to the Ypres area was not too soon. The 29th Division and to a lesser extent the 2nd Monmouths had suffered sufficient casualties during July to make them far less than a fully effective fighting force. On the 24th July, 1916, the battalion moved, via Bus-le-Artois to Amplier where it remained for two days. Whilst here the men received some drill and practice for the entraining of the night of the 27/28th July at Doullens which was to move them northwards and back to Ypres. The Ypres sector at this time was a relatively quiet sector, as much as the Salient could ever be said to be quiet, and it was considered to be satisfactory area to allow the 29th Division a chance to rest and to fill its depleted ranks with replacements. The 2nd Monmouths reached Proven, to the west of Ypres on the afternoon of the 28th July and on the following day were split into two, such that Headquarters and A and C companies were billeted in Brandhoek and B and D companies were billeted in cellars in Ypres. It was a year since the battalion had last seen Ypres and how different it must have seemed to them. In 1915 they had been part of the 4th Division holding the line against concerted German attacks, now in July, 1916, they were attached to the 29th Division as pioneers and Ypres was considered to be almost a 'rest' area. One thing that hadn't changed was the weariness that follows involvement in a major battle and as in their last visit they were to see Ypres through tired eyes. Many of the men were veterans of 2nd Ypres and for them this visit was likely to have been a time of some reflection on the events of a year before and there can be little doubt that thoughts were cast to those comrades they had left behind following that fight. It would certainly have been strange to these men to think of Ypres as a place to recover - but then, the Somme had also been a quiet sector once!

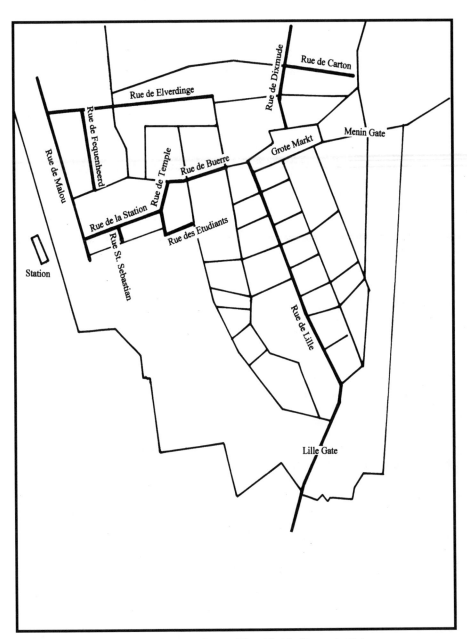

Sketch Street plan of Ypres Showing Streets Identified in Bowen's Notes

The problem of billeting two companies, at this time about 300 men, in Ypres was amongst the first to be faced by Lieut. Col. Bowen and in the days following their return to the area Bowen carried out a survey of the ruined town to ascertain the suitability of the cellars as billets for his men. His notebooks give details of the various streets he visited near the town centre and his estimates for accommodation, for example:

> Rue de la Station
> No.44 big basement good condition accommodate 30 - house above standing
> No.42 good basement accommodate 10
> No.38 good cellar accommodate 20
> No.34 cellar good condition (accommodate) 10
> No.32 small basement wants repairing (accommodate) 8
> No.39 S. corner of Station Rd. - Rue St. Sebastian, basement condition fair
> wants strengthening.

In this methodical manner Bowen visited most of the streets surrounding the Grande Place of the mediaeval market town until sufficient billeting was found for his men. Initially this would have been for B and D companies but as work in the area progressed the companies would have changed places periodically.

The conditions within the Salient would have been, for the most part, new and different to anything the troops of the 29th Division had encountered in Gallipoli or on the Somme. It must have come as quite a shock to the men of all units to realize that trenches were always wet and in need of drainage and that breastworks were needed to construct most trenches to a safe depth. It was no new experience to the Monmouths. The entire Division was put to the task of improving the trench system of their sector lying between the Menin road and the Langemark road to the east of Ypres. The task allotted to the 2nd Monmouths was the construction of a communication trench which was to be known as Piccadilly and would eventually join the area of Hussar and Dragoon Farms near Potijze to the front line 1500 yards to the east of the village. Bowen was, as ever, specific in his orders to his company commanders over this work:

> O.C. B Coy. 1/2 Monmouth Reg.
> The 20 men working tomorrow will carry out task 2, i.e. fitting in U frames
> and galvanised sheets, nailing down trench boards so that they are 3" below
> ground level. 10 of the men will work for D Company under Cpl. Cox.
> They will report to O.C. D Coy at 8.30 a.m. tomorrow, they will take with
> them mauls, hammers, saws and nails. The remaining 10 will work in
> the trench your Coy was digging tonight. You will inspect the work early
> tomorrow morning and satisfy yourself that it is being correctly carried
> out. They will carry the same tools as above and fill in all material now
> in the trench. They will all take haversack rations and full water bottles.
> 15.8.16
> 1.35 a.m.
> URGENT

In a similar manner he was to write the following order:

O.C. C Coy
You will continue work on PARK LANE and NEW TRENCH from
SUPPORT LINE to PICCADILLY tonight. New Trench is now on average
4' wide and 3' deep. 30 men (exclusive of Sgts) will widen it to 4'6" and
deepen to 4'6" to take U frames. The earth will be thrown on the SE side
forming a parapet 3' high and leaving a berm of 2'. They will work in 10'
lengths. They will place U frames in position and drive pegs for wiring.

There was little room for error with such precise instructions. Bowen knew
exactly what was expected of him and he relayed the information as precisely as
possible and consequently expected his subordinates to carry out their work
thoroughly and correctly. It is clear that not all his orders were followed as he
would have liked and this is demonstrated when the commander of B Company
was to get a written dressing down only a day after the order above had been
issued:

O.C. B Coy.
PICCADILLY
The day work in this trench is not being satisfactorily carried out and it is
evident that there is a lack of supervision and energy. The trench must be
finished off as it moves eastwards, at present not a yard is floored and one
cannot (walk) from X Line. The U frames must be picketed and wired. In
future day parties will breakfast early and start work by 6 a.m., an NCO
will remain in the trench from the night party and point out the work to be
done and hand over material to the officer or NCO i/c Day Party. The Day
Party must be i/c of an officer or visited twice by an officer during the work.
I will inspect the trench today at about noon and will call at your HQ for an
officer to accompany me.
16.8.16. 2.45 a.m.

There is no attempt to mince words here and the officer in charge of B Company
(Captain S.R. Hockaday) can have been left in no doubt that he had incurred the
displeasure of his colonel. At this stage it is clear that Bowen was keen to maintain
discipline at the highest level. Although the battalion were out of the main
fighting they were still in the front line and the fact that it was a quiet area and the
battalion was awaiting replacements were not reasons to allow a change in the
standards he had expected of them in the heat of the Somme fighting. In any event
the work done by the Division as a whole in building a satisfactory trench system
did not go unnoticed since when the King of the Belgians visited Brigade
Headquarters he insisted on visiting the front line and the divisional history
records with some pride that he was able to do so without getting his royal
feet wet!

During the stay in the Ypres area there were other problems of discipline
which needed to be dealt with and in one incident Bowen writes to the Division
administration to ask the specific charge in which a soldier should be charged. The
soldier in question had been arrested at Blaenavon as a deserter. There must have
been some doubt in Bowen's mind as to this and although there is no record of
the response from Division, it would appear that the soldier was not tried as a
deserter and was later transferred to the Royal Engineers. In another incident a

sergeant of some considerable service was charged with 'Falling out without permission from a working party'. Again the soldier is transferred, this time to a labour unit, presumably where his recalcitrant behaviour would cause less of a problem! These minor incidents show that even under active service conditions there were certain details that the commanding officer of the battalion needed to handle. It made no difference that there was heavy fighting elsewhere the battalion's internal discipline was to be maintained, for on this unit lay the army's strength. This was probably even more so the case when Bowen himself came in for criticism:

> O.C. A, B, C, D Coys 1.2 Monmouths
> The Head Censor has drawn my attention to the fact that letters censored have been received at Base which contain references to places where the Battalion is or recently has been. This shows that there is a serious neglect of duty on part of some officers. Please draw the attention of all your officers to the Censorship Regulations and the responsibility resting on officers to see that these regulations are strictly and loyally complied with.

For this action to have been taken it would appear that a number of letters had slipped through battalion censorship to Base and although the kind of information that could have been gleaned form them is likely to have been of limited significance, Bowen was not going to let it continue. No doubt the Head Censor had already had a 'quiet' word with the colonel when the issue was brought to his attention.

Throughout the month of August enemy action was limited but on the night of the 8th August there was a cloud phosgene attack against the Division. According to the divisional historian it had very local effects with the Royal Inniskilling Fusiliers bearing the brunt of the effect where it caused most of the 300 casualties suffered by the Division. For the 2nd Monmouths good gas drill helped limit the casualties to four. The men immediately donned their gas helmets and stood still, as instructed, while the white dense mist of the gas cloud blew over them. Fortunately, the Germans did not follow the gas with an infantry assault for, in all probability, that would have caused substantially more casualties for the Division. That apart the action by the Germans was that which had become considered normal, with sniping and periodic shelling. In the middle of August the battalion was to lose Captain Edward Edwards when he was killed by a rifle bullet whilst directing the work of D Company, presumably the victim of a sniper. This was a considerable blow to the battalion and possibly to the army for not only was he a respected and well liked officer he also had the experience the army was looking for. Two weeks before his death he had been recommended by Bowen to the Division as follows:

> In reply to A1397 I beg to recommend Capt. E. EDWARDS of the battalion under my command for appointment as commandant of a Pioneer School. He has been in France from May 1915 to the present date continually acting as Company Commander and 2nd in command at various times. Before the war he was a surveyor to an Urban District Council and has a thorough knowledge of civil engineering in addition to his military knowledge. He is 33 years old.

It was a sad loss to the battalion since Edwards was 'a real good sort and liked by everyone'. But on previous visits, Ypres had claimed lives of Monmouths and before the end of the month the battalion was to lose another company commander when Captain S.R. Hockaday of B Company was severely wounded while directing the work of his company, no doubt to the guidelines that Bowen set down, and died of his wounds some days later. The following account of the incident was given by 2nd Lieut. Greenland a fellow company officer:

> Besides night work we always have a day party out and Hock and Lawlor had gone up to see the work this morning. A shell exploded just on the trench. Hock got two ghastly holes in the left shoulder, a Sergeant got it in the arm and a man got it in the thigh. I cycled down the shell scarred road to the dressing station - a ruined chateau - this afternoon to see him. There he lay, white as death, and still on a stretcher, covered with blankets. His hair, always so immaculately parted, was ruffled and without the usual sheen. He was almost sleeping, but when I went in he said in such a weak little voice 'Good-bye Greenland' Oh! since then I have felt so very fed up! He was wounded at 11.30 this morning but owing to that part being under observation by the Boche our ambulance will not take him from the dressing station until 10.30 tonight. The doctor says he will pull through with tremendous luck, but will probably lose his arm.

Captain Sainsbury, medical officer to the battalion, spent time with Captain Hockaday after he was wounded, one source saying he hardly left his side, and wrote to his brother, Percy Hockaday who was also serving with the 2nd Monmouths, to break the news. In part of the letter he writes:

> HE shrapnel. It has damaged his shoulder and chest badly - but has not injured his lung I think. He could not be moved until 10.30 p.m. He was wounded at 11.30 a.m. He was seen as soon as possible by 2 M.D's. who gave him morphia at once. I saw him as soon as possible afterwards and went with him to the CCS. I have been with him all day today.

In spite of the ministrations of Captain Sainsbury, Captain Hockaday died on the 2nd September, 1916, aged 24. It was a sad blow at a time when enemy action was slight and casualties were very light indeed. The loss of officers was worsened when another officer, Captain G.E. Foster, was wounded and returned home. He survived his injuries, however, and returned to the battalion in 1917.

In September with the Somme fighting continuing in its ferocity the battalion received news which probably amused or at least confused them. Pte. Heare was to write:

> The news sheet says the tanks are doing good work on the Somme. We all wonder what the tanks are. No one here knows.

The impact of this new weapon was just being felt and before too long there would be many soldiers, now ignorant of their use and purpose, who would have reason to be thankful for the invention of the tank. For the time being the work of the battalion was to continue in Ypres and they carried on a variety of trench and road works throughout September. Probably they were thankful to be away from the Somme and the tanks but there were those who expected the call back to the Somme at any moment.

In early October the battalion was ordered to prepare for a move. The 29th Division was replaced by the 55th Division and its pioneers, the 4th South Lancashires, took over the work from the Monmouths. The battalion was ordered to occupy a camp near Montauban, a village that had fallen as planned on the opening day of the Battle of the Somme. As the battalion history put it:

> *The camp site was found to be a bare patch of ground pitted with shell holes. The Pioneer Battalion Coldstream Guards had spent the morning filling in the worst holes, and they proved helpful friends when tents arrived and had to be pitched.*

In some aspects the Somme battlefields hadn't changed since they were there last in July. It was still very muddy and wet but the blasting away of houses and trees in the captured areas had made it a very stark landscape. Initially the battalion was kept busy by Corps and completed their quota of road building and repair whilst the Division was engaged in the fighting around Gueudecourt. Towards the end of October they came back under the control of the 29th Division as it prepared for an attack on the 25th October which was eventually cancelled as a result of the bad weather and ground conditions. The Division was relieved on the 30th October but, as was to become normal, the pioneers were kept in the line to continue their work. At this stage there is some evidence to suggest that the battalion, or at least part of it, came under the control of the 1st Australian Division. Pte. Alex Mitchell, who had begun his service with the 3rd Monmouths, remembered that the Australians were a rough and ready bunch of soldiers but easy to get on with and always ready for a fight! Pte. Heare was to write:

> *Black and I report to them. What a lot of lads, give or share anything. Their pay 6 shillings a day, private, when they gamble its heavy, a bit of luck and you're made.*

The stay with the Australians was short but long enough for a number of the battalion to have a bit of luck and carry off some of the Australian cash when they left.

The conditions had deteriorated rapidly as winter deepened. The battalion history records that the corded roads they were sent to repair were often found floating on a couple of feet of liquid mud. Working in these conditions can only be imagined by anyone who was not there - imagined to be dreadful with a continuous struggle against the cold and the wet with no real hope of success and all the time the threat of death or terrible injury. There are stories of men disappearing in the muddy shell holes and never being seen again. Whether or not these stories are apocryphal does not matter, since they serve to indicate the popular concept amongst the men of the Somme mud. Conditions were undeniably bad but the men of the battalion carried on as best they could to carry out the orders of their superiors, learning a few new tricks along the way to help make their lives that little bit easier. One of these tricks was the cutting up of rubber waterproof sheets to make waterproof puttees. For this remedy they were able to thank the Australians and there were those in the know in the battalion who made as many puttees as they could get hold of rubber sheets since waterproof puttees were considered to be 'handy'.

During this part of the stay on the Somme the battalion came under the control of the Guards Division and were working alongside the 4th Coldstream Guards the pioneers to the division. Life with the Guards was very different, described by one of the Monmouths as 'real soldiering'. Ptes. Heare and Black working in the orderly room got themselves into a number of scrapes as they tried to get round the strict discipline of the Guards, for compared to the Guards, even Bowen would have been considered relaxed. However, it appears that Pte. Heare took some pleasure at one of the visitors to the Divisional HQ:

> The Prince of Wales is frequent visitor to the Guards Division Headquarters at Trones Wood. He seems cool enough out here, sometimes he comes up on an old bicycle other times he walks up. No one notices him much out here.

Whilst work with the Guards was very disciplined both Black and Heare were enough of veterans to survive without getting into any serious trouble and Heare put that down to the fairly strict training he had had from Col. Cuthbertson, a regular officer, when he had commanded the 2nd Monmouths at the outbreak of the war and the subsequent command of Bowen.

Compared to their earlier visit to the Somme this tour proved to be somewhat quieter. There was still fighting going on but as winter hardened the battle gradually came to a standstill and officially closed on the 18th November, 1916. That did not particularly lessen the work load or the danger for the pioneers. They continued to work and during their work came under shell fire from long range enemy guns. It is thought that the state of the ground at this time even helped reduce casualties the German shells tended to detonate well below ground level in the soft mud which deadened the effect of the explosion. Occasionally their camp in Montauban came under shellfire and on at least one occasion was bombed. On the 23rd October an enemy aeroplane dropped a bomb in the camp which killed one man, Pte. Thomas Rees, and wounded Captain J. Sainsbury the Medical Officer. A month later on the 23rd November, a direct hit from a long range gun on the mess hut of A Company gave Lieut. Ernest Victor Haggis a close escape as he counted the canteen takings. Fortunately for Haggis the shell was a dud but the money was scattered all round the camp. Two days later a direct hit on the tent of Captain Clive Warneford Taunton killed him instantly. Captain Taunton was one of the original battalion officers and his death was keenly felt amongst both officers and men.

Throughout November the battalion made slow progress with their work in the battle against the mud and the enemy's attentions and completed two long communication trenches known as Flers Alley and Flank Avenue. It was, however, work that was described as 'heartbreaking' since the weather conditions meant that a new stretch of trench could collapse or be full of water when the battalion returned to continue their work. It has been said that at night it was preferable to walk along the top of the trenches rather than risk the mud and water in the trench. And, as the winter weather worsened the work became harder. By December the battalion had been engaged on pioneer work for eight months. They had not had a break except from the time taken to travel between different parts of the line. This was having an effect on the efficiency of the battalion and many of the officers and men were becoming ill as a result of the strenuous work and the worsening conditions. In short the battalion was exhausted. The battalion historian states that the men were more worn at this period than at any other time during the whole of the war. This is probably not overstating the case, for eight months of more or less continuous front line work was far more than should have been asked of them and would be unthinkable in the army of today. Their parlous state had probably not gone unnoticed and by mid-December rumours had started that they were about to get some relief but no one was ready to believe it - there had been rumours before. However, for once the rumours turned out to be true and the battalion was relieved on the 19th December. The battalion entrained at Trones Wood on a bitterly cold December morning en route for Ville-sur-Somme. By the time they detrained in Ville-sur-Somme later that day, the effects of the cold in the unheated cattle wagons had been felt by some of the men as a number of cases of frostbitten feet were reported. The following day they continued their journey away from the front until they reached Foudrinoy where they were to be billeted for the next three weeks. There was to be no trench digging, no danger of being shelled and no wet clothes for the next three weeks. Added to this, the Christmas season was upon them and all these factors must have done much to ease the tired spirit and lift the flagging morale of the battalion. Of the Christmas celebrations Pte. Heare recorded the following:

> *I am invited to D Company Mess with the servants. We have a glorious time, owing to continually drinking rum. It takes a lot to affect us now, without it we would have failed. The day after Christmas was cruel. Our Colonel not being of a merry making sort, orders every man on parade. I am feeling rough. On passing the parade, what a sight, some of the men not sober and the officers looked rough. Our Colonel dished out punishment after the parade. How the men swear over it. Even the officers are sorry for the men.*

The officers had been entertained to dinner on Christmas Day by Lieut. Col. Bowen and all were reported to have had a very good time there and at the concert party organized in the Sergeants Mess afterwards. Bowen had undoubtedly relaxed the discipline for Christmas Day celebrations but was not prepared for that to continue beyond the day and he resumed the daily training regime immediately the festivities were over. Training was carried out on a daily basis throughout the rest period but it was not over-zealous consisting of company drill and some weapons practice. It was during bombing practice that RSM J. Noble, who had been attached from the South Wales Borderers and was highly respected, was wounded in the chest by a small fragment of a mis-handled Mills bomb and had to leave the battalion. It was a sad incident in an otherwise successful period of rest for the battalion. To replace Noble, Sgt. C. Love was made up to Acting RSM for the next few weeks. All too soon the rest came to an end. Following an inspection by the G.O.C., Major General H. de B. de Lisle, on the 9th January, 1917, the battalion was ordered back to the forward area with the Division. On the 12th January they began their journey back to approximately the same position they had vacated just before Christmas.

Throughout the winter the enemy and the weather had taken their toll amongst the battalion. Unfortunately, the replacements that were arriving in France at that time were not always as ready for their duty as some of the more experienced soldiers would have liked:

> *The strength of the Battalion was diminishing owing to sickness (it was terribly cold and wet between the thaws) and killed and wounded. A lot of extra work fell upon the old hands because the new drafts were not hardened to the work and furthermore were not strong enough. I complained to the C.O. about this and he promised (if he had time) to inspect the next batch of reinforcements from base, and he did while I was acting RSM. Of the 65 that arrived I could not pick one able and strong enough to do the work that was required of him. Our C.O. was a great believer in work. In fact he gave the impression that the result of the War depended on him and his Battalion. He gave orders that every available man was to proceed to the line that night, and out of the 65 only 30 reported for work the following night.*

It was not the best way for the battalion to get its work done but there was much work to do as the British army continued in its attempt to take the war to the Germans. It was, also, a situation that was causing some concern amongst the battalion officers so much so that on the 9th February the War Diary records:

> *A large number of men have been reporting sick daily and, in consequence the MO submitted a report to the CO, which was forwarded to Div. HQ, on the class of men who were coming to the Battalion as reinforcements.*

It is highly unlikely that anything arose from this report and there would appear to be no record of a response to the report in the War Diary. The men arriving at the Battalion were probably all that were available at the time bearing in mind the losses the infantry had sustained in the second half of 1916. It was certainly not a situation that the officers would have wanted but they had no option since the battalion was required to carry on with the work that was allotted to it.

Although the Battle of the Somme had officially finished there was a philosophy in the British army that insisted on continual pressure upon the German army in the area, particularly the salient in their lines on the River Ancre. The 29th Division were ready to do just that for they had not forgotten the punishment they had received at the hands of the German machine gunners on the opening day of the Battle of the Somme. Not only was the Division ready to fight, it was able to fight, and following the success it had achieved at Gueudecourt and the rest period over Christmas the morale of the men was excellent. With these facts in mind a plan was established for what was really a large scale trench raid using no more than three battalions and with limited objectives. The plan was to capture a section of the German front line and second line over a length of approximately 1,000 yards in the area of the village of Le Transloy. The attack had been carefully planned and information that the Germans had a regular Stand To time of 5.30 a.m. gave the time for zero hour for the intense artillery barrage supplied by the divisional artillery of the 29th Division and of those divisions adjacent to it. The infantry assault was to be made by the 87th Brigade of the Division. It was further planned that the 1st Royal Inniskilling Fusiliers, under Lieut. Col. R.R. Willis V.C., would attack on the right whilst the 1st Border Regiment, under Lieut. Col. F.G. Morris, would attack on the left. The Newfoundland Regiment was to hold the extreme left of the line and the 2nd South Wales Borderers would be used for mopping up or as Brigade reserve as required. As part of the preparation for the attack the 2nd Monmouths received the following instruction from Brigade Headquarters:

> Instructions from 87 Bde:
> CT's (Communication Trenches) to be dug from T6 B9 5.40 to N36 D 3.2 and from T5 B 6.6 to T5 B 9.9. Report at once Bde HQ Bull Dump 2 p.m. 27th. Personnel to be ready to move off at 4.30 p.m. from railhead 27th.

These brief instructions, issued four days before the attack, indicated the consolidation works that were expected of the battalion. The attack, as always, was expected to be successful and all the fighting was expected to be completed by the evening to allow the Monmouths to complete their task of consolidation during the night. The attack opened as planned and was a great success. The artillery barrage was followed closely by the attacking infantry and the Germans offered limited resistance. In this action Sergeant E.J. Mott of the Border Regiment was to win a V.C. for disabling a machine gun although already wounded himself and CSM C. Gardiner of the Newfoundlands was awarded the DCM for capturing 70 Germans who had little fight left in them. The success of the attack was complete when the attackers sent back a total of 394 prisoners. This had cost the Brigade 132 men killed and wounded, which in terms of the Somme fighting, should be considered light. More casualties occurred the following day when the Brigade had to withstand a German barrage but for the present there was the pleasant feeling of success. There is no official name for this action though the divisional historian suggests that it should be called 'The Kaiser's Birthday Raid' for such was the 27th of January.

The Monmouths were ready to commence work B and C companies being detailed. B Company, under Captain A.L. Coppock. were detailed to dig the right hand communication trench while C Company, under Captain John Trevor George, were to dig the left trench. The weather conditions were in some respects better than they had been for some time. It was very cold and there had been a succession of penetrating frost which had turned the mud rock hard to a depth of eighteen inches or so and there had been a substantial fall of snow. This meant that it was likely to be better for digging, though the work would be hard, but also that the conditions underfoot could be treacherous. With the former in mind D Company were told to stand by with additional men should they be required.

By the time that B Company reached the old front line it was about 8 p.m. The garrison of that trench were not certain of the exact position of things in front of them. Coppock sent out Sergeant A. Hodges and a party of six bombers in an attempt to find out. They were fired on immediately and the sergeant and one of the bombers became casualties. A further party was sent out only for it to return with the disturbing news that the Germans were still holding the point in the line where the communication trench was to finish. Clearly the attack had not fully removed the defenders. It was from this point that B Company had come under fire and it was speculated by the battalion historian that this was the result of the Germans having fixed rifles since the night, though moonlit, was quite dark. Capt. Coppock being uncertain of the next move and, quite rightly, not wishing to risk any more of his company unnecessarily left it in charge of Lieut. Rees Thomas Saunders and went back to Battalion Headquarters to seek information and new orders. Shortly after he left Lieut. Col. Bowen appeared in the trench occupied by B Company. It was by then 11.30 p.m. and Bowen wanted to get on with the job so he climbed over the top, accompanied by Lieut. Morgan Thomas Howells, and made his way steadily towards the captured trench. He eventually found a post held by the 2nd South Wales Borderers and from that point he taped a line back towards the old front line. Whilst the line deviated by some 30 degrees from the planned line it was sufficiently close to be of service and, perhaps more to the point, it enabled the work to be completed that night. The deviation also made the line longer and consequently additional men from D Company were called up to assist in the work. With time getting on the men attacked their work with a will and largely ignored the harassing fire of the Germans and by 4.30 a.m. on the 28th the new trench had been completed to a depth of 4 feet. The success of this work was undoubtedly due to Bowen's timely arrival, his rapid assessment of the situation and, finally, to him taking the initiative to establish a new line for the trench. No doubt his own disregard for the danger all around helped to give the men the additional confidence they needed to complete the task in spite of the close attentions of the Germans.

C Company, at work on the left communication trench, were also to experience some difficulties before the night was through. Their work was taped out when they arrived at the old front line and the men set to their task without hesitation or incident. They had been digging for no more than ten minutes when the enemy put down a heavy barrage. The more experienced men had removed the snow and about a foot of the frozen ground and so had managed to create some cover before the barrage fell. Unfortunately, the company had a number of replacements who had little idea how to dig a trench in No Man's Land. As the barrage fell a number of these men became casualties. Sadly L/Cpl Harold Jones, a stretcher bearer who had been with the battalion since it landed in France, described by the battalion historian as 'one of the bravest and most devoted of that hard worked band' was killed whilst attending one of the wounded. Captain George acted immediately and dashed back to the old position through the barrage shouting the code word for artillery retaliation which on that night happened to be 'Tripe'. Soon afterwards the British artillery responded and the German barrage died down sufficiently for C Company's work to be completed to a depth of about six feet. Bowen had imagined the worst when he saw the barrage fall to his left where he knew his company should be working. He was relieved to find the company making good progress when he was able to pay them a visit later that night. During the night the battalion had suffered more casualties than they had for some time with B Company suffering ten killed and seven wounded and C Company having four killed and eight wounded. In spite of the casualties it had been a successful operation on which the 29th Division historian commented:

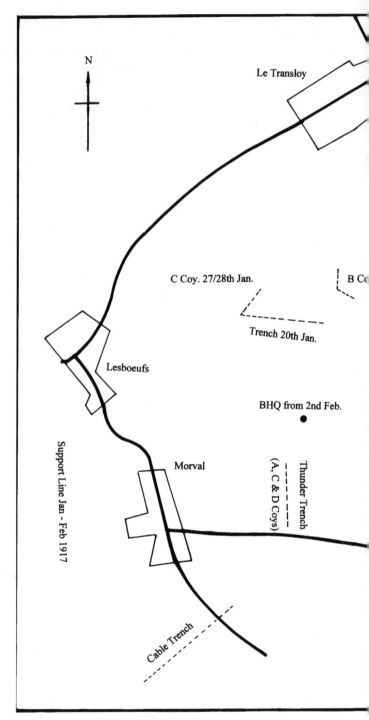

Sketch Map of Work Areas, January and February, 1917.

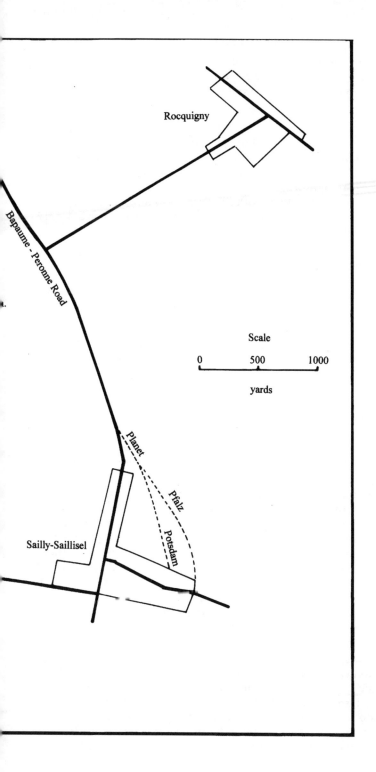

Rocquigny

Bapaume - Peronne Road

Scale

0   500   1000

yards

Planet

Pfalz

Potsdam

Sailly-Saillisel

The consolidation of the captured ground by the 2nd Monmouthshire Pioneers under Lieutenant Colonel Bowen's personal supervision was a remarkable feat. The ground was frozen to a depth of eighteen inches, and, of course, as hard as iron. Yet the line was dug in twenty minutes in the face of hostile fire at close range.

It was also a night of personal success for Bowen for he was to be awarded a Bar to the DSO he had won in 1915. For his part in the night's work Captain George was awarded the Military Cross. Awards of the Military Medal were made to Sergeant Charles Griffith, L/Cpl. Thomas Rose, L/Cpl. James Powell and Pte. John Lewis for their part in the action, full citations for these awards will be found in Appendix 3. The work of the Monmouths that night did much to enhance their reputation as a 'steady' unit and did no harm to the reputation of their Colonel as Pte. Heare was to point out:

Our Colonel is the talk everywhere. For his coolness, Col. Bowen is a good soldier everyone says. Our Colonel gets a bar to his DSO. He has earned the VC many times over, always the same, no five minute show with him.

The battalion was also noted at a higher level with Lieut. Col. Bowen receiving a message of thanks from Lord Cavan the Corps commander and the battalion was mentioned in the despatches published in England on the 1st February, 1917. The battalion historian further comments on the reply of an infantry sergeant when questioned on the most impressive part of the Le Transloy action:

The wonderful accuracy of our artillery and the remarkable bravery of Colonel Bowen and his Pioneers.

On the 9th February the Division was relieved and, for once, the battalion moved with them and were billeted in Meaulte, near Albert, where they continued to train in the safety offered at this distance from the front line. It was but a short break and ten days later they rejoined the Division and took over the Sailly-Saillisel sector of the line close to the Bapaume - Peronne road. Here, for two weeks, the battalion were involved in what had become the routine pioneer work of repairing and draining trenches and building of trench mortar pits with the added variety of the preparation of a 1,000 yards long telephone cable trench six feet deep in only four days. The battalion was duly thanked for its efforts in completing this work so rapidly - by a telephone message from Col. O.C. Mordaunt commanding XIV Corps Signals! Conditions by this stage of the winter had changed dramatically. The penetrating frosts had ended and the thaws of February had seen ground conditions reverting to a sea of mud so that the speed at which the cable trench was completed is noteworthy.

There was, within the upper echelons of command in the British army, the continuing desire to maintain pressure on the Germans in the area of the Somme and especially in the area south of the salient that had formed in their lines about the River Ancre as a result of the earlier fighting. It was considered that some large scale probing to the south would firstly, maintain the pressure and indicate the scale of German resistance in the area; secondly, provide some tactical advantage with the capture of the trenches around Sailly-Saillisel; thirdly, if successful it would improve the defences of the sector by providing better observation of the valleys to the east. Thus the capture of the trench system known as Potsdam Trench and its supporting Pfalz Trench to the east of the Bapaume - Peronne road in the village of Sailly-Saillisel was decided upon with these three objectives in mind. For this, a large scale raid similar to that at Le Transloy was decided upon with the responsibility for it falling on the 86th Brigade of the 29th Division. The attack, covering 1,100 yards of the enemy trench system immediately to the north of the road junction in the centre of the village was to be carried out with the 2nd Royal Fusiliers to the right and the 1st Dublin Fusiliers with a company of the Lancashire Fusiliers to the left. As at Le Transloy the 2nd Monmouths were detailed to begin consolidation works as soon as the trenches were under the control of the attacking battalions. The artillery preparation was to be supplemented by the use of trench mortars since much of the wire to be cut was on the reverse slope on the approaches to the German defences of Sailly-Saillisel. The attack was launched on the 28th February and, with the aid of a creeping barrage supplied by the Royal Artillery, the Royal Fusiliers, under Lieut. Col. G.A. Stevens, reached its objective on the right. To the left, portions of the wire remained uncut and parties of the Dublins and the Lancashires were held up. There was serious hand to hand fighting here as the remainder of the Dublins entered Potsdam Trench and bombed northwards to help their comrades who were eventually able to reach their objectives. The Royal Fusiliers were unable to extend their gain southwards along the trench system because of stubborn German resistance in both Potsdam and Pfalz trenches. Therefore, defensive blocks were erected in both trenches and the Royal Fusiliers stood by in anticipation of German counter attacks which continued through the afternoon of the 28th February. By 6.30 p.m. all attacks had ceased and the Monmouths were called upon to begin their work but not before Bowen had issued the following instruction to Captain A.L. Coppock of B Company:

> Situation at present; we do not hold Pfalz Trench from U8 D7.2 to the south. You cannot, therefore, dig the C(ommunication) Trench originally ordered. You will report to O.C. 2nd Royal Fusiliers with your Comp. and he will issue orders direct to you. Be prepared to hold the line reinforcing the RF's. Guides will be at Brigade HQ to take you to Bn HQ at U14 B 4.8. Inform the Bn Commander that you have two bombs per man and rations.
> 4.45 p.m.
> 28.2.17

At the same time A Company, under Captain W.D. Howick was ordered to dig a communication trench to the captured portion of Potsdam Trench. Both these companies came under a heavy barrage put down by the Germans in an attempt to prevent the reinforcement of the men in Potsdam and Pfalz Trenches. A Company was fortunate in so far as they only had three men wounded during this barrage whilst B Company escaped casualties completely. Both companies began the task of digging the communication trenches. Here the water and the mud became a nightmare for the men working under fire. Reinforcements were called upon from C Company in an effort to speed up the work and even then the allotted tasks were not completed until almost dawn the following day. The

German shelling had been severe and when portions of C Company were ordered to garrison the old front line they found that it had been totally obliterated. They then occupied two strong points known as Cushy and Sailly Posts.

Whilst, in a general sense, the attack of the 28th February had been a success the fighting did not end there and it was necessary to bring up reinforcements to maintain the line against renewed German counter attacks on the following day. The Divisional historian comments:

> The work of the Monmouths in consolidating the ground captured was beyond praise. Thanks to their labours and the gallantry of the Newfoundland, who had been attached to the 86th as a reserve battalion, two attacks on the 1st March and two more on the 2nd against the northern and southern barricades were frustrated.

On the 2nd March, 1917, B Company were ordered to dig a trench to act as flank defence for the position recently won from the enemy. Bowen issued the orders for this work at 7.20 p.m. and by 3 a.m. the following morning the work had been completed. Also on the evening of the 2nd March C Company were ordered to dig a new front line trench some 60 yards from the enemy in front of the position that had been captured two days before. Bowen wrote the detailed instructions for Lieut. Saunders, as follows, before leaving for the front line with Captain J.T. George O.C. C Company:

> 1. Your Coy. with 15 men of B Coy will continue the work done last night on POTSDAM by digging a trench NW to U8 d$2^{1}/_{2}$ - $5^{1}/_{2}$ from U8 d $3^{1}/_{2}$ - 4, that is left of A Coy's work last night as shown on the attached sketch.
> 2. Dimensions 5' deep, 4' wide at the top 3' at the bottom. The bays are to be fire stepped.
> 3. Care must be taken that the enemy don't surprise the working party.
> 4. The sandbags to be carried up are to be handed to the NFLD's at the junction of the right CT with Potsdam Road.
> 5. Leave (written) report and sketch of trench dug at Bde. HQ for me.
> 2.4.17
> 7.30 p.m.

Whilst it was not unusual for Bowen to give detailed written instructions to his company commanders, Lieut. Saunders recalled later that the Colonel had said to him 'Well, Saunders, I'm afraid its going to be a sticky night, so I will write out detailed orders for you.' Whether or not this was a premonition of the events to come is hard to say but before 8 p.m. that night Lieut. Col. A.J.H. Bowen had been killed - his last written order being that given to Lieut. Saunders. The story of the events that unfolded are best told in the words of Lieut. Saunders:

> About 8 p.m. I led the company up and finding no guide awaiting me, I went along the front line where I met a Newfoundland officer, who told me Colonel Bowen had been killed and Captain George wounded. I went forward to the covering party and withdrew them, not finding any tape. After consultation with the Newfoundland officer, I set the men to work in the front line and

proceeded to the headquarters of his battalion. Here I found George who had been blown up by a shell. Despite the fact he was badly shaken, he gave me the exact location of Colonel Bowen's body and details of what had happened. I returned to the company, found the Colonel, and had his body carried down. He had been shot through the left arm, the bullet penetrating his heart.

It was a tremendous blow to the battalion, for over two years Bowen had served in the thick of things, from the early days as a Captain and into his command of the battalion. He had been wounded at 2nd Ypres but to some of the men he seemed to be indestructible and one soldier even commented that 'his bravery was frightening'. He had gained a reputation for himself and his battalion and the words of the 29th Division historian are relevant here:

He was not a regular soldier, but so completely a soldier by temperament and self culture that he was indistinguishable from the very finest type the British army can produce. The G.O.C. was not exaggerating when he said Bowen's death was a loss to the whole army.

It was, indeed, a sad loss but the war would continue and there were mixed feelings about who his successor was likely to be. Bowen may not have been liked by all his men but most respected him because he led by example. His expectations of his men were no less than of himself and that had made him a good leader. The men needed someone they could respect and trust. The Division was relieved of duty in Sailly-Saillisel on the 4th March and when the battalion returned to billets in Meaulte they were joined by Major John Evans, second in command, who took over command of the battalion and was duly promoted to Lieutenant Colonel. To some in the battalion this marked the best possible choice since in John Evans they saw a continuity of the standards that had been set by Bowen and on which the good name of the battalion had been founded.

Whilst at Meaulte there was time to recover from the rigours of a tough tour of the trenches. There was also time for officers and men alike to adjust to the new commander and for him to get to know his command. There was the usual training in bayonet fighting and bombing and there was also experimentation in trench digging. This latter exercise must have seemed pointless to the men involved. The idea was that a number of different systems of digging allowing men to rest while others continued should be compared to the system operating which allotted a man a task to be completed as quickly as possible. The result of the work of the battalion was that the existing system was the most efficient and, therefore, it was continued. On the lighter side the 88th Brigade organised a football competition for all the companies of the Brigade. The Monmouths joined in this enthusiastically but while C Company was carrying off the trophy by beating a company of the Worcesters, the other companies of the battalion were to show their talents varied from average to poor. It was, however, good for the morale of the battalion as a whole.

Later in the month a number of awards were made to men of the battalion for their good work during the action at Sailly-Saillisel. These included the award of the MC to Lieut. W.D. Howick and the MM to Sgt. J. Jones, Cpl. R. Trew and L/Cpl. Williams. The ribbons to these awards were presented when the battalion was inspected by the G.O.C. on their training ground to the south of Meaulte on the 17th March.

It was during this period in Meaulte that the battalion was issued with new regimental numbers, a fact noted with some amusement by Pte. Heare:

> *New numbers are given to us, 2nd Mons. 1927 was my number now it is 265371. More to carry says the boys.*

Unknown to the men of the battalion it was not simply the issuing of new numbers that was concerning the commanders of the army. Plans were already well under way for the offensives of 1917 that would continue to carry the war to the Germans. As part of the general redistribution of troops, and partly because the 29th Division had such a high reputation and was earmarked for future use, the battalion was to move twice before the end of the month. Initially they moved to Foudrinoy where they found themselves in billets they had occupied in January, 1917. Here they continued with training which included exercises in both 'open warfare' and trench digging. Every eventuality was being considered or so it would seem, for the coming assault on the Germans. In the last few days of March the battalion was billeted in Flesselles, their last stop before being moved into the heat of the first of the battles of 1917 - the Battle of Arras.

Chapter Ten

'Monchy-le-Preux'

(April to June 1917)

The year of 1917 has been seen by some as the year in which the war was intensified beyond all that which had gone before. To some extent this argument is easily sustained when it is realized that 1917 was the year of Arras, Passchendaele and Cambrai. The men of the 2nd Monmouths were involved in all three offensives, usually as part of the 29th Division but occasionally attached to other units as the need arose. Each of these ventures is dealt with in the appropriate place but before any of the battles are discussed it is, perhaps, important to consider briefly the situation on the Western Front in the early months of 1917.

To understand the situation in 1917 it is necessary to look to the relative fortunes of the belligerents in 1916. For all concerned 1916 had been an expensive year as both men and material were thrown into the fighting but yielded little by way of result. The war was still locked in stalemate at the beginning of 1917 and whilst it had been possible for one side or the other to gain a little ground at terrific cost it was clear to all concerned that the war was no nearer to a conclusion than it had been at the start of 1916. For the British and the French the continuation of the war meant offensive action - there was no place in their thinking for a defensive war. To the Germans the offensive was, perhaps, less important as they saw the possibility of simply wearing out both the French and British armies by staying put behind carefully constructed defences as successive waves of Allies crashed against them in one futile attack after another. Further, the Germans appear to have understood that 1917 would see renewed allied offensives. Both von Hindenburg and Ludendorff sought to deal with this inevitability in as an efficient manner as possible. As early as September 1916, before the fighting on the Somme had died down and shortly after Falkenhayn had been replaced, they had begun to draw up plans that would improve their position for the assaults they saw as inevitable.

The German High Command looked with some envy at the allies since there seemed an almost limitless resource of fresh troops coming from the colonies of both the main allied nations. Of course, it was not an inexhaustable resource and the drain of 1916 had told as heavily on Britain and her Empire as it had on France and her colonies. However, the Germans saw their own resources as rather more limited and their allies as less reliable and of inferior quality and there can be no doubt that uppermost in the thinking of the High Command was the conservation of manpower, particularly of German manpower. For two years the Germans had fought from a position of strength on the Western Front. As the fighting of 1914 subsided into trench warfare the Germans had chosen their defensive positions with care. And, for two years the allied effort had been directed at knocking a dent in the German fortress that was, in fact, their Western Front.

As mentioned earlier, German planning had started in September, 1916, and the construction of a new defensive line, known to the Germans as the 'Siegfried-Stellung' and to the British as the 'Hindenburg Line', had begun. At this time the Germans looked on it as little more than a precautionary measure, they needed to know they could fall back on a well-prepared position and that they could meet the onslaught of the Allies from there. This defensive line extended from Arras through St. Quentin to Vailly on the River Aisne and this was to become the main defensive line to face a large part of the British Army through much of the remainder of the war. Although the *Siegfried-Stellung* had been originally constructed as a line of defence in the event of a withdrawal forced upon the Germans by a determined allied attack, the High Command realized early in 1917 that conditions on the Western Front were such that a withdrawal was almost inevitable if they were to conserve sufficient forces to maintain their war effort in that theatre. Thus, it was in the early months of the year that the Germans commenced a voluntary withdrawal of their forces along this portion of the Western Front. This had the effect of shortening the line they were to defend and hence released a number of divisions for reserve purposes. The Germans were not withdrawing to a point of weakness but to an immense defensive zone some six to eight thousand yards deep with outposts, strong points, deep reinforced concrete dugouts and belts of barbed wire totalling some fifty yards in depth. They had thought out the defences well and now in early 1917 they had decided to make use of them.

The scale of the works being undertaken by the Germans would not have gone unnoticed by the British and French intelligence units since the work involved would have been recognized as a major construction project with large quantities of men and material being required to bring it to completion. The strength of the defences were, correctly, assessed as being great and it was realized by the Allies that, even if the Germans did withdraw to it, it was impossible to attack such a zone until such a time as there had been sufficient artillery preparation. Whilst the Allies may have realized the purpose of the *Siegfried-Stellung* they could not have been expected to know that the Germans were preparing to use it as soon as they eventually did. Indeed, had the Allies been aware of the general depression in the German Army as 1917 started, there can be little doubt that it would have done much to have boosted their own flagging morale - this was particularly true of the French Army which had suffered so terribly in the early years of the war, and was on the verge of mutiny. Gradually the responsibility for conducting the war in

Flanders and Picardy was falling squarely on the the British Army and it is not suprising that the Germans believed the defeat of the British was likely to be of prime importance to their own conduct in the war. The preparation of the heavily defended zone of the *Siegfried-Stellung*, whilst entirely defensive, was considered absolutely necessary if there was to be any hope of the Germans wearing out the British Army and effectively defeating it without necessarily committing their forces to a major offensive.

The sorry state of the German morale from the highest to the lowest level following the very heavy fighting of 1916 meant that the withdrawal to the *Siegfried-Stellung* was begun in February 1917. Initially this took the form of the evacuation of the less essential forces from the old front line area followed by the artillery and ultimately by the infantry holding the line. The entire movement was completed by mid-March all along the front that was to be evacuated. The areas that were evacuated were, in some sectors of the front, left in such a state that rapid advance by the Allies was impossible. In some areas water supplies, including wells, were polluted with large quantities of horse dung though, as this was against the strict meaning of the Hague Convention, this was not a universal occurrence. In other areas efforts were made to block roads and there were instances of church towers being toppled into the entrances into villages to create as many problems as possible for advancing troops. Further, there were many devices set with some sort of trip wire or delay fuse which were to create problems for the troops occupying the former German areas and these were, to say the least, often very inventive.

This withdrawal of the Germans behind their defences caused some consternation among the allied military planners since they had expected to attack in the same area in early 1917 to drive the Germans back. The French plan, devised by General Nivelle, was to attack in the area of the Aisne and force the Germans to retire. To achieve this he had asked for, and received, the support of the British in making an attack in the area around Arras. This was to be the first major operation of 1917. The plan, put simply, was for the British to tie up as many of the German forces in the fighting at Arras whilst Nivelle concentrated his forces for a major assault on the Aisne that was to effect the eventual break through that was needed to bring about the early conclusion of a war that was devastating France and stripping the nations involved of the youth that would be needed to build the peace. Of course, the political background for the support that was to be given to the French was complex and had as much to do with the relationships between people such as Lloyd George and Haig as it had to do with any real military objectives. But, nonetheless, the Allies agreed on a plan and it was into this environment that the forces of the British Army were being drawn in the early days of the Spring of 1917. Amongst the forces being concentrated around the Arras sector was the 29th Division including its pioneer battalion the 2nd Battalion the Monmouthshire Regiment.

The 2nd Mons arrived in the town of Arras on the 8th April, 1917, as the final stages of the preliminary bombardment for the Battle of Arras were taking place. The battalion historian remarks that guns and howitzers were firing from every garden and every street corner and that 'The noise reverberating among the buildings was ear shattering'. The battalion was attached to the 3rd Army at this time since there was no plan to use the 29th Division in the opening phases of the attack. Preparation for the attack was considered to be thorough and, with the use of the creeping barrage as the attack began, it came as no surprise when progress was made and large numbers of German soldiers were seen coming back as prisoners guarded by the lightly wounded. The battalion was employed largely in the repair of the Arras to Cambrai road which had been cut by numerous trenches prior to the attack. The filling of these trenches became a top priority since it was essential to allow the artillery and material to advance in close support of the attacking troops. Initially the effort was directed at filling the trenches to a standard that would allow for the passage of horse-drawn transport, and hence the artillery, towards the front. This was achieved quite rapidly with two companies employed continuously filling the trenches and shell holes with almost anything available and, in particular, using railway sleepers in especially soft spots. It was, however, no mean feat since it was necessary to provide a road wide enough to allow two lanes of traffic going towards the front and one coming from the front. The work was hampered initially by a German long range gun which, according to the battalion historian, fired armour piercing shells at intervals. The gun was heard before the shell arrived and this gave the men some opportunity to find cover. Fortunately, the ground was so soft in much of the area that the shells landed harmlessly giving the road repairers little more than a fright and a thorough splashing with mud. The weather conditions during the work were not good as it snowed heavily during the afternoon of the 9th April to cause additional problems for the attacking troops and not inconsiderable ones for those troops in support as cold and wet both groups struggled to maintain the momentum of the battle. The battalion worked steadily throughout the day and by 5 am on the 10th April the road was of a sufficiently high standard to allow motor vehicles to pass without difficulty. The battalion War Diary records some of the work carried out by the battalion in this opening phase of the battle as follows:

> Owing to the heavy shelling of the roads A Company was unable to commence work until nearly noon and then not further than 100 yards E of G30c 4.3. B Company was not able to start work as soon as A Company but at 12.30 pm reinforced A Company on the north and gradually moved forward as the shelling abated. C and D Companies relieved A & B at 2.30 pm and were able to work to the TILLOY ROAD junction. By 10 pm the road was in a condition for horse transport. Orders were received about midnight 9/10 that two companies were to be placed at the disposal of the TANKS (Machine Gun Corps, Heavy Branch) together with as much of our transport as was available

The following day C Company provided 50 men for the purpose of rescuing tanks that had succumbed to the ground conditions on the first day of the attack and during nine hours of labour, were able to restart eight tanks. During the day the weather continued to deteriorate and A Company were returned to billets as a snow storm prevented them even finding the tanks they had been sent to help!

For the rest of the week, until the 16th April, the battalion was employed on similar work to be completed quickly enough for the artillery to move forward into support. Initially the work was completed without much in the way of interference from the enemy. As the artillery was brought forward however, it began shelling the Germans from the new positions and this brought some retaliation as the Germans commenced counter-battery fire, making life very unpleasant for the pioneers attempting to maintain a serviceable road. Thus, as in previous battles, the opening days of the first offensive of 1917 had passed away and it had not met with all the success that had been hoped for.

The 29th Division were brought into the fighting on the 14th April when they took over the village of Monchy-le-Preux from the 12th Division. Monchy had been part of the objective of the first day of the attack but it was not captured until the 11th April when it fell to the 37th Division who had been relieved by the 12th Division the following day. The importance of the village should not be underestimated since it formed a high point in the area to the south and east of Arras from which commanding views of the battlefield could be gained. The Germans saw it as important to hold Monchy if at all possible and even when it fell they saw it as necessary to recapture it if they could. On the 14th April, an event unusual, though not unknown in modern warfare, was to occur. The 88th Brigade of the 29th Division were ordered to attack at 5.30 am and to capture Infantry Hill to the east of Monchy. The creeping barrage was not as great a success as it had been on earlier days during the battle but the troops made some progress until such a time that the Newfoundland and Essex Regiments realized that they were becoming surrounded by German infantry who were also attacking. The Germans gained the upper hand, capturing or killing large numbers of both regiments. Lieut. Col. J. Forbes-Robertson of the Newfoundland Regiment, together with a small party from HQ were able to hold the Germans on the south east of the village for over four hours, whilst the 4th Worcesters prevented the advance at the south of the village. It is said that Forbes-Robertson was a competent marksman and accounted for over thirty of the enemy himself with a rifle. It was at this point in the battle for Monchy-le-Preux that the 2nd Mons were to rejoin the 29th Division.

Half the battalion was transferred from road repair duties and on the 16th April C and D companies were in the line east of Monchy for the purpose of constructing a new defensive line. Whilst in the line, the companies were accommodated in the trench that had been identified as the Brown Line of the initial attack. Needless to say it had come in for some heavy treatment from British guns during the artillery preparation and was in a very poor condition. Whilst pioneers in all divisions had built some reputation for trench repair, the condition of the Brown Line and the fact that it began to rain, together with the absence of suitable revetting material, eventually defeated the best efforts of the battalion. Added to these problems was the fire from the enemy which a nearby British battery was attracting. Two days later A and B companies relieved them in the line and the defensive line was completed shortly afterwards which allowed the battalion to concentrate in Arras relieved to be away from the persistent shellfire of the last week or so.

This period of continuous shelling had, in fact, marked a lull in the fighting and later was used to separate the First Battle of the Scarpe from the Second Battle of the Scarpe which started on the 23rd April, 1917. Not that this meant anything to the men involved. To them it was all part of the ongoing offensive to break the German lines. Following the occupation of Monchy the village had been shelled incessantly so that by the time of the Second Battle of the Scarpe commenced there was little of the original village standing. It was just as well that the Germans had fortified the town with deep concrete shelters which were now used to the best effect by the men of the 29th Division. On the night of the 23rd April, A Company of the 2nd Mons was detailed to dig communication trenches in the sector occupied by the 88th Brigade to the south of Monchy-le-Preux. When they arrived to commence the work Capt. W.D. Howick, the company commander, was informed by Brigade HQ that the work outlined in operation orders could not be carried out since the Germans were still holding the positions concerned. A Company was then assigned to carry out work as directed by the 4th Worcesters of the same Brigade. This battalion was holding the line on the right of the divisional area between Monchy itself and La Bergère on the Arras to Cambrai road. It would have been, under normal circumstances, a simple task for Capt. Howick to report to the CO, Lieut. Col. Kerans, of the 4th Worcesters but the conditions on the night of the 23rd April were far from normal even for the Western Front. The shelling was intense. Not only could Capt Howick not make the rendezvous with the 4th Worcesters but he also lost contact with his own platoons at various times throughout the night. Lieut. R.G. Noble, a platoon commander in A Company, was to record:

> I had sent out a couple of runners to try and get orders, but these not returning, I sent my sergeant - an Ebbw Vale man whose name I cannot recall - with a companion. Not even these returned, and as the shelling was the heaviest I had ever been through, I was afraid they had all been killed. I did not like ordering any more to go out, so went myself, leaving a corporal in charge. A stretcher bearer came voluntarily with me, and we worked our way forward, eventually getting near one of the tanks stranded in the first attack. Hearing someone calling, we moved over and found Colonel Evans and Major Comely. They had just arrived, and were overjoyed to see us and know that my platoon at least was intact.

Nonetheless, later that night the shelling subsided and Capt. Howick was able to get his men to work so that by the early hours of the 24th April they had been able to improve about 100 yards (90 m) of the position.

For B company the night started badly. Their work had been clearly taped out but while they were waiting to start work two heavy shells fell in their trench killing twelve of their number including 2nd Lieut. R.A. Cruickshank. Colonel Evans was to write to the young Lieutenant's wife in the following manner:

> Your husband has proved himself a stout hearted good soldier, and by his devotion and always capable discharge of his duties had won for himself the respect and regard of the NCO's and men under his command, and all the brother officers of the battalion who now mourn his loss. He died while leading his platoon. On the night of his death his platoon was employed on very important work in connection with present operations; he was instantly killed by a shell, but was not disfigured, his body was brought some distance back by his men and later was reverently buried and a cross now marks his resting place.

This letter, though well meaning, is somewhat typical of the letters sent to the relatives of the casualties of the fighting. It gives very little in the way of detail and, perhaps, did little to comfort the young soldier's wife; it was, however, the duty of the Commanding Officer to write such letters. Today 2nd Lieutenant Cruikshank lies in the British Cemetery at Dury some miles from where he fell. Although his company had suffered casualties before their work started they were able to finish their work on that night in good time so that further casualties were avoided.

Trenches near Le Bizet in April, 1915. Note the structure of the trench - partly excavated and partly in breastwork. Note also the revetting and the partially timbered fire step.

(Photo: SWB Museum)

Trenches near Le Bizet in April, 1915.   (Photo: SWB Museum)

Captain I.E.M. Watkins outside a shelter in the trenches near Le Bizet, Spring 1915.

Fortified cottage near Le Bizet in April 1915. The officer seated on the right is Capt. A.J.H. Bowen.

(Photo: SWB Museum)

Trench scene near Le Bizet in April 1915. Note the boxes of SAA and the rum jar in the foreground.

(Photo: SWB Museum)

Trench scene near Le Bizet in April 1915. The man second from the camera is holding a likeness of the Kaiser which was used to draw sniper fire. (Photo: SWB Museum)

Capt. A.J.H. Bowen outside a shelter which was known as 'Rose Villa' in the Le Bizet sector, April 1915.

Capt. A.J.H. Bowen making notes seated on a stretcher in the Ypres area April/May 1915.

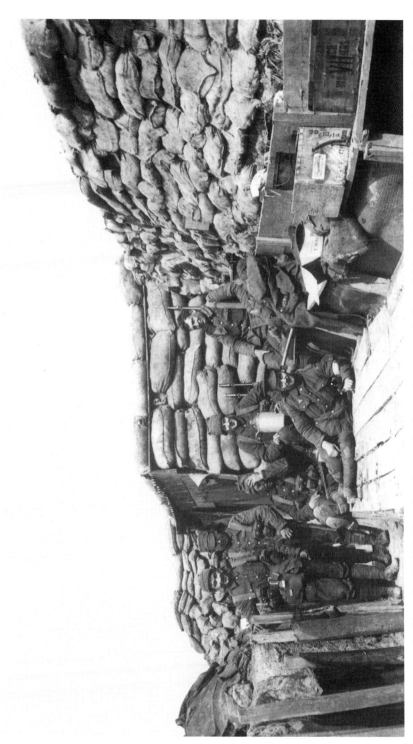

Trench scene near Le Bizet, April 1915. Note that the stretcher bearer is wearing the Imperial Service Badge. Note, also, the fondly cradled rum jar!

(Photo: SWB Museum)

Trench scene near Le Bizet, April 1915. Note trench construction with timbered floor. Note also the feet of resting men sticking out from their 'dugouts'. (Photo: SWB Museum)

The War Diary comments on the events of the night as follows:

> *While B Company was waiting to commence work two heavy shells fell in the trench and killed 2/Lieut. Cruickshank and 11 other ranks and wounded 5 other ranks. 2/Lieut. Shimmin and 3 other ranks were wounded at work by shell splinters. The enemy was shelling Monchy and the neighbourhood very heavily all through the night.*

The battalion remained in the line supporting the division for the next four days and were relieved when the division came out of the line on the 27th April. There was time for a brief rest at Couin, some 15 miles south west of Arras. It was a brief respite from the hardships of the trenches but nonetheless welcome for all that. During this rest Colonel Evans received a letter from Brig. Gen. H.G. Joly de Lotbinière, Chief Engineer of the XVIII Corps, under whom the battalion had served during part of the time in the Arras sector. The letter thanked Col. Evans and his men for the...

> *..really good work they have performed since the battle of the 9th April. I have not yet met officers and men who have tried harder to carry out their instructions, and I consider the work they accomplished on the Tilloy - Wancourt road as very fine.*

At least someone had appreciated their efforts! Perhaps this letter to the battalion had been triggered by a request to the CRE from Col. C.S. Fuller of the 29th Division staff, dated 25th April, 1917, and which ran:

> *As the Pioneer Battalion of the Division (1/2 Monmouthshire) has been engaged since the commencement of the Offensive Work under your supervision, the GOC would be glad to learn whether their work has been satisfactory in all respects.*

At the height of the Battle of Arras the 29th Division staff officers had sufficient time to check up on the battalion and the response by the Chief Engineer is instructive and demonstrates the respect that the battalion had earned:

> *The battalion have been working under my orders on the ARRAS - TILLOY and TILLOY - WANCOURT roads. They have also done very useful work in digging out tanks.*
> *Both officers and men have done exceptionally good work and I am much impressed by their keenness and thoroughness. The OC has gone most carefully into every detail of the work, and he could not have done more to than he did to assist me in every possible way.*

It would appear that this reponse satisfied the GOC for it is accompanied by the comment: <u>Most satisfactory</u> and signed by Major Gen. H.B. de Lisle.

The rest in the back area lasted until the 2nd May when the battalion returned to the Arras area coming under the direct command of the XVIII Corps for the next two weeks where they were employed in road repair and maintenance work. When the 29th Division was ordered back to the area in the second half of May the battalion rejoined it and moved forward with it. As might be expected the 29th Division had been brought back to the line to be part of a renewed attack which

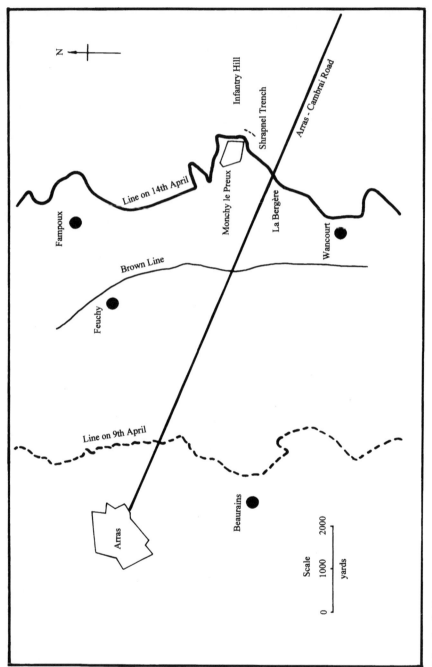

Monchy-le-Preux 1917.

was to be directed at Infantry Hill to the east of Monchy-le-Preux. This objective had held out since the early days of the April attack and was to remain a thorn in the side of the British Army for a little while longer. On the 19th May an attack against the Hill, in which the 2nd Mons were detailed for consolidation works, failed and it was not until the 30th May that the enemy line was eventually broken. On that occasion C Company had moved into Shrapnel Trench some 500 yards or so to the east of Monchy to be in close support of the attacking troops and during the night the company was to come in for some rough treatment at the hands of the Germans. The enemy opened up an accurate and heavy artillery fire some ten minutes before the planned attack was to commence and continued the fire even as the attack made progress. At 12.30 a.m. on the 31st May C Company were moved forward understanding the position to be captured was already in British hands. Apart from the shelling conditions were bad with the trenches knee deep in mud and, understandably, progress was not as fast as it might have been. When the company reached the position they found it had also been abandoned by the attacking British troops for the trench was in bad shape and full of water; it could also be easily enfiladed by the German machine gunners. The company managed to withdraw from this dangerous position but during the course of the night they had twenty-five men, including 2nd Lieut. A. King, killed and wounded with a number of men severely shaken and bruised, 'and nothing in the end to show for it' as the battalion historian was to state somewhat ruefully. The death of 2nd Lieut. King prompted Col. Evans to write to his parents with the following details:

> On the night in question he was acting as a guide to a platoon of another Company, attached for the night to his Company, for the purpose of carrying out some very important work south east of Monchy-le-Preux; he, together with a sergeant of the attached platoon, were instantly killed by a shell. Both were reverently buried near the spot where they fell.

The similarities with this letter and that to the family of Lieut. Cruickshank are obvious but no doubt it went some way to comforting the grieving family. The bodies of 2nd Lieut. King and Sgt. William George Hopkins were never recovered after the fighting in this area and today they are both commemorated on the Memorial to the Missing in the Faubourg d'Amiens in Arras along with many of their commrades-in-arms who fell in the fighting of the Battles of Arras in the spring of 1917.

The company was withdrawn from the area the day after Lieut. King fell and marched to Arras where it rejoined the battalion. The battalion left Arras on the 5th June, 1917, and moved by train and march to Le Meillard on the southern flanks of the valley of the Authie some 28 miles (45 km) west of Arras. Here the battalion rested for twelve days and it was noted as a village where officers and men were able to relax in the pleasant company of the locals. The officers were billeted with Madame Le Grand in Le Meillard. This lady did everything she could for the officers and organized tennis parties and gave them the freedom of her home. It was much appreciated by the officers and, unusually for a civilian her kindness is recorded in the battalion War Diary.

> On the 14th June the battalion held a sports with the 87th Field Ambulance:
> The Quartermaster had arranged for tea to be served on the field. The whole

arrangements were very successful and everyone spent a most enjoyable afternoon. The prizes were given away by Madame Le Grand who thoroughly enjoyed herself although she spoke very little English. Her husband, the Mayor of the village, was also present.

It should also be recorded that, as on previous occasions, D Company carried off most of the honours. However, a day or two later the battalion failed to gain any recognition at the Division Horse Show held in the nearby village of Gorges although it entered in all the classes possible.

The divisional HQ was at Bernaville, the next village, about which Pte. Heare was to record:

The battalion are in the next village, Le Meillard, plenty of sports and concerts, the weather is ideal, we sleep out in an orchard. In the morning the birds sing, thrush and blackbirds, in the fruit trees. It is so peaceful here and so strange to hear the birds whistle. We are able to get eggs and milk, chips and coffee here. It is the best place the Div. HQ has been to. Division sports, we all take part. After a glorious fortnight new drafts arrive, a lot of old hands come back to the battalion at Le Meillard. Our popular adjutant, Capt. Ibbs, has the MC presented to him here. He has earned it many times over. We all like him, always pleasant, wake him any time at night and he never grumbles and never seems to take this war serious.

It was not all relaxation for the men of the battalion as training was continued throughout the rest period. Mostly the training was carried out at a company level and at Le Meillard there were facilities for the battalion to practice all the skills required - a field had even been set aside 'for the training of inexperienced diggers'.

The pleasure the men got from the days out of the line is obvious from the comments of Pte. Heare and those in the War Diary. The Army were planning other things and the rest was soon to come to an end. On the 17th June the battalion together with the 29th Division was ordered to be prepared to move by train on the following day. The move, taking longer than expected carried the Mons back to the north and back to the Ypres sector where it was planned that another effort was to be made to take the fight to the Germans. The battalion eventually de-trained at Proven some miles behind the front and were marched to tented billets in St. Sixtus some 2 miles (4 km) to the north of Poperinge. The 2nd Mons were familiar with the Ypres area since they had seen fighting there in 1914, 1915 and 1916 and it is difficult to imagine the feelings of the survivors of those struggles as they moved to the area again. Pte. Heare had no doubts in his mind:

I fear this place. Black says 'You don't seem pleased here'. I tell him this is my place I fear for one. 'Why worry' says Black, 'Every time we move from rest I say this is my last but here we are again'.

It would appear that at least some of the men were able to take it in their stride but perhaps that would have been more difficult if they had realized they were to be involved in the battle that was later to be called Passchendaele by those who were fortunate to survive.

Chapter Eleven

'This is About the Worse of the War'

(July to November 1917)

It is probably fair to say that, in spite of the great endeavour and loss of life, the Battle of Arras was not the success that had been hoped for. But it was only the beginning of the campaign for 1917. Even before the Battle of Arras had begun the Chantilly conference of November 1916 between the allied general staffs had recognized and accepted the need for action on the Flanders part of the front. It was, however, Nivelle's bold plan to attack in Artois that had lead to the abandonment of the proposals of the Chantilly conference and although by early January, 1917 Nivelle's plan was in full preparation, Haig was still preparing for what appeared to him as the inevitable confrontation in Flanders. Whilst Haig's planning for the attack in Flanders required success in the Nivelle offensive in front of Reims, its failure only made the fighting at Ypres in 1917 more of an inevitability since it became an even more important issue to carry on the wearing out of the enemy and to break his fighting capabilities at the earliest possibility. This approach was the embodiment of Haig's strategy of attrition. Attack the enemy and wear him down. Right or wrong it was a clear and established policy, not always approved of by his political masters, but clear in his own mind. It is worth pointing out that in early 1917 Haig had the full support of Lloyd George in this matter - it was only later in the year that the politician began to oppose the strategy. In early 1917 Haig preferred the idea of attacking in Flanders to anywhere else. It was an opportunity to break out of the Salient around Ypres and to recapture the ground lost in 1915 and, perhaps, go far beyond. There have been many critics of the policy and plan adopted by Haig. The plan to attack at Ypres was bold and, at least in his own mind, thoroughly prepared. Critics have said that the plan was flawed in that it was too late and in the wrong part of the line - most of these have had the benefit of hindsight. The plan was to attack the ridges to the east of Ypres and to gain the Passchendaele Ridge by the end of the first day. The preparation was to be a large scale bombardment of the German defences for a number of days before the attack commenced and then with every resource at its disposal, including tanks, the British army was to sweep forward hopefully creating the breach in the line on the Passchendaele Ridge area and from that point rolling up the German line. The need for the latter was driven by the need to remove the Germans from the Belgian coastal towns and hence reduce the U-Boat menace which was having a major effect on the allied shipping. Perhaps the plan was simple and, with hindsight, it may seem to be full of folly. However, the British army had defended a tight salient since May, 1915 and there had been a large drain on resources, both men and material, during the two years since the 2nd Battle of Ypres. During those years, as the men of the Monmouthshire Regiment could testify, the salient was never truly a quiet sector. There was more or less constant fighting with trench raids heavy shelling and sniping, all of which brought a steady stream of casualties estimated by some to have been in the thousands every week of the war! The Ypres Salient was probably the most difficult part of the entire British sector of the line to defend and was a major problem throughout much of the war. To some extent Haig's plan for 1917 must be seen in this light; it was an effort to bring an end to the problems of defending the area where his men could be fired on from all directions all the time. In that respect it may be seen as a struggle to regain a measure of control in the area and in so doing once more take the war to the enemy - further, the drain on the resources would be lessened though, paradoxically, to achieve this much energy and life would need to be expended.

It was in preparation for this battle that the 2nd Monmouths were torn from their pleasant rest at Le Meillard on the 17th June, 1917 and became the first troops of the 29th Division which were moved in readiness for the coming offensive. It was, perhaps, a feeling of foreboding that had made Pte. Heare feel so bad when he heard that the destination of their march was to be the Ypres Salient. The battalion had not been in the area since August 1916 and had not been involved in heavy fighting there since the dark days of May 1915. Many of those who had survived the 2nd Battle of Ypres were still with the battalion but many had died since on the Somme and Arras battlefields. There can only have been apprehension amongst those who remembered the Salient - too much had happened for it to be otherwise and Heare was probably expressing the feelings of some of those who knew what the Salient could hand out.

The battalion arrived in the Salient rear areas on 19th June, 1917, and after two nights in the camp at St. Sixtus were moved again to Woesten about a mile further east where they were to bivouac whilst working in the area

> An advance party of 1 officer and 20 men per company went forward in the morning with the Quartermaster to pitch the camp. The day was very wet and the wood very thickly covered with undergrowth which made everything very uncomfortable. The companies moved up independantly followed by the transport.

During these first few days back in the Salient they came under the direct orders of the CE of the XIV Corps, Brig. Gen. C.S. Wilson and were employed to begin with in constructing tracks in the area of St. Sixtus. On the 23rd June, in the absence of its own division, the battalion was attached for work to the 38th (Welsh) Division then holding the line to the north of Ypres along the Yser Canal. Here the battalion was engaged in road repair and track laying as the 38th (Welsh) Division was preparing for what is considered by some to have been its finest hour. Three days later the battalion relieved the 19th (Glamorgan Pioneers) Welsh, the pioneers to that division and continued to work in the canal area. The first spell in the area lasted about a week but it was not without incident since Pte. Heare was to record:

> *The Germans drop gas shells on the far side of the canal. The shells plop like dud shells and the wind blows the gas across the canal to our dugouts. We drop the dugout door blanket and use the flaps to beat it off and put our gas masks on but the cursed stuff hangs around and gets in our eyes hours after.*

The squalor of life in the Salient had begun again for the battalion but the build up for the offensive continued unabated.

The 29th Division arrived in the area on the 25th June and the battalion moved to rejoin it in Poperinge. Together with the Guards Division and the 20th and 38th (Welsh) Divisions they became part of the XIV Corps. Two days later the Monmouths were back in dugouts in the canal bank to the north of Ypres this time near Essex Farm. These dugouts had been a safe haven for Monmouths before. At the end of 1915 the 3rd Monmouths had worked in the same area when serving as pioneers to the 49th Division. The 2nd Monmouths had been in the same general area when they had been part of the 4th Division. It is hardly suprising that they were immediately reminded of their previous visit there when they found the graves of comrades lost on that occasion in the cemeteries near the canal especially at Bard Cottage.

Once more attached to their division, the Monmouths were involved in trench improvements and the construction of the Bard and Marengo causeways and associated tracks. The causeways and tracks were to be of suitable quality to carry both men and equipment form the rear areas, across the wide Yser Canal, to the front line to the north of Ypres where the 29th Division were in the line. On the 3rd July the War Diary records:

> *C Company worked on the MARENGO CAUSEWAY and B Company on the BARD CAUSEWAY. The work consisted of cutting through the banks of the canal and putting the earth in the canal to make a track across about 15 feet wide. The companies worked on the causeways in 3 eight hour shifts. MARENGO CAUSEWAY was shelled from 8 am to 4 pm and considerable damage was done. After the shelling the next shift repaired the damage and carried on with cutting through the banks. BARD CAUSEWAY was shelled for 1/2 hr from 7.45 am*

The work was, as may be expected, difficult since the battalion could come under the observation of the Germans at any time and as, seen from the above entry, they were able to destroy it all with a few well aimed shells from guns that had been registered for some two years or so. This became a particular problem on the Bard Causeway, being constructed by C Company, so much so that the company commander, Capt. R.B. Comely, decided on the use of camouflage. Shell

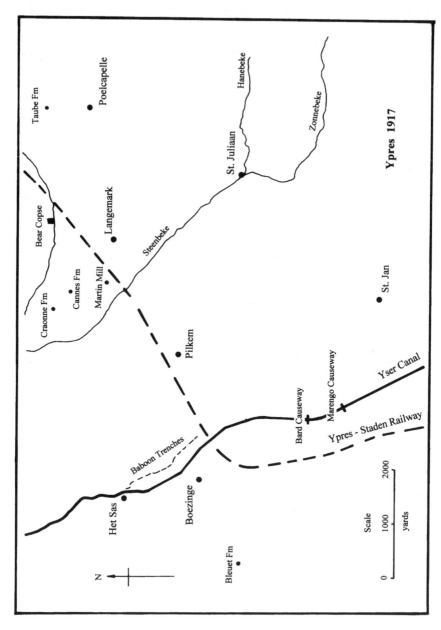

Ypres Sector 1917.

holes in the causeway were carefully noted before they were filled in at night and then before dawn planking was laid over the repair and buckets of mud from the canal was spread in circles upon the surface so as to appear as a shell hole from a distance. The Germans were deceived by this and it must have appeared to them that the work on the causeway had been abandoned but some weeks later, as the offensive opened, guns were able to travel forward across Capt. Comely's 'shell holes'. An indication of both the importance attached to the work and the danger involved can be gained by the fact that during this period of preparation the battalion won a number of gallantry awards including a Bar to the MC for Capt. Comely. The citation for the award of the DCM to CSM T. Johnson states that the working parties were 'under continuous bombardment' and clearly demonstrates the danger a pioneer faced while carrying out his work. Sgt. J. Hale was awarded a MM under similar trying circumstances. It was, however, also a period when the battalion had a number of casualties both from the shelling of their work and from gas:

> 4 men of C Company and 1 man of D Company were admitted to Field Ambulance, GASSED, as the result of gas shells penetrating deep into the earth behind a dugout and the gas working through to the men while they were asleep.

The conditions in the forward area taken over by the 29th Division were bad and the history of the division explains the need for a further two miles of trenches that needed to be constructed in the lead up to the planned assault. To achieve this end, and prepare other works, the division put on nightly working parties of about 600 strong - that is almost a battalion involved in duties other than holding the line. In the course of the coming weeks a total of 3,040 tons of trench stores was manhandled to the front line. The efforts of the Monmouths should be seen in this context - the importance of their maintenance and construction work should not be underestimated and it is certain that when strong backs were needed to assist the working parties, they were to be found amongst the pioneers. This work continued throughout the early part of July and the battalion remained in and around the front line until the 20th July when they were relieved to Caribou Camp near Proven for a rest. After a month of almost continual work in the forward area, in more or less constant danger, there can be little doubt that they needed a rest. Whilst out of the front line the battalion historian records that a divisional boxing tournament was organized in which the battalion won the most bouts. More unusually, perhaps, the battalion was also visited by Major General de Lisle, the division GOC, who presented them with a post horn. This was to mark his recognition of the fact that in spite of being on active service and frequently in danger the battalion had made special efforts to maintain a battalion band!

The date fixed for the opening of the attack was the 31st July, 1917. It had been decided that the 29th Division would not be talking part in the opening exchanges of the great battle. However, the 2nd Monmouths were not to be left out of the event and were attached to the Guards Division which was to be engaged on that opening day on the extreme left of the British line to the north of Ypres between Boezinge and Het Sas. The divisional artillery was also involved in the preparatory work for the attack made by the Guards, a preparation on which Capt. Arthur Gibbs of the Welsh Guards was to comment as follows:

I should think the guns could have easily been heard in England. The noise on the Somme was terrific, but the noise during today and all through last night was still more stupendous.

A and B Companies of the battalion were to follow the Guards Division over and begin the immediate work of road repair to enable that division to bring supplies forward as needed and were to be ready to move as soon as the attack commenced. In this extreme left of the sector the Germans had withdrawn from some of their trenches some days before and the Guards had moved forward in a 'bloodless advance' to occupy Baboon and Baboon Support Trenches. This meant that they were somewhat further forward than the 38th (Welsh) Division to their right and consequently needed to remain in their trenches for almost forty minutes after the 3.50 a.m. zero hour to allow the adjacent division to catch up with them. The initial phases of the attack went well and the Guards moved forward in three waves maintaining a distance of as little as fifty yards (45 metres) from their own barrage as it rolled forward. The 2nd Monmouths followed close on their heels to begin their consolidation works. The work of the battalion was not grand like that of the battalions they followed, indeed, this was the action in which Sgt. Robert Bye of the Welsh Guards was to win the first VC for that regiment, but it was essential work that brought them into the zone of German shelling as the attack continued. However, in the steady manner which was, by that time, their watchword the first two companies of the battalion commenced their work as the shelling continued all around them as the Germans responded to the early rush of the British army. A and B Companies were relieved by C and D Companies at 2 p.m. after some nine hours working under fire. At about the time the relief was taking place the Germans were redoubling their efforts to halt the advance and the shelling increased. Sgt. R.J. Powell who had won an MM on the Somme, fell wounded and Capt. R.B. Comely and Pte. J.H. Pickford went to his assistance. In a matter of moments another shell fell in the same place and Powell and Pickford were killed. By some strange quirk of fate Capt. Comely was uninjured and was able to carry on his duties. The battalion suffered only six fatalities during the day which must be considered fortunate when the scale of the fighting around them is considered. The Germans may have been forced to concede ground but they had not done so cheaply as the Guards had swept forward. Further south, casualties amongst the British divisions had been heavy as the first day of fighting in the 3rd Battle of Ypres progressed. However, the Guards were full of confidence for Pte. Heare was to comment:

The Guards attack for our Corps. They say next day it's easy, we could have gone to Berlin, no opposition, but they stopped when taking their objective.

It was not quite as simple as this and slowly and surely over the next few days the advance became bogged down in most appalling conditions as the rains of a very wet August turned the battlefield into a bloody quagmire. The 29th Division relieved the Guards Division on the 8th August and their historian was to comment as follows:

Compared with Flanders, the Monchy Plateau was dryness itself and the wintry gloom of the Somme was forgotten.

Pte. Heare was to comment much more graphically:

> *This is about the worse of the war, mud everywhere and dead lying in hundreds. An artillery man with a pack mule passes me going up, then suddenly they disappear. I lose my footing and fall in a shell hole full of mud and water, up to my neck. I try to scramble out. I catch a loose duck board, an orderly says 'Hello Taff, shipwrecked?' smiling, but he pulls me out. I am sure there are bodies in that hole and I have been treading on them. I tell the orderly of the man and pack mule and he says he saw them fall in a shell hole full, but they didn't get out.*

Conditions such as these were a direct response to the heavy shelling of a clay soil where the water table was high followed by the heavy rain of August. The shelling served to destroy the local drainage patterns turning narrow streams such as the Steenbeke into a morass of perhaps half a mile wide whilst the rain could no longer get away and simply gathered into shallow depression and shell holes. It was under these conditions that the battalion was expected to function as road repairers and, where it became necessary, to construct raised duck board tracks supported on long piles driven into the deep mud. Even the battalion historian was to comment some years later that:

> *Sad was the fate of any man who slipped from these boards when no comrade was near to pull him out.*

The next phase of the 3rd Battle of Ypres in which the battalion was involved was the attack to capture the ground around Langemark. The 29th Division had relieved the Guards Division on the 8th August for this purpose and it was to be this division's first involvement in the offensive. Of prime importance to the attack was the crossing of an area of swamp that had once been the Steenbeke. This stream which was normally no more than 10 yards wide had become a difficult obstacle hundreds of yards wide. It was clear that the only way to supply and sustain the planned large scale assault across this waterlogged area was on raised track ways and bridges and these needed to be constructed as soon as possible. The 86th Brigade of the Division were able to clear the vicinity of enemy by a limited assault and this allowed the construction of the tracks before the main assault would begin. The 2nd Monmouths, as pioneers to the division, were heavily involved in this work during the days immediately before the attack was launched. The attack by the division was planned for the 16th August and there was no time to spare in the preparation. It is generally accepted that the halt in the offensive caused by the exceptional weather in the opening days of August had done much to assist the German defenders in their preparation for renewed assault. Nevertheless, nothing but success was expected and the attack was set two objectives. The first was to capture a line running north west from Martin Mill, on the northern outskirts of Langemark, to the boundary of the French 2nd Division on the left of the British line. The second objective was some 500 yards (480 metres) distant running through Cannes Farm and Craonne Farm. Much of the ground was waterlogged and 'the going was awful, in places men sank over their knees in the swamps' but the attack was pressed vigorously and the attacking battalions engaged the enemy and succeeded in overcoming the numerous block houses and strongholds. Two platoons of A Company, commanded by 2nd Lieut. H.J. Hopkins were detailed to go forward with the attacking troops so that they could tape the most suitable way through the area of swamp for the following units. The attack was a success and both objectives were reached by noon of the 16th August and there was a feeling of pride for a job well done. It had been costly with the division suffering well over two thousand casualties though the Official Historian puts the figure significantly lower at a little over one thousand four hundred. Throughout the operation the 2nd Monmouths had been involved in consolidation works and as usual there was a trickle of casualties for the battalion. Once again the importance of their support rôle should not be underestimated as they worked to ensure that the successes of their division could be consolidated in a very short time.

During the next ten days the battalion continued its work while the 29th Division held the front line it had captured on the left of the British sector north of Ypres. The weather conditions deteriorated, the rain continued in heavy blustery downpours and the mud got deeper as the shelled area turned into a sea of mud. The work of the pioneers became increasingly difficult but, at the same time, increasingly necessary as the need to move and ensure the ground was held became obvious as minor attacks to the south met with limited success. The plight of some of the soldiers asked to attack can barely be imagined as men were asked to stand for hours and hours in mud, often above the knee, while waiting the order to attack. In these conditions the 2nd Monmouths were able to carry out all manner of pioneering tasks from road repair to the laying of light railway tracks. The latter method of transport has been described by Col. E.F.W. Lees, CRE Guards Division, 'as the most efficient form of transport under the circumstances' and, thus, no little effort was expended on their construction and maintenance. Pte. Heare was to comment that at least there was a positive side to the prevailing conditions:

> It seems we old hands are able to tell a bullet or a shell, safe or otherwise, by the sounds, but if it wasn't for the mud there would be a lot more casualties. The shells go deep in the mud before they explode. It is a common thing to get a shower bath of mud and not hurt otherwise.

On the 28th August, 1917, the 29th Division were relieved by the Guards Division and spent the next month out of the line recovering from their efforts. Life was not so kind to the 2nd Monmouths for they were attached to the Guards and remained in the forward areas to carry on their work including constructing tracks and wiring sections of the line as defence against anything the Germans may be planning. During much of the time the battalion was forced to carry out work at night for even in areas not in direct view of the enemy line, they were coming under observation from enemy observation balloons. If there was any delay in finishing a night's work they were immediately shelled off as the Germans reacted to the pressure being put on them by the offensive. The battalion was billeted about six miles away from the working area and the nightly march to and from the front along congested tracks was completed under the grimmest of conditions. The battalion history remarks that on one night two men of another unit were spotted weaving about between the files of men and transport in what appeared to be a drunken state. When the men were questioned it became clear that they were far from drunk and were in fact the blinded victims of a gas attack who were trying to make their way to the nearest dressing station as best they could. A guide was provided immediately by the battalion and the blinded men were taken to the relative safety of a dressing station. The Salient of 1917 still had horrors to offer even the most hardened of troops! During this period the Germans were active in the skies above the British advance and regularly bombed the areas immediately behind the front line. Even when the resting companies of the battalion were attempting to get a little sleep they were often disturbed by air raids. It is recorded that there were nightly air raids made by four flights of German aircraft each of five aeroplanes and each of which dropped four bombs. Pte. Heare's account is a little more detailed as to the effects of these raids:

> The German aeroplanes are giving us socks. One bombing plane came over so low we could see the Germans in the plane. I felt so low, this bomber blew up two guns and caught the transport on the road. The number of horses and mules killed was tremendous..... That night the German planes came over again, four of us were out hours helping to shoot disabled horses and in some cases getting wounded men from under horses.

The battalion returned to the 29th Division when it returned from rest to relieve the Guards on the 22nd September, 1917. The 2nd Monmouths had now been in the line on constant work since the beginning of August and the general state of the battalion can only be guessed at. It cannot have been functioning at optimum efficiency since both officers and men were bound to be tired to the point of exhaustion. It is true to say that they had had very little involvement in the real fighting like the infantry battalions but they had been in the forward areas for a long time and at all times they were subject to shelling, gas and the sniper's bullet. The toll in terms of morale and efficiency will have been a heavy one and after two months of this sort of work it is likely that the battalion was as battle fatigued as any unit that had been heavily engaged in the fighting. Nonetheless when the division was involved in a minor holding action on the left of the battle that was to become known as the Battle of Broodseinde the battalion was there carrying out its pioneering duties. The front held by the division was consolidated as the ground was won when the Australians involved in the major part of the fighting to the right captured and held the ground expected of them.

The offensive ground its way painfully forward, small gains were made at enormous cost as the principle of attrition was applied relentlessly. Conditions did not improve as autumn set in and by early October movement within the front line area was becoming so difficult as to be almost impossible. The last major part that the 29th Division was to play in the 3rd Battle of Ypres took place on the 9th October in an action that was to become known as the Battle of Poelcapelle. As an indication of the poor conditions prevailing in the area, units marching to their jumping off points for the battle took several hours to travel the last few miles and arrived in position already tired before even a shot had been fired. The 29th Division attacked astride the remains of the Ypres - Staden railway line from the vicinity of Bear Copse to beyond Taube Farm. The fighting was intense as the assault progressed and by the end of the day the division had been able to secure most of the objectives that had been set. Once again the 2nd Monmouths were involved in consolidation works preparing the way for the following troops and supplies to get to the front line to ensure that the ground so expensively won could be held. It was not glamorous work, it was tiring, back breaking work but it was necessary and it was something that the battalion was very good at. Lieut. H.L. Hughes, who was wounded during the day's fighting, was to have his own opinion of the events of the early part of the day:

> *Zero on the 9th was at 5.20 a.m., and before that hour we were waiting in a trench on the slopes looking down onto Langemark, when suddenly a German 'plane suddenly swooped from low clouds to within fifty feet and began spraying us with machine-gun bullets. It was remarkable that only two or three of the men were hit, but we opened fire at him and he soon disappeared into the early morning mist. It was most disturbing for a few moments, and I recall having the same feeling of utter helplessness at Montauban in 1916, when an enemy 'plane appeared over camp dropping flechettes. A tin hat seemed very inadequate protection on such occasions!*

By the end of the 9th October, however, the work of the battalion had allowed men and materials to move forward to support those units who had captured the ground. On the 11th October the 29th Division was relieved and took no further part in the fighting around Ypres of 1917. For the 2nd Monmouths, however, it was not quite the end of things at Ypres. They remained in forward areas for another four weeks carrying out essential work attached to other divisions and were not relieved until the 5th November, 1917. During the early part of this period the battalion was assisted in its work by A and D companies of the Royal Guernsey Light Infantry a newly formed unit only recently arrived in Flanders. These two companies joined B and C companies of the 2nd Mons to form a composite battalion coming under the direct orders of Lieut. Col. Evans and worked on the preparation of tracks in the Langemark area. It was not a happy introduction to the front line for the new men for while they were helping the Monmouths with road construction in the area around Langemark, Major A. Davey and four Guernseymen were killed on the 14th October and became that unit's first casualties. Later the unit was withdrawn and joined the 86th Brigade of the Division with which they served until April, 1918.

When the Monmouths were finally withdrawn they had been in the line continuously from the very start of the great battle until almost its conclusion. There can be no one who doubted their need for a short period of rest before they were to rejoin their division to take part in the next phase of blood-letting that was to be known as the Battle of Cambrai. It is by virtue of the 2nd Monmouths presence at Ypres during 1917 that the Regiment was able to boast the battle honours 'Pilkem', 'Langemark', 'Poelcapelle' and 'Ypres 1917'. For the battalion it had been a very trying four months with little break in their work and very little in the way of recognition for their efforts but at least they had the satisfaction of knowing that they had been able to achieve all that was asked of them during one of the greatest battles ever fought by the British army.

Chapter Twelve

'They Took Their Picks and Shovels and Came on With Us'

(November to December 1917)

The tank had been a weapon in the arsenal of the British army for almost a year when the idea of a large scale tank attack was first suggested in August of 1917. At first little notice was taken of the idea because the tanks had not been a towering success in the fighting of the 3rd Battle of Ypres (Passchendaele) to that date and besides the British effort was firmly focused on the battles around Ypres. The tank commanders, for their part, were not surprised by the events around Ypres as they had suggested that tanks could serve much more effectively in the rolling chalk down-lands further to the south. Initially a proposal was put forward by General H. Elles and Col. J.F.C. Fuller that a large scale 'tank raid' should be organized that would have limited objectives to 'destroy the enemy's personnel and guns, to demoralize and disorganize him and not to capture or hold trenches'. The place suggested for this raid was in front of Cambrai. General Sir Julian Byng took the decision to adopt the outline of the plan but saw it being so much more. In his hands the plan was developed to set somewhat grander objectives to capture Cambrai and Bourlon Wood and hence create a significant breakthrough that could be exploited by cavalry which would, in turn, allow the Germans to be rolled back in the area of the town. It is, perhaps strange to think that planning for this attack was proceeding whilst the fighting at Ypres was continuing and not making the expected progress. It is even stranger to think of the attack opening with the tank, the most modern of weapons, creating the gap to be exploited by cavalry. However, the British command was intent on breaking their enemy and in the planning for this attack they were simply continuing that process as far as they were concerned. It is also interesting to note that the command was learning its trade and that relatively new concepts were being adopted and tried out. The use of the tank at Cambrai must be seen as another step in the re-education of the leadership - it must also be borne in mind that the enemy was also learning from such tactics.

The 29th Division were withdrawn from the fighting around Ypres in October 1917 so that they could begin training to take part in the great battle that was in preparation and when the 2nd Monmouths were finally withdrawn from the Ypres Salient to rejoin their division, it was to resume their pioneering role in the Battle of Cambrai as the first large scale tank battle was to be known.

When the 2nd Monmouths were withdrawn, tired and battle weary, from the Ypres Salient on the 5th November their condition as a fighting unit can only be guessed. The weariness of front line service for almost three straight months would have taken its toll and, most likely, the men of the battalion really needed a rest to recover. That could not be so. They were destined to take part in the events further south. Without any sort of rest or time to recover from their experiences at Ypres they were ordered to start for the Cambrai sector of the line in north France - a march of almost one hundred miles. To say that the battalion was treated badly at that stage is, perhaps, to overstate the case since they were not on their own in this situation. However, after emerging from the trenches of the Ypres sector it should be expected that the men were not best pleased at the thought of such a long march which was only to carry them to yet another battle zone. With these thoughts in mind the comments made by Pte. Heare are more readily understood:

> The whole Corps are getting relieved now, at last. We start on a march, five days, marching every day. Our battalion passes about a hundred busses on the road side, nice and clean, the men happy getting 6/- (30p) a day, all poshed up. How our boys swear over these busses standing there and all the boys are footsore. The 2nd Mons have never had a bus ride since they came out, the busses are good ornaments. That night all busses are burnt to the ground, what a fire! The 2nd Mons are in the next village. All the food stores of the bus drivers are gone. All sorts of enquiries are made but no one can find out anything of it.

There is no evidence to suggest that the battalion had anything to do with the incident but there is little doubt from the tone of the comments that the soldiers saw it as a kind of justice and were not in the least dismayed - after all if they had to walk to their destination why shouldn't everyone else? It was a tiresome march and at Arras some of the men got into a bit of bother with their new Regimental Sergeant Major. Fortunately, the company officer understood the men's difficulties rather better than this soldier fresh from home and straightened out both the awkward situation that was developing and the RSM. The mental and physical toll of the last few months was beginning to show. Tempers were short though there appeared to be no lack of morale in the battalion since this incident tends to show that the battalion officers looked out for their men who looked out for each other. In this respect the battalion had become a close knit unit so much so that it could lead to the almost total exclusion of newcomers who were seen as being almost outsiders. The Mons, with three years service overseas, had learned their lessons the hard way and were not about to be second guessed. This attitude was probably healthy since they knew their job and would follow an officer who understood this almost anywhere. It is interesting to note that the unnamed RSM in this incident was replaced by Sgt. George Yearsley before the fighting of

Cambrai commenced. Yearsley had been with the battalion since 1914 and had done much to earn the respect of the men.

Their march took them via Arras and Bapaume to Equancourt some 15 miles (20 km) to the south west of Cambrai. The battalion spent one night at Bapaume where they were treated to a 'good concert party' which helped relieve the difficulties of the march but it was a short stop and then on again. It soon became clear to the men that something big was about to happen. No one was allowed to move during the day and even at night great care was taken not to create extra noise as masses of troops were brought into the area in front of Cambrai. On arriving in the 29th Division area the Mons were put to work on the construction of a light railway track running up to the front line. The importance attached to these light railways has already been pointed out and in the coming battle it was thought that they would be of great value again. However, as will become clear, emphasis of their importance was to have a considerable effect on the battalion. One night some of the men saw tanks being unloaded at a railway siding and soon realised that whatever was happening was going to happen soon.

The arrival of the tanks was but a small part of the build up of men and material in the area. Over the previous few weeks thousands of men and masses of equipment of all descriptions had been moved into the forward area. All of it had been done under the cover of darkness and much use of woodland and camouflage was made so that the enemy was unaware that anything was going on. The British Third Army was in place by the third week of November and it comprised 19 divisions in six Army Corps. The 29th Division, and hence the 2nd Monmouths, was attached to the III Corps which was to take a central position in the attack when it eventually took place. The British had chosen their place for attack wisely since the area had been a relatively quiet area which, although forming part of the Hindenburg Line, was relatively thinly manned by units of the German Second Army. The Germans actually saw the Cambrai sector as a kind of rest area and units that had been in the heavy fighting at Ypres were sent there to recover. Initially there was no reason to suspect that there was to be a British offensive in the area though the German High Command had warned that the lack of British success in Ypres might lead to further attacks elsewhere. However, on the 16th November the commander of the Second Army was to report to his superiors that 'hostile attacks on a large scale against the Army front are not to be expected in the near future'. Suspicions were aroused a day or so later when men of the 36th Division were taken prisoner by the Germans, but no idea of when the attack could be expected was gained from these prisoners. Nonetheless, the Germans did send some reinforcements to the area in readiness. They believed that any attack on their positions would commence with a substantial bombardment which would give them sufficient time to bring even more defenders to the area. This turned out to be an error of judgement on their part, an error which was to have a major influence on the conduct of the battle during the opening phases.

By the 19th November everything was set for the attack, men and machinery were in place for a large scale offensive with a difference. There was to be no long preparatory bombardment and for the first time tanks were to be used in large numbers - a total in excess of 300 had been gathered for the attack. The III Corps was to take the sector from Beaucamp to Gonnelieu with the objective being to create a breakthrough in the Hindenburg Line and to capture the two small towns of Marcoing and Masnières and then proceed to the Masnières-Beaurevoir Line and Cambrai itself. The 12th Division was on the right of the sector, the 20th

Division in the centre and the 6th Division was on the left. This meant that the 29th Division was in reserve. The latter division had been training hard and was ready for action but there was a problem. The secrecy surrounding the attack meant that troops had been kept out of the forward areas until as late as possible. For the 29th Division this meant marching on three consecutive nights to get to their reserve position in the rear areas of III Corps. Then, on the morning of the attack they were to march six miles (9.5 km) to their assembly position to await the order to pass through the assaulting troops of the first wave - this entailed a march of another four miles (6.5 km). The last ten miles (16 km) or so would be completed in full fighting order which entailed the men carrying packs of between 60 and 70 pounds (27 - 30 kg). Understandably the divisional commander was questioned as to whether his men were capable of completing the task asked of them and then be able to hold any positions taken for another day. Major General de Lisle was able to assure the Chief of the General Staff that his men were able to deal with all the rigours that could be put before them. His faith in the men of his division was not unfounded as the events of the following two weeks were to show. Of course, as divisional pioneers the 2nd Monmouths were included in this general arrangement although they were not expected to press forward with the infantry brigades.

On the 20th November, 1917, the attack opened at 6.10 a.m. when the tanks began to move. Ten minutes later the artillery opened up with smoke, gas and high explosives. By this time the 29th Division had already been on the move for about four hours so that they could reach their assembly points. The divisions in the front line swept forward and were soon through the Hindenburg Line and heading towards Marcoing and Masnières. The tanks were showing their worth as they crushed all the wire before them and allowed the infantry to make progress in the zone where, in earlier battles, it had been held up. The opening phase of the attack was a great success as tank and infantry overran positions and broke through the Hindenburg Line on a seven mile (11 km) front. It could have been even worse for the Germans but for the bravery of pockets of defenders - in particular Field Marshal Haig, in his dispatches, was to single out one German artillery officer who manned his field gun until he was killed and in doing so had destroyed a number of the attacking tanks.

By 10 a.m. the 29th Division were ordered forward to exploit the gap. Their orders were to capture Marcoing and Masnières and to force a crossing of the St. Quentin Canal and by making that bridgehead allow the cavalry to come forward to exploit the gains made up to that time. The 2nd Monmouths were to follow up closely on the heels of the attacking brigades and commence consolidation work at once. A Company was placed under the direct control of the Divisional Artillery Commander (Brig. Gen. E.H. Stevenson) and were to construct the tracks to allow the guns and ammunition to be brought through the Hindenburg Line and thereby allow the artillery to keep in touch with the advance. Some members of the battalion received their orders direct from Lt. Col. H. Biddulph, CRE of the 29th Division, who spelled out what he wanted of them as part of his instructions to the division:

> O.C. 1/2nd Monmouthshire Pioneers will detail (under orders already issued) 3 taping Parties, each under an officer, to lay forward tape lines from the present front line system to Advanced Brigade Headquarters. These officers will report to their respective GOC on 'Y' day.

The remainder of the battalion was employed constructing a light railway as fast as they could to keep pace with the advance and to allow all manner of trench stores and ammunition to be brought forward as quickly as possible. It was an attack the like of which none had experienced. They were all moving forward and at a pace that was almost unthinkable - it was, for a brief period of time, 'open warfare' in all but name.

For the Mons the sight of the Hindenburg Line *(Siegfried Stellung)* was something special as Pte. Heare was to record:

> *The Germans are taken by surprise. It is easy, hardly any Germans (from) here to Marcoing. The Hindenburg Line is perfect, large dugouts, electric light, cooking stoves, chairs, beds, tables, like small palaces. The Germans have done themselves well here.*

and as the battalion historian was to comment:

> *These dugouts were particularly elaborate. They were reached by staircases of 20 to 25 steps down, and consisted of long corridors below ground with rooms leading off. Some were heated by carbon stoves provided with chimneys to clear the fumes, and were lighted, in German times, by electricity. The walls of officers quarters were lined with panelling evidently taken from churches.*

No evidence for the last comment was offered but it is obvious from both comments that no one had seen the like of the Hindenburg Line dugouts before. Clearly the Germans had not planned on being removed so quickly.

For their part, the 29th Division were able to move forward rapidly and to get into both the towns of Marcoing and Les Rues Vertes, the southern suburb of Masnières. In the area of Nine Wood, however, the 86th Brigade were involved in some heavy fighting before being able to move on. In this action the Royal Guernsey Light Infantry were in action for the first time as part of that Brigade and acquitted themselves very well indeed. The capture of the canal and its bridges was of next importance. Some of the bridges had already been destroyed when the division reached the canal banks. The bridge on the main Masnières-Cambrai road was still intact but when a tank of F Battalion, Flying Fox, commanded by Lieut. E. Edmundson, attempted to cross it collapsed taking the tank with it into the canal. Quick thinking by the men of the 2nd South Wales Borderers of the 87th Brigade, commanded by Lt. Col. G.T. Raikes, allowed a passage to the east of the canal to be gained by the lock halfway between Marcoing and Masnières. This allowed the Royal Inniskilling Fusiliers to follow and the bridgehead was established. Later this makeshift bridge was used by the Newfoundland Regiment of the adjacent Brigade as they threw their weight behind the attack. The 4th Worcesters (88th Brigade) on the south east side of Masnières crossed the canal by yet another lock and they too were able to establish a bridgehead as did the 2nd Hampshires still further to the east. Once parts of the Division were across the canal it became a race for the Masnières-Beaurevoir Line - the Germans' last defensive line of the system in front of Cambrai. The Germans were bringing up support as rapidly as possible and in the event their relatively fresh 107th Division was able to save the line and beat off the assault of the British forces. It had been a successful day for the British troops, they had achieved almost as much as had

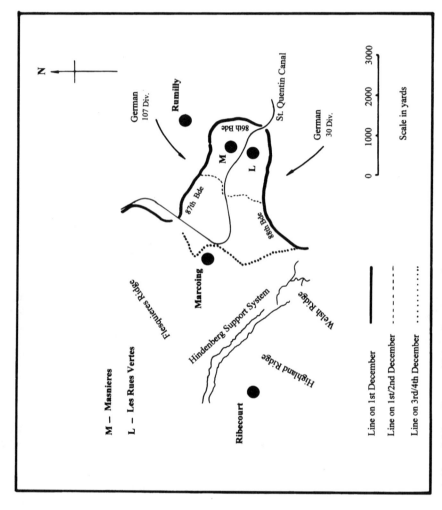

Action at Masnières and Marcoing 1st - 4th December, 1917.

been hoped for and, perhaps, more than had been truly expected. But for the tired men on that cold and wet winter's night the day was not quite over as the assaulting troops dug themselves in so as to be better prepared for any German counter attack. In the coming days the news of the effects of this attack on the people at home reached the men at the front:

> *One of the fellows just back off leave says 'The bells are ringing in England and the people are saying 'The Byng Boys are at 'em''*

No doubt the success must have done much to lift the morale of the men at the front and of those at home but although losses had been relatively light more men would be wanted to fill the once more depleted ranks of the successful divisions.

Fighting continued on the following day and an attempt was made to gain the Masnières-Beaurevoir Line by the 87th Brigade of the Division. It was not a success and resulted in significant casualties. Elsewhere counter attacks were beaten off and mopping up operations were carried out. By the end of the day the first phase of the Battle of Cambrai, marked by the successful assaults, was over. The 29th Division historian sums up the situation at the end of that day:

> *So ended this well-thought-out offensive, which resulted in a signal defeat for the Germans, but failed to achieve the very important result hoped for. How nearly it succeeded we now know. It is easy to criticize after the event, but there is little doubt that historians of the future will attribute failure to gain full advantage of the victory at Cambrai in 1917 to the want of 'weight behind the spear'.*

For those men who had taken part it was clear that there should have been a greater effort made at Cambrai and that more resources should have been used. However, the British army had been fighting hard all year and was showing the signs, particularly after the arduous Passchendaele campaign and, mindful of this the command was not prepared to take the necessary risks at that time.

For the next week there was a period of relative calm in this section of the front. The 2nd Mons continued their work, particularly on the construction of the light railway. One officer of the battalion was to remark upon the effect of the tank on the German infantry as he followed the tracks of one of these metal monsters into a small ravine which was littered with the bodies of the better part of a company who had defended to the last. The battalion were working long hours in an effort to get the railway into a state of readiness. Such was the urgency attached to this task that the divisional commanders insisted that the battalion was not to carry rifles or equipment other than gas helmets. The men were not entirely happy with this arrangement but since it did allow for them to carry heavier loads of materials and tended to speed up the track laying they had to put up with the decision. There was some logic in the thinking of the divisional officers, after all it was very likely that in the event of an attack the pioneers would receive at least some warning and hence some time in which to re-arm themselves. It was, however, a mistaken belief which came very close to costing the battalion dearly.

On the 30th November the Germans launched a huge counter attack and although it cannot have been totally unexpected it did come as a full scale surprise to the defenders. In no time at all there was confusion as the blow struck at the salient formed in the line by the British advance. In the south eastern part of the salient the Germans made rapid progress and pushed deeply back into the area they had given up a week earlier. To the right of the 29th Division the 20th Division came under intense pressure and were forced to give ground. Dick Williams, a gunner with the 20th Division was to comment:

> *Everything went well until the 30th, then Bang! Jerry made a counter attack and took back most of what he had lost. We were lucky to get our guns out, the 92nd Brigade lost theirs.*

For Pte. Heare and his comrades the shock of the German attack was almost too much to believe:

> *Black and I meet up at 86th Brigade HQ one morning about seven....'Let's scrounge a bit of breakfast before we go back', says Black, so we stay in a dugout with the signallers until breakfast is ready. Looking out of the dugout I see Germans passing by, I cannot believe my eyes....I say to one of the signallers, 'There are Germans out there'.*
> *'Go away Taffy', he says, 'We don't have a match with them today'.*
> *Then more Germans go by and their artillery starts and German aeroplanes flying low. The Germans had made a surprise attack. Capt. Gee, the staff captain, rushes out (and) he shouts 'The Germans are through'.*

It was a fact, they were through in places all along the southern flank of the salient and Capt. Robert Gee was to play an important part in holding them up. Capt. Gee had risen through the ranks of the Royal Fusiliers and had 22 years of pre-war experience to call upon. He had been wounded at Gallipoli and by 1917 he needed a stout metal pointed stick to help him get around. This did not hamper him in any way for he was a resourceful and courageous officer and during the next hours he arranged barricades and cleared the Germans out of Masnières with the help of an assortment of all the men he could gather together. His action was to save the 86th Brigade and win him the Victoria Cross. Pte. Heare, admitting to having the 'wind up' gives the following account of his part in the action:

> *Capt. Gee gets out into a trench with a machine gun. 'Shoot anyone in front'.*
> *It is a mix up here. I hear our RSM, George Yearsley, in front. Capt. Gee had said shoot all in front! I say to Capt. Gee, 'The RSM of the 2nd Mons is in front, Sir', then I hear Col. Evans' voice, 'and our Colonel, Sir.'*
> *'Are you sure.'*
> *'Yes Sir'.*
> *'Shout to them then', says Capt. Gee.*
> *So forgetting I call, 'Hi George, is that the Mons.'*
> *'Allo', says his voice, 'got any rations?'*
> *'Who's George?' says Capt. Gee.*
> *'Our RSM, Sir.'*
> *Didn't he tell me a tale of discipline, he's a ranker, so Black shouts, 'Are the 2nd Mons there, Sgt. Major?'*
> *'Yes', comes the RSM's voice, 'wanting some rum, have you got any?'*
> *Black looks at me expecting it off Capt. Gee. We join them. It appears our*

Battalion HQ have been rushed up. No one is sure where to find the Germans. Col. Evans says, 'Heare, you and Black go back to Division HQ, take this report'. So we go back, just as we are leaving our RSM says he can see someone moving in a bush. He crawls out and throws a couple of bombs and catches a German machine gun and crew.

Things were not much better at Division HQ at Gouzeaucourt. The German breakthrough had swept through the right flank and in short order was threatening Gouzeaucourt to such an extent that Major General de Lisle and his staff were forced to make a hasty withdrawal. Black and Heare witnessed this and, having just come from the sharp end of the fighting, were not impressed by the actions of some of the senior officers.

The battalion, less A company, had set off early for its tasks leaving only a handful of men at their billets in Gouzeaucourt. This small group was totally surprised by the 'grey-clad hoard of men sweeping over the hill'. Lieut. L.B. Rosenbaum gathered as many of the men together as he could and directed them toward Fins, to Battalion HQ, where he hoped they could be put to good use. As the town was overrun the men of the battalion became involved in the desperate fighting and a number were made prisoners - the first prisoners that the battalion had lost during the war to that date. Also Capt. Christopher Comely and Capt. Henry North were wounded and captured. The men of B Company were deep in the Cambrai salient, unarmed as ordered, working as usual. When the news was received that Gouzeaucourt had fallen they continued towards their tasks under the cover of thick fog. They hoped to be of use in any defence that may be required and so began to look for weapons amongst the dead that were already on the battlefield. As the fog lifted it became clear that the Germans were closer than anyone had thought - no more than 400 yards (365m) to be precise. The company dumped their tools and material and since they had very little to fight with they had no choice other than to withdraw in extended order maintaining 400 yards between themselves and the Germans. As they withdrew towards Gouzeaucourt they were pleased to see the 1st Battalion the Irish Guards coming towards them advancing 'on the enemy as if at Chelsea Barracks'. The Guards had been called up to assist in the defence of the area when it was realized that the flank was in peril. Brig. Gen. C.R. Champion de Crespigny, commanding the 1st Guards Brigade, had ridden to within sight Gouzeaucourt and had rapidly assessed the situation in the area. He decided that he should commit his men to the attack of Gouzeaucourt, which was by that time overrun, even though he did not have any artillery support. He ordered the Brigade to advance in extended order with the 2nd and 3rd Battalion the Coldstream Guards to the south of the Metz - Gouzeaucourt road and the Irish Guards to the north. The Guards fixed bayonets and walked determinedly towards the enemy. One of the Irish Guards was to be reported in Rudyard Kipling's history of that battalion as saying:

There was men with blankets round 'em an' men with loose puttees wavin' in the wind, and they told us 'twas a general retirement. We could see that. We wanted to know for why they were returnin'. We went through 'em, fairly breastin' our way and - we found Jerry on the next slope makin' prisoners of the Labour Corps with picks and shovels. But some of that same Labour Corps took their picks an' shovels and came on with us.

Was this Guard mistaken into thinking that the unarmed 2nd Mons was the Labour Corps? After all they had no equipment for fighting whatsoever, as they had been ordered, and they did lose a number of prisoners at that time. When B Company saw the Guards they offered their services but this was declined. For all that, throughout the next hour a number of men of B, C and D companies are known to have found rifles and gone along with the Irish Guards. In little more than an hour the Irish Guards had retaken Gouzeaucourt and had moved beyond the town. Both Capt. Comely and Capt. North, who had been taken by the Germans were rescued for since they were both wounded the Germans had seen fit to leave them behind. Both officers were shown suitable consideration and their wounds had been dressed by their captors.

Meanwhile, back at the 29th Division front things were becoming perilous as their flanks around Marcoing and Les Rues Vertes were coming under pressure. The 1st King's Own Scottish Borderers were sent from the 87th Brigade reserve to plug the gap between Welsh Ridge and Les Rues Vertes and succeeded in pushing back the Germans as units of the 88th Brigade arrived to lend weight to the defence. Eventually the 29th Division established a flank facing roughly south east between the canal near Les Rue Vertes and the Hindenburg Support Line. At about 5 pm the Germans made their final attack for the day and this was beaten back. It was, by this time, a dark winter's evening and it is probable that the Germans thought better of attacking over unprepared ground at night. However, they had dealt a severe blow to the British in the Cambrai salient and although they had not wiped it out completely the Germans could feel satisfied with their day's work. For their part the 29th Division could also be satisfied for in due course, when the official despatches were released their part in the defence was commented on thus:

> On the Masnières front the 29th Division, composed of English, Scottish, Welsh, Irish, Guernsey and Newfoundland battalions, although seriously threatened as the day wore on, by the progress made by the enemy farther south, where their battery positions had been taken in reverse, most gallantly beat off a succession of powerful assaults and maintained their line intact.

The following day, the 1st December, the position of the 29th Division became even more dangerous as the 86th Brigade took most of the onslaught. At 7.15 am the enemy opened up a severe bombardment of the Brigade and an hour later followed up with waves of infantry. By 9.50 am it was clear to Brig. Gen. Lucas that without support the position could not be held. He sent a message informing the division of this but unknown to him the Division HQ was also under fire and had been forced to move from Villers Plouich to Trescault which further lengthened lines of communication. This message, and subsequent ones from Lucas, were severely delayed by the conditions of the battlefield. Even if they had reached their destination immediately Maj. Gen. de Lisle had almost no reserves at hand with which to help the beleaguered division except for the 2nd Mons and some of the RE field company which had not been committed to the fight. Before too long these units were also sent into the battle. In this fighting the 2nd Mons were used as infantry though only in a piecemeal fashion. A Company were sent to support the 1st KOSB of the 87th Brigade whilst B and C Companies supported the 1st Royal Inniskilling Fusiliers and the 2nd South Wales Borderers respectively of the same brigade. It was a time of great strain for everyone as the division fought to hold every inch of ground it had won ten days earlier. For Col. Evans there was little hope of keeping a clear picture of where and what his men were doing at any particular time as they came under the orders of the battalions to which they were attached. Pte. Heare, still acting as a battalion messenger, was to write of the events as follows:

> *Up goes our battalion again, not as pioneers, but to take the line. All the boys are played out. Black and I are kept busy, orderlies and motorcyclists are short, day and night going, the motorcycle seems to be moving on its own. Everyone is dead beat, there are a lot of dead about, of all divisions, killed on the road. The German artillery got the road to an inch. The Germans have almost all their ground back. It appears they came over on our left and caught the reserves first and are in the back of our front line.*

The situation was indeed much as Pte. Heare had gathered from his running about the battlefield delivering messages. During the 1st December, 1917, A Company were involved in some heavy fighting particularly the half company under Lieut. D.G. Cockrill as they defended part of the old German line. The German defensive system had been well supplied with barbed wire entanglements and the company was able to make good use of these in its defence of the line. Sgt. A.J. Cross, the battalion's best shot, was positioned opposite a break in the wire and as the Germans tried to trickle through the gap Sgt. Cross picked them off one by one and prevented any momentum being gained in their thrust towards the Monmouths position. Lieut. Cockrill was to comment on the events of the day:

> *We were attacked several times that first day and we repulsed each effort, I suppose - anyway the bursts seemed to more fade away than be repulsed. We had a strong position, and had a feeling of security after we got settled down.*

Even as darkness fell the Germans maintained their efforts to force the British back in this area continuing bombing attacks for some time. These were successfully beaten off. It had been a tense time for the company and over 24 hours without food or rest had taken a toll but at least they had completed all that had been expected of them before they rejoined their comrades for a short respite.

By the end of the day as the fighting all across the front subsided for the second time, the order was issued that the 86th Brigade would withdraw from its unsatisfactory position. To allow the brigade to go into reserve it was necessary for the line to be shortened by the 87th Brigade and the 88th Brigade turning their flanks to meet on the canal near the lock about 800 yards (730 m) to the west of Masnières. The biggest problem was to disengage the enemy without him becoming aware of the withdrawal. The first troops of the 86th Brigade left at 11pm on the 1st December and were followed by the rest throughout the night - the Germans were never aware of the manoeuvre. As the 87th Brigade turned its flank on the north of the canal two companies (B and C) of the 2nd Monmouths were ordered into the line on the extreme right of the brigade such that they were immediately against the canal. It should be noted at this point that during the first two days of the German counter stroke, the 29th Division had not given up any ground, in fact it had done much to stabilize the line when the situation had seemed hopeless. This has been put down to good leadership and thorough training such that all the men of the division knew how to behave almost instinctively. In this the 2nd Mons had played their part and during the coming days, as the Germans forced further withdrawals from in front of Cambrai the Mons behaved with great credit. By the end of the following day, the 2nd December, Field Marshal Haig had instructed Gen. Byng to 'select a good winter line'. It had been recognized that it would be wrong to hold or attempt to hold any positions of weakness and Haig believed that when the weather broke after the winter now upon them, the Germans would launch even stronger attacks. Haig further recognized that his army was tired after the large scale fighting of 1917 and this gave him limited scope to continue in front of Cambrai. Thus the withdrawal from the Cambrai salient was put into motion. On the 3rd December the order was issued that a general withdrawal would take place on the night of the 4th December. The line chosen as the 'winter line' for defence ran from Welsh Ridge in the south around Flesquières to the Bapaume-Cambrai road at Boursies and then to the line of the 20th November. Where possible every use was made of the Hindenburg Support System as the British settled down to a winter in defence. The 2nd Mons were withdrawn, along with the battalions they had supported, on the 4th December and, like the 29th Division, they had been in action every day of the battle and were now in need of a period of rest.

> Absolutely dead beat, all of us. We are off for a rest. Col. Evans and Adjutant Ibbs beg for a ride, for the boys. Everyone, officers and men, are played out. So at last after three years our battalion gets a ride, back in a bus instead of marching.

During the fighting for Cambrai the 2nd Monmouths had acted as pioneers and as infantrymen and had acquitted themselves well. During the period of the battle they had suffered one officer and 32 other ranks killed and a large number of wounded. Their service was recognized by the award of Military Medals to Sgt. A.J. Cross, Sgt. E. Wagstaff and Pte. I.J. Griffiths for their part in the action. It is interesting to note that Pte. I.J. Griffiths MM was one of those originally posted as missing since he had become detached from his company in the confusion of the battle. He had been ordered by a senior officer to man a machine gun and it was for this action that he was awarded the MM. He was to remain detached from the 2nd Mons for five days and during that time he continued fighting with the 16th Middlesex Regiment.

On balance the Battle of Cambrai cannot be said to have been a great success but it had demonstrated quite clearly the usefulness of tanks. However, the 2nd Mons, as part of the 29th Division, had been involved in some of the most gallant actions of the whole fighting and perhaps the following letter of thanks from Field Marshal Haig to the Division sums up the situation clearly:

> Please convey to General de Lisle and men of the 29th Division my warm congratulations on the splendid fight successfully maintained by them against repeated attacks by numerically superior forces. Their gallant defence of Masnières throughout almost two days of almost continuous fighting has had important results upon the course of the battle, and is worthy of the best traditions of the British Army.

Chapter Thirteen
'With Our Backs to the Wall'
(December 1917 to April 1918)

The 2nd Mons were marched away from the fighting of Cambrai to a well earned rest along with all the 29th Division. They were billeted in the villages around Doullens to the west of Arras immediately after the fighting and here they were to spend almost two weeks during which they were allowed to rest with little emphasis being placed upon training or parades. The value of the work done by all of the 29th Division during the Cambrai fighting was recognized and appreciated by the military commanders. The weather changed rapidly as December progressed and before they left the area on the 16th December, 1917, they all saw their first snows of winter when a storm blanketed the countryside in white - in places two feet of snow fell. This hindered movement between the companies and between brigade and division headquarters but since there was little pressure on the tired troops at this time it was much less of a problem than it would have been had they been still actively involved in some front line action. As usual the rest soon came to an end - too soon most soldiers would have said - and the battalion entrained on the 16th December and headed northwards to Wizerne. This village had been their first billet in 1914 and now, much as then, the battalion had been moved to begin training again so as to be ready for their recall to the line. They were also able to absorb drafts to fill the gaps left by the battle casualties of November and December. Christmas, the fourth that the battalion had spent overseas, was celebrated whilst out of the line and it left the usual 'heavy heads' the next day - the resting soldier did not miss a chance to grab what little pleasure he could as and when it was offered! The break from trench duty was short enough in any case and most knew what sort of dangers they would be facing again when they were returned to trench duty in the not too distant future.

135

On the 6th January, 1918, the battalion entrained for the familiar territory of the Ypres Salient and they found themselves at La Brique where some of the men had been with the battalion in 1915. The Ypres of 1918 was far worse than any of them would have imagined in 1915. Three years of war had reduced the town to little more than a pile of shattered rubble. The consequences of the fighting and untold numbers of corpses around the area had given the place a deathly air which was only worsened by the ever multiplying numbers of rats. There were rats everywhere and soldiers who knew Ypres at this time remark upon the quantities that added to the squalor of the conditions. Rats were killed in their hundreds but it did little to alleviate the conditions in which the troops were expected to live and fight. It was an unpleasant start to the year for the battalion but they were no strangers to Ypres or the awfulness that it could offer.

During this spell in Ypres the battalion historian remarks that the Salient was quiet. As far as there were no concerted efforts by either side to launch a large scale attack that would be a fair assessment of the situation. But the Salient was never 'quiet' and throughout the early part of 1918 the 29th Division, and hence the 2nd Mons, were involved in the existence that was holding the line in front of Ypres. The fighting of 1917 had left the battlefield in a state of almost complete chaos. There was debris of battle everywhere, often human, and there was little by way of a formal line since the heavy shelling had almost obliterated the landscape in the area of the Salient. To say that the conditions were terrible is probably an understatement and it is not unrealistic to say that the conditions cannot be truly imagined or believed by anyone who did not experience them. The battalion's work in these conditions was to put together some kind of defensive system in the area held by its division in the vicinity of Passchendaele. This included the construction of the Goudberg defences and the digging and draining of the Army Line of Defence at Weiltje. Throughout the divisional area they also constructed numerous duck board tracks in an effort to assist movement over the morass that was now the Ypres Salient. This work was further hampered by the fact that every few yards during the course of digging the defensive line a body, British or German, was found which had to be removed for burial. The grisly nature of the task can be better realized when it is remembered that a large portion of these bodies would have been lying out on the battlefield for a number of months. Ironically, part of the defensive line they completed at this time was to be known as the Belle Vue Line! This line was linked to the Gravenstafel road by a road which the battalion was also to be involved in constructing. The first step in the construction of the road required the construction of a drainage ditch to one side which was achieved by linking up shell holes many of which had first to be emptied of the debris of war. The next stage of the work required that the shell holes on the line of the road were drained into the ditch and then filled with any material that could be found:

> In one hole, full like the others of liquid mud, were found a dead horse and a field gun, which gives an impression of the size of the cavities and the immensity of the task. Objects such as these were removed and the holes filled with fascines and such road materials as were available.

Whilst this work continued the line was held in the most appalling conditions and there was, by now, the usual amount of sniping, shelling and raiding by both sides as each sought to assure the other that things were far from over. It was during one large scale German trench raid that the Royal Guernsey Light Infantry, of the same division, sustained over fifty casualties. This gives an indication of the fact that it was far from quiet in the Salient and, also, that it was not an easy time for anyone concerned. The 2nd Mons were fortunate in this respect in so far as the casualties from enemy action were relatively light throughout this stay at Ypres. Nonetheless they still lost Lieut. W.M. Sankey and five other ranks during their tour of duty. Although casualties were light the strain of working under these conditions was considerable. This was recognized by Lieut. Col. Evans who took all the opportunities he could to ensure that his men got some relaxation and organized sporting events whenever he could. This was especially successful during February since Pte. Sammy Thomas the battalion light heavyweight champion beat all challengers to win the 2nd Army title to add to his others. Opportunity was also taken to challenge other Welsh battalions in the area to a variety of sports and all of this was to help the general morale of the battalion through the early months of 1918. For many soldiers the small town of Poperinge offered a haven for, although it had been shelled from time to time, it was considered to be 'a good place for food' much as it is today. For some of the lucky ones of the battalion this period of relative 'quiet' was the opportunity to be granted leave. Unfortunately, some of the men returned from leave almost as unhappy as they had been before they went. Britain, home, was feeling the effects of the war and food shortages were a common feature remarked upon by returning soldiers. To many it would appear that the front line had become their home and at least there a resourceful soldier could always 'scrounge' a bit of food.

During February there was a reorganization of the British army, brought about, at least in part, by the manpower shortages arising from the repeated offensives of 1917. One of the effects of this reorganization was to reduce infantry brigades from four to three battalions. A direct result of this was for the 2nd Mons to reduce its establishment to three companies with D Company disappearing. This was also the result of the lack of replacements to the pioneers and there was no problem for the personnel of D Company to be absorbed into the depleted ranks of the other three companies. This internal reorganization was completed on the 28th February, 1918.

The winter passed slowly into spring and the battalion continued with its duty in the Salient. On the 21st March, 1918 the Germans launched what they called the 'Kaiserschlacht' and which became known to the allies as the Spring Offensive. The Spring Offensive is generally seen as the Germans final effort to win the war as the result of troops being released from their Eastern Front as the Russian war effort collapsed into revolution and civil war. Whilst there is some truth in this, it should be realized that much of the liberated manpower did not have an effect on the Western Front until well after the Offensive had commenced. Nonetheless the Germans were aware that many more divisions would become available to them on the Western Front as the Offensive developed. The initial moves on the opening of the Offensive were in the Somme region and in a matter of days they had recaptured all the ground they had lost to the British in 1916 and were able to make significant advances. There can be no doubt that within a short time of the Offensive being launched things were looking black for the allied cause in France. To the Monmouths billeted in Ypres this all seemed far away but they were aware that the Germans were making progress on the Somme front and there were those amongst them who recognized that it would not be long before they would be back in the thick of the action. This point was confirmed when, in early April, the 29th Division was told to stand ready to go back to the Somme to be added to the defence of the area against the continued German offensive.

This state of readiness lasted for some days and then the battalion's stay in the Ypres sector was brought to an abrupt end. It had been hoped, by all concerned, that the relief from the trenches to School Camp, near Poperinge, would bring about a period of rest and re-equipping of the battalion. That belief lasted no more than forty-eight hours when on the 10th of April the battalion was ordered to travel to La Crèche some miles from Bailleul where for a number of days the 34th Division and adjoining units had been under pressure from the expansion of the German offensive. As part of the wider objectives of the German High Command it was considered essential for further attacks to be made in the area of the Franco-Belgian border and an offensive, code named Georgette by the Germans, was launched on the 9th April commencing with the Battle of Estaires. In this fighting the British Divisions, tired from the fighting of the Somme, came under increasing pressure and at the junction of the British and Portuguese troops there was a breakthrough which worsened the situation immediately. The largely untried Portuguese troops were hammered by a superior German force and collapsed and the British divisions were compelled to withdraw and form defensive flanks as best they could. One of these divisions, the 34th, had suffered heavily in the fighting on the Somme in March and had, effectively, been withdrawn from that theatre of operations to allow it to recover. For it to be involved in another major attack was bordering on the disastrous and it was for this reason that the 29th Division, and hence the 2nd Monmouths became involved in the fighting around Bailleul in the second week of April, 1918.

There is always a fear among commanders that his force of trained men will be broken up or used piecemeal in action so that they no longer fall directly within the control of those who have been responsible for the training and organization. This fate befell the 29th Division now. As soon as the situation on the 9th of April was understood the 87th Brigade was ordered south and left the Ypres Salient and was followed early on the morning of the 10th April by the 86th Brigade whilst the 88th Brigade were still holding a sector of the Ypres Salient until well into the afternoon of the 10th. However, its release from this duty signalled a rapid move south. It was part of this general move to meet the enemy in a different area that brought about the end of the short rest for the Monmouths and their attachment to the 88th Brigade. The 29th Division was reformed in the crisis area on the 10th April with the two Brigades that had been withdrawn early from the Ypres area and it was some time before the 88th Brigade would rejoin its comrades. The 88th Brigade were briefly attached to the 25th Division but the same day came under the control of the 34th Division together with two other Brigades. Thus it was that the Monmouths were, for a period, involved with the heavy fighting experienced by that division.

The battalion were moved from their camp by lorries and buses and in no time at all they were heading south towards Armentieres. Pte. Heare was to comment as follows:

> *Refugees are coming down the road. The Germans have broken through the Portuguese on the Armentieres front. The lorries start to turn around before we can get out. The lorry drivers start to yell 'Get out quick'. They are in a panic. Col. Evans came to them and stopped their nonsense. 'Stop here', says*

our Col to the Lieut. in charge, 'until I tell you to go'. They are almost in tears. Our fellows keep asking them if they want some paper. At last we all get out and Col. Evans tells all the wounded and refugees to get in the lorries, then he tells them to go - they fly!

As a result of their rapid move the 2nd Monmouths arrived in the area in advance of the Brigade to which it was eventually to be attached. On the night of the 10/11th April the Battalion was ordered to dig a defensive line along the side of a railway line south of Rabot facing Le Veau. Here the countryside is flat much like the rest of the Flandrian plain as it extends northwards to Belgium. The vistas are wide and the country is broken up by steep sided drainage ditches and, in general, poor quality roads and tracks. Today the railway runs, as then, on an embankment standing about two metres above the surrounding area and as such it forms a marked feature running across the landscape. The defensive line that the Monmouths dug that day was effectively on the reverse side of a low ridge and would give them such advantage as was available to an out-manned force under threat of imminent attack. It should be noted that this line was facing south - such were the conditions during the day that attack was expected from this direction.

This line was no more than a temporary defensive line and at midday on the 11th April, by which time they had been joined by the rest of the 88th Brigade, the battalion was ordered to establish a line between Papot and Rue du Sac. As the men withdrew across the open fields there was the imminent fear of the arrival of the Germans into the area before the new line - now facing more or less east - could be constructed. There would be little in the way of cover since the country is open and whilst it gave a good field of fire for a defending force, one caught in the open would be more or less at mercy of the artillery and machine guns. This line was to be established at all costs, that is, the Monmouths were expected to launch an attack if it was necessary to gain the line ordered. This line was effectively a support line for the 34th Division who were holding the area immediately to the south east in front of Pont d'Achelles. An indication of the uncertain nature of the line at this time can be gained from the order that the Monmouths received in that they were told to attack the enemy if necessary in an area that was still some distance behind the main defending force of the 34th Division. However, the area appears to have been free of enemy, for the Monmouths had established the line by 3.30 p.m. and had begun to dig in. A Company was on the right nearest Papot while B Company held the left with C Company in the centre. As the fighting continued C Company was to be withdrawn from the centre and was to form the only support that the battalion could expect. It was not long before they came under harassing fire as they scratched some hasty defensive positions. The level of ground water in the area probably hindered the establishment of the line and bearing in mind the limited time available to the men it is very likely that the trenches were shallow and muddy affairs.

Within a matter of hours the troops in front of the battalion began to withdraw and rumours were heard that a general withdrawal had been ordered and A Company, not unnaturally, proceeded with an orderly withdrawal. The withdrawal had not been ordered, however, and Battalion Headquarters soon put A Company straight and they went back into their position on the right and stuck to their task. A Company were not alone in believing the order had been issued. Pte. Heare, now at Brigade Headquarters in his usual work of orderly was to comment:

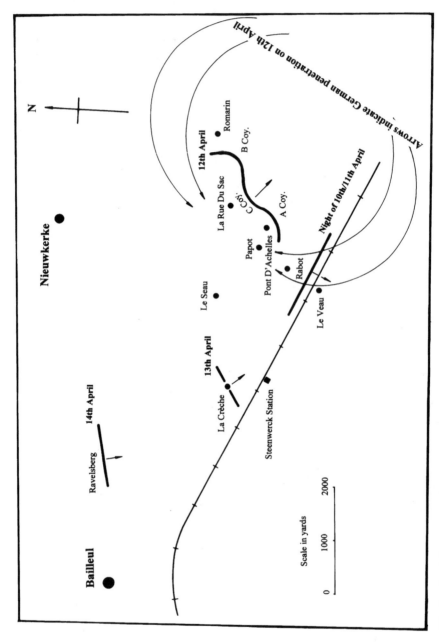

The Battle of the Lys, April 1918. Movements of the 2nd Monmouths.

No Man's Land of Christmas, 1914. This photograph is taken looking towards the lines held by the 2nd Monmouths over the period of the Christmas Truce. The cottages mark the approximate position of the line and the foreground was the area where the men gathered to 'fraternize' with the enemy.

Mouse Trap Farm as it is today. This area was defended by the Battalion during the 2nd Battle of Ypres and the German attack came at them from beyond the present farm buildings. A drainage ditch in front of the building may be all that remains of the 'moat' that Dmr. White swam to seek assistance and in so doing earned himself the DCM.

Trenches at Newfoundland Park. This trench may be remains of one of those constructed by the Monmouths in the days following the initial attack on Beaumont Hamel and Y-Ravine

The junction of 88 Trench and 2nd Avenue on the outskirts of Auchonvillers. The German lines would have been on the horizon. 'A' Company assembled in this area on 30th June, 1916.

The St. Quentin Canal near Marcoing, looking approximately north in the area defended by the Monmouths during the German counter attack of early December, 1917.

Four unidentified casualties of the Monmouthshire Regiment at Gouzeaucourt New British Cemetery - casualties of the Cambrai offensive.

The area defended by the Battalion on 12th April, 1918. Pont D'Achelles is on the left, the line ran towards La Rue Du Sac in the distance, B Company would have defended this area and the Germans attacked from the right.

The view the battalion had of the battlefield from La Crèche on 13th April, 1918.

Outtersteene Ridge, the scene of the attack on 18th August, 1918. The Meteren Becque lies in the tree lined depression at the foot of the ridge which was captured on that date.

A general comes to Brigade Headquarters, hears that they are all retiring,
takes me with him and rushes across fields to stop the tide. I think he must
be mad. He collects all troops together then advances to (the) Newfoundland
trench - to hold out at any cost.

It is believed that this General was Brigadier General Freyberg VC commanding officer of the 88th Brigade and more shall be heard of him later since Pte. Heare was to come across him again before the battle was over.

The Germans were close on the heels of the retreating men but came under rapid rifle fire from the line held by the Monmouths and decided not to press the attack resorting to shelling the line instead. The trenches were completed rapidly to provide at least some cover from the shelling but nonetheless casualties occurred with one shell killing one man and wounding fifteen in B Company. At Brigade Headquarters the casualties were also mounting as, one after another, orderlies fell as they attempted to deliver their messages to groups of troops that were continually changing position.

One Newfoundland orderly named Tizzard says 'Taffy, watch those trees by
the cross-roads. They are under fire.' Poor old Tizzard was shot there the
next time he went down.

Pte. G. Tizzard's body was never recovered and he is named on the Beaumont Hamel Memorial along with so many of his countrymen.

The situation was further complicated by the fact that contact with flanking troops had not been established. To the left the 25th Division could not be induced to extend their line towards the Monmouths and Lieut. Col. Evans attempted to solve the problem by sending two platoons from his support, C Company, to the left to provide at least some flank. This was further improved by B Company falling back at an angle on the left along the road in front of Rue du Sac though B Company were in no shape to dig yet more trenches in such a short space of time and satisfied themselves with improving the ditch along the roadside and since these ditches are fairly deep they probably served well as temporary trenches. In this manner the gap on the left was shortened somewhat.

Nonetheless the left flank was weak. To the right the situation was worse. Lieut. Col. Evans received orders from Brigade that he should extend his right so as to make contact with the Hampshires who were known to be there. However, they were much further back than anticipated and, with the resources at his disposal it was impossible for Evans to make contact. He did, however, do all that he could by sending a further platoon of C Company to the right to hold as much of the line as they could. Lieut. Col. Evans realized that this was not good enough and that there was a gap on his right flank - but there was nothing else he could do. The battalion frontage at this time was over 1,000 yards, held with only three companies, and it formed a shallow salient. In this position with one weak and one non-existent flank and with only one platoon in reserve the 2nd Monmouths faced the dawn of the 12th April, 1918. It is interesting to note that it was on the 11th April that Field Marshal Haig had issued a Special Order Of The Day in which he wrote:

There is no other course open to us but to fight it out. Every position must
be held to the last man: there must be no retirement. With our backs to the

wall and believeing in the justice of our cause each one of us must fight on to the end. The safety of our homes and the Freedom of mankind alike depend upon the conduct of each one of us at this critical moment.

It is unlikely that the men of the Monmouthshire Regiment were aware of this Order and it is unlikely that it would have made any difference if they had. For all the skill of the Order the men in the line could only do their duty and there can be little doubt that the men of the Monmouths and the 88th Brigade as a whole, had no intention of doing otherwise.

Dawn broke on the 12th April and was followed by a concerted German attack all along the front of the 88th Brigade from Steenwerck Station to Rue du Sac. The Monmouths, in their exposed position held on well but suffered heavily. Trench mortar and machine-gun fire was causing havoc in the Monmouths positions and in no time at all their casualties amounted to four officers and seventy-five other ranks killed and wounded. To begin with the battalion's stretcher-bearers did magnificent work and were able to get most of the wounded away. As time passed the battlefield became more and more heavily swept by fire until it was impossible for anyone to move and the wounded were treated as best as the conditions would allow. The Germans eventually attacked the positions, presumably believing the positions to have been sufficiently prepared, and received a shock as the Monmouths and the neighbouring units met the advance with Lewis-gun and rifle fire. The Germans were kept at bay for a time but not for long as they adopted an alternative method of attack with small groups of men infiltrating the lines especially around the weakened flanks of the Monmouthshires. It was a cautious but persistent approach and the fighting continued all morning in the effort to prevent the Germans gaining any ground. At about midday Lieut. Col. Evans was told that he was expected to hold the line for another twenty-four hours and that he would receive a company of the Royal Newfoundland Regiment to lend support. Further, the remainder of the latter regiment would move up to his aid later in the afternoon from positions in the region of Steenwerck Station. With the latter plan in mind it was agreed that the two commanding officers, Lieut. Col. Evans and Lieut. Col. Woodruffe of the Newfoundlanders, would meet at about 4 o'clock that afternoon to arrange the defences in detail. The meeting was to take place in a dugout in the embankment of a light railway approximately half a mile behind the front line. This was to prove to be a fortuitous arrangement as later events were to show.

As the afternoon wore on the fighting continued unabated and although the battalion was losing men it was still causing the Germans some problems. The weakness of the flanks was a continuing problem and was, ultimately, the downfall of the defence of the area. The commanders held their meeting, which lasted no more than a quarter of an hour, and as they emerged from the dugout they saw a mixed band of Newfoundlanders and Monmouths withdrawing with the Germans hot on their heels. Enemy infiltration had not been stemmed on the right and gradually the enemy had been able to work around in a pincer-like movement. As they closed the pincers they pressed home a strong attack in the area of Pont d'Achelles - Lampernisse. Some of the defenders recognized the situation and were able to withdraw but a mixed group of men, largely from B Company the Monmouthshire Regiment, did not give ground and chose to fight until they were totally surrounded and their ammunition had all but failed.

142

Once they were cut off there could be no hope for them as the Germans followed up on their attack and as a consequence the battalion was to lose eight officers and over four hundred men, many of whom became prisoners, before the day was out. Captain G.E. Foster, C.O. of B Company, wrote to Lieut. Col. Evans shortly after his capture and was to say:

> I tried or rather wanted to reinforce the people on my right, but before I could do so I saw the troops on my left retiring. Our front we had kept clear, but our lines were enfiladed from both flanks, and we, being almost sideways to the main attack, could not bring sufficient fire to bear. Enemy machine guns were already in the road behind us. However, I am quite satisfied with the damage we did - the men proved themselves splendid and disciplined soldiers.

At about this stage of the attack it was becoming clear to all concerned that the battle was not going well. At Brigade Headquarters General Freyberg attempted to notify his commanding officer of the situation at which point he uses Pte. Heare as a go between:

> General Freyberg VC loses his voice. At Brigade HQ only the Division wire is in use all other work done by the orderlies. General Freyberg says, 'Quick, take the phone and repeat what I say - 34th Division, all our men played out, ask for the general.' A voice answers, 'Your message is delivered, the general is having dinner'. I am hoping his dinner will choke the swine, hang on at all costs comes back the order. But General Freyberg says 'The men are all done in they will only be taken prisoners'

But, although prisoners were lost and the British troops were forced to retire, parties of men continued to fight even as they withdrew.

For those of the 88th Brigade who got away from the line the fight was not over because Lieut. Col.'s Evans and Woodruffe rallied the men they saw retiring and made a stand along the line of the railway embankment where they had held their meeting. This was the line they were to hold for the rest of the day. It was during this episode that Lieut. Col. Evans witnessed what he considered in later years to be the most gallant behaviour he was to see during the war. Whilst the battalion, together with the Newfoundlanders, were forming the line there were a number of casualties. Evans saw one of his officers fall, wounded in the head and unable to move but clearly still alive. The chances of rescuing the officer, believed to have been Lieut. Rosenbaum, was slim since the German fire was considerable. However, the officer's plight was witnessed by a Newfoundland sergeant who was standing close by Evans. Eventually the officer's spasmodic movements got to the sergeant and he said to Lieut. Col Evans 'I can't stick it any more, sir; I'm going'; and in spite of the heavy fire he launched himself out of the cover and went towards the officer by crawling from one shell hole to the next until he was with the officer. In a similar manner he was able to bring the wounded man back in behind the line. The sergeant, who remained nameless, must have realized that the officer's wounds were fatal but had not given a thought to his own safety in getting the wounded officer back. Lieut. Rosenbaum died of his wounds several days later. At midnight the battalion was ordered to dig-in at La Crèche by which time the battalion's bayonet strength was one hundred and fifty with four officers. Another officer who fell on that day was the battalion Lewis-gun Officer, Lieut. Ifor Evan Owen. 'Dicky' as he was known to his fellow officers, was an experienced soldier and had been with the battalion for some time in France. He was an officer who was popular with all ranks and never tired in his duty and even when out of the line did all he could to provide entertainment for the men by way of organizing such things as boxing matches. He was mortally wounded during the breakthrough in the Monmouths positions while he was rallying his men.

The stay at La Crèche was short with the position being held until the evening of the 13th April when the battalion was ordered to move forward to cover the withdrawal of the Brigade. The depleted battalion was on the move again by 2 a.m. of the 14th and marched to a position on the Ravelsberg Ridge, to the east of Bailleul, where it arrived at about four in the morning. The fighting in this area did not really abate on the 14th but the 88th Brigade was not heavily involved in it as the artilleries of both sides blasted away at each other for all they were worth. Late in the day the 88th Brigade was relieved, such had been the casualties of the Brigade that it was replaced with one battalion of the Lincolns from the 59th Division. The battalion marched back to Croix de Poperinge where they awaited orders. Later in the day news was received that the Germans had made a break-through along the line of the Lincolns that had replaced the 88th Brigade and had almost wiped out that battalion. Consequently the 88th Brigade, together with the Monmouths were rushed back into the fighting. The entire Brigade was employed in digging a defensive line, this time Bailleul was in front of them and not behind them. The following day the German attack was held and the Monmouths, in support of the 4th Worcesters saw little in the way of shelling and did not take any more casualties. Over the next few days the fighting continued and there was little chance of relief since the British army had very little by way of reserves at this stage. However, the Germans were held, probably because the incessant attacking over the period of weeks had exhausted them as much as it had drained the allied forces. On the 20th April the situation was such that it was possible for a portion of the area to be taken over by the French and the 29th Division was one of those relieved. The Monmouthshires were marched through Abeele and to a camp at Staple where they were able to rest and re-equip for ten days. The fighting of the Battle of Lys had been hard on the troops. The 2nd Battalion the Monmouthshire Regiment had marched into the battle area on the 9th April twenty-four officers and eight hundred and ninety-three men. By the 20th April their numbers had been reduced to ten officers and about three hundred and eighty other ranks. For a pioneer battalion they had been in the thick of things and for them it had been the worst fighting of the war. All along the British line the story was similar and in many divisions battalion strengths were about half of the normal establishment. The fighting had been heavy but the German advance had been stemmed and the Monmouths had played a full and active part in the defence of the line.

Chapter Fourteen

'Well Done Mons'
(May 1918 to November 1918)

The Battalion rejoined the 29th Division at Hondeghem on the 21st April, 1918. Now that the Germans had exhausted themselves in a month of spectacular advances there was a little time for the tired units of the British army to rest and get themselves back to something like fighting strength. For four days the battalion cleaned itself up and then, suitably rested, went back to the front line to start working on a defensive system in the area west of Bailleul that was known as the 2nd Zone of Defence. Now Bailleul was in front of them as their division took the line covering the area from the Nieppe Forest to the Hazebrouck-Bailleul railway line. The battalion remained in the area, billeted in L'Hoffand, for almost two months. During that time they were constantly working on the defences to ensure that the near disasters of March and April would not happen again. They were constantly harassed in their work by gas shell bombardment which brought an inevitable number of casualties. One such incident occurred on the 3rd May when A Company were working on the defences around Petite Sec Bois to the east of Hazebrouck and came under fire and lost six men killed. The deaths of these men serve to demonstrate how intermingled the battalions of the regiment had become. It is recorded that three of these men had served in only the 2nd Battalion while one had served in the 1st Battalion and one in the disbanded 3rd Battalion. One, Pte. J. Clancy a veteran of the South African war, is recorded as having served in the 4th Battalion which was essentially a home service battalion. These six men are buried in Cinq Rues Military Cemetery a little to the west of Hazebrouck.

It may not have been the same level of fighting as earlier in the year but working in the forward zone was always dangerous even when there was not a major attack to contend with. After two years of pioneer work the battalion was well aware of the dangers and their experience as front line soldiers probably helped to keep the casualties to a minimum. There was one advantage of working in this area; since the Germans had succeeded in pushing the British line so far to the west the battalion was working in an area that had not suffered greatly from the ravages of the mechanised warfare of the Western Front. This meant that the billets were much better than the battalion had become accustomed to and, generally, that helped to keep the morale good amongst the men.

Although, by comparison to early April, conditions were much better for the battalion it was not without incident. On the 4th June, 1918, C Company of the battalion was employed in consolidation work in an area that had been captured by the Royal Fusiliers and the Royal Dublin Fusiliers of the 86th Brigade when they attacked both Lug and Ankle (also known as Anchor) Farms. The Germans opened up a heavy shell fire as the work progressed which both interrupted the work and hampered the few infantry carrying parties that were available. Nonetheless the Monmouths carried on their work throughout the night and suffered a number of casualties including Major A.H. Edwards who was severely wounded during the work. The loss of the second-in-command meant that the Adjutant, Captain T.L. Ibbs was promoted to major and Captain R.T. Saunders took over the duties of the Adjutant.

The battalion was relieved on the 20th June, along with the division, and moved back to Staple, some 7 km (5 miles) west of Hazebrouck. This was meant to be a period of rest and training but, as usual, the manual labour of the war demanded that one company at a time of the battalion was kept in the forward areas working on the Hazebrouck defences. It was, for all that, a welcome relief and for a month the battalion was given a better time than normal when they were entertained by a Divisional Horse Show on the 9th July and a Divisional Boxing Competition later in the same month. In both events the Monmouths gained prizes including a first prize to Sgt. J. Roberts DCM for the best turned out mounted NCO at the horse show and the light weight title in the boxing competition. On the 11th July the battalion were entertained by the Divisional Concert Party, the Diamond Troupe, who had gained sufficient fame to have had a short run on the London stage at the Royal Court Theatre in January of 1918. All in all the period out of the line did much for the morale of the division.

On the 22nd July, 1918, the battalion was moved further west to Noordpeene, to the west of Cassel where they spent a further three days training, billeted in rather overcrowded conditions amongst local farms, before they moved back towards the front line to Eecke. Here they were once again within artillery range and the Battalion Headquarters and each company was billeted, under canvas, in separate fields to minimise the effects of enemy shelling. Here, for the remaining days of July the battalion came under the command of the X Corps Signals and were employed in digging cable trenches forward from Mont des Cats to artillery headquarters. Subsequently, when the division took over the Merris sector of the line on the 2nd August the battalion rejoined the division with Battalion Headquarters and C Company being established at Le Pueplier, whilst A Company was stationed at Courte Croix and B Company at Pradelles in the area to the north of the Bailleul - Hazebrouck road. Here the battalion resumed divisional responsibilities as pioneers until they were moved back to L'Hoffand on the 10th August, 1918.

By this stage of the war the fortunes of the belligerents were changing. On the 8th August the Allies launched a major attack, far to the south of the Monmouths work area, that was to become known as the Battle of Amiens. To the Germans the

8th August, 1918, became known as the 'black day for the German Army'. This was by virtue of the fact that the attack was a great success, probably even greater than had been expected, as the Germans were forced back along all of the sector attacked. This battle should be seen as the beginning of the end of the war and although there was still a lot of fighting to come, and many lives to be lost, from the start of August the allied forces were in the ascendancy and the Germans were continually withdrawing, often to hastily prepared positions from which they were ousted the following day. Although the 29th Division took no part in the events unfolding in front of the Amiens part of the old Somme battlefield, it was to be involved in the work of driving the Germans out of Belgium as they, and other divisions like them, were given the task of chasing the Germans by following closely and leaving them no time to establish another strong line of defence. During the coming months the 29th Division was involved in a series of short sharp actions as the enemy withdrew and the 2nd Monmouths were fully involved in these actions in both a supporting and fighting rôle.

The first of these actions was to involve the capture of a low ridge on which the village of Outtersteene is situated. The need for this action had come about since the movement of the XV Corps was being hampered by the Germans holding the ridge. It is not a large feature but it does dominate the flat land of the area and in August 1918 effectively barred the way to the British army towards both Bailleul and the River Lys to the east. It was an important strong-point for the Germans and even if it was to be a small scale action when compared to the events taking place further south, success here was still a necessity if the momentum of the offensive was to be maintained. The western approaches to the ridge are, to some extent, protected by a muddy stream, the Meteren Becque, which, though only 10 feet (3m) wide was a sufficient obstacle to prevent the entire attack on the ridge coming from the west. As luck would have it, a little to the north of the ridge the Becque swung through the British lines making an attack from the north an easier option since no stream would need to be forded. Thus the plan was that the 9th Division would attack roughly southwards completely to the east of the Meteren Becque whilst the 29th Division was to attack astride the Becque in a roughly south easterly direction. The first objective of the attack was to be a line including Hoegenacker Mill and Belle Croix Farm. The units assigned for this task were the 9th Scottish Rifles, the 6th King's Own Scottish Borderers and the 11th Royal Scots of the 9th Division together with the 1st King's Own Scottish Borderers and two platoons of A Company the 2nd Monmouths. The right flank of the attack was to be extended as needed by the 2nd South Wales Borderers and the 2nd Hampshires also of the 29th Division. There was to be no preliminary bombardment but the preparation of the artillery plan was no less thorough for that. The artillery of the 9th Division was to open with smoke shells and after the first round a quarter of all shells fired were to be smoke. The 29th Divisional Artillery was to fire a creeping and rolling barrage while maintaining some enfilade fire on the German lines. To this was added the smoke fired by the artillery of the 36th Division to the north to keep the attack out of sight of the Germans in Bailleul. On top of all this was a machine gun barrage which was to commence as soon as the attack began providing long range harrassing fire to assist the attacking troops.

The attack was planned for the 18th August and every effort was made to ensure that the Germans were unaware of what was going on. Even the time of the attack, which was set at 11 am, was chosen with a view to catching the enemy completely off guard. It is clear from the German sources that the attack was unexpected. The enemy's own patrols had found everything quiet and had found nothing suspicious in the days leading up to the attack. The timing of the barrage was critical as evidence had suggested that the Germans would fire a counter preparation barrage on the British lines within minutes of their own barrage descending. It was decided, therefore, that the barrage would commence at Zero minus one minute and that the infantry would start to move at Zero plus one minute. This meant that even if the Germans responded as quickly as they possibly could their shells would only find the empty trenches recently vacated by the assaulting troops.

The two platoons of A Company of the 2nd Monmouths to be involved in the action were to be commanded by Lieut. H.J. Hopkins and he was, together with Lieut. R.H. Watkins and eighty-five other ranks, to keep in close contact with Captain J. Hayton's company of the 1st King's Own Scottish Borderers. They were to carry spades and barbed wire to enable consolidation works to commence immediately the objectives were captured. The following words of Lieut. Hopkins set the scene for the battlefield:

> At the time the corn was almost ripe, standing quite four feet high, and although farming had ceased through the evacuation of the peasantry, the countryside had the calm and peaceful appearance of a typical Belgian harvest-tide. Shell holes and the usual marks of war were hidden by the tall, ripening corn which coloured the landscape.
>
> Looking towards Outtersteene, the scene presented a complete contrast. No Man's Land and the area in front and behind showed the picture so common to the eye of the British soldier - smashed houses, shell torn soil, discarded limbers, graves with wooden crosses and the waving lines of upturned earth of the trenches. To the left front the ground sloped down to Meteren, a heap of tumbled masonry. In the foreground the Meteren Becque rippled over the worn stones, its water sparkling in the sun as it splashed on its course. On the right the ground rose gradually to where Merris once stood, now ruins in the debris of battle.

The platoons gathered their equipment on the evening of the 17th August and moved into their assembly trench to await zero hour. This trench, known as Africa Trench, had been prepared in advance and, according to the Official History of the Great War, was camouflaged by the use of screens of coconut matting which were pulled over the top to hide the assembled troops from the prying eyes of the German airmen. That also meant that the position could not be relayed to the enemy artillery and although the hours passed very slowly for the men hidden in this way it helped to keep the intentions hidden and consequently prevented any unnecessary loss of life.

At 10.59 am on the 18th August the British barrage opened up as planned and within two minutes the two platoons of the 2nd Monmouths were moving forward with the 1st King's Own Scottish Borderers towards their objective. The plan was to keep up with the barrage which moved accurately ahead sweeping the ground with such intense fire that virtually nothing escaped. The enemy were surprised by the attack, but their counter barrage came soon enough and began to

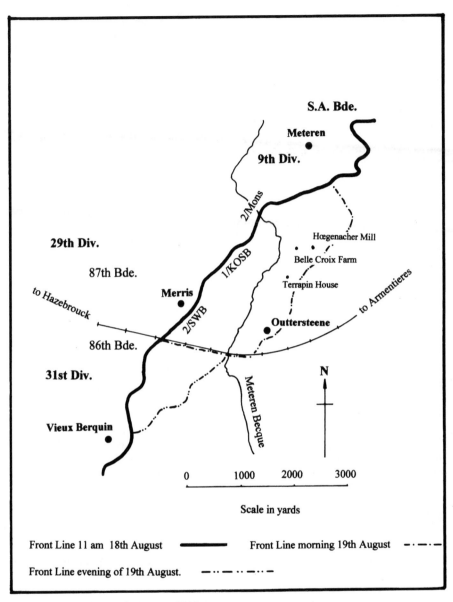

Outtersteene Ridge 18th August 1918.

cause casualties among the assaulting troops who were managing to keep up a good pace and remain in contact with their own barrage. Soon they found themselves amongst the enemy's machine gun posts which, because of the effects of the smoke shells, had done very little by way of their usual damage. Now they began to work and held up the advance, but only fleetingly since the attacking troops were close enough to charge the posts and dispatch the enemy with the bayonet. The machine gun fire and the counter barrage had created a gap in the KOSB line which was spotted by Lieut. Watkins who immediately led his own platoon into the gap. Capt. Hayton spotted this and shouted his encouragement with a 'Well done, Mons!' and the attack proceeded.

At this point of the attack the creeping barrage halted at the foot of the Outtersteene Ridge to allow the infantry to keep pace with it. Capt. Hayton and Lieut. Watkins spoke briefly to confirm their exact position on the map and as they spoke the barrage began to move again, wheeling to the left, and the men moved in to action once more. For their part the Germans had little fight left in them and those not killed by the barrage on the flanks of the ridge emerged from the safety of their dugouts to surrender to the advancing troops and Lieut. Watkins and his men rushed a machine gun post capturing an officer and men of the 49th Saxon Regiment and two machine guns.

The objectives set the KOSB and the Monmouths were soon taken and the Monmouths main task of consolidating the ground won commenced. A counter attack was anticipated since the Germans had always fought dearly for every scrap of ground surrendered and that fact made the work of the Monmouths all the more important as trenches were dug and a wiring party, under Sgt. D. Dallimore, made use of the barbed wire they had carried into the battle. Lieut. Hopkins made use of one of the enemy machine guns captured and mounted it in a suitable spot to defend his portion of the line when the Germans counter attacked. In about five hours the trench and defences were completed sufficiently for there to be cover for everyone and although, at this point, the work of the Monmouths was completed a request from the commander of the KOSB to Lieut. Hopkins to stay was immediately accepted. The ranks of the KOSB had been thinned somewhat in the attack and both Hopkins and Watkins recognized the need for their continuing support. This situation was made worse when the KOSB lost further men to fire from three enemy aeroplanes that swooped over the trenches late in the afternoon. However, the party of Monmouths were also reduced in number and when at about 6 pm that evening they were asked to go out in front of the main line to act as lookout posts the party was only 24 strong. Once again Hopkins was happy to offer assistance and he took the small party some 350 yards (320 m) in front of the trench and, in a position suitable for rifle fire, formed two mutually supporting posts. The expected counter attack had still not arrived though the account of the action in the Official History states that, according to German records, the counter attack had been launched at 5 pm. It would appear that the German records were in error because the Monmouths did not face any serious challenge until 9 pm. At that time the German gunners opened up and their infantry began their assault. The Monmouths, in their forward position, were even able to hear the shouts of the German officers urging their men forward but their posts were never really threatened since the British artillery had the position ranged accurately and were able to create havoc amongst the advancing German formations. It is recorded that one battalion of the 49th

Saxon Regiment was completely destroyed during the counter attack - only 29 men returned, and two companies of the 62nd Regiment were also wiped out. It had not been a good day for the enemy since they had been forced to give ground and their counter attack had failed with great loss of life. When the Monmouth party was relieved at midnight on the 18th August it had lost over 60 casualties, wounded or gassed and of this number ten are known to have been killed. It had been a day of heavy fighting and although successful, it had not been without considerable sacrifice to the attacking troops.

During the period where part of A Company was heavily engaged in the fighting the rest of the battalion had been stood ready to follow the attacking battalions for consolidation work. There had been some delay as the Germans shelled the area heavily, but when they started they were kept hard at work digging trenches and wiring until dawn of the 19th August when the assault on Outtersteene recommenced with the KOSB, the Border Regiment the SWB and the Hampshires finally capturing the whole for the ridge crest and the village of Outtersteene. Once again the battalion was assigned consolidation works and moved forward behind the main assaulting troops and were kept busy throughout the night of the 19th August until the new line was in a satisfactory state and ready for use as a defensive line.

For the next couple of weeks the battalion was employed in the Outtersteene area working on wiring and generally improving the trenches. During this period the Battalion Headquarters were at Pradelles though the companies were mostly billeted as close to their work as they could be. Throughout the Western Front the month of August had been generally successful for the Allies whilst the Germans had suffered a succession of defeats, notably in the area of the old Somme battlefields. The continuing pressure put on the Germans at every opportunity was having an effect and in the Bailleul area they had made no serious attempt to regain any of the ground they had lost. This was not a typical response and, although this may not have been realized at the time, this was certainly a good sign for the future conduct of the war. On the 30th August, 1918, it was discovered that the Germans had evacuated the salient they had formed in the Bailleul sector and had withdrawn approximately five miles. If pressure was to be maintained on the enemy then it was necessary that the British divisions in the area followed up immediately. The 29th Division did just that and the Monmouths were once again called upon in their rôle as divisional pioneers to prepare the roads for the heavy trafficking that the advance would produce. The progress was good and the battalion headquarters were moved on an almost daily basis to keep up with the rest of the battalion as it worked its way steadily forward. Their work was varied including many aspects of repair and building of the communication network needed as the division moved forward. In early September A Company was involved in the construction of a bridge over the Style Becque in the region of Steenwerk Station. They were now heading back into the area they had defended so bravely in April, 1918 and it must be imagined that the survivors gave some thought to the friends they had lost in those dark days when the outcome of the war seemed to be swinging in favour of the enemy. So much had changed in the intervening four months. Then they had been defending with their 'backs to the wall', now they were part of an attacking force trying to stay in close contact with the enemy as he withdrew. As they moved into the Steenwerck area Lieut. Hopkins received information that there could be German mines in and around the village. He went forward with Sgt. Parsons to establish if any Germans remained in the village and as his men followed he warned them not to enter any of the houses because of the danger of mines. Hopkins and Parsons ensured that Steenwerck was free of Germans though they came under some rifle fire from beyond the eastern edge of the village. Hopkins and his sergeant returned through the village to commence their work on the bridge building with material recovered from the ruins of the local brewery. There was some shelling during their work but the company had no casualties from it or, because of the earlier warnings, from the explosions of delayed action mines in two nearby houses. This kind of work, often under fire, was typical of the work carried out by the Battalion for the first two weeks of September but they were not always so lucky as to escape without casualties. On the 10th September they were ordered to return through Bailleul ready to be sent to another part of the front. On that day Pte. Heare was to record:

> *Off again, but I am sent with a message to our battalion not to move through Bailleul until 1700 hours. While the 2nd Monmouths waited the Germans shell the battalion. Drummer Ball, an old friend of mine gets killed. I some how feel guilty delivering that message.*

The battalion had got off lightly for Ball was the only fatality but, nonetheless, the sense of guilt that Heare felt is, perhaps, understandable, and made worse by the fact that the battalion was being relieved of its duty in the area. Later that day the battalion moved to Hazebrouck before moving, on the 16th September, to St. Jan Ter Biezen in Belgium to take part in the offensive actions in the Ypres area planned for that autumn.

The success of the operations in the southern part of the British sector needed a similar action in the north and, as part of this, the 2nd Monmouths, together with the rest of the 29th Division, were moved to Ypres in preparation for an attack to take place at the end of September. The division moved to take over the sector of the line lying between Zillebeke Lake and the Menin Road on the 21st September, 1918. The 2nd Monmouths moved to Brandhoek where they established Battalion Headquarters and where billets were found for the Companies except B Company who proceeded to Ypres ready to begin their work. This move had been in response to an order issued on the 19th September which instructed a break through along the Passchendaele Ridge followed up by the immediate exploitation of any successes gained. In view of the similar optimistic orders that had been issued at various stages throughout the war, it is possible that the concept of breaking through on the ridge was viewed with some scepticism. There was however, a somewhat different situation in the early autumn of 1918 to any other time of the war. The German tide had been stopped in April of the year and since early August there had been little but success for the Allied armies as they pushed the Germans back across the countryside of France and Flanders.

The attack planned for Flanders was to involve close co-operation between Belgian, French and British units and for the British Second Army the attack was to be on the Passchendaele Ridge between Broodseinde in the north and Wytschaete in the south. For the 29th Division, forming part of II Corps of that army, the front of attack was to be along the Menin Road towards Gheluvelt. The orders issued on the 19th September also stressed the need for secrecy and for gathering as much artillery as possible, though any new guns brought into the area would not be allowed to fire until Zero-hour on the day of attack. All preparations for the attack were in place by the 25th September and Zero-hour was set for 5.30 am on the 28th September. To the left of the British were the Belgians who were keen to have a substantial artillery preparation but following recent successes the British commanders realized that a better chance of success would be gained if the Germans were caught completely unaware. The British commanders further realized that the real strength of the German positions lay in their superior observation that the ridge gave them and thus a sudden barrage together with a creeping barrage as the attack proceeded where infantry were able to follow close behind tended to invalidate this advantage. In the event a compromise was reached which now seems a little odd since the Belgians were granted a three hour bombardment of the lines they were about to attack. It is hard to believe that the length of this bombardment did not warn the Germans of a pending attack - nonetheless the planning for the attack was continued on this basis. The British were insistent that they would not open their barrage until Zero-hour on the 28th September. It is interesting to note, also, that there was information to suggest the Germans had reduced their numbers in the Ypres sector and the French even went so far as to suggest that the enemy was about to evacuate their line. Crown Prince Rupprecht was to comment on the state of the German army in the area thus:

> .... what is worse is that according to a report from the 4th Army the troops will no longer stand up to serious attack.

It cannot be doubted that the Germans still had plenty of fight in them but perhaps for the first time the optimism displayed by the allied commanders had a sufficient basis in fact.

From the 21st September to the 28th September the 2nd Monmouths were employed in preparatory works for the attack working mainly on constructing and repairing the roads of the divisional area that would eventually carry the artillery pieces forward as the attack proceeded. It was the sort of work to which they were well accustomed and it was carried out as speedily as possible using all the materials that were at their disposal for filling shell holes and moving the roads and tracks onwards. The recent successes in the south and those in which they had been involved in themselves were not wasted on the men of the battalion as they worked to meet the time for the attack

On the 28th September the weather was poor and it rained heavily. To some this would typify the past efforts of the British Army in the Ypres Salient. This time, however, the weather played a much less important part as the attack commenced:

> At the appointed moment the barrage opened. It was perfect and the infantry were able to advance behind it as behind a wall.

In the 29th Division the attack was led by the 86th and 87th Brigades until about half way to the final objective of the ridge when the 88th Brigade passed through them and continued the attack. It was a resounding success for in a matter of hours, all along the front, the Allies were in possession of the ridge from north of Passchendaele to Wytschaete. There had been casualties but compared with the dreadful attrition of 1917 they were light and the ridge that had taken three months to capture then had fallen in as many hours. A short time later the 29th Division reached the ruins if the village of Gheluvelt - it was by that time no more than a pile of rubble marked by a German signpost identifying that as the village. The first troops into the village were the 4th Worcestershires almost four years after the 2nd battalion of that regiment had captured and defended it during the fighting of the 1st Battle of Ypres.

An advance of this scale, though welcomed by everyone, did present a problem to the British. The advance had been over shell torn battlefields that had seen repeated fighting over four years. There was little by way of a road network so the supply of the troops and getting guns and ammunition forward became increasingly difficult as the advance proceeded. The construction and repair of roads in the battle zone then became a high priority and in the 29th Division the work fell on the Royal Engineers and the 2nd Monmouths though all available men were set to work with them including the Trench Mortar Battery which was moving forward with the division. The rain that had persisted all through the day had, as usual in the Salient, turned everything into a morass and the supplies and guns needed to be brought up through about three miles (5 km) of it. The Monmouths worked hard, the successes of earlier in the day had at least allowed them to get on with their work, and hour by hour the main supply road, the Menin Road, improved sufficiently to allow at least some pack transport to get through, but conditions were far from ideal and must have moderated the feeling of success throughout the division. The 29th Division historian comments as follows:

> Thanks to the spirit in which all worked, the road improved every hour, but all in front had to depend on the services of pack transport. It was impossible to move cookers and vehicles carrying greatcoats, so that those in front, in the wet and cold, were not likely to have had a comfortable time, especially in the absence of all shelter, except a few habitable, but filthy, pill boxes.

During the next few days the attack was continued. There was less success than on the first day but the attack proceeded and the battalion was kept busy constantly on improving the communications to the front. Pte. Heare was to comment of this period:

> At last we get to the top of the ridge, there is a six inch howitzer just under the ridge: 'I wonder how many times, Charley, that gun has made us run and put the fear of Hell up us' says Black. No wonder they could shell Ypres. We can see Ypres square from here and men and horses moving about. I stand here on my own for over half an hour looking at Ypres, thinking of the wreck of it and wondering. I always thought I would get mine at Ypres.

By the 2nd October, 1918, the attack had lost some of its momentum and the German resistance had hardened somewhat. The 29th Division was, by that time, occupying the edges of Gheluwe. At 7.45 pm on that day General H. Plumer issued an order which effectively brought the battle to a close. The gist of the order was that it was necessary to consolidate the positions gained and to improve the communications sufficiently to allow the artillery forward to begin the next phase of the attack. It had been a successful battle for the allies, the Germans had been forced to withdraw from the ridges to the east of Ypres and they had been forced to do so quickly. On the 4th October the 29th Division were relieved by the 41st Division but the 2nd Monmouths were left in the forward area to continue with their work on improving the roads and drainage of the supply routes to the new front line.

During this time out of the line for the division some of the men were billeted in and around Ypres. Although some distance from the front line Ypres was still subjected to intermittent shelling from German guns firing at extreme range which meant that it was still not a safe place to be. Pte. Heare was to witness one incident arising from this shelling which took place shortly after the Division had been ordered back to the front line:

> One (shell) drops amongst our motorcyclists. There is panic, the petrol catches fire, the motorcycles burn fiercely. The men in the flames are yelling and screaming, expecting another shell. At last we get them out. What a terrible sight, one has his leg blown off and burnt, four dead, what an awful smell burnt flesh is. A KOSB orderly, Thurston, is killed; someone says Black is there but he has been out. It upsets us all. It takes me days to get right - off my food as well.

Records show that Clement Percy Thurston died of wounds on the 10th October, 1918 which clearly dates the incident recorded by Pte. Heare and which serves to indicate the dangers in Ypres which was at that time some miles behind the advancing British Army.

The period of consolidation for the attacking troops before the next move was very short. The 29th Division was back in the line on the 6th October where they were joined by the 2nd Monmouths. The next phase of the operations against the Germans in Flanders that last autumn of the war was to take place on the 14th October and it was seen as part of the continuing pressure upon the withdrawing German army all along the front. The first task of the operation was to capture Ledeghem before pressing on to the much larger town of Courtrai (Kortrijk). Zero-hour was set for 5 am and a platoon from each of A and B Company was assigned to the attacking 88th Brigade. These platoons were to carry footbridges, essentially elongated duck boards 12 feet (3.7 m) to 14 feet (4.25 m) in length, to assist the attacking troops cross the Heulebeck beyond Ledeghem. The morning, for once, was a fine morning but there was some low lying fog in places and the confusion that this may have caused on its own was worsened by the use of smoke shells. Nonetheless the attack proceeded rapidly and in about two hours Ledeghem was in the hands of the 29th Division though fighting continued as the Germans were cleared from their dugouts and cellars. Prior to the battle the town had still held a civilian population and unfortunately, despite the care of the attacking troops, many were to become victims of the war - the 29th Division historian lays the finger of blame firmly on the German artillery for indiscriminate shelling. The sight of dead women and children in this town is said to have spurred on the men of the division to ensure that it could be cleared as quickly as possible and prevent any further unnecessary death of civilians.

Once Ledeghem had fallen the open ground towards Courtrai lay beyond but the enemy proceeded to add his own smoke screen to make observation and control of the battle even more difficult. Lieut. J.T. Phillips, in charge of B Company's platoon, lost half his command killed or wounded by shell fire and machine gun fire at this stage of the attack. In the confusion he had also gathered some men who had become detached from their units. However, the Heulebeck was reached without further incident and the footbridges were thrown across the stream immediately for the use of the infantry as they rushed forward. During the ensuing fighting several small and rather disorganized groups of Germans were encountered by these platoons but only one machine gun post of a dozen men put up any sort of real resistance. Sergeant J. Dowding rushed forward on his own to prevent any further hold ups and quickly silenced the post. By the time the platoons had returned to the battalion they had gathered about 30 prisoners. Sergeant Dowding was given the immediate award of the Distinguished Conduct Medal for his quick thinking in silencing the machine gun. The day's fighting had cost the battalion eleven men killed and a number wounded mostly as a result of the fighting in Lieut. Phillips area. Overall it had been a successful day for the Division for it had advanced some 6,000 yards (5,500 m) and had taken over 1,000 prisoners.

The next major obstacle to the advance of the British Army in this part of the line was the River Lys at Courtrai and although the advance continued on the 15th October it was the following day before the 29th Division reached the banks of the Lys. The Lys was the widest river they had encountered up to that date and it presented a sizeable obstacle being approximately 30 yards (27 m) wide and about eight feet (2.4 m) deep. On the evening of the 17th October a number of men of the division had succeeded in getting across the river but they failed to establish a suitable bridgehead and were withdrawn. It was not until the 19th October that the troops were sufficiently prepared to make the necessary assault in force. During the night a footbridge was constructed under cover of parties of men who had been ferried across the river in small groups and by dawn the attack had commenced. The Royal Engineers and the 2nd Monmouths then proceeded to construct a pontoon bridge and its approaches so that by 8 am the artillery was able to move across in support of the infantry. This bridge could not be observed by the Germans directly and because of early morning mist could not be observed by artillery spotters working from aeroplanes. The bridge did not receive any attention from the German guns for some little time and when the mist had cleared, the shelling that the Germans were able to bring to bear was never accurate enough to cause any damage to the bridge.

With the crossing of the Lys the capture of Courtrai was almost complete. The inhabitants of the town were overjoyed to see the Germans leave, so much so that they actually became something of a problem as they, good naturedly, offered food and drink to their liberators as they pushed on after the Germans. It was an unexpected obstacle to the men of the division but not an entirely unpleasant one and even if some soldiers did stop for some quick refreshment with the friendly locals, the overall progress of the attack was not impaired. Later that day Pte. Heare and his comrades from the divisional signals were in Courtrai and noticed towns folk carving up many of the dead horses in the area that had resulted from the fighting, including those of Divisional Headquarters, that had been killed by German shelling as they retired. They were undoubtedly a bit bemused by this but attached no specific importance to the action. All they knew was that the townsfolk were friendly and very hospitable at that moment and so they decided to see if they could get some kind of a meal with someone:

We go to a house and ask for coffee. Scottie can't speak French so I parley, 'Oh, come in', says the man. They are cooking chips and steak. 'What luck', says Scottie, 'We have struck it here.' I talk of the war and the Germans in my best French, the man asks us to have some supper. I tell Scottie to sit down.... Now we are down to it, the girl, about our age, puts chips on our plate, her mother puts steak and gives us coffee. We stuff. 'Come tomorrow', says the girl. 'How long are you staying, don't forget tomorrow night'. We have fed well. 'Oh,' I say, 'I expect we shall move tomorrow morning but as our horses have been killed we may have to stay for horses to pull our things.' 'You can do without horses', says the girl. 'You two pull, you have just eaten some of the horses so you ought to be able to pull.' I feel my stomach go all about. 'What's wrong', says Scottie. 'We have eaten horse flesh'. Out rushes Scottie and he has it all up, I manage to keep mine down!

The towns folk had probably been short of food for some time and although some had been seen butchering the dead horses it had not occurred to Heare or his companion that it would be for food. For a moment the horrors of four years of war were forgotten for the immediate, and particularly British, horror of eating horse flesh!

On the 23rd October the division and the 2nd Monmouths were withdrawn from the action and sent to the Roubaix area for a rest period. The battalion was billeted in St. Andre to the west of the town and whilst there, the men were treated well by the populace who could not do enough for them. Billets were comfortable and the men appreciated the rest after two months of strenuous front line activity. Whilst at St. Andre, on the 5th November, the officers of the battalion were able to dine together to mark the fourth anniversary of the arrival of the battalion in France. At this time also, rumours were starting to fly that there was to be a cessation of the hostilities and that there was to be a signing of an armistice; the offensive across France and Belgium was now going so well that even the most battle hardened veterans were beginning to believe that the end was in sight. There was one more obstacle which it was expected would need to be taken before that could happen. That was the crossing of the River Scheldt. This river was at least twice as wide as the Lys and was known to be very deep. It was thought that this would create a major problem to the advance particularly if the Germans chose to defend it in strength. On the 7th November the battalion moved up with the division in preparation for the attack and preparations were completed ready for the attack planned for the 10th November. However, on the 9th November it was noticed that the Germans had withdrawn and the division, led by the 88th Brigade, were across the Scheldt and advancing as fast as they could. This marked the end of the fighting for the Monmouths and as the division moved forward they followed closely behind repairing roads to allow the transport to keep pace with the quickening advance. By the 11th November the battalion had reached Celles and the 'war to end all wars' was over.

Chapter Fifteen
'Wind Up The Watch On The Rhine'
(November 1918 to July 1919)

News of the Armistice arrived whilst the battalion was at Celles. The Battalion War Diary records in a very matter of fact way that:

> The news was received that GERMANY has signed the armistice laid down
> by the allies and that hostilities would cease at 1100 hrs today (11th). The
> Coys were employed on road repairs

There can be little doubt that amongst those companies there was relief and excitement, perhaps all the more for those men who had arrived in France in 1914. Pte. Heare was to comment:

> We are told on the road, at 11 o'clock, the war is over, 'What's to become of
> us now' says Black. 'We have lived this life, now we shall have to start over
> again'. I think the same. It all seems strange.

For four years there had been only one kind of existence for Heare and his comrades. Many of his friends of 1914 had not made it to the Armistice and those men who had been out since 1914 probably considered themselves very lucky to have survived.

The Armistice had been signed and brought about the end of the fighting. It was not the end of the war since the original Armistice of 11th November, 1918 was for no more than 36 days with the option for extensions should this be considered appropriate. The details of the Armistice are beyond the scope of this work but it should be made clear that there was a need for swift action on behalf of the Allies. To this end plans were rapidly drawn up to ensure that the initiative was not lost in the relatively short period of the initial Armistice. These plans were to include both the movement of the Allied troops forward to Germany and the simultaneous surrendering of arms and equipment by the Germans. The scale of the project was enormous and it is hardly surprising that many of the deadlines for the hand over of equipment were extended to allow for the quality and quantity of the equipment concerned to be checked to the complete satisfaction of the Allies. The extensions were only partly due to the size of the task because there was a general reluctance of the Germans to hand over anything that could be used later. Within days of signing the Armistice the Germans were attempting to claw back some of the lost ground that had been agreed to under the conditions of the Armistice. The Official Historian intimates that even at this early stage the German military hierarchy were already mindful of the next war! It can be imagined that the Allies were in no mood to be generous on anything and the terms of the Armistice were enforced as rigorously as possible.

The stance necessarily adopted by the Allies meant that for the ordinary soldier it was pretty much business as usual. There was now less chance of sudden death but the army routine continued. An order was issued by G.H.Q. on the 11th November to the effect that:

> *All commanders are to pay the strictest attention to discipline, smartness and well being of their troops, so as to ensure the highest state of discipline....*
> *Troops will be given every opportunity for rest, training, recreation and leave.*

This would probably have been good news for all concerned but in reality there was little chance for rest because the need to follow up the German withdrawal meant days of marching for most of the infantrymen. There was, however, some scope for recreation. Pte. Heare was to record:

> *A man comes out of a cafe and says we are the first troops in the village. He gives us wine and champagne, which he says he has kept hid, drinks for nothing. A woman comes in the cafe all excited. I hear her talking about a convent. The landlord asks us to go with her and shaking us by the hand 'Vive Le Anglay (sic)' they shout. We are the first English troops they have seen, the Germans only left last night. We arrive at the convent, the Mother Superior welcomes us in. I say we are not Catholic, does it matter? 'Come in' says a sister, we enter, what a spread, best butter, brown bread, cakes, coffee, what a feed.*

This village would have been in the vicinity of Celles, possibly Renaix, but Pte. Heare does not identify it. For the inhabitants it was a dream come true for them also since they had felt the weight of the occupation for four years. The battalion spent one night and moved on the following day. Initially the welcome was the same as the battalion moved through the south Belgian countryside. At Tubize, Major General D.E. Cayley was reportedly given the Freedom of the Town and the men of his division, the 29th, were treated to a party with a band and singing and dancing. In these towns, reached early in the advance to Germany, there were refugees from the front line towns and villages. Whilst these people were happy that the war was over one can only imagine their reaction as they learned their towns and homes had become victims of war. The stops in the days immediately after the Armistice were brief as the army moved to keep pace with the withdrawing Germans. The battalion left Tubize after the party and passed through Braine-l'Allaud before reaching Waterloo a little to the south of Brussels.

A party of us ride on and see the Germans leave the town. We keep back. The people here go mad, cafes open, no pay, all night dancing. A man calls a party of us in English, he is English, his wife Belgian, and they have one son. They give us tea and food and take us up to see the panorama of the Battle of Waterloo. General Cayley and Freyberg are there. Its a fine sight. Now we go up to the Lion. What a shock. Our papers have said for four years that the Germans have melted this lion down for munitions, but it's still here, and a wonderful view of where the the Battle of Waterloo was fought. From here I see a sight which impresses me. My battalion, the 2nd Mons, marching up the road, all of them. I am above them. It looks good to see them all at once.

The lion Heare is referring to here is situated on top of a tall conical mound on the spot where the Prince of Orange was wounded during the battle of 1815 and the plinth of the lion does provide a good vantage point to view the battlefield or, indeed, a suitable spot to watch your comrades march past. Much of the time the troops were engaged in marching to a new destination as the advance to the German frontier maintained pace. It is recorded in the Official History that the troops were also employed on the repair of roads and railways which, according to the Armistice, were to be left untouched by the Germans as they withdrew. There were breeches in this agreement as the withdrawing German troops, either by design or accident, caused a variety of kinds of damage to the Belgian transport infrastructure. In this repair work as many men as could be spared were used to ensure that the momentum of the advance was kept up thereby keeping the pressure on the Germans leaving them in no doubt of the intentions of the Allied armies. As early as the 20th November the battalion became split up to serve the brigades of the division. They formed part of the advance guard of each of the brigade groups and were employed in road repair to ensure the smooth advance of the division. At this stage A Company was serving with the 88th Brigade, B Company with the 86th Brigade whilst Battalion HQ and C Company were part of the 87th Brigade. The battalion remained split in this way until after it had crossed into Germany.

As part of the Armistice agreement it was necessary for the withdrawing Germans to leave quantities of weapons and ammunition which were stockpiled in France and Belgium. These were to become part of the arms and armament penalties incurred by the Germans as a result of their capitulation. Mostly it would appear that this was adhered to and the advancing troops found many dumps of equipment in the back areas through which they were marching. The 2nd Mons marched south from Waterloo towards Virginal-Samme and, in the words of Sgt. W.G. Sweet:

..were billeted in a school which had been a German bombing training place, and all kind of grenades were left lying about. Our boys must play with them and one exploded. Corporal Richards, who came up on mobilization as a band boy playing the triangle in 1914, was mortally wounded and died that night. Richards had tried to get the grenade out of the room, but it had exploded just outside the door. Whilst they were attending the wounded and giving first aid, and old man came out of the house opposite and kicked up a row because some glass was broken in his windows. Our lads said nothing, but one of them clocked him hard.

Whether this unfortunate incident was really an act of regrettable folly or simply the men of the section trying to follow Sgt. Sweet's original orders to pack them away is not recorded. Cpl. William John Richards died on the 22nd November, 1918 and was the last fatality of this kind to be suffered by the battalion some eleven days after the Armistice had taken place.

The route of the 29th Division and hence the battalion, was southwards and at each place of rest the welcome got more and more enthusiastic. At Ottignies the battalion were fed stew by the locals though some of the men were openly suspicious of the meat contained in it. Here the men were to witness the feelings of the majority of the locals towards those who had been 'friendly' with the Germans and windows were smashed in one house as a large crowd exacted some revenge. Beyond Ottignies the battalion marched to Huy, a medium sized industrial town, where they were to cross the Meuse. Again there was an enthusiastic welcome and a party where the wine flowed all night. It was recorded by Pte. Heare that even at this stage after the Armistice there were some of the men who were finding the peace unreal and were, in the quieter moments, convinced that they could hear the guns banging away in the distance. After four years of being in the sound of the guns men were likely to have problems in adjusting to the new environment. Today the symptoms that some of the soldiers were feeling would be called post-traumatic stress disorder.

The march was taking them nearer the German border and from Huy it was to become more difficult since their route lay through a portion of the Ardennes Forest where the landscape is one of steep sided valleys with, sometimes, dense forest. Routes were less direct but nonetheless they were heading steadily towards Germany. The British Army as a whole had been assigned a particular area of operations which ultimately led it to Cologne. To their north were the Belgians and to their south the Americans and beyond them the French. All were moving towards the German frontier and all were moving to pre-designated positions as they marched such that a unified front could be presented to the Germans. The lines chosen for pauses in the march served the purpose of keeping the armies together and also allowed the Germans time to withdraw. After four years of fighting the importance of avoiding unnecessary confrontation was recognized. Most of the Allied soldiers in the advance never saw a sign of a retreating German column though there were reports of large bands of stragglers being encountered, some of which were considered to be responsible for a measure of looting. These bands, however, did not generally cause any trouble for the advancing Allies.

To administer the terms of the Armistice a Permanent International Commission was formed. This Commission comprised British, French and German delegates and it was set to convene in the Belgian town of Spa which was thought to be convenient since it had been a German Headquarters during the war. Its purpose was to ensure that, as far as possible, the terms of the Armistice could be met. The Germans attempted to modify the terms of the agreement at every opportunity but met with little success as the Allies pressed them for the delivery of such materials as set out in the Armistice by the agreed dates. There can be no doubt that the Germans did all they could to hinder the process but the steady insistence of the Allies brought about a considerable measure of success. It was in this general area that the battalion saw for the first time the effect of the war on the locals and it is quite clear that food had been short for some time. Where possible members of the battalion helped out by contributing food to the families where they were billeted. The welcome received by the British troops was, however, more reserved than they had become accustomed to in the rest of Belgium. This was probably partly due to the presence of the German delegation to the Permanent International Commission. Sgt. Sweet was to record in his memoirs that:

> ....*going along a tree lined avenue I saw a stationer's shop, and asked the driver to stop up the road for me to go and buy some postcards. I dived into the shop and, to my surprise, came up against two German staff officers. The atmosphere froze. The old lady left them and came and served me quickly. Just after rejoining the lorry, we passed the old German HQ, with German soldiers still on guard. They looked at us as black as ink, and as we passed we got our rifles handy, but everything was O.K.*

Sgt. Sweet's company rested for two days at Spa and no doubt found it strange to see German Staff Officers and sentries at various points throughout the town. Discipline was strict on both sides and the stay in Spa passed without incident though the famous waters of the town did cause a few stomach problems amongst some of the troops who tried them for the first time!

The rest in Spa was short lived and the battalion was soon off to move another step closer to the German Frontier when they were halted at Francorchamps where they were to rest for two days before entering Germany. This was a time when spit and polish took over and the condition of boots was of prime importance to a battalion who had marched approximately 150 miles (240 km) since the Armistice. Billeting in Francorchamps was a problem since there was a number of units in the town at that time and by the time the 2nd Mons had arrived most of the best billets in the area had been taken. Sgt. Sweet was an old soldier by that time and did not miss much and a group of four villas in a side street caught his attention because although they appeared neater and tidier than many of the others and there was evidence of straw which he knew the Germans used in their billeting. He continued:

> *That was enough for me, as the Germans usually strawed their billets. Going up I found both villas empty, and looking through the windows saw the floors were strawed. These I booked for our lads, and from the end house a Belgian limped over and asked if I wanted a place for officers. I promptly booked his place for them. Our officers were delighted as he had a lot of wine hidden and they had quite a party. The Colonel had only a small room in a cafe and when he saw what our officers had he was very angry with our billeting officer.*

Sgt. Sweet's ability for the job of billeting was further recognized when on the 3rd December, 1918 he was part of the large billeting party organized by the Quartermaster General's Staff which included representatives of Brigade and Divisional troops. He was told to draw a bicycle and that:

> *You will be crossing into Germany today, so keep alert. It doesn't matter who you shoot as long as you are all right yourself.*

Perhaps this over dramatizes the situation but it is a fact that at this time the troops who were about to enter Germany were lectured on their conduct in Germany and were warned to carry rifles loaded with ten rounds in the magazine and a further fifty in the bandolier. Whilst this cannot be taken that trouble was expected it should be taken as understood that no risks were to be taken by any of the troops crossing the frontier on the 4th December, 1918, a day after Sgt. Sweet's bicycle ride to look for billets.

After four years of fighting it is, perhaps, understandable that the troops did not feel particularly friendly towards the Germans and no doubt the lecture on their conduct was designed to show just how far they could go in their dealings with the Germans. The troops themselves would appear to have been somewhat apprehensive expecting 'groans and curses not smiles and welcome'. This was, in all probability, an understandable reaction bearing in mind the often near rapturous welcome they had received in their march across Belgium. The battalion crossed the frontier into Malmedy, which was then in Germany though is now a Belgian town, and sure enough they were met with at least some indication that they were now in a different country, a fact that Pte. Heare recorded:

> .....We see the German flag, a large one, hanging down from an upstairs window. We all stop, get off our bicycles. 'Let's burn it' says one 'Let's pull the B thing down' says another. 'Let's cheer old Fritz for his pluck' says one, which we do. The German is on the doorstep. He beckons us up to his house. In we go. He gives us coffee bad as it is. We all shake hands with the German and his wife and, coming out of the door, kiss his three daughters for fun. How they laughed. On the road again Black starts to swear, what's up? 'There goes four years resolutions' he says, 'I always said what I would do to German man or woman or child. Now we have cheered the German flag, shook hands with a German and his wife, drank coffee with them and kissed their three daughters, so no more resolutions for me'. We all agree he is right.

At least for some of the soldiers who were to occupy Germany there was some realization that the civilians of the country were not too different from themselves. Perhaps it would take a little longer to accept the German who had been a soldier.

From Malmedy the 29th Division marched to Elsenborn which had been a German garrison town and was capable of providing accommodation for 25,000 men. The camp with its barracks was neatly laid out each group of buildings being separated by a neatly trimmed hedge about eight feet high. To the newcomers there was some difficulty in finding the way around the camp and NCO's responsible for billeting were told off to bring in their companys. It was whilst carrying out this duty that Sgt. Sweet had a close call.

> A car full of German officers came along, flying a white flag. They had evidently been arranging details of the takeover. As the car came up to me, it suddenly swerved in and tried to run me down. I quickly sprang to one side, and they missed. Thinking to fire on them, I swung round to the right, but in my line of fire were a lot of canvas huts which were occupied by German women and children, so I could not risk hitting them.

Sgt. Sweet's introduction to Germany had been less than pleasant but it did not seem to have affected his judgement. The attitude shown by the officers in the car may not have been universal in the German Army but the Armistice had not been welcomed by all the Germans as later events were to show. The stay in Elsenborn camp was short and the next day the troops prepared to move on. Sgt. Sweet was to comment that:

> One of the stores nearby had a great heap of German helmets, thousands of them, with pre-war badges. On the march the next day nearly everyone had a helmet in his pack, but in the course of a few days not many were to be seen.

At this stage of the occupation of Germany little was known as to how the Germans would react to the presence of British soldiers. All men were ordered to carry their rifles and officers were to carry revolvers. The need for caution in the approach was further outlined by the proclamation, or *Anordnungen* as it was known, of Gen. Sir Herbert Plumer dated the 2nd December, 1918 which set out strict controls on such things as the movement of civilians, the sale of alcohol, the appearance of local newspapers, the issue of identity cards and so on. In total it set out nineteen rules which were to be used to control the German population during the early days of the occupation. It was added that 'any act of disobedience will be punished in a manner set forth in the proclamation first above mentioned' which referred to the proclamation made by Haig the day before. The Germans were to be left in no doubt who would be running things and this approach was adopted in the other allied areas to the west of the Rhine.

The route of the 29th Division now took it north east from Elsenborn through provincial towns such as Montjoie, Thum, Zulpich and ever nearer to their final destination of Cologne.

In Cologne things were different for the men of the battalion. It was the first time they had been in a big city for some time and Cologne was big at that time with a population of in excess of 600,000 souls. The occupation of Cologne and the formation of a bridgehead on the eastern side of the Rhine was the limit of the ambition of the occupation. It has been said that the reason for these limited objectives was that the Allied armies were simply too tired to go any further. Judging by the scale of the operation to achieve this limited goal it is easy to understand this concept but there is no official record of such a thought amongst the military or political rulers of the day. In any event similar limited bridgeheads were established by other allied armies to the south of the British sector. The bridgehead was effectively a defended area enclosed by a radius of 30 km (19 miles) centred on Cologne. The area was not rigidly semicircular since some towns were excluded, other included, to assist in the local administration and management of the area. Beyond the defensive area was a neutral zone of 10 km (6 miles) depth from which armed forces of either side were to be excluded.

The Official History remarks that at this stage of the occupation there was little in the way of food shortages in Germany:

> *All, particularly the children, looked well clothed and nourished, a striking difference from the French villages which had been occupied by the Germans, just as smug, food-and-drink satisfied inhabitants of Cologne, Bonn and Düren offered a marked contrast to the haggard figures of the people of Lille, Roubaix and Tourcoing, with their clothes hanging loosely on them scarecrow fashion.*

There may have been some truth in this statement but some members of the battalion may have argued differently. By the time the battalion reached Cologne there would appear to have been food shortages and several of the men became involved in preparing or supplying food for German families. This does not seem to have been for any profit since it was usually the children who benefited from the kindness of the soldiers who had probably seen all the suffering they wanted. Pte. Heare also recorded that when he acted as a cook for a while he was preparing some of the army food for the daughters, young women, of a local hotelier in the town who had showed them some kindness. Pte. Heare was to spend time talking to the eldest of the daughters who taught English in one of the local schools:

I tell her of the gas at Ypres, 1915, the shelling, sniping, air raids. How I got to hate her people for it, what a hell they made of our lives. How I swore what I would do if I got to Germany and what I done when I got to Malmedy, cheer the flag and all, how she laughs over this part, of England I know little, only three leaves in four years.

Of course the young woman was reasonably well educated and offered Pte. Heare, who incidentally admitted to being rather afraid of her, her version of the war as seen from her position as a teacher in a German school:

Well I am still here and you are English and I am a German girl alone yet you haven't done anything desperate, why? Now I will tell you my side. I am a school teacher, my sister works in the hotel, helps Dad. I speak English, French and German, of course, my sister speaks French and German. We have lost no one in the war, Dad is too old and I have no brothers. As a teacher, when I saw the children's faces getting thin and pale, how I used to pray a plague would settle on France and England and wipe you all out and what I would like to do if I had a chance. I have thought awful things and you have said some awful things. I like what you say - only what you know or have seen not what (the) papers say, yet here we are speaking like old friends. Isn't it awful what we are led to believe of one another, yet left alone we are only natural human beings, led by the papers we get into this state. You have never done me any harm, only good, neither have I done you any harm, yet we get in this bad state led by capitalist people and papers.

Pte. Heare declined to enter into the proffered political discussion but the comments of the schoolteacher reflected the mood of Germany and Cologne immediately following the Armistice. There was much civil unrest in Germany, many of its people felt that they had been badly let down and following the events in Russia of 1917 it was hardly surprising, perhaps, that there was a feeling that it was time for social change. The British Army were called upon to assist in restoring order but there were problems some, apparently, instigated by the so called 'Red Militia' hurriedly set up to maintain order. These men wore arm bands bearing the insignia 'Stadt Koln' which seemed to carry with it some authority. At about the same time as Pte. Heare was having his conversation with the schoolteacher Sgt. Sweet was to encounter, much more closely, the feeling of political unrest and dissatisfaction in Germany. Sgt. Sweet was dropped off one morning to find billets for the men on the outskirts of Cologne when he came face to face with a band of the 'local police':

These civilian patrols were of the regime who had taken over the city, and were in parties of ten. Four of them were walking in single file on the side of the road. They were quickly hedging me in on a narrow part of the pavement, so seeing a gap between (the) two parties I just walked quickly through, and got to the middle of the road where I had more room to manoeuvre if anything happened. Didn't they look at me! Walking through I was able to size them up, and came to the conclusion that they were not trained soldiers but looked like factory hands. Their rifles were of a small carbine type, with new leather slings, and they did not have any equipment, so I supposed that they carried ammunition in their pockets. If they had started anything I should have opened up at once, as after what I had come through I didn't intend to be shot by a bunch of revolutionaries.....

165

Although a young man, barely twenty four years of age, Sgt. Sweet had been on the Western Front for four years and could, undoubtedly, handle himself in a tight corner. He carried on billeting but expected more trouble from the patrol. But to his unashamed relief they had disappeared. He puts their rapid departure down to the fact that:

> I heard the bagpipes and around the corner came a Scottish regiment, I believe it was the Black Watch, bagpipes playing and swirling kilts, and very welcome they were too.

It is likely that this was the 8th Black Watch who had already taken a dislike to these armed bands and in the nearby town of Düren had rounded them all up and locked them in the local jail. Thus the soldiers of the occupation were faced with new dangers but both Pte. Heare and Sgt. Sweet got the impression that generally the people of the country were happy to see them. Sgt. Sweet asked why this was so:

> The answer was that war was better than revolution, and they knew everything would be all right when we came.

Cologne was a big city and the opportunity to sample its pleasures was not wasted by the men who had fought long and hard to get there. They took advantage of its shops and cafés and as can be imagined large quantities of German beer were consumed by the off duty soldiers. The British soldiers rode the trams for free but the German drivers were not always happy to wait for stragglers. It was a source of amazement, and amusement, to the soldiers that the German male did not give up his seat to the women on crowded trams. Pte, Heare was to note:

> The German treats the women strange, man first. A man sits down and a woman stands, our fellows swear over it. This night on this tram some of the lads had (had) many drinks (and) saw women standing. They threw all the German men off and gave the women the seats - unfortunately we had thrown most of the women's husbands off, but it passed over all right - the women seemed to like our ways of women first.

But things were not all good for the civilians of occupied Germany. There were food shortages as the occupation progressed and, as mentioned, some had continued for some time. Pte. Heare was very embarrassed when his landlady openly cried at the sight of the army food he had taken back to his billet. The German papers had insisted that things were every bit as bad for the Allies and that their army was starving also. The children naturally suffered more and were the first to be attended to by the British soldiers and soon it appears that all the soldiers of the Battalion were involved in feeding the German children in some shape or form. Sgt. Sweet recorded:

> The men in the school where they were billeted had many children for visitors and at dinner time they queued up for their food and the German children filed in behind with basins to get what was over. Men were asked if they wanted more, but when they saw the waiting hungry children they said: 'No', and let the kids have it.

166

It was some time before the allied governments accepted this situation and continued to insist that the troops did not feed the civilian population. It was not until mid January 1919 that it was agreed that essential foodstuffs such as bread, cereals and pork, should be supplied to the German populace. This shortage was not what the war had been about and although there were efforts to stop the soldiers supplying the Germans, they were largely ignored. Too many of the soldiers had families of their own at home to stand by and watch people going hungry when there was food readily available to them.

By mid December the preparations were complete for the official march into Cologne and across the Rhine. This was spelled out to the men of the 2nd Mons by Operation Order No. 94 which gave all the details of the parade such as the type of dress - marching order with soft caps - and the order of the companies in the march which was to be HQ followed by A, B, C Company and then by the transport and all following the Band. Item three of this order is instructive in its attention to detail and reads as follows:

> The Battalion saluting point will be at the western end of the Hohenzollern Bridge. The 2nd Army Commander will take the salute. All ranks must be warned to look the Army Commander straight in the face. The compliment must be paid from six paces before reaching the saluting point to six paces beyond. The Band will wheel to the left opposite the Army Commander and counter march to form up facing the Army Commander playing the Regimental march the whole time and then join on behind the transport. The Band will cease to play as it joins on behind the Battalion striking up again when 300 yards past the saluting point. At the first halt afterwards the Band will resume its position at the head of the Battalion.
> The attention of all ranks must be drawn to pulling their caps on straight when marching to attention.

As far as the soldiers of the battalion were concerned the order translated into getting themselves sorted out. Sgt. Sweet was to provide the following details of the event:

> Next, we had spit and polish for the official march through Cologne. It was stormy so we had to wear ground sheets, and with fixed bayonets we marched past the cathedral and on to the Hohenzollern Bridge on the 13th December, 1918. At the entrance under the statue of the Kaiser was the saluting point with Gen. Fergusson, the Military Governor, and our Divisional General commanding the 29th Division. Marching in step was too much for the beautiful bridge, and we had to break step, unfix bayonets, and march at ease. Then the order came down, 'Everyone with a watch, wind it on the Rhine', referring to the German song 'When They Wind Up The Watch On The Rhine'.

In a similar vein Pte. Heare was to record in his diary:

> We all have to be over the Rhine before eleven o'clock, we get to the Rhine at eleven, we all pull out our watches and sing 'we wind up our watches on the Rhine'. We go over the Hohenzollern Bridge. It's a fine bridge, two footpaths, two tram lines, a wide road and two railway lines. It's almost as wide as it is long. We stop at the far end to watch the march past of the 29th

Division held on the bridge. All German men to take their caps off to our officers, one fellow refuses to do so, General Freyberg tells the man to take off his cap for the march past, the German laughs and spat at the troops passing. General Freyberg knocks him down, discipline every time for General Freyberg V.C.

For the next ten days or so the battalion was billeted in and around Dellbruck a suburb of Cologne on the east bank of the Rhine. During this time the Colours were brought from Pontypool under the escort of Lieuts. L.E. Ford and H.T. Nelmes, 265363 Sgt. Williams DCM, MM and L/Cpls Dyke MM and Wooding. Sgt. Sweet and Sgt. Mansell Davies were billeted with a family at 21, Thurnver Strasse where the eldest daughters were schoolteachers. During this period Sgt. Sweet was able to relax and indulged himself in reading the family's copies of the Waverly novels. Once again there is some evidence of the discussion of the causes of the war. Here there was the opinion that the British had become involved because it had wanted the German colonies overseas. Sgt. Sweet expressed the opinion that the Empire was big enough and that to add more colonies was simply adding more trouble. It is, perhaps, ironic that two young people of two powerful imperial nations were able to sit calmly and discuss such matters after one of the bloodiest wars in history that, in fact, was to mark the beginning of the end of the old imperial order in Europe and the start of the rise to power of those nations that were to dominate the world during the second half of the twentieth century.

By Christmas the battalion had moved again to Burscheid about 26 km (16 miles) north east of Cologne. In the run up to Christmas the troops themselves had suffered from supply shortages particularly clean shirts and underclothes. Sgt. Sweet states that it had been weeks since they had had a change of clothes and that they were as louse ridden then as at any time in the trenches. The need for a clean shirt had become so great to some men that it had become quite a game to see who could buy a clean shirt from someone returning to the battalion from hospital. Some men went even further and stole women's blouses from clothes lines in the town leaving their lousy shirts in exchange. Apparently the Germans considered this to be a fair deal!

Nonetheless at Christmas the battalion did its level best to have a good time and in the words of Pte. Heare:

Now come Christmas 1918, we are to have a good do. The German celebrates Christmas like us, not New Year like the French. Our signal Sgt., Sgt. King, gets a small hall and a piano, dinner at eight. The interpreter goes to Cologne in the signal lorry and gets Vermol and other things. We have half a sheep, plenty of pudding, make custard, plenty of potatoes and cabbage and a jar and a half of rum. I am busy until it is all ready the signal sergeant says 'Now Charley, take off your apron and clean up and sit down, we NCO's are waiting on you tonight.' What a tuck in, everyone lets themselves go and eat and drink, real soldiers songs until the pianist got too dazed to play and that don't stop us, on we go until morning. I get to my billet singing and happy. It appears my landlord and landlady put me to bed. How bad I feel, now all of a do, after struggling hard to make a drink of tea, I take it to the hall, what a sight, the lads had fell down some sick - lying in it, some done worse, I shout tea up, such cries 'Let me die' 'Oh my head' 'Wet a towel and bathe my head'. After a drink of tea they begin to brighten up a bit. I don't cook breakfast, none ask for it. I go to my billet, how my landlord, landlady and his sister, Lena, laugh at me and show me how I came home. I get dinner but little of it is touched. The nippers of the village have a feast, they fetch their mothers as well. They all have their plates full.

The Battalion War Diary records that at Christmas the Sergeants' Mess held a concert and that all the officers were able to dine together which was probably the first time that had occurred for some time.

The battalion began another year overseas but at least now there seemed to be some light at the end of the long dark tunnel. Attitudes were relaxed and some advantages were taken that would not have been risked in wartime. Sgt. Sweet was to recollect as the following:

I had to take over the duties of the RQMS, and found that a lot of things were missing and going out of the stores that shouldn't, so had to stop the flogging. One stunt was, at the baths men would leave their underclothes in the billet, draw clean ones, then on return put on the dirty linen and sell the clean ones to the Germans. So those who came with no underclothes went back without.

Sgt. Sweet helped to tighten things up at the stores but it is unlikely that even an old soldier such as Sweet could have prevented all the dodges of the men of the battalion. It was early January when the effects of the 1918 influenza pandemic was felt by the battalion and Sgt. Sweet was one of the men to find himself in hospital. He recovered and it was his belief that most of the tough old soldiers did recover but the men who had gone out for the 'last lap' were the ones who became casualties of this very different war.

Things in the army were changing. Immediately after the Armistice the demobilization of many of the units who were to remain in France and Flanders had begun. For the Army of Occupation the demobilization plans were not put in place until mid January, 1919, though small numbers of men had left their units some weeks before. There was a controlled run down of units as those men whose occupations were essential for the industry of the nation, such as miners, were allowed home followed by those with family commitments or those who had 'been out' since 1914. Naturally, the battalion had men from both the coal and iron industries and gradually these men were sent home. This is likely to have had a demoralizing effect on the men who remained behind. Many friendships had been made on the battlefields of France and Flanders and were broken by the demobilization. Added to this, of course, was the fact that the Army of Occupation had reached its destination. There were no plans to go further than the Rhineland so there was a sense amongst the men of a job finished. Pte. Heare recorded that at this time 'I feel ashamed of my khaki uniform and soldiering'. He was among an early draft to apply for demobilization and since he had been overseas since 1914 he was given a fair hearing by the Adjutant, Major Ibbs, although he did not fit into any special category at this time. Major Ibbs attempted to persuade him to stay with the battalion by the promise of promotion. This was of little attraction to the young man who had seen over four years of active service. Major Ibbs conceded defeat and arranged for his demobilization and for that of Pte. Black who had seen much of the action with Pte. Heare, they were to leave at the same time.

The trip home for the demobilized men was the final hardship. Once again they were herded into cattle trucks, no comfort, no heating, no place to wash and in short order they were a lousy unshaven mob. The journey from Cologne to

Calais took a long time for troops eager to get home. Troop trains leaving for home were given a low priority on the rail network now gearing itself up for peaceful purposes as industry and commerce were coming back to life. The journey was very much one of stop-start across Belgium and as Heare and his party neared the Ypres area and the scene of so much fighting and devastation he was to record:

> At last we get to the land we knew over the Ypres sector, how strange it all seems, all smashed up, 'What was it for?' says one in the truck 'What have we got for it, or anyone else?' How strange it all seems, I am held spellbound, I can't shake this feeling off me. 'How do you account for us living through it all?' I ask Black, 'Luck, a lot, good hearing, a good sense of danger and the first six months at Le Bizet to get used to it and a month in Ypres in 1915 to wake us up and get settled to it', he says. This Ypres has a hold on me and I am not sorry when we stop at Hazebrouck station.

By the time they reached Calais after their long slow journey Heare reported that he is lousier and dirtier than at any time during the war but how after a bath and a shave they are like 'new men' and all eager to get home. Eventually Heare and his companion reach Newport where they have a long wait for a train to Pontypool:

> Black says 'How do you feel about it Charley?' 'Oh, alright' says I. 'I am thinking' says Black, 'We have had to protect one another from danger, share our sleep and food, we have saw a lot happen, saw many killed, thousands of dead as many dying, we have had romping good times, and horrid bad ones together but now we must part and to start a new life.' Well let's hope we have lived through it all for a good purpose. Pontypool at last. My discharge in my pocket and my sandbag of goods on my shoulder, back home.

This story would have been repeated by numerous groups of men from the battalion as gradually it was reduced in strength. In early March the battalion was relieved from the Army of Occupation and reduced to cadre strength. A large draft of retainable men was transferred to the 9th Cheshires and some volunteered for service in the Army of Occupation. By the end of March the battalion strength had been reduced to 10 officers and 102 other ranks. The cadre was reduced further by mid April to 5 officers and 40 other ranks. This party was eventually to leave for home on the 27th May, 1919. They travelled via Antwerp and Tilbury and arrived in Pontypool on 7th June, 1919 to a civic reception. In early July this cadre was finally disembodied almost five years after the outbreak of war had sent them off on an adventure that none had survived unscathed. The battalion was represented at the Great Peace Demonstration on the 19th July, 1919 by its colour party comprising Lieutenants H.T. Nelmes MC and H. Llewellyn Hughes together with Sergeants W. Williams DCM MM and C. Hayes DCM.

During the war the battalion had been present at most of the major engagements on the Western Front and were duly awarded the appropriate battle honours by the Battle Nomenclature Committee. During the service of the country it had suffered 24 officers and 420 other ranks killed in action with at least 1626 other ranks wounded. The battalion also had the distinction of being one of only ten Territorial Force battalions to be awarded the 1914 Star and were the only Territorial battalion to be part of the Occupation of the Rhineland. The service was one of which the Regiment and the people of Monmouthshire could be justly proud.

Appendix 1
Roll of Honour

The Roll of Honour lists all those soldiers who died during the Great War and are believed to have served with the 2nd Battalion the Monmouthshire Regiment. The list has been complied using *'Soldiers Died in the Great War'* together with *'Officers Died in the Great War'* to which additions have been made as a result of the present research. Whilst it is considered that this represents a comprehensive listing it should be remembered that in certain instances where soldiers may have served with a number of units, errors and omissions are likely to occur.

Each entry in the list takes the following form:

1. The soldier's name, rank and number. These details are generally those that applied at the time of death.

2. Where another unit is indicated in italics it is indicative of a unit in which the soldier served at some time during his service during the Great War. In many cases this will have been service after the service with the 2nd Monmouths.

3. Abbreviations relating to the nature of death and theatre of war are: K.I.A. - killed in action; D.O.W. - died of wounds; F. & F. - France and Flanders; D.O.W.G.H. - died of wounds in German hands; D.O.S. - died of sickness.

4. The final resting place of the soldier. In the absence of a known grave the memorial bearing the name of the soldier is given.

It should be noted that only official battlefield memorials are included in the list. Many of the fallen have memorials in their home towns and many readers will be aware of those in their own areas. The research in this particular area has not been exhaustive and is, therefore, not included.

ACKROYD, Richard. Pte. 266134 D.O.W. F. & F. 19.8.18. Buried: Longeunesse (St. Omer) Souvenir Cemetery, France.

AINSWORTH, Alexander. Pte. 15096 K.I.A. F. & F. 28.1.17. Buried: Believed to be buried in Guards Cemetery, Les Boeufs, France.

ALLSOPP, William John. CQMS 120 K.I.A. F. & F. 17.3.15. Buried: Calvaire (Essex) Military Cemetery, Ploegsteert, Belgium.

ARCHER, Percy. Pte. 2156 K.I.A. F. & F. 5.5.15. Buried: No Known Grave. Memorial: Menin Gate Memorial to the Missing, Ypres, Belgium.

ASPINALL, James. Pte. 227032 *1st Mons., South Lancs.* D.O.W. 15.4.18. Buried: Lindenhoek Chalet Military Cemetery, Kemmel, Belgium.

ATKINS, John. Pte. 2696 *137693 178th Tun. Coy. R.E.* K.I.A. F. & F. 1.6.16. Buried: No Known Grave. Memorial: Thiepval Memorial to the Missing, Thiepval, France.

ATKINSON, Harold. Pte. 291282 *3rd Mons.* K.I.A. F. & F. 12.4.18. Buried: No Known Grave. Memorial: Hyde Park Corner Memorial to the Missing, Ploegsteert, Belgium.

AURTHER, William Albert. Pte. 2236 K.I.A. F. & F. 3.5.15. Buried: La Brique Military Cemetery No.2, St. Jan, Belgium.

BADGER, James Christopher. Pte. 266714 K.I.A. F .& F. 3.5.18. Buried: Cinq Rues Military Cemetery, Hazebrouck, France.

BADHAM, George Charles. Pte. 2803 D.O.W. F. & F. 11.5.15. Buried: No Known Grave. Memorial: Menin Gate Memorial to the Missing, Ypres, Belgium.

BAGGS, Andrew (Arthur) Charles. Pte. 2949 *265888* K.I.A. F. & F. 12.4.18. Buried: Pont d'Achelles British Cemetery, Nieppe, France.

BAILEY, James. Pte. 226017 *1st Mons.* D.O.W. F. & F. 12.4.18. Buried: Aire Communal Cemetery Extension, Aire, France.

BAKER, Frederick Samuel. Pte. 267596 D. F. & F. 5.9.17. Buried: Longuenesse (St. Omer) Souvenir Cemetery, St. Omer, France.

BALL, Albert. Dmr. 3281 *266093* D.O.W. F. & F. 10.9.18. Buried: La Kreule Military Cemetery, Hazebrouck, France.

BALSOM, Frederick. Pte. 2476 K.I.A. F. & F. 23.11.14. Buried: Calvaire (Essex) Military Cemetery, Ploegsteert, Belgium.

BARKER, Richard. Pte. 228338 *1st Mons.* D.O.W. F. & F. 24.8.18. Buried: Longuenesse (St. Omer) Souvenir Cemetery, Longuenesse, France.

BATESON, John. Pte. 291235 *3rd Mons.* K.I.A. F. & F. 31.7.17. Buried: Artillery Wood Military Cemetery, Boesinge, Belgium

BATSTONE, Hubert. Pte. 3047 K.I.A. F. & F. 5.5.15. Buried: No Known Grave. Memorial: Menin Gate Memorial to the Missing, Ypres, Belgium.

BAYNTON, Thomas. Pte. 267595 K.I.A. F. & F. 12.4.18. Buried: Le Grand Beaumart British Cemetery, Steenwerk, France.

BEATTY, Leyland. Pte. (Rfn.) 228763 *1st Mons.* K.I.A. F. & F. 12.4.18. Buried: No Known Grave. Memorial: Memorial to the Missing Faubourg D'Amiens Cemetery, Arras, France.

BEBBINGTON, Charles. Pte. 15304 *SWB* K.I.A. F. & F. 16.1.17 Buried: No Known Grave. Memorial: Thiepval Memorial to the Missing, Thiepval, France.

BECKETT, Richard Joseph (James). Pte. 228604 *5135 K. Liverpool Reg.* K.I.A. F. & F. 20.1.18. Buried: Oxford Road Cemetery, Ypres, Belgium.

BEDDIN, Ralph Spencer. MM Sgt. 15668 *SWB, 3rd Mons.* K.I.A. F. & F. 28.1.17. Buried: No Known Grave. Memorial: Thiepval Memorial to the Missing, Thiepval, France.

BELL, James. Pte. 30648 *13810 Border Reg.* K.I.A. F. & F. 12.4.18. Buried: Le Grand Beaumart British Cemetery, Steenwerk, France.

BENNETT, Worthington Wanford. Pte. 3030 D.O.W. F. & F. 1.6.15. Buried: St. Marie Cemetery, Le Havre, France.

BENNION, George. Pte. (Rfn.) 227060 *1st Mons.* K.I.A. F. &F. 12.4.18. Buried: No Known Grave. Memorial: Memorial to the Missing Faubourg D'Amiens Cemetery, Arras, France.

BERROW, Granville. Sgt. 2390 K.I.A. F. & F. 24.1.17. Buried: Combles Communal Cemetery Extension, Combles, France.

BEVAN, John. L/Cpl. 267423 D.O.W. F. & F. 4.6.18. Buried: Ebblinghem Military Cemetery, Ebblinghem, France.

BEVAN, Sidney. Pte. (Rfn.) 226392 *1st Mons.* K.I.A. F. & F. 12.4.18. Buried: No Known Grave. Memorial: Memorial to the Missing Faubourg D'Amiens Cemetery, Arras, France.

BEVAN, William George. Pte. 267428 K.I.A. F. & F. 12.7.17. Buried: Bard Cottage Military Cemetery, Boesinge, Belgium.

BIBEY, James. Pte. 3061 *260058 2/6 Royal Warwicks.* K.I.A. F. & F. 6.12.17. Buried: No Known Grave. Memorial: Cambrai Memorial to the Missing, Louverval, France.

BIGGS, Thomas. Pte. 3117 *265995* D.O.W. F. & F. 14.10.18. Buried: Ypres Reservoir Cemetery, Ypres, Belgium.

BIRKIN, Arthur. L/Cpl. 1288 K.I.A. F. & F. 6.12.14. Buried: Calvaire (Essex) Military Cemetery, Ploegsteert, Belgium.

BIRT, Henry Charles. Cpl. 2120 *264469* K.I.A. F. & F. 28.1.17. Buried: No Known Grave. Memorial: Thiepval Memorial to the Missing, Thiepval, France.

BLACKWELL, Sidney Harold. Pte. 288001 D.O.W. F. & F. 1.12.17. Buried: Rocquigny - Equancourt Road British Cemetery, Manancourt, France.

BLANCHARD, Stanley. Pte. 267429 *3rd Mons.* K.I.A. F. & F. 23.4.17. Buried: Vis-en-Artois British Cemetery, Haucourt, France.

BLEWITT, Frank. Pte. 1905 K.I.A. F. & F. 22.7.16. Buried: No Known Grave. Memorial: Thiepval Memorial to the Missing, Thiepval, France.

BOARDMAN, Joseph. Pte. 291636 *3rd Mons.* D.O.W. F. & F 4.12.17. Buried: Etaples Military Cemetery, Etaples, France.

BOND, Charles, Henry. Pte. 2169 D.O.W. F. & F. 13.6.15. Buried: Elsenwalle Brasserie Cemetery, Voormezele, Belgium.

BOWEN, Alfred John Hamilton. DSO & Bar, Lieut. Col. K.I.A. F. & F. 2.3.17. Buried: Guards Cemetery, Combles, France.

BOWEN, Howard Thomas. CQMS 265585 *2/2 King's African Rifles.* D.O.S. East Africa 3,9.17. Buried: Kilwa Kivinje Cemetery, Tanzania.

BOWEN, John. L/Cpl. 26/423 D.O.W. F. & F. 1.6.18. Buried: Ebblinghem Military Cemetery, Ebblinghem, France.

BOWEN, Oliver. Pte. 227373 *1st Mons.* K.I.A. F. & F. 22.11.17. Buried: No Known Grave. Memorial: Cambrai Memorial to the Missing, Louverval, France.

BOWEN, Thomas. L/Cpl. 1817 K.I.A. F. & F. 4.5.15. Buried: La Brique Military Cemetery No. 2 St. Jan, Belgium.

BOWEN, William. Pte. 266782 Died. Home. 9.4.17. Buried: Tarrington (St. Philip & St.James) Churchard.

BRADFORD, Albert Harold. Dmr. 265362 K.I.A. F. & F. 13.7.17. Buried: Bard Cottage Military Cemetery, Boesinge, Belgium.

BRAY, Thomas Mursell. Pte. 228963 K.I.A. F. & F. 11.3.18. Buried: Nine Elms British Cemetery, Poperinge, Belgium.

BRIDLE, Percy William. Pte. 2205 *265518* D.O.W.G.H. 20.5.18. Buried: Berlin South Western Cemetery, Stahnsdorf, Germany.

BRIMBLE, Henry C. L/Cpl. 1814 *265322* K.I.A. F. & F. 12.4.18. Buried: No Known Grave. Memorial: Hyde Park Corner Memorial to the Missing, Ploegsteert, Belgium.
BROOKS, George Frederick. Pte. 2076 K.I.A. F. & F. 22.7.16. Buried. Hamel Military Cemetery, Beaumont-Hamel, France.
BROTHERTON, James. Pte. 265770 K.I.A. F. & F. 30.11.17. Buried: Flesquières Hill British Cemetery, Flesquières, France.
BROWN, Albert. Pte. 266660 K.I.A. F. & F. 12.4.18. Buried: No Known Grave. Memorial: Hyde Park Corner Memorial to the Missing, Ploegsteert, Belgium.
BROWN, Charles Alexander. Pte. 265901 K.I.A. F. & F. 11.3.18. Buried: Oxford Road Cemetery, Ypres, Belgium.
BROWN, Thomas. Pte. 3400 K.I.A. F. & F. 20.7.16. Buried: Hamel Military Cemetery, Beaumont Hamel, France.
BROWN, William James. Pte. 267818 K.I.A. F. & F. 27.1.17. Buried: No Known Grave. Memorial: Thiepval Memorial to the Missing, Thiepval, France.
BRYANT, George Charles. Pte. 3454 K.I.A. F. & F. 28.1.17. Buried: No Known Grave. Memorial: Thiepval Memorial to the Missing, Thiepval, France.
BULLOCK, Arthur John. Pte. 3238 K.I.A. F. & F. 1.7.16. Buried: No Known Grave. Memorial: Thiepval Memorial to the Missing, Thiepval, France.
BULLOCK, Edwin George. Pte. 4876 *203014 R.West Kent.* D.O.W. 26.5.18. Buried: St. Sever Cemetery, Rouen, France.
BURNETT, James George. Pte. 2097 *265454* K.I.A. F. & F. 1.7.16. Buried: No Known Grave. Memorial: Thiepval Memorial to the Missing, Thiepval, France.
BURNS, Samuel. Pte. 1981 D.O.W. F. & F. 9.4.17 Buried: Hazebrouck Communal Cemetery, Hazebrouck, France.
BUTCHER, John. Sgt. 1936 D.O.W. F. & F. 26.7.16. Buried: Couin British Cemetery, Couin, France.
BUTCHER, Thomas John. Sgt. 2344 *265588* D.O.W. F. & F. 7.7.17. Buried: Lijssenthoek Military Cemetery, Poperinge, Belgium.
BUTCHER, William. Pte. 3121 K.I.A. F. & F. 22.7.16. Buried: Knightsbridge Cemetery, Beaumont-Hamel, France.
BUTLER, Francis G. Pte. 3095 D.O.W. F. & F. 16.6.15. Buried: Wytschaete Military Cemetery, Wytschaete, Belgium.
BUTLER, Victor. L/Cpl. 265425 K.I.A. F. & F. 2.12.17. Buried: No Known Grave. Memorial: Cambrai Memorial to the Missing, Louverval Military Cemetery, Louverval, France.
BUTTERWORTH, William. Pte. 266809 K.I.A. F. & F. 21.8.17. Buried: Bard Cottage Military Cemetery, Boesinge, Belgium.
BUXTON, Henry Charles. Pte. 291337 *3rd Mons.* K.I.A. F. & F. 31.7.17. Buried: Artillery Wood Military Cemetery, Boesinge, Belgium.

CAINES, Frank. Pte. 1358 K.I.A. F. & F. 10.3.15. Buried: Calvaire (Essex) Military Cemetery, Ploegsteert, Belgium.
CANTLE, Richard George. Pte. 2217 *77285 Tank Corps.* Died F. & F. 13.1.18. Buried: Bucquoy Road Cemetery, Ficheux, France.
CAREY, William. L/Cpl. 1369 K.I.A. F. & F. 6.7.16. Buried: No Known Grave. Memorial: Thiepval Memorial to the Missing, Thiepval, France.
CARMAN, Thomas Parkin. Pte. 267390 D.O.W. F. & F. 11.7.17. Buried: Lijssenthoek Military Cemetery, Poperinge, Belgium.
CARPENTER, George. Pte. 267825 *3rd Mons.* K.I.A. F. & F. 12.4.18. Buried: No Known Grave. Memorial: Hyde Park Corner Memorial to the Missing, Ploegsteert, Belgium.

CAWSEY, William Henry. Pte. 1877 K.I.A. F. & F. 21.1.17. Buried: Guards Cemetery, Les Boeufs, France.

CHAMP, Arthur. Pte. 291292 *3rd Mons.* K.I.A. F. & F. 31.7.17. Buried: Artillery Wood Cemetery, Boesinge, Belgium.

CHAMP, Joseph. Sgt. 268270 *2nd SWB* K.I.A. F. & F. 15.10.18. Buried: Dadizele New British Cemetery, Dadizele, Belgium.

CHANCE, Walter George. Pte. 3332 *266123* K.I.A. F. & F. 12.4.18. Buried: No Known Grave. Memorial: Hyde Park Corner Memorial to the Missing, Ploegsteert, Belgium.

CHARLES, George. Pte. 3250 *266737 14th Welsh* K.I.A. F. & F. 20.10.18. Buried: Montay-Neuvilly Road Cemetery, Montay, France.

CHISNALL, William. Pte. 30718, *SWB, 18139 North Lancs.* K.I.A. F. & F. 12.4.18. Buried: No Known Grave. Memorial: Hyde Park Corner Memorial to the Missing, Ploegsteert, Belgium.

CHIVERS, George Frederick. Pte. 285033 D.O.W. F. & F. 3.3.17. Buried: Sailly-Saillisel British Cemetery, Sailly-Saillisel, France.

CHIVERS, John. Pte. 267608 K.I.A. F. & F. 23.2.17. Buried: Sailly-Saillisel British Cemetery, Sailly-Saillisel, France.

CIANTAR, Antonio. Pte. 267774 K.I.A. F. & F. 2.2.17. Buried: No Known Grave. Memorial: Cambrai Memorial to the Missing, Louverval Military Cemetery, Louverval, France.

CLANCY, Joseph. Pte. 316452 *4th Mons.* K.I.A. F. & F. 3.5.18. Buried: Cinq Rues Military Cemetery, Hazebrouck, France.

CLANCY, (Clansey) Michael. Pte. 1687 *265258* K.I.A. F. & F. 24.5.17. Buried: Monchy British Cemetery, Monchy-le-Preux, France.

CLARKE, Albert Reginald Pte. 499 *265036* K.I.A. F. & F. 23.4.17. Buried: No Known Grave. Memorial: Memorial to the Missing Faubourg D'Amiens Cemetery, Arras, France.

CLARKE, Edward. Pte. 266639 K.I.A. F. & F. 12.4.18. Buried: No Known Grave. Memorial: Hyde Park Corner Memorial to the Missing, Ploegsteert, Belgium.

CLARKE, Richard. Pte. 266998 *41444 K. Liverpool Reg.* K.I.A. F. & F. 22.11.17. Buried: No Known Grave. Memorial: Cambrai Memorial to the Missing, Louverval Military Cemetery, Louverval, France.

CLARKE, William. Cpl. 2597 *2nd SWB* D.O.W. F. &. F. 17.8.17. Buried: Dozinghem Military Cemetery, Westvleteren, Belgium.

CLASSON, Ermot. Pte. 5089 *41432 K. Liverpool Reg. 260074 2/6 Royal Warwicks.* K. I. A. F. & F. 4.9.17. Buried: No Known Grave. Memorial: Tyne Cot Memorial to the Missing, Passchendaele, Belgium.

CLEE, Thomas. Pte. 43283 285365 15th Welsh D.O.W. F& F 16 8 17. Buried: No Known Grave. Memorial: Tyne Cot Memorial to the Missing, Passchendaele, Belgium.

CLEMENTS, Joe. Pte. 227050 Died, F. & F. 13.12.18. Buried: Belgrade Cemetery, Namur, Belgium.

COCKILL, Richard. Pte. 291523 *3rd Mons.* K.I.A. F. & F. 3.5.18. Buried: Cinq Rues British Cemetery, Hazebrouck, France.

COLE, Richard. Pte. 3861 D.O.W. F. & F. 28.1.17. Buried: Guards Cemetery, Les Boeufs, France.

COLE, Raymond Henry. Pte. 2295 K.I.A. F. & F. 23.11.14. Buried: Calvaire (Essex) Military Cemetery, Ploegsteert, Belgium.

COLEMAN, Thomas C. Pte. 267433 K.I.A. F. & F. 3.5.18. Buried: Cinq Rues Military Cemetery, Hazebrouck, France.

COLLETT, Frederick John James. L/Cpl. 6275 *242131 2/8th Worcs* D.O.W. F. & F. 28.8.17. Buried: Wieltje Farm Cemetery, Ypres Belgium.

COLLINGS, Walter. M.C. Lieut. *3rd Mons., 12th K.O.Y.L.I.* K.I.A. F. & F. 10.4.18. Buried: Le Grand Hasard Military Cemetery, Morbeque, France.

COLLINS, Frank. Sgt. 528 K.I.A. F. & F. 25.12.14. Buried: Calvaire (Essex) Military Cemetery, Ploegsteert, Belgium.

COLLINS, William. 2nd Lieut. *8th Gloucesters* K.I.A. F. & F. 30.7.16. Buried: No Known Grave. Memorial: Thiepval Memorial to the Missing, Thiepval, France.

COMPTON, Harry. Pte. 267606 *3rd Mons.* D.O.W. F. & F. 29.6.17. Buried: Ferme Olivier Cemetery, Elverdinge, Belgium.

CONIBEAR, Ernest Edmund. Pte. 2905 Died Home. 19.8.15. Buried: Bristol (Arno's Vale) Cemetery, Bristol.

CONNOR, John. Pte. 267952 *1st Mons., 20902 K. Liverpool Reg.* K.I.A. F. & F. 8.10.18. Buried: Sequehart British Cemetery No.1, Sequehart, France.

CONNOR, John. Pte. 20153 *27332 Royal Defence Corps.* Died Home. 18.9.17. Buried: Neath (Llantwit) Cemetery, West Glamorgan.

COOK, George William. Pte. 265113 K.I.A. F. & F. 23.8.17. Buried: Bleuet Farm Cemetery, Elverdinge, Belgium.

COOK, Reginald Gilbert Henry. Pte. 285702 D.O.W. F. & F. 7.12.17. Buried: Tincourt New British Cemetery, Tincourt, France

COOK, William Trevor. Pte. 267573 *1447 3rd Mons.* K.I.A. F. & F. 30.11.17. Buried: No Known Grave. Memorial: Cambrai Memorial to the Missing, Louverval Military Cemetery, Louverval, France.

COOPER, Edward. Pte. 2165 K.I.A. F. & F. 22.7.16. Buried: Knightsbridge Cemetery, Beaumont-Hamel, France.

COOPER, George. Pte. 31013 *11th RWF, SWB, 22nd Rifle Brigade.* D. Salonika. 10.10.18. Buried: Sarigol Military Cemetery, Greece.

COOPER, James. Pte. 267607 *1924 3rd Mons.* K.I.A. F. & F. 12.4.18. Buried: No Known Grave. Memorial: Hyde Park Corner Memorial to the Missing, Ploegsteert, Belgium.

COOPER, William John. Cpl. 1924 *40562 1st Worcs.* K.I.A. F. & F. 31.7.17. Buried: No Known Grave. Memorial: Menin Gate Memorial to the Missing, Ypres, Belgium.

CORBETT, Charles Archibald. Pte. 15707 K.I.A. F. & F. 23.11.16. Buried: A.I.F. Burial Ground, Grass Lane, Flers, France.

CORKE, James Ernest. Pte. 47671 *5054 RWF* K.I.A. F. & F. 14.10.18. Buried: Dadizele New British Cemetery, Dadizele, Belgium.

COTTLE, Richard George. Pte. 2420 *260059 2/6th Royal Warwicks* K.I.A. F. & F. 24.9.17. Buried: Brown's Copse Cemetery, Roeux, France.

COX, Arthur John. Pte. 3344 *39474 6th SWB* K.I.A. F. & F. 6.6.17. Buried St. Quentin's Cabaret Military Cemetery, Ploegsteert, Belguim.

COX, George Lambert. Pte. 2665 K.I.A. F. & F. 28.3.15. Buried: Calvaire (Essex) Military Cemetery, Ploegsteert, Belgium.

COX, Samuel. Cpl. 2266 *265550* K.I.A. F. & F. 1.7.16. Buried: No Known Grave. Memorial: Thiepval Memorial to the Missing, Thiepval, France.

CRABB, Walter. Cpl. 1925 *265369* K.I.A. F. & F. 12.4.18. Buried: No Known Grave. Memorial: Hyde Park Corner Memorial to the Missing, Ploegsteert, Belgium.

CRICKMORE, Harry Alfred Richard. Pte. 228816 *1st Mons.* D.O.W. Home 26.4.18. Buried: Acle (St. Edmund) Churchyard, Norfolk.

CROWLEY, M. Pte. 266117 Died Home. 25.5.20. Buried: St. Woollos Cemetery, Newport, Monmouthshire.

CROWLEY, William. Pte. 1684 K.I.A. F. & F. 22.11.14. Buried: Le Touquet Railway Crossing Cemetery, Warneton (Waasten) Belgium.

CRUICKSHANK, Raymond Alfred. 2/Lieut. *3rd Mons.* K.I.A. F.& F. 23.4.17 Buried: Dury Crucifix Cemetery, Dury, near Arras, France.

CUDBY, John Cpl. 1946 D.O.W. Home. 6.6.15. Buried: Aylesford (St. Peter) Churchyard.

DACEY, Davis. Pte. 267449 D. F. & F. 24.4.18. Buried: La Kreule Military Cemetery, Hazebrouck, France.

DACEY, George. Pte. 2939 *40137 6th SWB* K.I.A. F. & F. 15.6.17. Buried: Kandahar Farm Cemetery, Neuve Eglise (Nieuwkerke), Belgium.

DANIEL, E. Reginald. Pte. 1274 *265344* K.I.A. F. & F. 19.4.17. Buried: No Known Grave. Memorial: Memorial to the Missing Faubourg D'Amiens Cemetery, Arras, France.

DARBY, Harry. Pte. 266723 D.O.W.G.H. 18.4.18. Buried: Tournai Communal Cemetery Allied Extension, Tournai, Belgium.

DARE, George Henry Williams. Pte. 2433 K.I.A. F. & F. 4.4.15. Buried: Calvaire (Essex) Military Cemetery, Ploegsteert, Belgium.

DAVIES, Arthur. Sgt. 1172 D.O.W. F. & F. 26.5.15 Buried: No Known Grave. Memorial: Menin Gate Memorial to the Missing, Ypres, Belgium.

DAVIES, Arthur George. Pte. 1724 K.I.A. F. & F. 6.12.14. Buried: No Known Grave. Memorial: Hyde Park Corner Memorial to the Missing, Ploegsteert, Belgium.

DAVIES, Charles George. L/Cpl. 265143 K.I.A. F. & F. 18.4.18 Buried: Merville Communal Cemetery Extension, Merville, France.

DAVIES, David. Pte. 267441 K.I.A. F. & F. 12.4.18. Buried: No Known Grave. Memorial: Hyde Park Corner Memorial to the Missing, Ploegsteert, Belgium.

DAVIES, David Llewellyn. Pte. 266472 K.I.A. F. & F. 6.8.17. Buried: Bleuet Farm Cemetery, Elverdinge, France.

DAVIES, Ellerton Osborne S. 2nd Lieut. K.I.A. F. & F. 2.4.15. Buried: Calvaire (Essex) Military Cemetery, Ploegsteert, Belgium.

DAVIES, Frederick. Pte. 266700 D.O.W.G.H. 29.4.18. Buried: Cologne Southern Cemetery, Cologne, Germany.

DAVIES, George. Pte. 3059 K.I.A. F. & F. 7.5.15. Buried: No Known Grave. Memorial: Menin Gate Memorial to the Missing, Ypres, Belgium.

DAVIES, George Thomas. Pte. 4399 K.I.A. F. & F. 28.1.17. Buried: No Known Grave. Memorial: Thiepval Memorial to the Missing, Thiepval, France.

DAVIES, Gerald Rees. Pte. 4671 *39875 5th SWB* D.O.W. F. & F. 11.6.17. Buried: Lijssenthoek Military Cemetery, Poperinge, Belgium.

DAVIES, Gwilym Rees. Pte. (Rfn.) 228274 *1st Mons.* K.I.A. F. & F. 11.4.18. Buried: No Known Grave. Memorial: Memorial to the Missing Faubourg D'Amiens Cemetery, Arras, France.

DAVIES, H. Pte. 227299 K.I.A F. & F. 26.3.18. Buried: La Brique Military Cemetery No. 2, St. Jan, Belgium.

DAVIES, John Henry. Pte. 2616 K.I.A. F. & F. 7.5.15. Buried: No Known Grave. Memorial: Menin Gate Memorial to the Missing, Ypres, Belgium.

DAVIES, James John. Pte. 265737 D.O.W. F. & F. 27.5.17. Buried: Duisans British Cemetery, Etrun, France.

DAVIES, John. Pte. 4582 *39902 2nd SWB* K.I.A. F. & F. 11.4.18. Buried: No Known Grave. Memorial: Hyde Park Corner Memorial to the Missing, Ploegsteert, Belgium.

DAVIES, John Penry. Pte. 267613 *3rd Mons.* K.I.A. F. & F. 12.4.18. Buried: Tourcoing (Pont-Neuville) Communal Cemetery, France.

DAVIES, Josiah James. Pte. 4705 *39551 2nd SWB* K.I.A. F. & F. 23.4.18. Buried: No Known Grave. Memorial: Arras Memorial to the Missing, Faubourg D'Amiens Cemetery, Arras, France.

DAVIES, Lewis. Pte. 1435 Died F. & F. 15.3.15. Buried: St. Sever Cemetery, Rouen, France.

DAVIES, Lewis John. Pte. 2525 K.I.A. F. & F. 7.5.15. Buried: No Known Grave. Memorial: Menin Gate Memorial to the Missing, Ypres, Belgium.

DAVIES, Percy. L/Cpl. 267583 *3rd Mons.* K.I.A. F & F. 30.11.17. Buried: No Known Grave. Memorial: Cambrai Memorial to the Missing, Louverval Military Cemetery, Louverval, France.

DAVIES, Samuel Gwyn. Pte. 266150 K.I.A. F. & F. 28.1.17. Buried: No Known Grave. Memorial: Thiepval Memorial to the Missing, Thiepval, France.

DAVIES, William Evan. Pte. 267445 K.I.A. F. & F. 6.5.17. Buried: Faubourg d'Amiens Military Cemetery, Arras, France.

DAVIES, William Ewart. Pte. 3114 *37702 12th Gloucesters.* K.I.A. F. & F. 25.4.18. Buried: No Known Grave. Memorial: Hyde Park Corner Memorial to the Missing, Ploegsteert, Belgium.

DAVIS, Grosvenor Alfred. Pte. 2422 *265627* D.O.W. F. & F. 12.7.17. Buried: Etaples Military Cemetery, Etaples France.

DAY, Arthur W. Pte. 2192 K.I.A. F. & F. 3.2.15. Buried: Calvaire (Essex) Military Cemetery, Ploegsteert, Belgium.

DAY, John. Pte. 1745 *265289* K.I.A. F. & F. 12.4.18. Buried: No Known Grave. Memorial: Hyde Park Corner Memorial to the Missing, Ploegsteert, Belgium.

DENNON, William. Pte. 291076 *3rd Mons.* K.I.A. F. & F. 2.12.17. Buried: No Known Grave. Memorial: Cambrai Memorial to the Missing, Louverval Military Cemetery, Louverval, France.

DESMOND, P. (served as John Shea). Pte. 2216 Died Home 3.10.16. Buried: Llantarnam Cemetery, Newport, Monmouthshire.

DIX, Albert. Pte. 3233 *266067* D.O.W. F. & F. 18.8.18 Buried: Longuenesse (St. Omer) Souvenir Cemetery, France.

DIXON, John. Pte. 291908 *3rd Mons.* K.I.A. F. & F. 12.4.18. Buried: No Known Grave. Memorial: Hyde Park Corner Memorial to the Missing, Ploegsteert, Belgium.

DORAN, Edward. Pte. 285054 K.I.A. F. & F. 12.4.18. Buried: No Known Grave. Memorial: Hyde Park Corner Memorial to the Missing, Ploegsteert, Belgium.

DOWNEY, William. Pte. 267446 K.I.A. F. & F. 6.8.17. Buried: Bleuet Farm Cemetery, Elverdinge, Belgium.

DOWNES, Albert Henry. Pte. 1442 D.O.W. F. & F. 21.12.14. Buried: Cité Bonjean Military Cemetery, Armentieres, France.

DOWSE, Henry Walter. CSM 2755 K.I.A. F. & F. 12.7.16. Buried: Hamel Military Cemetery, Beaumont Hamel, France.

DRAPER, Phillip. Pte. 15526 *SWB* K.I.A. F. & F. 28.1.17. Buried: No Known Grave. Memorial: Thiepval Memorial to the Missing, Thiepval, France.

DRUMMOND, Thomas Edward. Pte. 2835 K.I.A. F. & F. 5.5.15. Buried: No Known Grave. Memorial: Menin Gate Memorial to the Missing, Ypres, Belgium.

DUKES, Albert Edward. Pte. 4405 K.I.A. F. & F. 28.1.17. Buried: No Known Grave. Memorial: Thiepval Memorial to the Missing, Thiepval, France.

DURBIN, William Gabriel. Cpl. 1429 D.O.W. F. & F. 10.7.16. Buried: St. Sever Cemetery, Rouen, France.

EACUPS, Frank William. Pte. 267617 *3rd Mons.* K.I.A. F. & F. 12.4.18. Buried: No Known Grave. Memorial: Hyde Park Corner Memorial to the Missing, Ploegsteert, Belgium.

EASTOP, Charles Henry. Pte. 267295 K.I.A. F. & F. 14.10.18. Buried: Dadizele New British Cemetery, Dadizele, Belgium.

EDWARDS, Charles. L/Cpl. 1516 K.I.A. F. & F. 7.5.15. Buried: No Known Grave. Memorial: Menin Gate Memorial to the Missing, Ypres, Belgium.

EDWARDS, Edward. Capt. K.I.A. F. & F. 17.8.16. Buried: Vlamertinge Military Cemetery, Vlamertinge, Belgium.

EDWARDS, Henry. Pte. 288012 D.O.W. F. & F. 6.3.17. Buried: Bray Military Cemetery, Bray-sur-Somme, France.

EDWARDS, Joseph. Pte. 1177 D.O.W. F. & F. 18.3.15. Buried: Bailleul Communal Cemetery Extension, France.

EDWARDS, Theophilus. Pte. 229949 *1st Mons.* D.O.W.G.H. F. & F. 21.4.18. Buried: Leuze Communal Cemetery, Belgium.

EDWARDS, Walter. Sgt. 740 K.I.A. F. & F. 4.5.15. Buried: La Brique Cemetery No.2, St. Jan, Belgium.

EDWARDS, William. Sgt. 267616 *3rd Mons.* K.I.A. F. & F. 12.4.18. Buried: No Known Grave. Memorial: Hyde Park Corner Memorial to the Missing, Ploegsteert, Belgium.

ELLIOT, Harold. Pte. 3925 *39857 2nd SWB* K.I.A. F. & F. 11.4.18. Buried: No Known Grave. Memorial: Hyde Park Corner Memorial to the Missing, Ploegsteert, Belgium.

ELSON, John Ernest. Pte. 2140 K.I.A. F. & F. 14.2.15. Buried: Calvaire (Essex) Military Cemetery, Ploegsteert, Belgium.

EMMOTT, Frank. Pte. 2456 *265643* D.O.W. F. & F. 18.4.18. Buried: Haringhe (Bandeghem) Military Cemetery, Rousbrugge-Haringhe, Belgium.

EVANS, Edward. Pte. 1682 K.I.A. F. & F. 30.12.14. Buried: Calvaire (Essex) Military Cemetery, Ploegsteert, Belgium.

EVANS, Edwin. Pte. 1085 K.I.A. F. & F. 5.5.15. Buried: No Known Grave. Memorial: Menin Gate Memorial to the Missing, Ypres, Belgium.

EVANS, Fred. Pte. 267451 D.O.W. F. & F. 5.10.17. Buried: Bethune Town Cemetery, Bethune, France.

EVANS, Frederick. Pte. 48428 *SWB, 36361 Border Reg.* K.I.A. F. & F. 18.8.18. Buried: No Known Grave. Memorial: Hyde Park Corner Memorial to the Missing, Ploegsteert, Belgium.

EVANS, Henry Herbert. Pte. 15535 *SWB.* D.O.W. F. & F. 21.10.16. Buried: No Known Grave. Memorial: Thiepval Memorial to the Missing, Thiepval, France.

EVANS, John. Pte. 3360 K.I.A. F. & F. 25.10.16. Buried: Bancourt Military Cemetery, Bancourt, France.

EVANS, John. Pte. 266739 K.I.A. F. & F. 23.2.17. Buried: Sailly-Saillisel British Cemetery, Sailly-Saillisel, France.

EVANS, John Henry. Pte. 1404 K.I.A. F. & F. 1.7.16. Buried: No Known Grave. Memorial: Thiepval Memorial to the Missing, Thiepval, France.

EVANS, John Thomas. Pte. 285124 Died Germany. 3.1.19. Buried: Cologne Southern Cemetery, Cologne, Germany.

EVANS, Sidney. Pte. 2363 K.I.A. F. & F. 26.5.15. Buried: Bailleul Communal Cemetery Extension, Bailleul, France.

EVANS, Thomas. Cpl. 265465 D.O.W. F. & F. 24.12.17. Buried: Rocquigny-Equancourt Road British Cemetery, Manancourt, France.

EVANS, Thomas Charles. Pte. 265452 K.I.A. F. & F. 30.11.17. Buried: No Known Grave. Memorial: Cambrai Memorial to the Missing, Louverval Military Cemetery, Louverval, France.

FLEETWOOD, Alfred. Pte. 2594 K.I.A. F. & F. 8.5.15. Buried: No Known Grave. Memorial: Menin Gate Memorial to the Missing, Ypres, Belgium.

FLELLO, T.H. Pte. 266133 Died Home 17.9.19. Buried: Garndiffaith (St. John's) Burial Ground, Varteg, Monmouthshire.

FLETCHER, Percy Leonard. Cpl. 2206 K.I.A. F. & F. 12.4.18. Buried: No Known Grave. Memorial: Hyde Park Corner Memorial to the Missing, Ploegsteert, Belgium.
FLETCHER, Percy Lyttleton. Cpl. 2294 *265565* K.I.A. F. & F. 6.7.17. Buried: Bard Cottage Military Cemetery, Boesinge, Belgium.
FLYNN, David. Pte. 267623 *3rd Mons.* Died Home. 10.4.18. Buried: North Ormesby (St. Joseph's) Roman Catholic Cemetery, Yorkshire.
FOLEY, James J. Pte. 385 K.I.A. F. & F. 8.7.16. Buried: Engelbelmer Communal Cemetery Extension, Engelbelmer, France.
FORD, William. Pte. 1843 D.O.W. F. & F. 27.5.15. Buried: Bailleul Communal Cemetery Extension, Bailleul, France.
FORREST, Firth. Pte. (Rfn.) 228928 *1st Mons.* K.I.A. F. & F. 12.4.18. Buried: No Known Grave. Memorial: Memorial to the Missing Faubourg D'Amiens Cemetery, Arras, France.
FRANCIS, John. Pte. 2263 D.O.W. F. & F. 21.7.16. Buried: Gezaincourt Communal Cemetery Extension, Gezaincourt, France.
FRASER, Alexander Evan. Lieut. K.I.A. F. & F. 2.5.15. Buried: La Brique Military Cemetery No. 2. St. Jan, Belgium.
FRASER, James Herbert. Lieut. *107 MGC* D.O.W. F. & F. 9.7.16. Buried: Puchevillers British Cemetery, Puchevillers, France.
FROST, Alfred Edward Watkin. Pte. 1300 K.I.A. F. & F. 12.4.15. Buried: Calvaire (Essex) Military Cemetery, Ploegsteert, Belgium.

GALLIVAN, Timothy. Pte. 1598 K.I.A. F. & F. 20.4.15. Buried: Calvaire (Essex) Military Cemetery, Ploegsteert, Belgium.
GARDNER, Ernest Owen. Pte. 3412 *285207 1/6th Gloucesters.* Died. F. & F. 9.10.17. Buried: No known Grave. Memorial: Tyne Cot Memorial to the Missing, Passchendaele, Belgium.
GARNETT, Joseph. Pte. 228548 *5678 Manchester Reg.* K.I.A. F. & F. 24.11.17. Buried: No Known Grave. Memorial: Cambrai Memorial to the Missing, Louverval Military Cemetery, Louverval, France.
GASKELL, Herbert. Pte. 53828 *2nd SWB, 31784 Welch Reg.* K.I.A. F. & F. 19.8.18. Buried: Borre Military Cemetery, Borre, France.
GAUGHAN, Patrick. Pte. 266603 K.I.A. F. & F. 26.9.17. Buried: Artillery Wood Cemetery, Boesinge, Belgium.
GEORGE, Levi. Pte. 2325 K.I.A. F. & F. 22.7.16. Buried: No Known Grave. Memorial: Thiepval Memorial to the Missing, Thiepval, France.
GEORGE, William. Pte. 2987 K.I.A. F. & F. 8.5.15. Buried: No Known Grave. Memorial: Menin Gate Memorial to the Missing, Ypres, Belgium.
GIBBS, Austin. Pte. 265931 D.O.W. F. & F. 18.8.18 Buried: Longuenesse (St. Omer) Souvenir Cemetery, France.
GIBBS, James Albert. Sgt. 290401 *3rd Mons.* K.I.A. F. & F. 12.4.18. Buried: No Known Grave. Memorial: Hyde Park Corner Memorial to the Missing, Ploegsteert, Belgium.
GIBSON, Edwin. Pte. 1699 K.I.A. F. & F. 1.7.16. Buried: Knightsbridge Cemetery, Beaumont Hamel, France.
GILBERY, Alfred William. Pte. (Rfn.) 226495 *1st Mons.* K.I.A. F. & F. 23.4.18. Buried: No Known Grave. Memorial: Memorial to the Missing Faubourg D'Amiens Cemetery, Arras, France.
GOFF, Ernest Fred. Pte. 3986 *39679 6th SWB.* Died. F. & F. 14.2.17. Buried: Bailleul Communal Cemetery Extension, France.
GOODALL, Edwin John. Pte. 2716 D.O.W. F. & F. 25.5.15. Buried: Bailleul Communal Cemetery Extension, Bailleul, France.

GOUGH, Enoch. Pte. 266730 K.I.A. F. & F. 12.4.18. Buried: No Known Grave. Memorial: Hyde Park Corner Memorial to the Missing, Ploegsteert, Belgium.
GOULDER, Charles. Pte. 1495 *265187* D.O.W. F. & F. 27.5.15. Buried: No Known Grave. Memorial: Menin Gate Memorial to the Missing, Ypres, Belgium.
GRAHAM, George. Pte. 285075 D.O.W. F. & F. 13.3.17. Buried: St. Sever Cemetery Extension, Rouen, France.
GRANGER, John Stanley. CSM 177 K.I.A. F. & F. 1.7.16. Buried: No Known Grave. Memorial: Thiepval Memorial to the Missing, Thiepval, France.
GRANT, Frank Edwin. Pte. 15900 K.I.A. F. & F. 23.11.16 Buried: A.I.F. Burial Ground, Grass Lane, Flers, France.
GREEN, Robert Walter. Pte. 268059 K.I.A. F. & F. 12.4.18. Buried: No Known Grave. Memorial: Hyde Park Corner Memorial to the Missing, Ploegsteert, Belgium.
GREENHALGH, John. Rfn. (Pte.) 260118 *4690 RWF.* K.I.A. F. & F. 31.7.17. Buried: No Known Grave. Memorial: Menin Gate Memorial to the Missing, Ypres, Belgium.
GREGSON, John. Pte. 288002 K.I.A. F. & F. 30.11.17. Buried: No Known Grave. Memorial: Cambrai Memorial to the Missing, Louverval Military Cemetery, Louverval, France.
GRIBBLE, William. Pte. 267323 *547 1/1 Welsh Horse, 1st Mons.* D.O.W. F. & F. 8.10.18. Buried: Tincourt New British Cemetery, Tincourt, France.
GRIFFITHS, Albert. Pte. 2565 K.I.A. F. & F. 18.3.15. Buried: Calvaire (Essex) Military Cemetery, Ploegsteert, Belgium.
GRIFFITHS, Cecil Ewart. Pte. 285129 D.O.W. Home. 25.8.17. Buried: Bettws-Cedewain (St. Bruno) Churchyard.
GRIFFITHS, David Gomer. Pte. 285128 *1/7 RWF, 2/SWB* K.I.A. F.& F. 5.10.17. Buried: Bleuet Farm Cemetery, Elverdinghe, Belgium.
GRINTER, Edwin George. Pte. 292056 *3rd Mons.* K.I.A. F. & F. 12.4.18. Buried: No Known Grave. Memorial: Hyde Park Corner Memorial to the Missing, Ploegsteert, Belgium.
GROVES, Arthur. Pte. 2335 Died Home. 10.11.14. Buried: Panteg Cemetery, Pontypool, Monmouthshire.
GUEST, Henry. Pte. 1345 K.I.A. F. & F. 11.12.14. Buried: Calvaire (Essex) Military Cemetery, Ploegsteert, Belgium.
GUNN, Austin Charles. Pte. 3493 K.I.A. F. & F. 22.7.16. Buried: Hamel Military Cemetery, Beaumont Hamel, France.
GUNN, George Robinson. Pte. 228618 *1st Mons. 23479 Sher. For.* K.I.A. F. & F. 14.10.18. Buried: Dadizele New British Cemetery, Dadizele, Belgium.
GWYN, Thomas Henry. Pte. 1917 Died Home. 16.9.15. Buried: Garndiffaith (St. John's) Burial Ground, Varteg, Monmouthshire.

HAINES, John White. Pte. 288008 D.O.W. F. & F. 13.4.18. Buried: Ebblingham Military Cemetery, Ebblinghem, France.
HALL, Alfred. Pte. 2749 *266731 18th Welsh* K.I.A. F. & F. 13.4.18. Buried: No Known Grave. Memorial: Hyde Park Corner Memorial to the Missing, Ploegsteert, Belgium.
HALL, George Alfred. Pte. 1545 *39503 2nd SWB* D.O.W. 28.4.17. Buried: Abbeville Communal Cemetery Extension, Somme, France.
HALL, Harry. Pte. 3216 *266055* K.I.A. F. & F. 1.7.17. Buried: Bard Cottage Military Cemetery, Boesinge, Belgium.
HALL, James. Pte. 226671 *1st Mons.* D.O.W. F. & F. 5.8.17. Buried: Etaples Military Cemetery, Etaples, France.
HAM, Frederick Charles. Pte. 1735 K.I.A. F. & F. 1.7.16. Buried: Auchonvillers Military Cemetery, Auchonvillers, France.

HANCOCK, Thomas George. Pte. 228971 *1st Mons.* K.I.A. F. & F. 14.10.18. Buried: Dadizele New British Cemetery, Dadizele, Belgium.

HAND, Herbert. Pte. 285149 K.I.A. F. & F. 16.8.17. Buried: No Known Grave. Memorial: Tyne Cot Memorial to the Missing, Passchendaele, Belgium.

HANSON, Vincent. Pte. 228889 *1st Mons.* D.O.W. F. & F. 15.4.18. Buried: Wimereux Military Cemetery, Boulogne, France.

HARDACRE, Joseph. Pte. 3029 D.O.W. F. & F. 5.5.15. Buried: No Known Grave. Memorial: Menin Gate Memorial to the Missing, Ypres, Belgium.

HARDINGE, Eustace William. Pte. 267467 K.I.A. F. & F. 1.7.17. Buried: Bard Cottage Military Cemetery, Boesinge, Belgium.

HARPER, Albert. Pte. (Rfn.) 230384 *1st Mons., 3rd Mons.* Died Home 17.11.18. Buried: Ebbw Vale Cemetery, Ebbw Vale, Monmouthshire.

HARRHY, Edgar. Cpl. 265902 D.O.W. F. & F. 25.6.17. Buried: Etaples Military Cemetery, Etaples, France.

HARRINGTON, David John. Pte. 1405 D.O.W. Home 23.7.16. Buried: Blaenavon (St. Peter's) Churchyard, Blaenavon, Monmouthshire.

HARRIS, Archie. Pte. 267784 Died F. & F. 21.3.17. Buried: St. Sever Cemetery Extension, Rouen, France.

HARVEY, Alfred. Pte. 265306 K.I.A. F. & F. 30.11.17. Buried: No Known Grave. Memorial: Cambrai Memorial to the Missing, Louverval Military Cemetery, Louverval, France.

HAVARD, Ernest. L/Cpl. 2833 *265827* K.I.A. F. & F. 2.12.17. Buried: No Known Grave. Memorial: Cambrai Memorial to the Missing, Louverval Military Cemetery, Louverval, France.

HAVARD, Thomas Benjamin. Pte. 2586 K.I.A. F. & F. 8.5.15. Buried: No Known Grave. Memorial: Menin Gate Memorial to the Missing, Ypres, Belgium.

HAWARTH, Herbert. Pte. 266305 *27622 South Lancs.* D.O.W. F.& F. 19.8.17. Buried: Dozinghem Military Cemetery, Westvleteren, Belgium.

HAYDEN, Joseph. Pte. 201389 K.I.A. F. & F. 30.11.17. Buried: No Known Grave. Memorial: Cambrai Memorial to the Missing, Louverval Military Cemetery, Louverval, France.

HAYMONDS, Thomas. Pte. 2748 K.I.A. F. & F. 8.5.15. Buried: No Known Grave. Memorial: Menin Gate Memorial to the Missing, Ypres, Belgium.

HAYWOOD, Nathaniel. Pte. 265943 K.I.A. F. & F. 12.4.18. Buried: No Known Grave. Memorial: Hyde Park Corner Memorial to the Missing, Ploegsteert, Belgium.

HERRINGTON, Frank Rowland. Pte. 15554 *SWB* K.I.A. F. & F. 28.1.17. Buried: No Known Grave. Memorial: Thiepval Memorial to the Missing, Thiepval, France.

HICKS, John Philip. Pte. 15470 K.I.A. F. & F. 21.11.16. Buried: Guards Cemetery, Les Boeufs, France.

HIGGINS, Tom. Pte. (Rfn.) 3274 *419041 9th London* K.I.A. F. & F. 24.9.18. Buried: No Known Grave. Memorial: Vis-en-Artois Memorial to the Missing, Haucourt, France.

HIGGINSON, George. Pte. (Rfn.) 228610 *1st Mons.* K.I.A. F. & F. 12.4.18. Buried: No Known Grave. Memorial: Memorial to the Missing Faubourg D'Amiens Cemetery, Arras, France.

HIGGS, William. Pte. 1344 K.I.A. F. & F. 1.7.16. Buried: No Known Grave. Memorial: Thiepval Memorial to the Missing, Thiepval, France.

HILL, J. Pte. 1269 K.I.A. F. & F. 13.4.15. Buried: Strand Military Cemetery, Ploegsteert, Belgium.

HILLIER, Cyril Anthony Hudson. 2nd Lieut. D.O.W. Home. 26.2.15. Buried: Stowmarket Cemetery, Suffolk.

HILLIER, Fred. Pte. 2134 *265476* K.I.A. F. & F. 18.7.17. Buried: Bard Cottage Military Cemetery, Boesinge, Belgium.

HINKSMAN, Frederick. Dvr. 3877 *T/294756 R.A.S.C.* Died. F. & F. 10.10.18. Buried: St. Sever Cemetery Extension, Rouen, France.

HITCHINGS, William Henry. Pte. 2311 K.I.A. F. & F. 30.12.14. Buried: Calvaire (Essex) Military Cemetery, Ploegsteert, Belgium.

HOARE, George. Pte. 1527 *15076 6th Welsh Reg.* K.I.A. F. & F. 26.9.16. Buried: Flatiron Copse Cemetery, Mametz, France.

HOCKADAY, Sidney Reginald. Capt. K.I.A. F. & F. 2.9.16. Buried: Lijssenthoek Military Cemetery, Poperinge, Belgium.

HOLDEN, Thurston. Pte. 47460 *SWB* K.I.A. F. & F. 1.5.18. Buried: No Known Grave. Memorial: Hyde Park Corner Memorial to the Missing, Ploegsteert, Belgium.

HOLLAND, William. Pte. 266469 K.I.A. F. & F. 12.4.18. Buried: No Known Grave. Memorial: Hyde Park Corner Memorial to the Missing, Ploegsteert, Belgium.

HOLLINSHEAD, William. Pte. 266770 K.I.A. F. & F. 12.4.18. Buried: No Known Grave. Memorial: Hyde Park Corner Memorial to the Missing, Ploegsteert, Belgium.

HOLMES, Augustus. Pte. 229019 *1st Mons.* D.O.W. F. & F. 20.8.18 Buried: Longuenesse (St. Omer) Souvenir Cemetery, Longuenesse, France.

HOLMES, Frederick. Pte. 267472 K.I.A. F. & F. 23.4.17. Buried: Vis-en-Artois British Cemetery, Haucourt, France.

HOLMES, Henry. L/Cpl. 266074 K.I.A. F. & F. 12.4.18. Buried: No Known Grave. Memorial: Hyde Park Corner Memorial to the Missing, Ploegsteert, Belgium.

HOLMES, Manley Walter. Pte. 3432 *3rd Mons.* K.I.A. F. & F. 28.1.17. Buried: A.I.F. Burial Ground, Grass Lane, Flers, France.

HOLT, George Arthur. Pte. (Rfn.) 263013 *1st Mons.* K.I.A. F. & F. 23.4.18. Buried: No Known Grave. Memorial: Memorial to the Missing Faubourg D'Amiens Cemetery, Arras, France.

HOLVEY, Sidney. Pte. 3313 *266111* K.I.A. F. & F. 1.7.16. Buried: Hawthorn Ridge Cemetery No.1, Auchonvillers, France.

HOOPER, Frederick. Pte. (Rfn.) 263014 *1st Mons.* K.I.A. F. & F. 23.4.18. Buried: No Known Grave. Memorial: Memorial to the Missing Faubourg D'Amiens Cemetery, Arras, France.

HOPKINS, William George. Sgt. 1015 *265006* K.I.A. F. & F. 31.5.17. Buried: No Known Grave. Memorial: Memorial to the Missing Faubourg D'Amiens Cemetery, Arras, France.

HORD, Horace. Pte. (Rfn.) 228817 *1st Mons. 9354 Lancs. Fusiliers.* K.I.A. F. & F. 12.4.18. Buried: No Known Grave. Memorial: Memorial to the Missing Faubourg D'Amiens Cemetery, Arras, France.

HORNBY, Bertram. Pte. 228560 *1st Mons., 5220 Liverpool Scots.* Died, Germany 29.4.18. Buried: Hamburg Cemetery, Ohlsdorf, Germany.

HORTON, Albert. L/Cpl. 2285 K.I.A. F. & F. 5.5.15. Buried: No Known Grave. Memorial: Menin Gate Memorial to the Missing, Ypres, Belgium.

HOUGH, John Prescott. Pte. 266516 K.I.A. F. & F. 2.12.17. Buried: No Known Grave. Memorial: Cambrai Memorial to the Missing, Louverval Military Cemetery, Louverval, France.

HOWELLS, William. Pte. 266180 K.I.A. F. & F. 3.7.17. Buried: Bard Cottage Military Cemetery, Boesinge, Belgium.

HUDSON, J. Pte. 2789 Died Home. 30.5.18. Buried: Billing Road Cemetery, Northampton.

HUGHES, Francis J. Pte. 2952 *265890* K.I.A. F. & F. 23.4.17. Buried: No Known Grave. Memorial: Memorial to the Missing Faubourg D'Amiens Cemetery, Arras, France.

HUMPHRIES, George E. Pte. 266717 *285060 9th Welsh.* K.I.A. F. & F. 23.3.18. Buried: No Known Grave. Memorial: Memorial to the Missing Faubourg D'Amiens Cemetery, Arras, France.

HUNT, Adolphus. Pte. 267787 K.I.A. F. & F. 12.4.18. Buried: Le Grand Beaumart British Cemetery, Steenwerk, France.

HURLE, Ralph. Pte. 3519 *39497 2nd SWB* K.I.A. F. & F. 29.9.18 Buried: Zandvoorde British Cemetery, Zandvoorde, Belgium.

ISHERWOOD, Ernest. Pte. 291242 *3rd Mons.* K.I.A. F. & F. 12.4.18. Buried: No Known Grave. Memorial: Hyde Park Corner Memorial to the Missing, Ploegsteert, Belgium.

JACKSON, Jonathan. MM. Sgt. 1996 K.I.A. F. & F. 1.7.16. Buried: No Known Grave. Memorial: Thiepval Memorial to the Missing, Thiepval, France.

JAMES, Brinley. Pte. 267645 K.I.A. F. & F. 23.4.17. Buried: Vis-en-Artois British Cemetery, Haucourt, France.

JAMES, Frank. Pte. 290991 *3rd Mons.* K.I.A. F. & F. 12.4.18. Buried: No Known Grave. Memorial: Hyde Park Corner Memorial to the Missing, Ploegsteert, Belgium.

JAMES, Henry Alfred. Pte. 1612 K.I.A. F. & F. 16.5.15. Buried: No Known Grave. Memorial: Menin Gate Memorial to the Missing, Ypres, Belgium.

JAMES, John. Pte. 3389 K.I.A. F. & F. 20.7.16. Buried: Hamel Military Cemetery, Beaumont - Hamel, France.

JAMES, James Morgan. Pte. 887 K.I.A. F. & F. 25.5.15. Buried: No Known Grave. Memorial: Menin Gate Memorial to the Missing, Ypres, Belgium.

JARRETT, George Maxwell. L/Cpl. 285060 K.I.A. F. & F. 14.8.17. Buried: Artillery Wood Cemetery, Boesinge, Belgium.

JAYNE, John. Pte. 1409 *265153* D.O.W. F. & F. 12.3.18. Buried: Nine Elms British Cemetery, Poperinge, Belgium.

JENKINS, Aneurin. L/Cpl. 2519 D.O.W. F. & F. 13.5.15. Buried: Boulogne Eastern Cemetery, Boulogne, France.

JENKINS, Alfred C. Pte. 1771 K.I.A. F. & F. 25.10.16. Buried: Bancourt Military Cemetery, Bancourt, France.

JENKINS, Edwin Francis. Pte. 315140 *4th Mons.* K.I.A. F. & F. 12.4.18. Buried: No Known Grave. Memorial: Hyde Park Corner Memorial to the Missing, Ploegsteert, Belgium.

JENKINS, Jehoiada. Pte. 2471 D.O.W. Home 19.5.15. Buried: Panteg Cemetery, Pontypool, Monmouthshire.

JENKINS, John. Pte. 2853 *428774 Labour Corps.* Died. Home. 11.3.18. Buried: Cwmbran Cemetery, Monmouthshire.

JENKINS, Percival A. Pte. 265887 K.I.A. F. & F. 1.3.17. Buried: Grove Town Military Cemetery, Meaulte, France.

JENKINS, Samuel. Pte. 267753 K.I.A. F. & F. 12.4.18. Buried: No Known Grave. Memorial: Hyde Park Corner Memorial to the Missing, Ploegsteert, Belgium.

JENNINGS, Frederick Giles. Sgt. 285054 *3rd Mons.* D.O.W. F. & F. 29.5.17. Buried: Duisans British Cemetery, Etrun, France.

JOHN, Edwin George. Pte. 1802 *265314* K.I.A. F. & F. 18.8.18 Buried: No Known Grave. Memorial: Hyde Park Corner Memorial to the Missing, Ploegsteert, Belgium.

JOHNS, John. Pte. 2004 K.I.A. F. & F. 25.5.15. Buried: No Known Grave. Memorial: Menin Gate Memorial to the Missing, Ypres, Belgium.

JOHNS, William C. Pte. 3137 K.I.A. F. & F. 23.11.16. Buried: A.I.F. Burial Ground, Grass Lane, Flers, France.

JOHNS, William Protheroe. Pte. 266260 Died Home. 27.12.17. St. Peter's Churchyard, Cockett.

JOHNSON, Herbert Robert. Pte. 2002 K.I.A. F. & F. 5.5.15. Buried: Tyne Cot Military Cemetery, Passchendaele, Belgium.

JONES, Alfred James. Pte. 2848 K.I.A. F. & F. 5.5.15. Buried: No Known Grave. Memorial: Menin Gate Memorial to the Missing, Ypres, Belgium.

JONES, Austin Wynne. Pte. 227678 *1st Mons.* K.I.A. F. & F. 3.5.18. Buried. Cinq Rues British Cemetery, Hazebrouck, France.

JONES, Arthur. Pte. 1611 *265229* K.I.A. F. & F. 1.7.16. Buried: No Known Grave. Memorial: Thiepval Memorial to the Missing, Thiepval, France.

JONES, Charles. L/Cpl. 2395 K.I.A. F. & F. 1.7.16. Buried: No Known Grave. Memorial: Thiepval Memorial to the Missing, Thiepval, France.

JONES, David Gomer. Pte. 202083 K.I.A. F. & F. 12.4.18. Buried: No Known Grave. Memorial: Hyde Park Corner Memorial to the Missing, Ploegsteert, Belgium.

JONES, Frederick Pte. 2366 K.I.A. F. & F. 8.5.15. Buried: No Known Grave. Memorial: Menin Gate Memorial to the Missing, Ypres, Belgium.

JONES, Fred. Pte. 3328 K.I.A. F. & F. 1.7.16. Buried: Knightsbridge Cemetery, Beaumont-Hamel, France.

JONES, Frederick Thomas Avery. 2nd Lieut. *3/1Herefords.* D.O.W. F. & F. 5.12.17. Buried: Peronne Road Cemetery, Maricourt, France.

JONES, George. Pte. 3312 K.I.A. F. & F. 21.11.16. Buried: Guards Cemetery, Les Beoufs, France.

JONES, Harold Burcher. L/Cpl. 1356 *265130* K.I.A. F. & F. 28.1.17. Buried: A.I.F. Burial Ground, Grass Lane, Flers, France.

JONES, Harry Owen. L/Cpl. 266459 D.O.W. F. & F. 3.2.18. Buried: Abbeville Communal Cemetery Extension, Abbeville, France.

JONES, Harold Leonard. Pte. 3240 *266071* D.O.W. F. & F. 3.7.17. Buried: Mendinghem British Cemetery, Proven, Belgium.

JONES, Jack. Cpl. 2368 *39514 2nd SWB* D.O.W.G.H. 23.7.18. Buried: Lille Southern Cemetery, Lille, France.

JONES, John. Pte. 1785 K.I.A. F. & F. 17.7.16. Buried: Hamel Military Cemetery, Beaumont Hamel, France.

JONES, John. Sgt. 265326 D.O.W. F. & F. 3.8.17. Buried: Duisans British Cemetery, Etrun, France.

JONES, Lewis. Pte. 267477 K.I.A. F. & F. 11.7.17. Buried: Canada Farm Military Cemetery, Elverdinge, Belgium.

JONES, Percy. L/Cpl. 2007 K.I.A. F. & F. 13.1.15. Buried: Calvaire (Essex) Military Cemetery, Ploegsteert, Belgium.

JONES, Robert Alfred. Pte. 2421 *265626* K.I.A. F. & F. 30.11.17 Buried: Gouzeaucourt New British Cemetery, Cambrai, France.

JONES, Rowland S. Pte. 538 K.I.A. F. & F. 16.6.15. Buried: Bailleul Communal Cemetery Extension, Bailleul, France.

JONES, Stephen Henry. Pte. 285099 K.I.A. F. & F. 11.4.18. Buried: No Known Grave. Memorial: Hyde Park Corner Memorial to the Missing, Ploegsteert, Belgium.

JONES, Thomas John. Pte. 267476 K.I.A. F. & F. 2.12.17. Buried: No Known Grave. Memorial: Cambrai Memorial to the Missing, Louverval Military Cemetery, Louverval, France.

JONES, William Edward. Pte. 2419 K.I.A. F. & F. 5.5.15. Buried: No Known Grave. Memorial: Menin Gate Memorial to the Missing, Ypres, Belgium.

JONES, William Henry. Pte. 285100 K.I.A. F. & F. 3.8.17. Buried: No Known Grave. Memorial: Menin Gate Memorial to the Missing, Ypres, Belgium.

JONES, Wyndham. L/Cpl. 266036 K.I.A. F. & F. 6.8.17. Buried: Bleuet Farm Cemetery, Elverdinge, Belgium.
JUKES, Thomas. Pte. 267644 *3rd Mons.* K.I.A. F. & F. 4.7.17. Buried: Bard Cottage Military Cemetery, Boesinge, Belgium.

KEEFE, William. L/Cpl. 2658 K.I.A. F. & F. 26.4.15. Buried: Calvaire (Essex) Military Cemetery, Ploegsteert, Belgium.
KELLY, James Joseph. Pte. 268324 *1st Mons., 41458 K. Liverpool Reg.* K.I.A. F. & F. 8.10.18. Buried: Sequehart British Cemetery No.1, Sequehart, France.
KENEALY, Thomas. Pte. 2846 K.I.A. F. & F. 5.5.15. Buried: Hop Store Cemetery, Vlamertinge, Belgium.
KENNEDY, Michael Cpl. 285061 *1st Mons.* K.I.A. F. & F. 29.8.17. Buried: Bard Cottage Military Cemetery, Boesinge, Belgium.
KENYON, Harold. Pte. 2490 D.O.W. F. & F. 23.7.16. Buried: Couin British Cemetery, Couin, France.
KILBY, Edward. Cpl. 1452 *39932 12th SWB* D.O.W. F. & F. 14.5.17. Buried: La Chapelette British and Indian Cemetery, Peronne, France.
KILMINSTER, Herbert William. Sgt. 1124 K.I.A. F. & F. 26.5.15. Buried: No Known Grave. Memorial: Menin Gate Memorial to the Missing, Ypres, Belgium.
KING, Albert. 2nd Lieut. *3rd Mons.* K.I.A. F. & F. 31.5.17. Buried: No Known Grave. Memorial: Memorial to the Missing Faubourg D'Amiens Cemetery, Arras, France.
KING, Herbert George. Pte. 1357 Died. F. & F. 7.12.14. Buried: Bailleul Communal Cemetery, Bailleul, France.
KING, William. Pte. 1557 K.I.A. F. & F. 15.1.15. Buried: Calvaire (Essex) Military Cemetery, Ploegsteert, Belgium.
KING, William James. Pte. (Rfn.) 228282 *1st Mons.* K.I.A. F.& F. 11.4.18. Buried: No Known Grave. Memorial: Memorial to the Missing Faubourg D'Amiens Cemetery, Arras, France.
KIRTLAND, Charles. Pte. 3373 K.I.A. F. & F. 1.7.16. Buried: Knightsbridge Cemetery, Beaumont Hamel, France.
KNIPE, George Edward. Sgt. 2561 *265701* K.I.A. F. & F. 28.2.17. Buried: No Known Grave. Memorial: Thiepval Memorial to the Missing, Thiepval, France.
KYNASTON, David. Pte. 285101 *1st Mons.* K.I.A. F. & F. 3.8.17. Buried: Bard Cottage Military Cemetery, Boesinge, Belgium.

LAMPARD, Henry Charles. Pte. 315217 *4th Mons.* K.I.A. F. & F. 12.4.18. Buried: No Known Grave. Memorial: Hyde Park Corner Memorial to the Missing, Ploegsteert, Belgium.
LAMPKIN, William Henry. Pte. 266907 *370737 Labour Corps* D.O.W. F. & F. 30.1.18. Buried: Grevillers British Cemetery, Grevillers, France.
LANE, Wiliam John. Pte. 1380 *265141* K.I.A. F. & F. 27.1.17. Buried: Guards Cemetery, Les Boeufs, France.
LANGLEY, John. Pte. 267658 *3rd Mons.* K.I.A. F. & F. 12.4.18. Buried: No Known Grave. Memorial: Hyde Park Corner Memorial to the Missing, Ploegsteert, Belgium.
LAWLOR, Edward Fred. 2nd Lieut. K.I.A. F. & F. 27.11.16. Buried: A.I.F. Burial Ground, Grass Lane, Flers, France.
LAWSON, Joseph. Pte. 260062 *1st Mons.* K.I.A. F. & F. 10.11.17. Buried: Passchendaele New British Cemetery, Passchendaele, Belgium.
LAWSON, Robert George. Pte. (Rfn.) 227697 *1st Mons.* K.I.A. F. & F. 12.4.18. Buried: No Known Grave. Memorial: Memorial to the Missing Faubourg D'Amiens Cemetery, Arras, France.

LAWTON, Alfred. Pte. 266689 *SWB* K.I.A. F. & F. 3.8.17. Buried: New Irish Farm Cemetery, St. Jan, Belgium.

LEDDINGTON, William George. Pte. 2649 *265743* K.I.A. F. & F. 23.4.17. Buried: No Known Grave. Memorial: Memorial to the Missing Faubourg D'Amiens Cemetery, Arras, France.

LEINTHALL, William. Pte. 267656 *3rd Mons.* K.I.A. F. & F. 18.8.17. Buried: Artillery Wood Cemetery, Boesinge, Belgium.

LESTER, George Thomas. Pte. 46 K.I.A. F. & F. 14.12.14. Buried: Calvaire (Essex) Military Cemetery, Ploegsteert, Belgium.

LEWIS, Frank. Pte. 266198 Died F. & F. 4.3.17. Buried: St. Sever Cemetery Extension, Rouen, France.

LEWIS, Godfrey. Pte. 265649 K.I.A. F. & F. 30.11.17. Buried: No Known Grave. Memorial: Cambrai Memorial to the Missing, Louverval Military Cemetery, Louverval, France.

LEWIS, Herbert. L/Cpl. 2255 K.I.A. F. & F. 3.5.15. Buried: La Brique Military Cemetery No. 2, St. Jan, Belgium.

LEWIS, Jack. Pte. 2437 K.I.A. F. & F. 17.6.15. Buried: Wytschaete Military Cemetery, Wytschaete, Belgium.

LEWIS, John. L/Cpl. 3178 *266030* K.I.A. F. & F. 30.11.17. Buried: No Known Grave. Memorial: Cambrai Memorial to the Missing, Louverval Military Cemetery, Louverval, France.

LEWIS, Joseph. Pte. 267490 K.I.A. F. & F. 1.7.17. Buried: Bard Cottage Military Cemetery, Boesinge, Belgium.

LEWIS, Nathan. Pte. 2515 D.O.W. F. & F. 30.11.15 Buried: Mailly-Maillet Communal Cemetery Extension, Mailly-Maillet, France.

LEWIS, Robert Kenneth. Cpl. 2634 D.O.W. Home. 8.6.15. Buried: Panteg Cemetery, Ponypool, Monmouthshire.

LEYSHON, William. Pte. 2994 D.O.W. F. & F. 13.5.15. Buried: Bailleul Communal Cemetery Extension, Bailleul, France.

LEYSHON, William John. L/Cpl. 1573 D.O.W. F. & F. 30.7.15. Buried: St. Marie Cemetery, Le Havre, France.

LILWALL, Arthur Edward. Pte. 2915 D.O.W. F. & F. 26.6.15. Buried: Etaples Military Cemetery, Etaples, France.

LINDLEY, Herbert. Pte. 3992 K.I.A. F. & F. 23.11.16. Buried: A.I.F. Burial Ground, Grass Lane, Flers, France.

LINNEY, Clifford. Pte. 265150 D.O.W. F. & F. 6.3.17. Buried: St. Sever Cemetery, Rouen, France.

LITTLER, John. Pte. 285104 K.I.A. F. & F. 31.7.17. Buried: No Known Grave. Memorial: Menin Gate Memorial to the Missing, Ypres, Belgium.

LLEWELLYN, William John. Pte. 3816 D.O.W. F. & F. 24.10.16. Buried: Heilly Station Cemetery, Mericourt l'Abbé, France.

LLOYD, Richard. Pte. 267652 *3rd Mons.* K.I.A. F. & F. 14.10.18. Buried: Dadizele New British Cemetery, Dadizele, Belgium.

LLOYD, William. Pte. 3091 K.I.A. F. & F. 11.4.15. Buried: Calvaire (Essex) Military Cemetery, Ploegsteert, Belgium.

LLYWARCH, John. L/Sgt. 1639 D.O.W. F. & F. 9.5.15. Buried: St. Sever Cemetery, Rouen, France.

LONG, Edward. L/Cpl. 2245 K.I.A. F. & F. 18.3.15. Buried: Calvaire (Essex) Military Cemetery, Ploegsteert, Belgium.

LONG, Ernest. Pte. 2405 K.I.A. F. & F. 1.7.16. Buried: No Known Grave. Memorial: Thiepval Memorial to the Missing, Thiepval, France.

LOVELL, Dudley. Pte. 2737 *204796 1st Somerset L.I*. K.I.A. F. & F. 14.4.18. Buried: No Known Grave. Memorial: Hyde Park Corner Memorial to the Missing, Ploegsteert, Belgium.

LOVELL, George. Pte. 1883 K.I.A. F. & F. 13.5.15. Buried: Bailleul Communal Cemetery Extension, Bailleul, France.

LOWE, Albert. Pte. 267495 K.I.A. F. & F. 12.4.18. Buried: No Known Grave. Memorial: Hyde Park Corner Memorial to the Missing, Ploegsteert, Belgium.

MACLAREN, Duncan. Pte. 285109 K.I.A. F. & F. 28.8.17. Buried: No Known Grave. Memorial: Tyne Cot Memorial to the Missing, Passchendaele, Belgium.

MAGNUS, (MAGNESS) Thomas. Pte. 267510 K.I.A. F. & F. 18.8.18. Buried: No Known Grave. Memorial: Hyde Park Corner Memorial to the Missing, Ploegsteert, Belgium.

MARSDEN, Herbert. Pte. 267374 D.O.W. F. & F. 12.4.17. Buried; Duisans British Cemetery, Etrun, France.

MARSH, John. Pte. 41977 *2nd SWB* Died. Germany 27.2.19. Buried: Cologne Southern Cemetery, Germany.

MARTIN, Thomas. Pte. 2962 D.O.W. F. & F. 26.5.15. Buried: No Known Grave. Memorial: Menin Gate Memorial to the Missing, Ypres, Belgium.

MATHER, Horace. Pte. 266182 K.I.A. F. & F. 5.10.17. Buried: Bard Cottage Military Cemetery, Boesinge, Belgium.

MATTHEWS, Edgar Walter. Pte. 265702 K.I.A. F. & F. 12.4.18. Buried: No Known Grave. Memorial: Hyde Park Corner Memorial to the Missing, Ploegsteert, Belgium.

McCARTHY, Edward. Cpl. 2826 Died. F. & F. 24.2.15. Buried: St. Sever Cemetery, Rouen, France.

McLAUGHLIN, Michael Lawrence. Pte. 228796 *1st Mons., 19282 Royal Lancs*. Died F.& F. 16.11.18. Buried: St. Andre Communal Cemetery, St. Andre, France.

MEADMORE, Edward William. Pte. 266688 K.I.A. F. & F. 12.4.18. Buried: No Known Grave. Memorial: Hyde Park Corner Memorial to the Missing, Ploegsteert, Belgium.

MEADMORE, George Morgan. Sgt. 540 K.I.A. F. & F. 8.5.15. Buried: Railway Dugouts Burial Ground (Transport Farm), Zillebeke, Belgium.

MELLOR, Percy. Pte. 291758 *3rd Mons*. D.O.W. F. & F. 21.4.18. Buried: Etaples Military Cemetery, Etaples, France.

MERCER, Albert. Pte. 266365 K.I.A. F. & F. 1.6.17. Buried: Monchy British Cemetery, Monchy-le-Preux, France.

MEREDITH, Daniel. Pte. 265479 K.I.A. F. & F. 10.7.17. Buried: New Irish Farm Military Cemetery, St. Jan, Belgium.

MEREDITH, Thomas George. Pte. 267737 *3rd Mons*. D.O.W. F. & F. 13.6.18. Buried: Pernes British Cemetery, Pernes-en-Artois, France.

MERRY, George. Pte. 1457 K.I.A. F. & F. 26.4.15. Buried: Calvaire (Essex) Military Cemetery, Ploegsteert, Belgium.

MICHAEL, Henry. Pte. 266391 K.I.A. F. & F. 12.4.18. Buried: No Known Grave. Memorial: Hyde Park Corner Memorial to the Missing, Ploegsteert, Belgium.

MIDDLE, Harold Herbert John. Pte. 3411 K.I.A. F. & F. 6.7.16. Buried: No Known Grave. Memorial: Thiepval Memorial to the Missing, Thiepval, France.

MILLER, William. Pte. 4336 *266689 14th Welsh* D.O.W. F. & F. Buried: Mendinghem Military Cemetery, Proven, Belgium.

MILLS, Clifford John. Pte. 265419 K.I.A. F. & F. 12.4.18. Buried: No Known Grave. Memorial: Hyde Park Corner Memorial to the Missing, Ploegsteert, Belgium.

MITCHELL, Edward John. Pte. 267351 K.I.A. F. & F. 12.4.18. Buried: No Known Grave. Memorial: Hyde Park Corner Memorial to the Missing, Ploegsteert, Belgium.

MOGFORD, John. Pte. 2764 K.I.A. F. & F. 8.5.15. Buried: No Known Grave. Memorial: Menin Gate Memorial to the Missing, Ypres, Belgium.

MOONEY, Robert. Pte. 291205 *3rd Mons.* K.I.A. F. & F. 12.4.18. Buried: No Known Grave. Memorial: Hyde Park Corner Memorial to the Missing, Ploegsteert, Belgium.

MOORE, John Maurice. Pte. (Rfn.) 263041 *1st Mons.* K.I.A. F. & F. 11.4.18. Buried: No Known Grave. Memorial: Memorial to the Missing Faubourg D'Amiens Cemetery, Arras, France.

MORGAN, Alfred William. Pte. 266949 235226 *1/4th South Lancs.* D.O.W. F. & F. 15.8.17. Buried: Lijssenthoek Military Cemetery, Poperinge, Belgium.

MORGAN, Charles. Pte. 2708 39337 *5th SWB* K.I.A. F. & F. 12.4.18. Buried: No Known Grave. Memorial: Tyne Cot Memorial to the Missing, Passchendaele, Belgium.

MORGAN, Francis Walter. Pte. 285024 K.I.A. F. & F. 12.4.18. Buried: No Known Grave. Memorial: Hyde Park Corner Memorial to the Missing, Ploegsteert, Belgium.

MORGAN, James Ambrose. Pte. 266772 K.I.A. F. & F. 28.2.17. Buried: Assevillers New British Cemetery, Assevillers, France.

MORGAN, John Lacey. Pte. 267501 K.I.A. F. & F. 12.4.18. Buried: No Known Grave. Memorial: Hyde Park Corner Memorial to the Missing, Ploegsteert, Belgium.

MORGAN, Phillip Ivor. Pte. 290285 *3rd Mons.* Died, Germany 16.11.18. Buried: Niederzwerhen Cemetery, Cassel, Germany.

MORGAN, Stephen. Pte. 2814 D.O.W. F. & F. 4.5.15. Buried: Klien-Vierstraat British Cemetery, Kemmel, Belgium.

MORGAN, Thomas H. Pte. 3136 D.O.W. F. & F. 31.8.16. Buried: Lijssenthoek Military Cemetery, Poperinge, Belgium.

MORGAN, William Henry. Pte. 2494 D.O.W. Home. 13.7.15. Buried: Netley Military Cemetery, Southampton.

MORRIS, Frederick. Pte. 14758 D.O.W. F. & F. 4.4.18. Buried: Nine Elms British Cemetery, Poperinge, Belgium.

MORRIS, Thoros. Pte. 1609 K.I.A. F. & F. 11.7.16. Buried: No Known Grave. Memorial: Thiepval Memorial to the Missing, Thiepval, France.

MORRIS, Thomas Edward. Pte. 15768 K.I.A. F. & F. 16.12.16. Buried: Guards Cemetery, Les Boeufs, France.

MORRIS, Walter David. Pte. 2151 K.I.A. F. & F. 6.7.16. Buried: No Known Grave. Memorial: Thiepval Memorial to the Missing, Thiepval, France.

MORSON, William John. Pte. 266784 K.I.A. F. & F. 12.7.17. Buried: Bard Cottage Military Cemetery, Boesinge, Belgium.

MORT, Henry. Pte. 267378 K.I.A. F. & F. 6.7.17. Buried: Bard Cottage Military Cemetery, Boesinge, Belgium.

MOSELEY, Henry. Pte. 2176 D.O.W. F. & F. 29.11.16. Buried: Grove Town Military Cemetery, Meaulte, France.

MULLARNEY, Ernest. L/Cpl. 1434 K.I.A. F. & F. 25.10.16. Buried: Bancourt Military Cemetery, Bancourt, France.

MURPHY, William. Pte. 769 K.I.A. F. & F. 3.5.15. Buried: No Known Grave. Memorial: Menin Gate Memorial to the Missing, Ypres, Belgium.

MURRAY, Colin. Pte. 266814 K.I.A. F. & F. 12.4.18. Buried: No Known Grave. Memorial: Hyde Park Corner Memorial to the Missing, Ploegsteert, Belgium.

MURRAY, Joseph Daniel. Pte. 1566 K.I.A. F. & F. 15.6.15. Buried: Elsenwalle Brasserie Cemetery, Voormezele, Belgium.

MURRAY, Thomas Henry. Pte. 1959 K.I.A. F. & F. 3.2.15. Buried: Calvaire (Essex) Military Cemetery, Ploegsteert, Belgium.

NEEDS, Walter. Pte. 266232 K.I.A. F. & F. 12.4.18. Buried: No Known Grave. Memorial: Hyde Park Corner Memorial to the Missing, Ploegsteert, Belgium.
NEWMAN, Reginald. Pte. 2386 K.I.A. F. & F. 20.1.15 Buried: Calvaire (Essex) Military Cemetery, Ploegsteert, Belgium.
NEWMAN, William. Pte. 3340 K.I.A. F. & F. 1.7.16. Buried: No Known Grave. Memorial: Thiepval Memorial to the Missing, Thiepval, France.
NICHOLAS, John Samuel. Pte. 2105 K.I.A. F. & F. 13.4.15. Buried: Strand Military Cemetery, Ploegsteert, Belgium.
NICHOLLS, Frank Phillip. Pte. 3275 *266090* K.I.A. F. & F. 12.4.18. Buried: No Known Grave. Memorial: Hyde Park Corner Memorial to the Missing, Ploegsteert, Belgium.
NICHOLLS, William. Pte. 210 K.I.A. F. & F. 15.12.14. Buried: Calvaire (Essex) Military Cemetery, Ploegsteert, Belgium.
NUNNERLY, Arthur. Pte. 3271 *266087* K.I.A. F. & F. 1.7.16. Buried: No Known Grave. Memorial: Thiepval Memorial to the Missing, Thiepval, France.
NURDIN, Alfred Stephen. Pte. 2678 D.O.W. Home. 20.6.15 Buried: Kensal Green (All Souls) Cemetery.

OATES, Dennis. Pte. 285025 D.O.W. Home. 6.11.17. Buried; Bankfoot (St. Matthew) Churchyard.
O'CONNELL, W. Pte. 267296 Died Home 6.7.20. Buried: Greenbank Cemetery, Bristol.
ORMESHER, Alfred. Pte. 266439 K.I.A. F. & F. 11.3.18. Buried: Oxford Road Military Cemetery, Ypres, Belgium.
OSBORNE, John. Pte. 2068 *266647* K.I.A. F. & F. 30.11.17. Buried: No Known Grave. Memorial: Cambrai Memorial to the Missing, Louverval Military Cemetery, Louverval, France.
OWEN, Griffiths John. Pte. (Rfn.) 229407 *1st Mons.* K.I.A. F. & F. 12.4.18. Buried: No Known Grave. Memorial: Memorial to the Missing Faubourg D'Amiens Cemetery, Arras, France.
OWEN, Ifor Evan. Lieut. D.O.W. F. & F. 13.4.18. Buried: Mendinghem British Cemetery, Proven, Belgium.
OWEN, Percy. Pte. 201869 K.I.A. F. & F. 2.12.17. Buried: No Known Grave. Memorial: Cambrai Memorial to the Missing, Louverval Military Cemetery, Louverval, France.

PADFIELD, James. Pte. 15964 *3rd Mons.* K.I.A. F. & F. 28.1.17. Buried: No Known Grave. Memorial: Thiepval Memorial to the Missing, Thiepval, France.
PALFREY, Ernest. Pte. 2341 K.I.A. F. & F. 25.12.14. Buried: Calvaire (Essex) Military Cemetery, Ploegsteert, Belgium.
PARFITT, James Henry. Pte. 2759 K.I.A. F. & F. 8.5.15. Buried: No Known Grave. Memorial: Menin Gate Memorial to the Missing, Ypres, Belgium.
PARKER, John. Pte. 2068 K.I.A. F. & F. 8.5.15. Buried: Perth Cemetery (China Wall), Zillebeke, Belgium.
PARRY, Tom. Pte. 266199 K.I.A. F. & F. 1.7.16. Buried: No Known Grave. Memorial: Thiepval Memorial to the Missing, Thiepval, France.
PARRY, William. Pte. 285113 K.I.A. F. & F. 3.8.17. Buried: No Known Grave. Memorial: Menin Gate Memorial to the Missing, Ypres, Belgium.
PARSONS, George. Cpl. 3143 *266007* K.I.A. F. & F. 8.7.17. Buried: Bard Cottage Military Cemetery, Boesinge, Belgium.
PARSONS, William. Sgt. 2160 D.O.W. F. & F. 13.1.15. Buried: Bailleul Communal Cemetery, Bailleul, France.

PASSANT, C. Pte. 20064 *SWB* Died Home 14.10.14. Buried: Llanfrechfa (All Saints) Churchyard, Monmouthshire.

PATON, John Edward. 2nd Lieut. Killed: 31.12.14. Buried: Calvaire (Essex) Military Cemetery, Ploegsteert, Belgium.

PATTEMORE, Samuel. Pte. 2800 *265815* K.I.A. F. & F. 1.7.16. Buried: No Known Grave. Memorial: Thiepval Memorial to the Missing, Thiepval, France.

PAUL, Albert, Edward. Pte. 266992 K.I.A. F. & F. 22.11.17. Buried: No Known Grave. Memorial: Cambrai Memorial to the Missing, Louverval Military Cemetery, Louverval, France.

PAUL, Richard. Pte. 15605 D.O.W. F. & F. 17.1.17. Buried: Grove Town Military Cemetery, Meaulte, France.

PAYNE, Clifford A. Pte.(Dmr.) 2195 *265509* K.I.A. F. & F. 30.11.17. Buried: Gouzeaucourt New British Cemetery, Cambrai, France.

PAYNE, Howard Wright. Pte. 2155 D.O.W. F. & F. 22.7.16. Buried: Couin British Cemetery, Couin, France.

PAYNE, John, L/Cpl. 1024 K.I.A. F. & F. 25.5.15. Buried: No Known Grave. Memorial: Menin Gate Memorial to the Missing, Ypres, Belgium.

PAYNE, Thomas. L/Cpl. 2453 K.I.A. F. & F. 6.5.15. Buried: No Known Grave. Memorial: Menin Gate Memorial to the Missing, Ypres, Belgium.

PEARCE, Albert. L/Cpl. 2330 K.I.A. F. & F. 8.5.15. Buried: No Known Grave. Memorial: Menin Gate Memorial to the Missing, Ypres, Belgium.

PERCIVAL, Reginald Frank. Lieut. K.I.A. F. & F. 12.4.18. Buried: No Known Grave. Memorial: Hyde Park Corner Memorial to the Missing, Ploegsteert, Belgium.

PERRETT, Francis Sidney. Spr. 3892 *450810 29th Div. Sig. Coy. RE* K.I.A. F. & F. 14.10.18. Buried: Dadizeele New British Cemetery, Dadizeele, Belgium.

PERRY, Albert Edwin. Sgt. 315083 *4th Mons.* K.I.A. F. & F. 12.4.18. Buried: No Known Grave. Memorial: Hyde Park Corner Memorial to the Missing, Ploegsteert, Belgium.

PHILLIPS, Alfred. Pte. 3977 *54658 MGC* K.I.A. F. & F. Buried: No Known Grave. Memorial: Nieuport Memorial to the Missing, Nieuport, Belgium.

PHILLIPS, Eli. Pte. 265828 K.I.A. F. & F. 23.10.17. Buried: Bard Cottage Military Cemetery, Boesinge, Belgium.

PHILLIPS, James Harold. Pte. 267759 *3rd Mons.* D.O.W. F. & F. 14.12.17. Buried: St. Sever Communal Cemetery Extension, Grand Quevilly, Rouen, France.

PHILLIPS, Thomas Herbert. Pte. 228229 *260132 13th Cheshire* K.I.A. F. & F. 10.8.17. Buried: No Known Grave. Memorial: Menin Gate Memorial to the Missing, Ypres, Belgium.

PHILLIPS, Soloman. Pte. 3255 K.I.A. F. & F. 1.7.16. Buried: Auchonvillers Military Cemetery, Auchonvillers, France.

PHILPIN, Joseph. Pte. 2109 Died Home. 28.3.15. Buried: St. Woollos Cemetery, Newport, Monmouthshire.

PHIPPS, William. Pte. 3335 D.O.W. F. & F. 15.1.16. Buried: Mailly-Maillet Communal Cemetery Extension, Mailly-Maillet, France.

PICKFORD, John Henry. Pte. 1310 *267676 3rd Mons.* K.I.A. F. & F. 31.7.17 Buried: Artillery Wood Military Cemetery, Boesinge, Belgium.

PIERCE, Ernest Frederick. Pte. 267800 *3rd Mons.* K.I.A. F. & F. 12.4.18. Buried: No Known Grave. Memorial: Hyde Park Corner Memorial to the Missing, Ploegsteert, Belgium.

PILKINGTON, William. Pte. (Rfn.) 229015 *1st Mons.* K.I.A. F. & F. 12.4.18. Buried: No Known Grave. Memorial: Memorial to the Missing Faubourg D'Amiens Cemetery, Arras, France.

POINER, Charles Thomas. Pte. 1410 K.I.A. F. & F. 4.5.15. Buried: La Brique Military Cemetery No. 2, St. Jan, Belgium.

PORTER, William. Pte. 265967 K.I.A. F. & F. 12.4.18. Buried: No Known Grave. Memorial: Hyde Park Corner Memorial to the Missing, Ploegsteert, Belgium.

POWELL, Charles. Pte. 265974 D.O.W.G.H. 19.7.18. Buried: Berlin South Western Cemetery, Stahnsdorf, Germany.

POWELL, David. Pte. 267687 *3rd Mons.* D.O.W. F. & F. 5.7.17. Buried: Bard Cottage Military Cemetery, Boesinge, Belgium.

POWELL, George. Pte. 267682 *3rd Mons.* K.I.A. F. & F. 30.11.17. Buried: No Known Grave. Memorial: Cambrai Memorial to the Missing, Louverval Military Cemetery, Louverval, France.

POWELL, Robert James MM. Sgt. 3180 *266032* K.I.A. F. & F. 31.7.17. Buried: Artillery Wood Cemetery, Boesinge, Belgium.

PREECE, Albert. Pte. 1656 K.I.A. F. & F. 22.11.16 Buried: Guards Cemetery, Les Beoufs, France.

PREECE, Ernest. Pte. 2771 *265801* K.I.A. F. & F. 26.3.18. Buried: La Brique Military Cemetery, No. 2, St. Jan, Belgium.

PRESTON, Colin. Pte. 266786 K.I.A. F. & F. 3.7.17. Buried: Bard Cottage Military Cemetery, Boesinge, Belgium.

PRICE, Arthur. Pte. 1892. K.I.A. F. & F. 21.10.16. Buried: No Known Grave. Memorial: Thiepval Memorial to the Missing, Thiepval, France.

PRICE, Bert. Edward Claud. Pte. 2252 K.I.A. F. & F. 6.5.15. Buried: No Known Grave. Memorial: Menin Gate Memorial to the Missing, Ypres, Belgium.

PRICE, David. Pte. 1879 *137699 178th Tun. Coy. R.E.* K.I.A. F. & F. 1.6.16. Buried: No Known Grave. Memorial: Thiepval Memorial to the Missing, Thiepval, France.

PRICE, David Richard. Pte. 15610 K.I.A. F. & F. 23.11.16. Buried: A.I.F. Burial Ground, Grass Lane, Flers, France.

PRICE, John Lewis. Pte. 1956 K.I.A. F. & F. 15.1.15. Buried: Calvaire (Essex) Military Cemetery, Ploegsteert, Belgium.

PRITCHARD, John. L/Cpl. 267518 K.I.A. F. & F. 12.4.18. Buried: No Known Grave. Memorial: Hyde Park Corner Memorial to the Missing, Ploegsteert, Belgium.

PROSSER, Ivor George. L/Cpl. 201304 D.O.W. F. & F. 20.4.18. Buried: Etaples Military Cemetery, Etaples, France.

PROSSER, Thomas James. Pte. 267683 *3rd Mons.* K.I.A. F. & F. 30.11.17. Buried: Gouzeaucourt New British Cemetery, Cambrai, France.

PROSSER, William H.J. Sgt. 3006 *265294* D.O.W. F. & F. 26.4.18. Buried: Etaples Military Cemetery, Etaples, France.

PUGH, David. Pte. 266616 K.I.A. F. & F. 12.7.17. Buried: Essex Farm Military Cemetery, Boesinge, Belgium.

PYE, James. Pte. 285123 K.I.A. F. & F. 3.8.17. Buried: No Known Grave. Memorial: Menin Gate Memorial to the Missing, Ypres, Belgium.

RAISTRICK, Sam. Pte. (Rfn) 260069 *1st Mons.* K.I.A. F. & F. 10.11.17. Buried: Passchendaele New British Cemetery, Passchendaele, Belgium.

RALPHS, Thomas. Pte. 285158 K.I.A. F. & F. 2.12.17. Buried: Flesquieres Hill British Cemetery, Flesquieres, France.

REECE, William. Pte. 292219 *3rd Mons.* K.I.A. F. & F. 12.4.18. Buried: No Known Grave. Memorial: Hyde Park Corner Memorial to the Missing, Ploegsteert, Belgium.

REED, Henry William Terrent. 2nd Lieut. K.I.A. F. & F. 2.5.15. Buried: La Brique Military Cemetery No. 2, St. Jan, Belgium.

REES, Henry Charles Stephens. Cpl. 1695 *265264* K.I.A. F. & F. 1.7.16. Buried: Hawthorn Ridge Cemetery No. 1, Auchonvillers, France.

REES, James. Pte. 290862 *3rd Mons.* D.O.W. F. & F. 26.4.18. Buried: Boulogne Eastern Cemetery, Boulogne, France

REES, Richard William. Pte. 130 K.I.A. F. & F. 3.12.14. Buried: Calvaire (Essex) Military Cemetery, Ploegsteert, Belgium.

REES, Robert William. Pte. 267528 D.O.W. F. & F. 11.7.17. Buried: Mendinghem British Cemetery, Proven, Belgium.

REES, Thomas. Pte. 15619 K.I.A. F. & F. 23.10.16. Buried: Bernafay Wood Cemetery, Montauban, France.

RENSHALL, William. Pte. 267022 *235227 1/4th South Lancs.* K.I.A. F. & F. 2.8.17. Buried: No Known Grave. Memorial: Menin Gate Memorial to the Missing, Ypres, Belgium.

REYNOLDS, David John. Pte. 2454 D.O.W. F. & F. 13.5.15. Buried: St. Sever Cemetery, Grand Quevilly, Rouen, France

REYNOLDS, Wilfred. Pte. 3606 *137109 52nd Bat. MGC* K.I.A. F. & F. 16.7.18. Buried: La Targette British Cemetery, Neuville St. Vaast, France.

RICHARDS, Charles. L/Cpl 290729 *3rd Mons.* K.I.A. F. & F. 27.9.17. Buried: Bleuet Farm Cemetery, Elverdinge, Belgium.

RICHARDS, David John. Pte. 15067 *SWB* K.I.A. F. & F. 28.1.17. Buried: No Known Grave. Memorial: Thiepval Memorial to the Missing, Thiepval, France.

RICHARDS, Frank Edgar. Pte. 4936 *7th Royal Fusiliers.* K.I.A. F. & F. 25.8.18. Buried: No Known Grave. Memorial: Vis-en-Artois Memorial to the Missing, Haucourt, France.

RICHARDS, William John. Cpl. 265395 Accidentally Killed F. & F. 22.11.18. Buried: Hal (Halle) Communal Cemetery, Brussels, Belgium.

RIGBY, John. Pte. 291246 *3rd Mons.* K.I.A. F. & F. 6.7.17. Buried: Bard Cottage Military Cemetery, Boesinge, Belgium.

RILEY, Clifford. Pte. (Rfn.) 228874 *1st Mons.* K.I.A. F. & F. 12.4.18. Buried: No Known Grave. Memorial: Memorial to the Missing Faubourg D'Amiens Cemetery, Arras, France.

RIMMER, George. Pte. 291895 *3rd Mons.* K.I.A. F. & F. 6.8.17. Buried: Bleuet Farm Cemetery, Elverdinge, Belgium.

ROBERTS, Alfred. Pte. 3208 *266051* K.I.A. F. & F. 23.4.17. Buried: No Known Grave. Memorial: Memorial to the Missing Faubourg D'Amiens Cemetery, Arras, France.

ROBERTS, Arthur. Pte. 2918 *39182 6th SWB* Died. F. & F. 23.10.18 Buried: Pont-de-Nieppe Communal Cemetery, Nieppe, France.

ROBERTS, Charles Joseph. Pte. 3199 *205137* K.I.A. F & F 16.8.17. Buried: No Known Grave. Memorial: Tyne Cot Memorial to the Missing, Passchendaele, Belgium.

ROBERTS, David Jenkins. Pte. 1585 K.I.A. F. & F. 14.12.14. Buried: Calvaire (Essex) Military Cemetery, Ploegsteert, Belgium.

ROBERTS, Edward. Pte. 267762 K.I.A. F. & F. 26.6.17. Buried: Ferme Olivier Military Cemetery, Elverdinge, Belgium.

ROBERTS, George. Pte. 15946 *3rd Mons.* D.O.W. F. & F. 27.11.16. Buried: Carnoy Military Cemetery, Carnoy, France.

ROBERTS, George Thomas. L/Cpl. 2797 K.I.A. F. & F. 18.3.15. Buried: Calvaire (Essex) Military Cemetery, Ploegsteert, Belgium.

ROBERTS, Hugh Pugh. Pte. 285138 *2/SWB* K.I.A. F. & F 16.8.17. Buried: Artillery Wood Cemetery, Boesinge, Belgium.

ROBERTS, John. Pte. 1891 D.O.W. Home. 25.4.16. Buried: Trevethin (St. Cadoc) Churchyard, Trevethin, Pontypool, Monmouthshire.

ROBERTS, Reginald Charles. Pte. 267529 K.I.A. F. & F. 22.5.18. Buried: La Kreule Military Cemetery, Hazebrouck, France.

ROBERTS, Thomas Herbert. L/Cpl. 1001 *265065* K.I.A. F. & F. 1.7.16. Buried: No Known Grave. Memorial: Thiepval Memorial to the Missing, Thiepval, France.

ROBERTS, William. L/Sgt. 1270 K.I.A. F. & F. 27.11.16. Buried: A.I.F. Burial Ground, Grass Lane, Flers, France.

ROCHE, Leo Francis. Pte. 5034 *T/242431 1st East Kent* K.I.A. F. & F. 21.3.18. Buried: No Known Grave. Memorial: Arras Memorial to the Missing, Faubourg D'Amiens, Arras, France.

RODEN, Stanley John. L/Cpl. 2943 *39366 5th SWB* K.I.A. F. & F. 6.5.17. Buried: Vlamertinge Military Cemetery, Vlamertinge, Belgium.

ROGERS, Jonah. Pte. 1565 K.I.A. F. & F. 8.5.15. Buried: No Known Grave. Memorial: Menin Gate Memorial to the Missing, Ypres, Belgium.

ROGERS, Sidney Thomas. Pte. 265463 K.I.A. F. & F. 12.4.18. Buried: No Known Grave. Memorial: Hyde Park Corner Memorial to the Missing, Ploegsteert, Belgium.

ROSENBAUM, Laurence Braham. Lieut. *3rd Mons.* D.O.W. F. & F. 17.4.18. Buried: Haringhe (Bandeghem) Military Cemetery, Roussebrugge-Haringhe, Belgium.

ROSEVERE, Frank. Pte. (Rfn.) 228374 *1st Mons.* K.I.A. F. & F. 12.4.18. Buried: No Known Grave. Memorial: Memorial to the Missing Faubourg D'Amiens Cemetery, Arras, France.

ROSS, Robert. Pte. (Rfn.) 228912 *1st Mons.* K.I.A. F. & F. 12.4.18. Buried: No Known Grave. Memorial: Memorial to the Missing Faubourg D'Amiens Cemetery, Arras, France.

ROWBERRY, Edwin Charles. Pte. 267530 K.I.A. F. & F. 17.8.18. Buried: Borre British Cemetery, Borre, France.

ROWLAND, Albert. Pte. 1991 K.I.A. F. & F. 22.1.15. Buried: Calvaire (Essex) Military Cemetery, Ploegsteert, Belgium.

ROWLAND, Ivor. Pte. 59839 *94159 17th RWF* K.I.A. F. & F. 29.10.18. Buried: Romeries Communal Cemetery Extension, Romeries, France.

ROWLANDS, Robert. Pte. 290993 *3rd Mons.* K.I.A. F. & F. 30.11.17. Buried: No Known Grave. Memorial: Cambrai Memorial to the Missing, Louverval Military Cemetery, Louverval, France.

ROWLANDS, Thomas. Pte. 267363 K.I.A. F. & F. 12.4.18. Buried: No Known Grave. Memorial: Hyde Park Corner Memorial to the Missing, Ploegsteert, Belgium.

RUCK, Sydney Robert. Sgt. 2681 K.I.A. F. & F. 8.5.18. Buried: No Known Grave. Memorial: Menin Gate Memorial to the Missing, Ypres, Belgium.

RUDDICK, Edgar. Cpl. 2893 *39367 5th SWB* K.I.A. F. & F. 2.8.17. Buried: Voormezeele Enclosure No. 3, Ypres, Belgium.

SAGE, William James. Pte. 1707 *265269* K.I.A. F. & F. 30.11.17. Buried: No Known Grave. Memorial: Cambrai Memorial to the Missing, Louverval Military Cemetery, Louverval, France.

SANKEY, William Manderville MC. Lieut. K.I.A. F. & F. 23.3.18. Buried: Ypres Reservoir Cemetery, Ypres, Belgium.

SAUNDERS, John Henry. Pte. 1163 D.O.W. F. & F. 17.5.15. Buried: Boulogne Eastern Military Cemetery, Boulogne, France.

SAUNDERS, Thomas George. Pte. 2836 D.O.W. Home. 22.7.16. Buried: Trevethin, (St. Cadoc) Churchyard, Trevethin, Pontypool, Monmouthshire.

SAVERY, Reginald. Pte. 3035 Died F. & F. 9.1.16. Buried: Villers-Bocage Communal Cemetery, Villers-Bocage, France.

SAVORY, Herbert Levi. Pte. 267698 *3rd Mons.* K.I.A. F. & F. 14.4.18. Buried: No Known Grave. Memorial: Hyde Park Corner Memorial to the Missing, Ploegsteert, Belgium.

SCANNEL, Percy James. Pte. 267368 K.I.A. F. & F. 26.8.17. Buried: Bleuet Farm Cemetery, Elverdinge, Belgium.

SCHOLES, George. Pte. 266531 K.I.A. F. & F. 3.5.18. Buried: Cinq Rues Military Cemetery, Hazebrouck.

SEABORNE, Joseph. Pte. 62690 1st Mons. *3rd Mons.* Died Home 10.12.18. Buried: Ebbw Vale Cemetery, Ebbw Vale, Monmouthshire.

SEAMER, Albert Victor. Pte. (Rfn.) 226422 *1st Mons.* K.I.A. F. & F. 12.4.18. Buried: No Known Grave. Memorial: Memorial to the Missing Faubourg D'Amiens Cemetery, Arras, France.

SHAW, Harry. Pte. 2130 K.I.A. F. & F. 12.3.15. Buried: Calvaire (Essex) Military Cemetery, Ploegsteert, Belgium.

SHAW, James Arthur Pte. 265860 K.I.A. F. & F. 12.4.18. Buried: No Known Grave. Memorial: Hyde Park Corner Memorial to the Missing, Ploegsteert, Belgium.

SHEA, John Pte. 2216 Died Home 3.10.16. Buried: Llantarnam Cemetery, Newport, Monmouthshire.

SHEEN, Joseph Stephen. Pte. 285078 Died. F. & F. 24.2.17. Buried: Heilly Station Military Cemetery, Mericourt-l'Abbé, France.

SHERRATT, Edwin. Pte. 285027 D.O.W. F. & F. 10.12.17 Buried: Tincourt New British Cemetery, Tincourt, France.

SHERRATT, James Grant. Sgt. 290387 *3rd Mons.* K.I.A. F. & F. 4.2.18. Buried: La Brique Military Cemetery No. 2, St. Jan, Belgium.

SHORE, E. Pte. 267700 K.I.A. F. & F. 7.7.17. Buried: Bard Cottage Military Cemetery, Boesinge, Belgium.

SHORT, Alexander. L/Cpl. 1285 K.I.A. F. & F. 8.5.15. Buried: No Known Grave. Memorial: Menin Gate Memorial to the Missing, Ypres, Belgium.

SIMONS, A. CQMS 265877 Died Home 20.4.21. Buried: Flixton (St. Michael) Churchyard.

SIMS, J. Pte. 265528 Died Home 31.10.18. Buried: Towcester Road Cemetery, Northampton.

SINNIAN, Arthur Wall. Pte. 5998 *T/202415 7th East Kent* Died F. & F. 16.7.18. Buried: Chauny Communal Cemetery British Extension, Aisne, France.

SKILLMAN, Frederick. Cpl. 2270 K.I.A. F. & F. 5.5.15. Buried: No Known Grave. Memorial: Menin Gate Memorial to the Missing, Ypres, Belgium.

SLACK, F. N. Pte. 285058 Died Home 29.10.18. Buried: Rake Lane Cemetery, Wallasey.

SLADE, Charles Henry. Cpl. 152 K.I.A. F. & F. 28.1.15. Buried: Calvaire (Essex) Military Cemetery, Ploegsteert, Belgium.

SMART, Stanley. Sgt. 265594 K.I.A. F. & F. 22.11.17. Buried: No Known Grave. Memorial: Cambrai Memorial to the Missing, Louverval Military Cemetery, Louverval, France.

SMITH, Charles. Pte. 2957 *39378 5th SWB* D.O.W. F. & F. 7.5.17. Buried: Vlamertinge Military Cemetery, Vlamertinge, Belgium.

SMITH, Edwin. Pte. 3296 K.I.A. F. & F. 1.7.16. Buried: No Known Grave. Memorial: Thiepval Memorial to the Missing, Thiepval, France.

SMITH, George. Pte. 3295 K.I.A. F. & F. 1.7.16. Buried: Auchonvillers Military Cemetery, Auchonvillers, France.

SMITH, Henry. Pte. 3256 *266080* K.I.A. F. & F. 12.4.18. Buried: No Known Grave. Memorial: Hyde Park Corner Memorial to the Missing, Ploegsteert, Belgium.

SMITH, James Edward. Pte. 267347 D.O.W. F. & F. 12.4.18. Buried: Ebblinghem Military Cemetery, Ebblinghem, France.

SMITH, John. Pte. (Rfn.) 229002 *1st Mons.* K.I.A. F. & F. 12.4.18. Buried: No Known Grave. Memorial: Memorial to the Missing Faubourg D'Amiens Cemetery, Arras, France.

SMITH, Stephen J. Pte. 3031 K.I.A. F. & F. 8.5.15. Buried: No Known Grave. Memorial: Menin Gate Memorial to the Missing, Ypres, Belgium.

SMITH, Thomas. Pte. 265963 *3068 2/Res.Bat.* Died Home 20.11.18 Buried: Tipton Cemetery, Birmingham, U.K.

SOUTHERN, Richard. Pte. 3032 *267136 8/Lancs. Fusiliers.* K.I.A. F. & F. 30.11.17 Buried: No Known Grave. Memorial: Cambrai Memorial to the Missing, Louverval Military Cemetery, Louverval, France.

SPANSWICK, James. Pte. 2786 *39382 5th SWB* D.O.W. F. & F. 19.5.17. Buried: Lijssenthoek Military Cemetery, Poperinge, Belgium.

SPENCER, Francis Leslie. Lieut. K.I.A. F. & F. 2.12.17. Buried: Flesquieres Hill British Cemetery, Flesquieres, France.

SPILSBURY, Herbert John. Sgt. 290432 *3rd Mons.* K.I.A. F. & F. 2.12.17. Buried: No Known Grave. Memorial: Cambrai Memorial to the Missing, Louverval Military Cemetery, Louverval, France.

STEPHENS, Arthur Edward. Pte. 267536 D.O.W. F. & F. 22.10.17. Buried: Dozinghem Military Cemetery, West Vleteren, Belgium.

STEVENS, George Thomas. Pte. 267803 K.I.A. F. & F. 10.7.17. Buried: Bard Cottage Military Cemetery, Boesinge, Belgium.

STIFF, Charles Wilfred. Pte. 2606 K.I.A. F. & F. 6.5.15. Buried: No Known Grave. Memorial: Menin Gate Memorial to the Missing, Ypres, Belgium.

STONE, William John. Pte. 1632 K.I.A. F. & F. 21.2.15. Buried: Calvaire (Essex) Military Cemetery, Ploegsteert, Belgium.

STOUT, James. Pte. 291910 *3rd Mons.* K.I.A. F. & F. 12.4.18. Buried: No Known Grave. Memorial: Hyde Park Corner Memorial to the Missing, Ploegsteert, Belgium.

STRONG, Thomas. Pte. 1832 *265332* K.I.A. F. & F. 2.12.17. Buried: No Known Grave. Memorial: Cambrai Memorial to the Missing, Louverval Military Cemetery, Louverval, France.

STROUD, William John. Dmr. 1312 D.O.W. F. & F. 9.12.16. Buried: St. Sever Cemetery Extension, Grand Quevilly, Rouen, France.

STURDY, Basil George. L/Sgt. 290093 1074 *3rd Mons.* K.I.A. F. & F. 4.7.17. Buried: Bard Cottage Military Cemetery, Boesinge, Belgium.

STURKEY, Robert. Pte. 285135 *3339 1/7 RWF* K.I.A. F. & F. 16.8.17. Buried: No Known Grave. Memorial: Tyne Cot Memorial to the Missing, Passchendaele, Belgium.

SULLIVAN, Thomas Joseph. Pte. 201855 K.I.A. F. & F. 30.11.17. Buried: No Known Grave. Memorial: Cambrai Memorial to the Missing, Louverval Military Cemetery, Louverval, France.

SYKES, Francis, George. L/Cpl. 2337 K.I.A. F. & F. 21.12.14. Buried: Calvaire (Essex) Military Cemetery, Ploegsteert, Belgium.

SYMONS, Frederick John. Pte. 2896 K.I.A. F. & F. 8.5.15. Buried: No Known Grave. Memorial: Menin Gate Memorial to the Missing, Ypres, Belgium.

TARLING, Thomas John. Pte. 2062 K.I.A. F. & F. 29.12.14. Buried: Calvaire (Essex) Military Cemetery, Ploegsteert, Belgium.

TAUNTON, Clive Warneford. Capt. K.I.A. F. & F. 25.11.16. Buried: Bernafay Wood Cemetery, Montauban, France.

TAYLOR, Arthur. L/Cpl. 3828 *37697 14th Gloucesters.* K.I.A. F. & F. 21.10.17. Buried: No Known Grave. Memorial: Tyne Cot Memorial to the Missing, Passchendaele, Belgium.

TAYLOR, Arthur. Pte. 265909 K.I.A. F. & F. 1.7.17. Buried: Bard Cottage Military Cemetery. Boesinge, Belgium.

TAYLOR, Francis Henry. 2nd Lieut. *3rd Mons.* K.I.A. F. & F. 30.11.17. Buried: Fifteen Ravine British Cemetery, Villers-Plouich, France.

TAYLOR, Frederick George. Pte. 3189 *53864 9th Welsh.* DOW. Home. 10.3.19. Buried: Aberbeeg Cemetery, Monmouthshire.

TAYLOR, Herbert. Pte. 266758 K.I.A. F. & F. 23.10.17. Buried: Bard Cottage Military Cemetery, Boesinge, Belgium.

TAYLOR, John William. Lieut. K.I.A. F. & F. 12.3.15. Buried: Calvaire (Essex) Military Cemetery, Ploegsteert, Belgium.

TAYLOR, Richard John. Pte. 1886 K.I.A. F. & F. 5.5.15. Buried: No Known Grave. Memorial: Menin Gate Memorial to the Missing, Ypres, Belgium.

TEAGUE, Wilfred Thomas Edward. Pte. 1478 K.I.A. F. & F. 3.5.15. Buried: La Brique Military Cemetery No. 2, St. Jan, Belgium.

THOMAS, Charles. Pte. 2941 K.I.A. F. & F. 24.5.15. Buried: No Known Grave. Memorial: Menin Gate Memorial to the Missing, Ypres, Belgium.

THOMAS. D.E. Pte. 18708 Died Home 5.11.18 Buried: Pant Cemetery, Merthyr Tydfil, Glamorgan.

THOMAS, Daniel Henry. L/Cpl. 1876 K.I.A. F. & F. 16.5.15. Buried: No Known Grave. Memorial: Menin Gate Memorial to the Missing, Ypres, Belgium.

THOMAS, Edgar. Pte. 265354 K.I.A. F. & F. 12.4.18. Buried: No Known Grave. Memorial: Hyde Park Corner Memorial to the Missing, Ploegsteert, Belgium.

THOMAS, Edmund. Pte. 2804 K.I.A. F. & F. 8.5.15. Buried: No Known Grave. Memorial: Menin Gate Memorial to the Missing, Ypres, Belgium.

THOMAS, Frederick. Pte. 2946 *39232 6th SWB* K.I.A. F. & F. 22.10.18. Buried: Lijssenthoek Military Cemetery, Poperinge, Belgium.

THOMAS, John. Pte. 202060 K.I.A. F. & F. 12.4.18. Buried: No Known Grave. Memorial: Hyde Park Corner Memorial to the Missing, Ploegsteert, Belgium.

THOMAS, John George. Pte. 2977 K.I.A. F. & F. 2.5.15. Buried: New Irish Farm Military Cemetery, St. Jan, Belgium.

THOMAS, Thomas John. Pte. 1658 D.O.W. F. & F. 4.12.16. Buried; Carnoy Military Cemetery, Carnoy, France.

THOMAS, William Henry. L/Cpl 332 *265030* K.I.A. F. & F. 12.4.18. Buried: No Known Grave. Memorial: Hyde Park Corner Memorial to the Missing, Ploegsteert, Belgium.

THOMPSON, Tom. Pte. (Rfn) 260078 *1st Mons.* K.I.A. F. & F. 10.11.17. Buried: No Known Grave. Memorial: Tyne Cot Memorial to the Missing, Passchendaele, Belgium.

THOMPSON, Walter. Pte. 15817 *3rd Mons.* D.O.W. F. & F. 28.11.16. Buried: Carnoy Military Cemetery, Carnoy, France.

TIBBS, John Henry. Pte. 60121 *94178 16th RWF* D.O.W. F. & F. 5.11.18. Buried: Caudry British Cemetery, Caudry, France.

TINDALL, George. Pte. 3217 K.I.A. F. & F. 30.1.17. Buried: A.I.F. Burial Ground, Grass Lane, Flers, France.

TOLMAN, Albert. Pte. 2968 *39179 6th SWB* K.I.A. F. & F. 15.4.18. Buried: No Known Grave. Memorial: Hyde Park Corner Memorial to the Missing, Ploegsteert, Belgium.

TOTTERDELL, William Charles. Cpl. 266381 K.I.A. F. & F. 12.4.18. Buried: No Known Grave. Memorial: Hyde Park Corner Memorial to the Missing, Ploegsteert, Belgium.

TREW, Reginald MM. L/Sgt. 2013 *265411* K.I.A. F. & F. 2.12.17. Buried: No Known Grave. Memorial: Cambrai Memorial to the Missing, Louverval Military Cemetery, Louverval, France.

TUNLEY, William John. Pte. 3372 D.O.W. F. & F. 1.7.16. Buried: Louvencourt Military Cemetery, Louvencourt, France.

TURNER, Charles Clifford. Pte. 60584 *94311 17th RWF* D.O.W. F. & F. 29.10.18. Buried: Awoignt British Cemetery, Awoignt, France.

TURNER, Isaac. L/Cpl. 1777 K.I.A. F. & F. 6.5.15. Buried: No Known Grave. Memorial: Menin Gate Memorial to the Missing, Ypres, Belgium.

UNDERWOOD, George. L/Cpl. 267349 *4168 South Lancs Reg.* K.I.A. F. & F. 12.4.18. Buried: No Known Grave. Memorial: Hyde Park Corner Memorial to the Missing, Ploegsteert, Belgium.

VAUGHAN, Albert. Pte. 267547 K.I.A. F. & F. 23.4.17. Buried: Vis-en-Artois British Cemetery, Haucourt, France.

VAUGHAN, Samuel. Cpl. 1302 K.I.A. F. & F. 15.1.15. Buried: Calvaire (Essex) Military Cemetery, Ploegsteert, Belgium.

VAUGHAN, Thomas Harold. Pte. 15820 K.I.A. F. & F. 27.11.16. Buried: Guards Cemetery, Les Boeufs, France.

VERNALL, Charles. Pte. 2675 K.I.A. F. & F. 8.5.15. Buried: No Known Grave. Memorial: Menin Gate Memorial to the Missing, Ypres, Belgium.

VERNALL, John. Pte. (Rfn.) 2412 *228011 1st Mons.* K.I.A. F. & F. 3.6.17. Buried: No Known Grave. Memorial: Memorial to the Missing Faubourg D'Amiens Cemetery, Arras, France.

VEYSEY, John Arthur. Pte. 2641 K.I.A. F. & F. 2.2.15. Buried: Strand Military Cemetery, Ploegsteert, Belgium.

VINCE, John. Pte. 2784 *39395 5th SWB* K.I.A. F. & F. 14.11.16. Buried: No Known Grave. Memorial: Thiepval Memorial to the Missing, Thiepval, France.

WALKER, Arthur. Pte. 15845 K.I.A. F. & F. 27.11.16. Buried: Guards Cemetery, Les Boeufs, France.

WALKER, Charles. Pte. (Rfn.) 229561 *1st Mons.* K.I.A. F. & F. 12.4.18. Buried: No Known Grave. Memorial: Memorial to the Missing Faubourg D'Amiens Cemetery, Arras, France.

WALTERS, Henry James. Lieut. K.I.A. F. & F. 5.5.15. Buried: No Known Grave. Memorial: Menin Gate Memorial to the Missing, Ypres, Belgium.

WARBRICK, George Robert. Pte. 268085 *22637 Loyal N. Lancs.* Died. Home. 7.10.17. Buried: Lancaster Cemetery, Lancs.

WARBURTON, W. Pte. 41906 K.I.A. F. & F. 14.10.18. Buried: Dadizele New British Cemetery, Dadizele, Belgium.

WARREN, William Joseph. Pte. 2487 *265661* K.I.A. F. & F. 23.10.17. Buried: Bard Cottage Military Cemetery, Boesinge, Belgium.

WARWICK, Stanley. Pte. (Rfn.) 227663 *1st Mons., King's Own* K.I.A. F. & F. 12.4.18. Buried: No Known Grave. Memorial: Memorial to the Missing Faubourg D'Amiens Cemetery, Arras, France.

WATERS, Ernest Griffith. Pte. 3227 *260357 12th Gloucesters.* D.O.W. F. & F. 7.10.17. Buried: Godewaersvelde British Cemetery, Godewaersvelde, France.

WATKINS, Edward. Pte. 1314 Died Home. 16.5.21. Buried: Blaenavon (St. Peter) Churchyard, Blaenavon, Monmouthshire.

WATKINS, Herbert J. Pte. 2385 K.I.A. F. & F. 3.5.15. Buried: La Brique Military Cemetery No. 2, St. Jan, Belgium.

WATKINS, Illtyd Edwin Maitland. Capt. K.I.A. F. & F. 7.5.15. Buried: No Known Grave. Memorial: Menin Gate Memorial to the Missing, Ypres, Belgium.

WATKINS, Vivian Holmes. Capt. D.O.W. Home. 20.2.15. Buried: Panteg Cemetery, Pontypool, Monmouthshire.

WATSON, Stanley Ivo. Pte. (Rfn.) 260216 *1st Mons.* K.I.A. F. & F. 10.4.18. Buried: No Known Grave. Memorial: Memorial to the Missing Faubourg D'Amiens Cemetery, Arras, France.

WATTS. James Robert. Pte. 2458 K.I.A. F. & F. 12.3.15. Buried: Calvaire (Essex) Military Cemetery, Ploegsteert, Belgium.

WATTS, William. Pte. 2704 K.I.A. F. & F. 30.1.17. Buried: Caterpillar Valley Cemetery, Longueval, France.

WAYGOOD, George. Pte. 265859 D.O.W. F. & F. 10.10.17. Dozinghem Military Cemetery, Westvleteren, Belgium.

WEAVER, Henry Percival. Pte. 266764 K.I.A. F. & F. 6.7.17. Buried: Bard Cottage Military Cemetery, Boesinge, Belgium.

WEBLEY, William Henry. L/Cpl. 266209 D.O.W. F. & F. 29.5.18. Buried: Ebblinghem Military Cemetery, Ebblinghem, France.

WEEKS, Percy. Pte. 266769 K.I.A. F. & F. 23.4.17. Buried: No Known Grave. Memorial: Memorial to the Missing Faubourg D'Amiens Cemetery, Arras, France.

WELSH, William. Pte. 267732 *3rd Mons.* D.O.W. F. & F. 5.4.17. Buried: Hazebrouck Communal Cemetery, Hazebrouck, France.

WEST, John. Sgt. 265780 *12th SWB.* K.I.A. F. & F. 25.11.17. Buried: Anneux British Cemetery, Cambrai, France.

WHATLEY, Charles Edwin. L/Cpl. 1744 D.O.W. F. & F. 16.2.17. Buried: Grove Town Military Cemetery, Meaulte, France.

WHATLEY, Charles. L/Cpl. 265288 K.I.A. F. & F. 16.2.17. Buried: No Known Grave. Memorial: Thiepval Memorial to the Missing, Thiepval, France.

WHATLEY, George. L/Cpl. 1722 D.O.W. F. & F. 11.3.15. Buried: Cité Bonjean Military Cemetery, Armentieres, France.

WHATLEY, Robert. Sgt. 290381 *3rd Mons.* K.I.A. F. & F. 12.4.18. Buried: No Known Grave. Memorial: Hyde Park Corner Memorial to the Missing, Ploegsteert, Belgium.

WHATMOUGH, George William. Pte. 4080 *291960 7th Welsh.* Died. Home. 5.11.18. Buried: Rochdale Cemetery, Lancashire.

WHITCOMBE, William James. Pte. 2365 K.I.A. F. & F. 25.5.15. Buried. No Known Grave. Memorial: Menin Gate Memorial to the Missing, Ypres, Belgium.

WHITE, Benjamin. Pte. 1449 D.O.W. Home. 15.1.16. Buried: Coleford Cemetery, Coleford, Gloucester.

WHITE, Charles. Pte. 267721 *3rd Mons.* Died. F. & F. 17.2.19. Buried: Etaples Military Cemetery, Etaples, France.

WHITE, Gerald. Pte. 266802 *27847 South Lancs Reg.* K.I.A. F. & F. 12.4.18. Buried: No Known Grave. Memorial: Hyde Park Corner Memorial to the Missing, Ploegsteert, Belgium.

WHITE, Thomas. Pte. 288019 D.O.W. F. & F. 20.4.18. Buried: Mont Huon Military Cemetery, Le Treport, France.

WHITLOCK, George. Pte. (Rfn.) 228585 *1st Mons. 12th SWB.* K.I.A. F. & F. 23.11.17. Buried: No Known Grave. Memorial: Cambrai Memorial to the Missing, Louverval, France.

WHITTAKER, Arthur. Pte. 285005 *27919 South Lancs Reg.* K.I.A. F. & F. 12.4.18. Buried: No Known Grave. Memorial: Hyde Park Corner Memorial to the Missing, Ploegsteert, Belgium.

WHITTINGTON, Herbert Henry. Pte. 1567 *265213* K.I.A. F. & F. 12.4.18. Buried: No Known Grave. Memorial: Hyde Park Corner Memorial to the Missing, Ploegsteert, Belgium.

WHITTLE, Charles. Pte. 267720 K.I.A. F. & F. 28.8.17. Buried: Hooge Crater Cemetery, Zillebeke, Belgium.

WILKINSON, James George. Pte. 228898 *1st Mons.* K.I.A. F. & F. 14.10.18. Buried: Dadizele New British Cemetery, Dadizele, Belgium.

WILLEY, George. Pte. 266200 K.I.A. F. & F. 12.4.18. Buried: No Known Grave. Memorial: Hyde Park Corner Memorial to the Missing, Ploegsteert, Belgium.

WILLIAMS, Albert Pte. 1424 D.O.W. F. & F. 7.5.15. Buried: Hazebrouck Communal Cemetery, Hazebrouck, France.

WILLIAMS, Alfred Victor. Pte. 15016 K.I.A. F. & F. 30.1.17. Buried: A.I.F. Burial Ground, Grass Lane, Flers, France.

WILLIAMS, Albert William. Pte. 265068 D.O.W. F. & F. 5.5.17. Buried: Duisans British Cemetery, Etrun, France.

WILLIAMS, Charles. Cpl. 65 K.I.A. F. & F. 17.3.15. Buried: Calvaire (Essex) Military Cemetery, Ploegsteert, Belgium.

WILLIAMS, Charles. L/Cpl. 265117 K.I.A. F. & F. 1.7.16. Buried: No Known Grave. Memorial: Thiepval Memorial to the Missing, Thiepval, France.

WILLIAMS, Charles. Pte. 2563 Died. Home. 6.10.14. Buried: Penygarn Baptist Burial Ground, Pontypool, Monmouthshire.

WILLIAMS, Charles James. Pte. 3141 K.I.A. F. & F. 23.2.17. Buried: Sailly-Saillisel British Cemetery, Sailly-Saillisel, France.

WILLIAMS, Emrys David. Cpl. 267359 *3rd Mons.* K.I.A. F. & F. 12.4.18. Buried: No Known Grave. Memorial: Hyde Park Corner Memorial to the Missing, Ploegsteert, Belgium.

WILLIAMS, Francis E. MM. L/Cpl. 2766 *265799* K.I.A. F. & F. 23.4.17. Buried: Vis-en-Artois British Cemetery, Haucourt, France.

WILLIAMS, Harry. Pte. 147 *252880 28th Durham L.I.* Died Home. 11.7.18. Buried: Colchester Cemetery, Essex.

WILLIAMS, Harry. Pte. 1615 K.I.A. F. & F. 8.5.15. Buried: No Known Grave. Memorial: Menin Gate Memorial to the Missing, Ypres, Belgium.

WILLIAMS, Harry W. Pte. 267719 *3rd Mons.* K.I.A. F. & F. 22.10.17. Buried: Bard Cottage Military Cemetery, Boesinge, Belgium.

WILLIAMS, Herbert. Pte. 267718 K.I.A. F. & F. 30.11.17. Buried: No Known Grave. Memorial: Cambrai Memorial to the Missing, Louverval Military Cemetery, Louverval, France.

WILLIAMS, John Frederick. Pte. 291107 *3rd Mons.* K.I.A. F. & F. 12.4.18. Buried: No Known Grave. Memorial: Hyde Park Corner Memorial to the Missing, Ploegsteert, Belgium.

WILLIAMS, John Rowland. Lieut. *MGC.* K.I.A. F. & F. 27.9.17. Buried: No Known Grave. Memorial: Tyne Cot Memorial to the Missing, Passchendaele, Belgium.

WILLIAMS, Llewellyn, Pte. 267568 D.O.W. F. & F. 2.6.17. Buried: Faubourg D'Amiens Cemetery, Arras, France.

WILLIAMS, Price. Pte. 2869 *37687 12th Gloucesters.* K.I.A. F. & F. 25.8.18. Buried: Queens Cemetery, Bucquoy, France.

WILLIAMS, Ralph. Pte. 2839 *265830* D.O.W. F. & F. 1.3.17. Buried: Grove Town Military Cemetery, Meaulte, France.

WILLIAMS, Reuben. Pte. 267557 D.O.W. F. & F. 29.6.17. Buried: Lijessenthoek Military Cemetery, Poperinge, Belgium.

WILLIAMS, Richard. Pte. 267768 K.I.A. F. & F. 2.12.17. Buried: No Known Grave. Memorial: Cambrai Memorial to the Missing, Louverval Military Cemetery, Louverval, France.

WILLIAMS, Samuel. Pte. 1362 K.I.A. F. & F. 5.5.15. Buried: No Known Grave. Memorial: Menin Gate Memorial to the Missing, Ypres, Belgium.

WILLIAMS, Thomas Henry. Pte. 227690 *1st Mons.* K.I.A. F. & F. 31.7.17. Buried: Artillery Wood Military Cemetery, Boesinge, Belgium.

WILLIAMS, Thomas John. Sgt. 3133 *325155 2/7th Royal Warwicks* K.I.A. F. & F. 24.10.18. Buried: Canonne Farm British Cemetery, Sommaing, France.

WILLIAMS, William John. Lieut. D.O.W. F. & F. 12.5.15. Buried: Boulogne Eastern Military Cemetery, Boulogne, France.

WILSON, Charles Robert MM. Pte. 267569 D.O.W. F. & F. 23.10.17. Buried: Dozinghem Military Cemetery, Westvleteren, Belgium.

WILTSHIRE, Edwin. Pte. 290705 *3rd Mons.* K.I.A. F. & F. 12.4.18. Buried: No Known Grave. Memorial: Hyde Park Corner Memorial to the Missing, Ploegsteert, Belgium.

WINSTONE, Edwin. L/Cpl. 1340 *227733 1st Mons.* D.O.W. Home. 28.2.19. Buried: St. Devereux (St. Dubricius) Churchyard.

WINWOOD, Henry Vaughan. Pte. 1200 K.I.A. F. & F. 21.12.14. Buried: Calvaire (Essex) Military Cemetery, Ploegsteert, Belgium.

WITCOMBE, Wlliam James. Pte. 2365 K.I.A. F. & F. 25.5.15. Buried: No Known Grave. Memorial: Menin Gate Memorial to the Missing, Ypres, Belgium.

WITHERS, James. Pte. 266411 K.I.A. F. & F. 12.4.18. Buried: No Known Grave. Memorial: Hyde Park Corner Memorial to the Missing, Ploegsteert, Belgium.

WOODFIELD, George. L/Cpl. 555 K.I.A. F. & F. 5.5.15. Buried: No Known Grave. Memorial: Menin Gate Memorial to the Missing, Ypres, Belgium.

WOODS, Harry. Pte. 796 K.I.A. F. & F. 23.12.14. Buried: Calvaire (Essex) Military Cemetery, Ploegsteert, Belgium.

WOODS, William John. Pte. 2828 K.I.A. F. & F. 24.5.15. Buried: No Known Grave. Memorial: Menin Gate Memorial to the Missing, Ypres, Belgium.

WOODWARD, Herbert. Pte. 78 *39257 6th SWB* K.I.A. F. & F. 13.2.17. Buried: Berkshire Cemetery Extension, Ploegsteert, Belgium.

WYATT, Harold Cray. Pte. 1544 *265200* D.O.W. F. & F. 22.10.17. Buried: Dozinghem Military Cemetery, Westvleteren, Belgium.

YARWORTH, Ralph. Cpl. 1543 K.I.A. F. & F. 1.7.16. Buried: No Known Grave. Memorial: Thiepval Memorial to the Missing, Thiepval, France.

YATES, Fred. Pte. 316440 *4th Mons.* Died F. & F. 12.11.18. Buried: St. Sever Cemetery Extension, Grand Quevilly, Rouen, France.

YOUNG, Edwin. Pte. 41962 D.O.W. F. & F. 14.10.18. Buried: Dadizele New British Cemetery, Dadizele, Belgium.

YOUNG, Gethin. Pte. 285069 K.I.A. F. & F. 30.11.17. Buried: No Known Grave. Memorial: Cambrai Memorial to the Missing, Louverval Military Cemetery, Louverval, France.

Appendix 2

Nominal Rolls

The following list of officers are all those officers who are known to have served with the 2nd Battalion of the Monmouthshire Regiment at some time during the Great War. Some of the officers served with other units during the period and where this is known the unit is shown in italics at the end of the entry. The rank shown is the highest rank attained by that officer whilst serving with the Regiment - many received promotion whilst with adopted units. The officers shown in bold type were killed or died as a result of their service and details of their burial or memorial will be found in the Roll of Honour (Appendix 1).

Lieutenant	Frederick Harold Allan *(3rd Mons.)*
2nd Lieut.	Walter Hedley Arthur *(1st Mons.)*
Captain QM	Samuel Henry Askew MC
Major	Horace William Elliott Bailey *(3rd Mons.)*
Lieutenant	Charles Percy Ballinger
Captain	Clare Banks *(1st Mons.)*
Lieutenant	Walter Searl Bartlett
Captain	George James Henry Beard
Lieutenant	Max Louis Beveridge *(MGC)*
Lieutenant	Cuthbert Edwin Birkett MC *(3rd Mons. & MGC)*
Lieutenant	Eric Gazzard Boucher
Lieutenant	Frederick Ivor Boucher
Captain	A.W. Bowen *(Labour Corps.)*
Lieut. Col.	**Alfred John Hamilton Bowen DSO & Bar**
Lieutenant	George Walter Bowler

Lieutenant	William Colwell Braddeley
Major	James G. Broackes
Lieutenant	Joseph Alfred Burgoyne *(Labour Corps.)*
Lieutenant	Charles Ernest Burton
Lieutenant	James Henry Bury
Captain	Hubert Oswald Butler
Captain	Evelyn Hook Byrde
Lieutenant	William Thomas Charles *(Major, 3rd Mons., 1942)*
Lieutenant	Donald George Cockrill
2nd Lieut.	**Walter Collings MC *(3rd Mons & 12th KOYLI)***
Captain	Ernest Ivor Streatham Colquhoun *(3rd Mons.)*
Captain	Christopher Comely MC
Captain	Richard Basil Comely MC & Bar
Lieutenant	Arthur Victor Cook
Lieutenant	William Reginald Doune Cooper *(1st Mons. and Welsh Reg.)*
Captain	A.L. Coppock *(3rd Welsh)*
Captain	Russel Coppock
Captain	Charles W.H. Cox *(MGC)*
Captain	Frank Spencer Crawford *(3rd Mons., 18th Middsx.)*
Lieutenant	Charles John Crawley MC *(MGC)*
2nd Lieut.	**Raymond Alfred Cruickshank *(3rd Mons.)***
Lieut. Col.	E. B. Cuthbertson MVO CMG
Major	Claud Edward Dansey KCMG
Lieutenant	Leonard V. Dart
2nd. Lieut.	**Ellerton Osborne Davies**
Captain	Geoffrey Hier Davies
2nd Lieut.	Horatio Glyn Davies
Lieutenant	Hubert Benron Davies MC
Lieutenant	Robert Stanley Davies
Lieutenant	Franklyn Noel Dayson
Lieutenant	John Bartram Deakin
Lieutenant	Gilbert Bennett Doré *(Indian Army)*
Lieutenant	Frederick Stanley Duck *(3rd Mons.)*
Lieutenant	Charles Percy Hogee Duncan
Lieutenant	John Edward Dunn
Lieutenant	Arthur Reginald Brayben Dunstan *(1st Mons., 6th KSLI)*
Major	Arthur H. Edwards MC
Captain	**Edward Edwards**
Captain	Noel Chamberlain Elstob BA
Lieutenant	David Morton Wayne Evans *(1st Mons.)*
Lieut. Col.	John Evans DSO TD
2nd Lieut.	Kenneth Parry Owen Evans *(Brecknocks, RAF)*
Lieutenant	John Victor Finn *(MGC, 4th SWB)*
Lieutenant	Leslie Ewart Ford
Captain	Ernest George Foster *(3rd Mons.)*
Lieutenant	George Edward Foster *(3rd Mons.)*
Lieutenant	John Fownes

Lieutenant	**Alexander Evan Fraser**
Lieutenant	**James Herbert Fraser** *(MGC)*
Captain	Walter Fryers *(5th Lanc. Fus.)*
Lieutenant	Cyril Leicester Gabell *(Hereford Volunteer Battalion)*
Lieutenant	John Trevor George MC
2nd Lieut.	Douglas Gilbert
Lieutenant	Alan Gledhill
Major	D.W. Graham
Lieutenant	Theophilus Gough
Lieutenant	Frederick William Gower *(3rd Mons.)*
Lieutenant	Leslie Lovell Green *(Cheshire Reg.)*
2nd Lieut.	Percy Arnold Green *(Indian Army)*
Lieutenant	George Wilfred Greenland *(MGC Heavy Branch)*
Lieutenant	Alfred William Gulliver *(1st Mons.)*
2nd Lieut.	Ernest Victor Haggis *(3rd Mons.)*
Lieutenant	Stanley John Harris
Major	George F. Hibbert
2nd Lieut.	**Cyril Anthony Hudson Hillier**
Major	R.A. Hobbs OBE
Captain	Percy Holland Hockaday *(Indian Army)*
Captain	**Sidney Reginald Hockaday**
Lieutenant	Arnold Reginald Hopkins *(1st Mons.)*
Lieutenant	Henry John Hopkins MC *(Brecknocks & 3rd Mons.)*
Lieutenant	Morgan Thomas Howells *(3rd Mons.)*
Lieutenant	W.D. Howick MC
Lieutenant	Hugh Llewellyn Hughes MBE
2nd Lieut.	Edgar Victor Hunt *(Labour Corps.)*
Major	Thomas Edward Ibbs MC & Bar
Captain	Cyril Prendegast Ingram *(1st Mons.)*
Major	John R. Jacob *(3rd Mons.)*
2nd Lieut.	W.N. James
Major	E.D.T. Jenkins
Captain	Edward George Jenkins
Lieut. Col.	John Charles Jenkins TD
Captain	Edward Jenkin John
Lieutenant	Charles Henry Johnson
2nd Lieut.	Archibald Basil Jones *(MGC)*
Lieutenant	Clifford Glanddu Jones *(3rd Mons.)*
2nd Lieut.	E.R. Jones *(SWB)*
2nd Lieut.	**Frederick Thomas Avery Jones** *(3/1st Herefords)*
Lieutenant	Stanley Victor Jones *(1st Mons.)*
Lieutenant	Norman Lucius Kelly *(1st Mons.)*
Lieutenant	Henry Vernon Kerr
Lieutenant	Alan Frederick Kimpton
2nd Lieut.	**Albert King** *(3rd Mons.)*

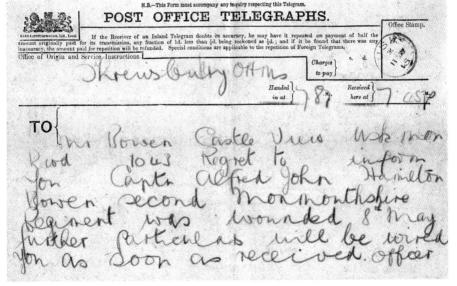

Telegram notifying Capt. Bowen's family of his wounds.   (Photo: SWB Museum)

The War of 1914-1918.

Monmouthshire Regiment [T.F.]
Capt. [T/Maj.] A. J. H. Bowen, D.S.O.

was mentioned in a Despatch from

Field Marshal Sir John D.P. French, G.C.B. O.M. G.C.V.O. K.C.M.G.

dated 30th November 1915

for gallant and distinguished services in the Field.

I have it in command from the King to record His Majesty's

high appreciation of the services rendered.

Winston Churchill

Secretary of State for War.

War Office,
Whitehall.S.W.
1st March 1919.

The first of three Mention in
Despatches certificates awarded
to Capt. (Lieut.Col.) Bowen.
(Photo: SWB Museum)

Replacements from the 3/2nd Battalion on Abergavenny station in September, 1915.

(Photo: SWB Museum)

Pte. David Gibbon of Aberavon joined up in January 1916 and served with the 2nd Monmouths in Flanders throughout the Battle of Passchendaele in 1917. He finished the war as a sergeant in the 25th KRRC. (Photo: Gareth Scourfield)

Officers in May, 1917. Back row: Lieut. Porter and Major C. Comely. Middle: Lieut. Col. J. Evans. Front: Capt. T.E. Ibbs and Lieut. P. Leighton RAMC. (Photo: SWB Museum)

This photograph is clearly signed by Major C. Comely and dated 28th May, 1917. (Photo: SWB Museum)

Lieut. P. Leighton Medical Officer to the battalion. The photograph was taken at the same time as the one above.

(Photo: SWB Museum)

Some of the officers in 1917 from the left: Lieut. H.V. Kerr, Lieut. W.C. Braddeley, Major A.H. Edwards, Lieut. Col. J. Evans, Capt. T.E. Ibbs, Lieut. W.M. Porter.

(Photo: SWB Museum)

Back row from left: Lieut. A.L.T. Robertson (machine gun officer), Lieut. R.T. Saunders (asst. Adj.), Lieut. H.V. Kerr (asst. Transport officer), Lieut. W.C. Braddeley (Transport officer), Capt. Steward (MO), Lieut. P.J. Hopkins (Signal officer), Lieut. C.W. Tacon (Bombing officer). Front row: Lieut. & QM W.M. Porter, Major A.H. Edwards, Lieut. Col. J. Evans, Capt. T.E. Ibbs (Adj.), Rev. G.C. Andrews, Chaplain. (Photo: Ian Griffiths)

No. 12 Platoon C Company in 1917.

(Photo: Ian Griffiths)

2nd Lieut.	**Edward Frederick Lawlor**
Lieutenant	John Jenkin Lewis
Lieutenant	Thomas Lister
2nd Lieut.	David Howard Lloyd

Captain	John Evan Temple Mathias
2nd Lieut.	William Gladstone McPherson
Lieutenant	Arthur Middenway *(Cheshire Reg.)*
Captain	Hanmer James Miers DSO *(Att. East Lancs.)*
Lieutenant	Leslie Alfred Mitchell TD
2nd Lieut.	David Walter Morgan
Lieutenant	Kevin Ivor Isaac Watkin Morgan
Lieutenant	Stanley Adin Morgan
Lieutenant	David Morris *(1st Mons.)*

Lieutenant	Harold Thomas Nelmes MC
Captain	Frank Leslie Newland
Captain	Albert Gordon Newman *(20th KRRC)*
Lieutenant	Reuben George Noble *(3rd Mons.)*
Captain	Henry Milward North
Lieutenant	Reginald Mathias Nott *(3rd Mons.)*

2nd Lieut.	James Oldham *(1st Mons.)*
Lieutenant	Douglas Alfred Onions
Lieutenant	**Ifor Evan Owen**

Lieutenant	Charles Elliot Fowlds Parker
2nd Lieut.	**John Edward Paton**
Major	Percy George Pennymore DSO
Captain	**Reginald Frank Percival**
Captain	Maurice George Perkins
Lieutenant	John Trevelyan Phillips *(Lieut.Col. 1.11.37. 3rd Mons.)*
Lieut. QM	Walter Morgan Porter MC *(1st Mons., 3rd Mons.)*
Captain	Arthur Lingham Hiscocks Power
Lieutenant	Augustus Herbert Welby Pugin

2nd Lieut.	**Henry William Terrent Reed**
Lieutenant	John E. Roberts *(1st Mons.)*
Lieutenant	Percival Alfred Roberts *(1st Mons.)*
Captain	Ashley Leicester Theodore Robertson
Captain	Stanley Percy Ashby Rolls DSO MC *(Dorset Reg.)*
Lieutenant	**Laurence Braham Rosenbaum *(3rd Mons)***
Major	Herbert Llewellin Rosser
Lieutenant	Robert Rutherford *(1st Mons.)*
Lieutenant	John Ruthven

Captain QM	Alfred Sale TD
Captain	Alfred Coirtney Sale *(Border Reg., 1st SWB)*
Lieutenant	**William Manderville Sankey MC**
Capt. Adj.	Rees Thomas Saunders

Lieutenant	James Horace Seccombe *(3rd Mons.)*
Lieutenant	Ernest Shimmin *(3rd Mons.)*
Lieutenant	John David Simpson *(9th Staffordshire Reg.)*
Lieutenant	Maurice Edwin Simpson *(Lieut. Col. 6.10.46)*
2nd Lieut.	Donald Frank Smith *(1st Mons., Indian Army)*
Lieutenant	Percy Archibald Martin Smith *(1st Mons.)*
Lieutenant	Charles Alexander Souper *(1st Mons.)*
Lieutenant	**Francis Leslie Spencer**
Captain	Richard Bassett Spencer *(3rd Mons.)*
Lieutenant	Cyril North Stafford *(3rd Mons., 12th KOYLI)*
Lieutenant	Tom Worton Stevens
Lieutenant	Frederick Charles Strong
Lieutenant	Charles Woodward Tacon
Captain	**Clive Warneford Taunton**
2nd Lieut.	**Francis Henry Taylor *(3rd Mons.)***
Lieutenant	**Frank Harding Taylor**
Lieutenant	John William Taylor
Captain	John George Thomas
Lieutenant	Cyril Kerridge Todd *(3rd Mons.)*
Captain	Maurice Finnemore Turner MC
Lieutenant	George Endell Tyler
Captain	Hugh Griffin Tyler *(3rd Mons.)*
Major	I.C. Vincent
Captain	John Evelyn Alexander Waddington
Lieutenant	Henry James Walters
Lieutenant	John Wightman Walters
Major	James Ward
Captain	Hubert Holmes Watkins
Captain	**Illtyd Edwin Maitland Watkins**
Lieutenant	Richard Henry Watkins *(1st Mons.)*
Lieutenant	Thomas Philips Watkins *(1st Mons.)*
Captain	**Vivian Holmes Watkins**
Captain	Leonard Digby Whitehead *(3rd Mons.)*
Lieutenant	Francis Henry Wigmore *(3rd Mons.)*
Lieutenant	Arthur Francis Williams
Captain	Benjamin Arthur Williams
2nd Lieut.	Bryn Davies Williams
Lieutenant	Frank Smith Williams
2nd Lieut.	Henry Howard Williams *(3rd Mons.)*
Lieutenant	John Henry Williams
2nd Lieut.	**John Rowland Williams *(MGC)***
Lieutenant	Leonard Langdon Williams *(London Reg.)*
Lieutenant	Robert Beresford Williams *(1st Mons.)*
Lieutenant	Thomas Edward Roper Williams
2nd Lieut.	**William John Williams**
Lieutenant	Walter Stutivillie Wilson *(1st Mons.)*

EMBARKATION ROLL

The following roll has been compiled from a number of sources. The Roll of Officers is largely the result of the information contained in the book by Brett but has been supplemented by the use of data from the South Wales Borderers and Monmouthshire Regiment Museum. The roll of other ranks is a synopsis of the data from the 1914 Star Roll held at the Public Records Office and is supplemented by such details as can be gleaned by study of the casualty lists of the early months of the War. The rolls contain 30 officers and over 920 men and, therefore, represents a substantial number of those soldiers who landed in France with the Battalion in November 1914. In the rolls the asterisk (*) indicates a soldier who died during his service, 'w' indicates a soldier who was known to have been wounded; 'p' indicates a soldier who was made a prisoner of war. The ranks shown are those that applied at the time of arrival in France.

ROLL OF OFFICERS

Cuthbertson	E.B.	Lieut. Col.	w
Dansey	Claud Edward	Major	
Rolls	Stanley Percy Ashby	Capt. & Adjutant	
Hobbs	R.A.	Captain	w
Edwards	Arthur H.	Captain	
Watkins	Vivian Holmes	Captain	*
Bowen	Alfred John H.	Captain	*
Ward	James	Captain	
Pennymore	Percy George.	Captain	
John	Edward Jenkin	Captain	
Miers	Hanmer James	Captain	
Watkins	Illtyd Edwin M.	Captain	*
Taylor	John William	Lieutenant	*
Walters	Henry James	Lieutenant	*
Hockaday	Percy Holland	Lieutenant	w
Dart	Leonard V.	Lieutenant	
Sale	Alfred Courtney	Lieutenant	
Power	Arthur L.H.	Lieutenant	
Fraser	Alexander E.	Lieutenant	*
Mason	G.W.	Lieutenant M.O.	
Williams	Benjamin Arthur	2nd Lieut.	
Hockaday	Sydney Reginald	2nd Lieut.	*
Comely	Christopher	2nd Lieut.	w
Comely	Richard Basil	2nd Lieut.	
Taunton	Clive Warneford	2nd Lieut.	*
George	John Trevor	2nd Lieut.	w

207

Newland	Frank Leslie	2nd Lieut.	
Perkins	Maurice George	2nd Lieut.	
Hillier	Cyril A.H.	2nd Lieut.	*
Paton	John Edward	2nd Lieut.	*

ROLL OF OTHER RANKS

1563	Absalom, A.	Pte.	
2099	Adams, F.	Pte.	w
1237	Adams, G.	Cpl.	
2210	Adams, W.H.	Pte.	
2219	Adams, W.H.	Pte.	
1583	Allcock, G.	Pte.	
1978	Allen, H.	Pte.	
120	Allsopp, W.J.	Col. Sgt.	*
1939	Andrews, W.	Pte.	
655	Anslow, G.	Pte.	
2156	Archer, P.	Pte.	*
1182	Arthur, W.	L/Cpl.	
2383	Ashman, J.	Pte.	w
1646	Atkins, A.	Pte.	
2696	Atkins, J.	Pte.	*
2161	Attwood, J.	Pte.	
2196	Baker, A.G.H.	Pte.	w
2123	Baldwin, M.	Pte.	Commission
2082	Ballinger, H.C.	Pte.	
1677	Balmer, I.	Pte.	
2476	Balsom, F.	Pte.	*
1556	Banks, S.	L/Cpl.	
2021	Barnes, G.C.	Pte.	
685	Barnes, W.	Pte.	
1219	Bartrum, J.	L/Cpl.	
1722	Bartz, D.	L/Cpl.	
2088	Batt, J.H.	Pte.	
1918	Baxter, T.	Pte.	
1827	Beal, C	Pte.	
2243	Benson, E.	Pte.	
1755	Berrows, E.	Pte.	
1872	Berry, F.	Pte.	w
2040	Bethel, S.E.	Pte.	
1702	Bevan, C.	Sgt. Dmr.	
1156	Bevan, W.L.	Pte.	
1476	Birch, S.	Pte.	
1931	Birchley, G.R.	Pte.	
1288	Birkin, A.	L/Cpl.	*
1218	Birkin, F.	Pte.	w
1308	Birkin, M.E.	Boy.	w, p

2212	Birkley, N.	Pte.		
2120	Birt, H.C.	Pte.	*	
1212	Bishop, T.G.	Pte.		
1555	Black, J.	Pte.		
2262	Bladen, J.	Pte.		
1414	Blake, E.	Sgt.		
1905	Blewitt, F.	Pte.	*	
2103	Blockley, A.W.	Pte.		
2116	Blower, F.	Pte.		
2116	Blows, F.	Pte.		
1638	Blunt, T.E.	Pte.		
1366	Bolt, E.H.	Pte.		
2020	Booth, W.J.	L/Cpl.	*	
2499	Bosley, A.	Pte.		
1805	Bowen, G.	Pte.	w	
1817	Bowen, T.	Pte.	*	
1782	Bowen, W.	Pte.		
911	Bowen, W.J.	O.R.Sgt.		
2462	Brace, B.	Pte.	p	
1913	Bradford, A.	Pte.	*	
1898	Bradley, A.	Pte.		
1985	Breeze, J.	Pte.		
1571	Brickley, J.	L/Cpl.		
1284	Bridges, G.	Pte.		
2146	Bridges, T.N.	Pte.		
2205	Bridle, P.W.	Pte.	*	
1814	Brimble, H.	Pte.	*	
1923	Britton, E.J.	Pte.		
2627	Brooks,N.	Pte.		
1453	Brown, F.A.	Sgt.	w	Commission
1916	Brown, L.	Pte.		
2315	Brown, L.	Pte.		
2223	Brown, R.	L/Cpl.		
1596	Buck, E.	Pte.		
2202	Bullimore, A.	Pte.		
1501	Burdge, I.L.	Pte.		
1620	Burge, E.	Pte.	w	
2287	Burgoyne, J.A.	L/Cpl.		Commission
1145	Burke, A.	Pte.	w	
696	Burnett, G.	Pte.		
2604	Burnett, G.	Pte.		
2507	Burns, M.	Pte.	w	
1981	Burns, S.	Pte.	*	
1807	Burr, F.	Pte.		
2240	Burr, J.	Pte.		
1808	Burr, W.	Pte.		
1812	Burton, F.	Pte.		
84	Butcher, C.	Sgt.		
1936	Butcher, J.	Pte.	*	

2344	Butcher, T.J.	Pte.	*
2047	Butcher, W.T.	Pte.	
2041	Butler, V.	Pte.	*
1244	Caddick, W.	L/Cpl.	
2241	Caffrey, R.	Pte.	
1358	Caines, F.	Pte.	*
1540	Cannon, J.	Sgt.	
2217	Cantle, R.G.	Pte.	
1396	Carey, W.	Pte.	*
2273	Carless, J.	Pte.	
1928	Carter, H.A.	Pte.	
1659	Catley, M.	Pte.	
526	Cavill, J.H.	L/Cpl.	
1877	Cawsey, W.H.	Pte.	*
2242	Chadwick, F	Pte.	
658	Challinger, W.H.	L/Cpl.	
2725	Challinger, W.H.	Pte.	
2014	Chick, W.H.	Pte.	
1687	Clansey, M.	Pte.	*
499	Clark, A.R.	Cpl.	*
1278	Clark, B.	Pte.	
1741	Clark, G.F.	Sgt.	
1349	Clark, J.	L/Cpl.	
2310	Clark, J.	Pte.	
2575	Clark, J.R.	Pte.	
2029	Clark, S.	Pte.	
2269	Clark, T.H.	Pte.	
2598	Clarke, A.J.	Cpl.	
1437	Clarke, C.E.	Pte.	
1671	Clarke, O.	L/Cpl.	
2597	Clarke, W	Cpl.	*
23	Cleaves, J.	Pte.	
24	Cleaves, J.	Pte.	
1750	Clinton, S.J.	Pte.	
1948	Clothier, T.	L/Cpl.	
765	Clothier, W.J.	Pte.	
2295	Cole, R.H.	Pte.	*
528	Collins, F.	Sgt.	*
1649	Constant, J.B.	Sgt.	
1318	Cook, G.W.	Pte.	*
1971	Cook, S.	Pte.	
1636	Coombes, E.	Cpl.	
1935	Coombes, W.	Pte.	
1834	Cooper, S.	Pte.	
2054	Cooper, W.	Pte.	
1924	Cooper, W.J.	Pte.	*
324	Cornock, J.	L/Sgt.	
1768	Cotterill, A.	Pte.	

1767	Cotterill, L.	L/Cpl.	
1819	Cotterill, J.	Pte.	
1800	Cotterill, S.	Pte.	
1343	Cornish, R.	Pte.	
1733	Cosgrove, W.	L/Cpl.	
1733	Counsell, W.	Pte.	
2843	Cousins, F.	Pte.	w
2173	Cox,A.E.	Pte.	
1551	Cox, G.	Pte.	w
2279	Cox, J.	Pte.	
2266	Cox, S.	Pte.	*
1925	Crabb, W.	Pte.	
2353	Crane, L.	Pte.	
1691	Crawford, A.	Pte.	
2699	Crees, T	L/Cpl.	w
302	Crew, T.	Pte.	
329	Crockett, T.J.	L/Cpl.	
134	Cross, A.J.	L/Cpl.	
1806	Cross, A.J.	Pte.	
135	Cross, H.	Sgt.	w
302	Crow, T.	Pte.	
1684	Crowley, W.	Pte.	*
1946	Cudby, J.	Cpl.	*
2125	Cummings, W.J.	Pte.	
421	Cunningham, P.	Sgt.	
1781	Currell, W.H.	L/Cpl.	
2124	Curtis, W.J.	Pte.	
67	Dacey, J.	Sgt.	
1274	Daniel, B.	Pte.	
1863	Daniel, R.	Pte.	*
1372	Davey, A.	Boy.	
1172	Davies, A.	Cpl.	*
1724	Davies, A.G.	Pte.	*
1377	Davies, A.J.	Pte.	
1826	Davies, A.J.	Pte.	
1351	Davies, C.A	L/Cpl.	
1382	Davies, C.G.	Pte.	
1427	Davies, D.	Pte.	
1538	Davies, D.J.	Pte.	
1845	Davies, E.	L/Cpl.	Commission
2309	Davies, D.H.	Pte.	
2211	Davies, H.	Pte.	
1754	Davies, J.	Pte.	
1713	Davies, J.	Pte.	
2230	Davies, J.	Pte.	
1710	Davies, J.T.	Pte.	
1435	Davies, L.	Pte.	*
1355	Davies, M	Pte.	

1562	Davies, W.	Pte.	
2148	Davies, W.	Pte.	
1794	Davies, W.H.	Pte.	
2535	Dawson, T.J.	Cpl.	
2192	Day, A.	Pte.	*
2369	Day, E.	Pte.	
1381	Day, W.G.	L/Cpl.	
1292	Dayton, J.A.	Pte.	
1299	Deacon, W.	L/Cpl.	
1519	Delaney, G.E.	Pte.	
2201	Derrick, E.	Pte.	
1501	Dix, T.	Pte.	w
2104	Dix, J.	Pte	
2382	Dixon, D.J.	Pte.	
2055	Donovan, D.	Pte.	
2028	Doogood, F.	Pte.	
1835	Doughty, S.	Pte.	
1549	Dowding, H.J.	Pte.	
1490	Dowle, A.E.	L/Cpl.	w
1791	Dowle, G.W.	Pte.	
1442	Downes, A.H.	Pte.	
2096	Downs, T.J.	Pte.	
2190	Drew, T.A.	L/Cpl.	w
1259	Drinkwater, G.	Pte.	
1258	Drinkwater, J.	Pte.	
1969	Driscoll, J.	Pte.	
1428	Durbin, D.	Pte.	
1980	Durbin, F.H.	Pte.	
1429	Durbin, W.	Pte.	*
2031	Durbin, W.J.	Pte.	
2249	Dyke, A.E.	Pte.	
1290	Earland, W.J.	Pte.	
1797	Eckley, E.	Pte.	
1287	Edwards, C.A.	Pte.	w
585	Edwards, C.F.	Col.Sgt.	
1177	Edwards, J.	Pte.	*
2238	Edwards, J.	Pte.	
738	Edwards, O	L/Cpl.	
1217	Edwards, P.	Pte.	
2676	Edwards, S.C.	Pte.	
1654	Edwards, T.	Pte.	
740	Edwards, W.	Sgt.	*
2320	Elliot, J.E.	L/Cpl.	
2140	Elson, J.E.	Pte.	*
2456	Emmott, F.	Pte.	*
2762	Evans, D.	Pte.	
1085	Evans, E.	Pte.	*
1682	Evans, E.	L/Cpl.	*

1938	Evans, E.	Pte.	
1342	Evans, G.	Pte.	
1404	Evans. J.H.	Pte.	*
2363	Evans, S.	Pte.	*
2114	Evans, T	Pte.	
2095	Evans, T.C.	Pte.	*
2247	Evans, T.H.	Pte.	
2208	Evans, W.	Pte.	
2321	Evans, W.A.	Pte.	
1751	Farr, C.J.	Pte.	
1291	Filer, B.	Pte.	
2244	Fish, J.F.	Pte.	
192	Fisher, W.	L/Cpl.	
2594	Fleetwood, A.	Pte.	*
2206	Fletcher, P.L.	Pte.	*
2294	Fletcher, P.L.	Pte.	*
910	Fletcher, R.G.	L/CPl.	
73	Floyd, G.H.	L/Cpl.	
385	Foley, J.	Pte.	*
2746	Ford, C.H.	Pte.	
2329	Ford, J.	Pte.	
2182	Ford, S.G.	L/Cpl.	
2379	Forrest, W.	Pte.	
2581	Fowler, H.J.	Pte.	
2308	Fowler, J.K.	Pte.	
2163	Fowler, S.J.	Pte.	
1157	Foxwell, J.	Pte.	
2263	Francis, J.	Pte.	*
1300	Frost, A.E.W.	Pte.	*
1542	Fuller, J.	Pte.	
898	Furlong, P.	Pte.	
1307	Furlow, E.J.A.	Pte.	
2355	Furnell, W.	Pte.	
1598	Gallivan, T	Pte.	*
603	Garland, W.A.	Sgt.	
2138	Garrett, V.	Pte.	
1422	George, A.J.	Pte.	
2325	George, L	Pte.	*
1699	Gibson, E.	Pte.	*
836	Gilbert, G.	L/Cpl.	
1250	Gill, A.	Pte.	
1982	Gillett, F.	Pte.	
1194	Gillman, A	Cpl.	w
811	Gittings, S.S.	L/Cpl.	
1732	Glover, S.	L/Sgt.	w
474	Goodall, E.	Cpl.	
2131	Goodare, A.	Pte.	w
675	Goode, S.	Sgt.	

1333	Goodwin, E.J.	Pte.		
1280	Goodwin, T.	Pte.	w	
2283	Gough, W.	Pte.		
1417	Gould, H.	Pte.		
1495	Goulder, C	Pte.	*	
1454	Grail, E.C.W.	Pte.		
177	Granger, J.S.	Sgt.	*	
2290	Granger, P.C.	Pte.	w	
2162	Green, J.J.	Pte.		
1326	Green, W.	Pte.		
1792	Greenslade, T.A.	Pte		
2340	Grey, C.H.	L/Cpl.		
2565	Griffiths, A.	Pte	*	
2754	Griffiths, A.G.	Pte.		
1319	Griffiths, C.	Pte.		Commission
1576	Griffiths, C.	Pte.		
478	Griffiths, G.	Sgt.		
29	Griffiths, J.	Cpl.		
2328	Griffiths, I.J.	Pte.		
2489	Griffiths, S.	Pte.		
2260	Griffiths, T.V.	Pte.		
1127	Griffiths, W.G.	Pte.		
1841	Griffiths, W.H.	Pte.		
2464	Griffiths, W.W.	Pte.		
1989	Gronow, W.J.A.	Pte.		
1345	Guest, H.	Pte.	*	
1917	Gwyn, T.H.	Pte.	*	
1894	Haines, A.	L/Cpl.		
1161	Haines, J	Pte.		
1953	Hale, J.	Pte.		
2700	Hale, J.	Pte.		
1742	Hale, S.	Pte		
140	Hall, C.W.	Sgt.		
2274	Hall, E.	Pte.		
2272	Hall, H.	Pte.		
1735	Ham, F.C.	Pte.	*	
2268	Harnett, T.	Pte.	w	
1697	Harrhy, A.	Pte.		
1405	Harrington, D.J.	Pte.	*	
2033	Harris, C.E.	Pte.		
1899	Harris, F.	Pte.		
2052	Harris, H.T.	Pte.	w	
1839	Harris, P.	Pte.	p	
1618	Harrison, O	Pte.		
1850	Hart, H.A.	Pte.		
1308	Hartley, S.	Pte.	w	
1783	Harvey, A.	Pte.	*	
661	Harvey, S.	Pte.		

1778	Harvey, W.	Pte.	
1621	Hathaway, C.	Pte.	
1537	Hatherall, B.	Pte.	
1233	Hatherall, H.T.	Pte.	
2586	Havard, T.B.	Pte.	*
1521	Hawkins, E.	Pte.	
2181	Hayes, A.B.	Pte.	
1774	Hayes, C.	Pte.	
1364	Hayes, J.	Pte.	
2416	Haymonds, G.	Pte.	
2748	Haymonds, T.	Pte.	*
2079	Haynes, G.	Pte.	
1443	Haynes, L.J.	Pte.	
2333	Hayward, J.	Pte.	
1927	Heare, C.P.	Pte.	
2064	Hedges, A.	Cpl.	
1607	Hemmings, H.	Pte.	
1608	Hemmings, W.G.	Pte.	
1630	Herbert, F	Pte.	
2292	Hewings, F.	Pte.	
2073	Hewings, J.	Pte.	w
2323	Hiatt, W.	Pte.	
1988	Higgins, W.H.	Pte.	w
1348	Higgs, D.	Pte.	
1388	Higgs, P.	Pte.	
1344	Higgs, W.	Pte.	*
1269	Hill, J.	Pte.	*
2134	Hillier, F.	Pte.	*
2091	Hine, W.	Pte.	
1507	Hipkins, D.J.	Sgt.	w
2311	Hitchings, W.H.	Pte.	*
77	Hite, C.	Pte.	
1553	Hoare, E.W.	Pte.	
1527	Hoare, G.	Pte.	*
2257	Hodges, A.	Pte.	w
2745	Hodges, J.D.	Pte.	
1910	Holder, A.E.	Pte.	
2451	Holland, G.	Pte.	
534	Hook, O.	L/Sgt.	
1129	Hopkins, A.	Pte.	
2077	Hopkins, D.	Pte.	
1015	Hopkins, W.G.	Sgt.	*
2285	Horton, A.	Pte.	*
2145	Howard, H.G.	Pte.	
2050	Howard, T.	Pte.	
1871	Howard, W.F.	Pte.	
1168	Howells, R.	L/Cpl.	w
1360	Hucker, C.V.	Pte.	
1998	Hucker, T.R.	Pte.	

2038	Hughes, C.T.	Pte.		
1888	Hughes, W.	Pte.		
1764	Hulbert, J.G.	Pte.		
2150	Humber, P.W.	Pte.	w	
2118	Humphrey, T.	Pte.		
2289	Humphreys, W.G.	Pte.		
1616	Humphries, F.A.	Cpl.		
535	Hunt, J.	Sgt.		
2248	Hunter, C.L.	Pte.	w	
2258	Hunter, T.	Pte.	w	
2327	Hurley, W.	Pte.		
1670	Insley, W.	Pte.		
1996	Jackson, J.	L/Cpl.	*	
1612	James, A.	Pte.	*	
1895	James, G.	Pte.		
1461	James, H.	L/Cpl.		
2011	James, J	Pte.		
1950	James, W.	Pte.		
1409	Jayne, J.	Pte.	*	
183	Jaynes, W.	Sgt.		
1752	Jeffreys, W.R.	Pte.		
1482	Jenkins, A.	Pte.		
1771	Jenkins, A.	Pte.	*	
2519	Jenkins, A.	Pte.	*	
1922	Jenkins, C.L.	Pte.		
1083	Jenkins, W.	Pte.		
1264	Jenkins, W.	Pte.		
2625	Jeremy, R.	Pte.		
2761	Jeremy, S.	Pte.		
1802	John, E.G.	Pte.	*	
2004	Johns, J.	Pte.	*	
2659	Johns, W.H.	Pte.		
1539	Johnson, F.	Pte.		
1228	Johnston, C.	Cpl.		Commission
1611	Jones, A.	Pte.	*	
1758	Jones, A.	Pte.		
2286	Jones, A.E.	Pte.		
1192	Jones, C.	Pte.		
173	Jones, E.	L/Sgt.		
773	Jones, E.	Pte.		
1674	Jones, E.	Pte.		
1779	Jones, E.	Pte.		
1823	Jones, E.	Pte.		
2154	Jones, E.	Pte.		
1371	Jones, G.	Pte.		
2189	Jones, G.	Pte.		
1356	Jones, H.B.	Pte.	*	
783	Jones, I	Pte.		

983	Jones, J.	Pte.	
1309	Jones, J.	Pte.	
1463	Jones, J.	Pte.	
1785	Jones, J.	Pte.	*
1822	Jones, J.	L/Cpl.	*
2012	Jones, J.	L/Cpl.	
2373	Jones, J.	Pte.	
2614	Jones, J.	Pte.	
1763	Jones, J.B.	Pte.	
2057	Jones, J.H.	Pte.	
2087	Jones, P.	Pte.	*
538	Jones, R.	Pte.	*
1820	Jones, R.	Pte.	
2179	Jones, R.W.	Pte.	
1421	Jones, S.M.	Pte.	
2128	Jones, T.	Pte.	
2756	Jones, T.H.	Pte.	
804	Jones, T.L.	Drmr.	
1833	Jones, T.W.	Pte.	
1240	Jones, W.	Pte.	
1550	Jones, W.	Pte.	
1736	Jones, W.	L/Cpl.	
2254	Jones, W.	Pte.	
1622	Jones, W.E.	Cpl.	
1166	Jordan, J.	Pte.	
119	Jordan, L	Pte.	
1489	Kear, T.	L/Cpl.	
2658	Keefe, W.	Pte.	*
1601	Keen, S.	Pte.	
1653	Kelly, J.	Pte.	w
849	Kidley, T.	Pte.	
1124	Kilminster, H.W.	L/Cpl.	*
1384	Kimber, D.J.	Pte.	
2016	Kimbrey, T.E.	Pte.	
1359	King, H.G.	Pte.	*
1557	King, W.	Pte.	*
480	Knill, J.	L/Cpl.	
1296	Kyte, T.	Pte.	
2252	Lainchbury, A.W.	L/Cpl.	
2492	Lane, A.	Pte.	w
1472	Lane, H.	Pte.	
1283	Lane, J.C.	Pte.	
2183	Lane, J.C.	Pte.	
1380	Lane, W.J.	Pte.	*
2071	Lanham, R.E.	Pte.	
314	Lavender, W.	Pte.	
2683	Lawes, C.H.	Sgt.	

1937	Lawler. A.	Pte.	
2210	Lawrence, W.	Pte.	
2226	Leek, F.	Pte.	
1740	Leek, W.A.	Pte.	
2233	Leighfield, A.	Pte.	w
46	Lester, G.T.	Pte.	*
1590	Lewis, E.	Pte.	
616	Lewis, G.	Pte.	
821	Lewis, G.	Pte.	
1208	Lewis, G.	Pte.	w
2256	Lewis, G.	Pte.	
2255	Lewis, H.	Pte.	*
1316	Lewis, I	Pte.	
469	Lewis, J	Pte.	
1865	Lewis, J.	Pte.	
1406	Lewis, J.W.	Cpl.	
1242	Lewis, M.	Cpl.	w
1634	Lewis, P.W.	L/Cpl.	
2679	Lewis, S.	Pte.	
1921	Lewis, W.G.	Pte.	
2322	Lewis, W.J.	Pte.	
1573	Leyshon, W.J.	Pte.	*
1399	Linney, C.	Pte.	*
2610	Llewellyn, J.	Pte.	
2467	Lloyd, J.	Pte.	*
2015	Lock, C. .	L/Cpl.	
2023	Lock, W.T.	L/Cpl.	
2405	Long, E.	Pte.	*
2245	Long, E.	Pte.	*
1613	Long, J.	Pte.	
2092	Long, J.H.	Pte.	
2121	Long, L.	Pte.	
2058	Love, C.	L/Cpl.	
1883	Lovell, G.	Pte.	*
2152	Low, W.	L/Cpl.	w
2045	Lucas, T.H.	Pte.	
2034	Lucas, W.J.	Pte.	
10	Luffman, R.H.	Sgt.	
1639	Llywarch, J.	Pte.	*
461	McCarthy, W.	Pte.	
1485	Madeley, S.	Pte.	w
262	Maggs, J.	Sgt.	
1054	Maggs, S.	Pte.	
1260	Maiden, M.	Pte.	
2298	Martin, G.H.	Pte.	
1588	Martin, J.	Pte.	
323	Mason, F.	Pte.	
2191	Mason, H.	Pte.	

1813	Mathias, E.	Pte.	
2153	Matthews, G.	Pte.	w
540	Meadmore, G.M.	Cpl.	*
2537	Meeham, J.W.	Pte.	
1471	Meek, C.F.	L/Cpl.	
1594	Meese, E.C.	Pte.	
6038	Mellsop, G.S.	C.Sgt.	(SWB) Commission
1257	Merchant, T.	Pte.	
1457	Merry, G.	Pte.	*
1635	Miles, C	Pte.	
2530	Miles, G.	Pte.	
2186	Mills, C.	Pte.	
2027	Mills, C.J.	Pte.	*
1393	Moore, E.	Pte.	
2450	Moreton, W.	Pte.	
2032	Morgan, A.	Pte.	w
1859	Morgan, A.H.	Pte.	
1853	Morgan, C.	Pte.	
1436	Morgan, E.	Pte.	
2293	Morgan, G.A.	Pte.	
691	Morgan, J.	Pte.	w, p
1251	Morgan, J.H.	Pte.	
2496	Morgan, J.J.	Pte.	
1717	Morgan, L.	Pte.	
1640	Morgan, P	Pte.	w
1352	Morgan, R.	L/Cpl.	
960	Morgan, T.	Pte.	
2083	Morgan, T.	Pte.	
1317	Morgan, T.F.	Pte.	
1368	Morgan, W.	Pte.	w
2288	Morgan, W.	Pte.	
2331	Morgan, W.F.	Pte.	
2277	Morris, A.	Pte.	
2222	Morris, A.E.	Pte.	
1265	Morris, J.	Pte.	
1609	Morris, T.	Pte.	*
2151	Morris, W.D.	Pte.	*
2682	Moseley, D.J.	Pte.	
196	Moseley, W.	Pte.	
2176	Moseley, W.	Pte.	*
2303	Moses, H.	Pte.	w
185	Moses, V.C.	Pte.	
1434	Mullarney, E.	Pte.	*
2601	Mullarney, J.	Pte.	
1327	Mullins, J.	Pte.	
1720	Munroe, J.	Pte.	
2225	Murphy, J.	Pte.	
769	Murphy, W.	Pte.	*
1566	Murray, J.	Pte.	*

1959	Murray, T.R.	Pte.	*	
1842	Murray, W.	Pte.		
1512	Nelmes, H.	L/Cpl.		Commission
2386	Newman, R.	Pte.	*	
2030	Newman, W.J.	L/Cpl.		
2132	Nichol, A.H.	Pte.		
2105	Nicholas, J.S.	Pte.	*	
210	Nicholls, W.	Pte.	*	
7440	Noble, J.	RSM	w	(SWB)
1412	Norman, E.	Pte.		
1355	Northcote, C.A.	Pte.		
2235	Norton, E.T.	Pte.		
1997	Orchard, A.	Pte.		
2742	Osborne, A.	Pte.		
1848	Owen, C.F.	Pte.	w	
2018	O'Shea, W.P.	Pte.		
1897	Owens, W.E.	L/Cpl.		
2578	Packwood, F.C.	Pte.		
2220	Padden, E.	Pte.		
2341	Palfrey, E.	Pte.	*	
1799	Palfrey, J.	Pte.		
2175	Palfrey, W.E.	Pte.		
1786	Palmer, T.	Pte.	w	
1464	Panting, S.	Pte.		
1864	Pardy, R	Pte.		
2639	Parfitt, T.M.	Pte.		
2068	Parker, J.	Pte.	*	
1912	Parker, R.	Pte.		
339	Parry, A.	Sgt.		
771	Parry, D.	Cpl.		
1954	Parry, I.	Pte.		
1336	Parry, J.	Pte.		
2408	Parry, J.	Pte.		
1955	Parry, H.	Pte.		
1721	Parsons, J.	Pte.		
2160	Parsons, W.	L/Cpl	*	
2187	Partridge, P.J.	Pte.		
2155	Payne, H.W.	Pte.	*	
2330	Pearce, A.	Pte.	*	
1788	Pearce, E.	Pte.		
2025	Pearce, H.R.	L/Cpl.		
1411	Pearce, T.J.	Pte.		
1447	Perkins, F	Pte.		
1533	Peters, B.	Pte.		
2231	Phelps, G.	Pte.		
2198	Phillips, A.	L/Cpl.		
2349	Phillips, F.H.	Pte.		

1854	Phillips, T.J.	Pte.	
2377	Phillips, T.J.	Pte.	
1900	Phillips, W.	Pte.	
543	Philpotts, H.	Sgt.	
2149	Pikes, E.J.	Pte.	
2542	Pilkington, G.E.	Pte.	
1599	Pinchin, A.E.	L/Cpl.	w
2307	Pitt, A.J.	Pte.	
1795	Pitt, G.F.	Pte.	
1410	Poiner, C.T.	Pte.	*
2024	Poole, F.J.	Pte.	
752	Poolman, W.J.	Sgt.	
1619	Pound, F.	Pte.	
2048	Powell, E.J.	Pte.	
545	Powell, J.	L/Cpl.	w
1994	Powell, T.	Pte.	w
862	Powell, W.	Pte.	
1656	Preece, A.	Pte.	*
2117	Preece, A.	Pte.	
1389	Preen, A.	L/Cpl.	w
1685	Price, A.	Pte.	
2669	Price, A.	Pte.	
1879	Price, D	Pte.	*
2352	Price, D.	Pte.	w
51	Price, G.	Pte.	
1956	Price, J.L.	Pte.	*
2599	Price, M.R.	Pte.	
1907	Price, R.	Pte.	
2482	Price, T.M.	Sgt.	
1266	Priddle, T.	L/Cpl.	
920	Prince, F.	Pte.	w
457	Pritchard, C.	Sgt.	
702	Pritchard, D.J.	Cpl.	
2007	Pritchard, E.	Pte.	
1432	Pritchard, T.	Pte.	
1581	Pritchard, T.	Pte.	
1367	Privett, T.J.	Pte.	
2338	Prosser, W.E.	Pte.	w
1500	Pugh, W.	L/Cpl.	
1694	Purchase, W.	Pte.	
1509	Ralph, H.	L/Cpl.	
1669	Randall, W.	Pte.	
1303	Rappell, G.	Pte.	
2234	Rapsom, F.J.	Pte.	
1603	Rawlings, G.	Pte.	
455	Redman, P.	Pte.	
125	Reece, A.J.	Sgt.	
1467	Rees, C.	L/Cpl	w
1695	Rees, H.C.S.	Pte.	*

130	Rees, R.W.	Pte.	*
1419	Rees, W.T.	Pte.	
1554	Regan, D.	L/Sgt.	
2297	Rhodes, W.H.	Pte.	
890	Reeves, P.	Pte.	
14	Richards, C.E.	Cpl.	
1693	Richards, G.	Pte.	
1838	Richards, S.	Pte.	
1704	Ricketts, G.	Pte.	
1770	Ricketts, H.R.	Pte.	
2080	Roberts, B.	Pte.	
2351	Roberts, C.H.	Pte.	
1585	Roberts, D.J.	Pte.	*
53	Roberts, J.	L/Cpl.	
1891	Roberts, J.	Pte.	*
2119	Roberts, L.	Pte.	
1315	Roberts, R.F.	Pte.	
1001	Roberts, T.H.	L/Cpl.	*
2141	Roberts, T.H.	Pte.	w
1270	Roberts, W.	L/Cpl.	*
1451	Roberts, W.B.	Pte.	
2371	Robertson, A.	Pte.	
861	Robinson, E.	Sgt.	
2251	Robinson, J.	Pte.	
1568	Robinson, J.H.	Pte.	
2296	Robinson, R.	Pte.	
1565	Rogers, J.	Pte.	*
1458	Rooke, I.	Pte.	
1992	Rose, W.T.	Pte.	
1561	Rowe, G.	Pte.	
1696	Rowen, E.A.	C.Sgt.	
1991	Rowlands, A.	Pte.	*
2005	Rowlands, C.	Pte.	
1728	Rowlands, J.	Pte.	*
1400	Rowlands, S	Pte.	w
1893	Ruck, A.	Pte.	
546	Rudge, A.H.	L/Sgt.	
1660	Russell, G.W.	Pte.	
548	Ryall, F.	Pte.	
1707	Sage, W.J.	Pte.	*
1815	Salter, W.	Pte.	
2229	Samuel, J.	Pte.	*
54	Sankey, T.	Pte.	w
1423	Sansom, D.	L/Cpl.	
390	Satherley, H.J.	C.Sgt.	
55	Saunders, A.	L/Cpl.	
2166	Saunders, F.	Pte.	
2836	Saunders, G.	Pte.	w

2346	Saunders, H.	Pte.	
1387	Saunders, I.W.	Pte.	w
1163	Saunders, J.H.	Pte.	*
2370	Saunders, M.C.	Pte.	
1164	Saunders, T.	Cpl.	
1433	Saunders, T.	Pte.	
2521	Sawyer, A.	Pte.	
1425	Scourfield, T.	Pte.	
1158	Scourfield, W.	Pte.	
4	Search, W.	Sgt.	
1821	Seymour, W.H.	Pte.	
2239	Sharkes, J.	Pte.	
2299	Sharley, F.J.	Pte.	
2130	Shaw, H.	Pte.	*
2216	Shea, J.	Pte.	*
1346	Shonk, C.	Pte.	w
1285	Short, A.	Pte.	*
1692	Simmonds, J.J.	Sgt.	
1365	Simmonds, W.	Pte.	
1852	Simpson, W.	Pte.	
1972	Sims, B.	Pte.	
2228	Sims, J.	Pte.	
1334	Skillern, G.	Pte.	
1337	Skillern, W.	Pte.	
2270	Skillman, F.	Pte.	*
2440	Skuse, T.	Pte.	
1247	Skyrme, W.J.	Pte.	
152	Slade, C.H.	Cpl.	*
1201	Smith, A.	L/Cpl.	w
1951	Smith, A.E.	Pte.	
1492	Smith, C.	Pte.	
2572	Smith, C.	Pte.	
153	Smith, C.H.	Pte.	
1564	Smith, H.	Pte.	
734	Smith, J.	Pte.	
1866	Smith, S.	Pte.	
2142	Smith, T.H.	Pte.	
1875	Smith, W.	Pte.	
2409	Smith, W.	Cpl.	
390	Sotherby, H.J.	C. Sgt.	
2664	Soward, B.	Pte.	
2239	Sparkes, J.	Pte.	
1386	Speers, W.H.	L/Cpl.	
1255	Squires, F.E.	Pte.	
1176	Stanton, F.	L/Cpl.	
2144	Stanton, J	Pte.	w
1610	Steele, L.	Pte.	
1460	Stephens, G.	Pte.	
1703	Stephens, H.	Sgt.	

2036	Stoat, A.E.	L/Cpl.	
1388	Stockham, P.S.	L/Cpl.	
2171	Stone, S.	Pte.	
1248	Stone, W.	Pte.	
2718	Stone, W.H.	Pte.	
1632	Stone, W.J.	Pte.	*
2523	Stone, W.J.	Cpl.	w
798	Stratton, W.	Drmr.	
2046	Strickland, A.	Pte.	
2135	Strong, D.	Pte.	
1832	Strong, T.	Pte.	*
1312	Stroud, W.J.	Dmr.	*
2490	Stubbs, W	L/Cpl.	w
1920	Styles, E.	Pte.	
1353	Sullivan, J.	L/Cpl.	
1766	Sullivan, J.	Pte.	
1357	Sweet, W.J.R.	L/Cpl.	
2337	Sykes, F.G.	Pte.	*
1929	Tamplin, W.	Pte.	
2062	Tarling, T.J.	Pte.	*
2319	Taylor, F.	Pte.	
1223	Taylor, G.	L/Cpl.	
1965	Taylor, H.J.	Pte.	
1858	Taylor, R.	Pte.	
1886	Taylor, R.J.	Pte.	*
843	Taylor, T.W.	Pte.	
2035	Taylor, W.	Pte.	
1478	Teague,W.T.E.	L/Cpl.	*
179	Tew, A.	Pte.	
180	Tew, C.	Cpl.	
2106	Thatcher, G.	Pte.	
1657	Thickpenny, J.	Pte.	
1796	Thomas, A.	Pte.	
1904	Thomas, B.J.	L/Cpl.	
1597	Thomas, B.T.	Pte.	
1876	Thomas, D.H.	Pte.	*
1889	Thomas, E.	Pte.	
2463	Thomas, F.	Cpl.	
2246	Thomas, F.G.	Pte.	w
1211	Thomas, G.	Pte.	
2261	Thomas, H.J.	Pte.	
2001	Thomas, H.S.	Pte.	
2093	Thomas, J.W.	Pte.	
510	Thomas, S.	Pte.	
1658	Thomas, T.J.	Pte.	*
2276	Thomas, W.	Pte.	
2345	Thomas, W.	Pte.	
332	Thomas, W.H.	L/Cpl.	w

1213	Thomas, W.J.	Pte.	
1243	Thompson, A.	L/Cpl.	
2361	Thompson, G.	L/Cpl.	
126	Thompson, J.	C.Sgt.	
2506	Thorne, A.E.	Pte.	
2304	Thorne, B.	Pte.	w
1860	Thorpe, F.	L/Cpl.	
2314	Tomlin, T.J.	Pte.	
495	Tooze, A.R.	Drmr.	
2013	Trew, R.E.	Pte.	*
1306	Trinder, A.	Pte.	
2037	Trinder, W.	Pte.	
170	Truman, W.T.	C.Sgt.	
2157	Turnbull, W.	Pte.	
2200	Turner, A.	Pte.	
1777	Turner, I	Pte.	*
1810	Turton, W.	Pte.	w
1930	Vaughan, E.L.	Pte.	
1302	Vaughan, S.	L/Cpl.	*
62	Vaux, A.	Pte.	
2675	Vernall, C.	Pte.	*
2641	Veysey, J.A.	Pte.	*
1711	Villis, F.J.	Pte.	
2144	Viner, R.	Drmr.	w
2332	Vinnecombe, A.L.	Pte.	
328	Waite, A.	Sgt.	
1530	Waite, A.	Cpl.	w
1934	Waite, T.E.	Pte.	
98	Waite, W.H.	Cpl.	
1339	Wall, F.	L/Sgt.	
1874	Wall, W.A.	Pte.	
663	Wallis, A.H.	L/Cpl.	w
1780	Walters, E.J.	L/Cpl.	
895	Walters, W.	Pte.	
1548	Walters, W.H.	Pte.	
2089	Wassall, E.	Pte.	
1962	Waters, F.	Pte.	w
1765	Waters, P.F.	L/Cpl.	
1059	Watkins, A.	Pte.	
2387	Watkins, A.	Cpl.	w
102	Watkins, D.	C.Sgt.	
1314	Watkins, E.	Pte.	
2385	Watkins, H.	Pte.	*
1748	Watkins, J.	Pte.	
1195	Watkins, T.R.	L/Cpl.	
588	Watson, R.	Sgt.	
1675	Watts, A.	Pte.	

2458	Watts, J.	Pte.	*	
2122	Way, B	Pte.		
1293	Weale, E.J.	Pte.		
2127	Webb, A.C.	Pte.		Commission
202	Webb, A.J.	Cpl.		
1824	Webb, E.G.	Pte.		
174	Webb, W.	Sgt.	w	
2213	Webb, W.	Pte.		
201	Weller, F.	Sgt.		
	West, A	Pte.		
1722	Whatley, G.	Pte.	*	
2207	Whitby, H.	Pte.		
1449	White, B.	Pte.	*	
450	White, D.	L/Cpl.		
505	White, E.	Pte.	w	
2129	White, T	Pte.		
2657	White, T.H.	Pte.		Commission
64	Whitfield, G.E.	L/Cpl.		
2147	Whitney, H.	Pte.		
1567	Whittington, H.H.	Pte.	*	
2399	Wigmore, B.J.	Pte.		
1486	Wilce, E.	Pte.	w	
2438	Willcocks, W.	Pte.		
1230	Williams, A.	Pte.		
1238	Williams, A.	Pte.		
1245	Williams, A.	Cpl.		
1321	Williams, A	Pte.		
1424	Williams, A.	Pte.	*	
2167	Williams, A.L.	Pte.		
1058	Williams. A.W.	Pte.	*	
1513	Williams, B.	Pte.		
65	Williams, C.	Pte.	*	
1328	Williams, C.	Pte.	*	
1947	Williams, C.	L/Cpl.		
1589	Williams, D.J.	Pte.		
156	Williams, D.W.	Pte.		
1231	Williams, E.J.	Pte.		
1154	Williams, F.	Pte.	*	
2056	Williams, G.	Pte.		
1615	Williams, H.	Pte.	*	
1179	Williams, J.	Pte.		
1945	Williams, J.	Pte.	w	
2414	Williams, J.	Pte.		
2697	Williams, J.	Pte.		
2164	Williams, J.L.	Pte.		
2384	Williams, J.R.	Pte.		
1868	Williams, R.	Pte.		
1362	Williams, S.	Pte.	*	
1311	Williams, T.	Pte.		

1552	Williams, T.	Pte.		
1587	Williams, T.	Pte.		
2081	Williams, T.	Pte.		
2633	Williams, T.	Pte.		
2017	Williams, T.G.	Pte.		
1914	Williams, W.	Pte.		
2203	Williams, W.	Pte.		
2280	Williams, W.	Pte.		
2375	Williams, W.	Pte.		
2411	Williams, W.J.	Pte.		*
2348	Willis, W.H.	Pte.		
2170	Wilson, G.E.H.	Pte.		
2529	Wilson, W.H.	Pte.	w	
1746	Wilson, W.J.	Pte.		
1574	Wiltshire, W.	Pte.		
1200	Winwood, H.V.	Pte.		*
157	Witts, E. A.	Pte.		
1676	Wood, W.	Pte.		
555	Woodfield, G.	Sgt.		*
1546	Wooding, F.	Pte.	w	
2158	Woodland, F.	Pte.		
2098	Woodland, S.	Pte.		
796	Woods, H.	L/Cpl.		*
2115	Woolfall, A.	Pte.		
1445	Worgan, A.L.	Pte.		
2326	Worthington, O.	Pte.		
2199	Wren, J.	Pte.		
2193	Wren, W.	Pte.		
1459	Wyatt, F.	Pte.		
1544	Wyatt, H.G.	Pte.		*
1543	Yarworth, R.	Pte.		*
1502	Yarworth, T.H.	Pte.		
894	Yates, T.	Sgt.		
1373	Yates, G.	Sgt.		
1370	Yearsley, G.	Pte.		
1346	Yorath, G.L.	L/Cpl.		

ROLL OF REINFORCEMENTS, 1915

The following roll has been compiled from a number of sources. It is a synopsis of the data from the 1914-15 Star Roll held at the Public Records Office and is supplemented by such details as can be gleaned by study of the casualty lists of the months of the War following the fighting of May, 1915. It gives the replacements to the battalion that occurred during 1915. The symbols used are the same as in the first part of the roll. Ranks shown are those that applied on arrival in France.

2752	Anderson, John David	Pte.	
2620	Angell, Samuel.	Pte.	
4858	Arnell, George.	Pte.	
3550	Arthur, Ellis.	Pte.	
2236	Arthur, William Albert.	Pte.	*
2543	Attwood, Edwin.	Pte.	
2803	Badham, George C.	Pte.	*
2949	Baggs, Arthur Charles	Pte.	*
2917	Baker, Alexander G.	Pte.	
2427	Baker, Horace,	L/Cpl.	
1976	Baker, Howard George.	Pte.	
3281	Ball, Albert.	Pte.	*
2959	Barnfield, Herbert.	Pte.	
3043	Barter, Reginald.	Pte.	
3047	Batstone, Hubert.	Pte.	*
3039	Beard, Stanley.	Pte.	
2886	Beniams, William C.	Pte.	
3030	Bennett, Worthington.	Pte.	*
2390	Berrow, Granville.	L/Cpl.	*
2278	Biby, Albert Edwin.	Pte.	
3117	Biggs, Thomas.	Pte.	*
1310	Blackman, Ernest.	Pte.	
2600	Blaney, Charles.	Pte.	
2169	Bond, Charles Henry.	Pte.	*
3269	Bond, Frank.	Pte.	
3174	Booth, Robert A.	Pte.	
3127	Bowyer, Herbert.	Pte.	
2852	Boyce, Thomas.	Pte.	
2076	Brooks, George F.	Pte.	*
3238	Bullock, Athur John.	Pte.	*
3304	Bullock, William Edwin.	Pte.	
2188	Burford, Albert Cecil.	L/Cpl.	
2097	Burnett, James George.	Pte	*
2851	Burnett, Stanley J.	Pte.	
2180	Burnett, William James.	Pte.	
3112	Butcher, Thomas G.	Pte.	
3121	Butcher, William J.	Pte.	*
3095	Butler, Francis W.	Pte.	*
13204	Byrne, James.	Pte.	
3262	Caddy, William.	Pte.	
2651	Carver, Willaim James	L/Cpl.	
10913	Champ, Joseph.	Pte.	*
3332	Chance, Walter George.	Pte.	*
2413	Chard, Alfred.	Pte.	w
3235	Clarke, W.H.	Pte.	

8721	Clifford, John.	L/Cpl.	
2174	Cobner, Austin.	L/Cpl.	
3286	Cole, John.	Pte.	
2845	Compton, Ernest W.	Pte.	
20902	Connor, John.	Pte.	*
3166	Cook, Victor.	Pte.	
2832	Coombs, John Henry,	Pte.	w
3017	Coombes, Thomas J.	Pte.	
2165	Cooper, Edward.	Pte.	*
2372	Cooper, Fred.	Pte.	
3082	Cordy, Thomas.	Pte.	
3153	Cotterrell, Albert H.	Pte.	
3339	Cotterrell, G.A.J.	Pte.	
2656	Cotterrell, Thomas.	Pte.	
2670	Coward, Wyndham.	Pte.	
24131	Cowell, Charles Edward.	Pte.	
2842	Cox, Henry Charles.	Pte.	
2665	Cox, George L.	Pte.	*
2930	Crook, Charles.	Pte.	
2367	Cuthbert, Arthur.	Pte.	
2729	Daly, Stephen F.	Pte.	w
2433	Dare, George Henry W.	Pte.	*
2958	Davey, William J.	Pte.	
2884	Davies, Bert L.	Pte.	
2922	Davies, Christopher.	Pte.	
3079	Davies, David.	Pte.	
3059	Davies, George.	Pte.	*
3253	Davies, Gilbert.	Pte.	
2422	Davies, Grosvenor A.	Pte.	*
2577	Davies, Henry.	Pte.	
9481	Davies, James.	Pte.	
2616	Davies, John Henry.	Pte.	*
2525	Davies, Lewis John.	Pte.	*
2642	Davies, Seth.	Pte.	
2793	Davies, Thomas.	Pte.	
1745	Day, John.	Pte.	*
2864	Deane, John Edward.	Pte.	
8833	Desborough, William H.	L/Cpl.	
3233	Dix, Albert.	Pte.	*
2980	Dowding, John.	Pte.	
3197	Dowle, William Wysome.	Pte.	
2755	Dowse, Henry Walter.	Pte.	*
2835	Drummond, Thomas E.	Pte.	*
2396	Eastman, Sam.	Pte.	
2645	Edmunds, Thomas G.	Pte.	
2870	Edwards, Rowley.	Cpl.	
3003	Edwards, William.	Pte.	
2818	Evans, Absalom.	Pte.	

1591	Evans, David.	Pte.	
3231	Evans, Oliver.	Pte.	
2392	Eyles, Stanley.	Pte.	
3370	Finney, Thomas.	Pte.	
1665	Fitzgerald, James D.	Pte.	
1843	Ford, William.	Pte.	*
2312	Forrest, John.	Pte.	
15597	Freeman, John.	Cpl.	
2373	Gaffney, Albert.	Pte.	
3016	Gardiner, James.	Pte.	
2448	Garland, Lemuel V.	Pte.	
3066	Gibbs, Meredith.	Pte.	
1626	Gibbs, Partick.	Pte.	
3182	George, Alfred.	Pte.	
2987	George, William L.	Pte.	*
2716	Goodall, Edwin James.	Pte.	*
2576	Goodreid, William.	Pte.	
2447	Gould, T.R.	Pte.	
2316	Gratton, Charles Henry.	Pte.	
2779	Green, Manley G.	Pte.	
2668	Green, Thomas.	Pte.	
547	Gribble, William.	Pte	*
2601	Griffiths, David G.	Pte.	*
2974	Griffiths, John A.	Pte.	
3135	Griffiths, William H.	Pte.	
2820	Gwatkin, William.	Pte.	
3216	Hall, Harry.	Pte.	*
3029	Hardacre, Joseph.	Pte.	*
2583	Harris, Percy.	Pte.	
3219	Harris, William.	Pte.	
3019	Harrison, Richard.	Pte.	
2512	Harwood, Stanley G.	Pte.	
2833	Havard, Ernest.	Pte.	*
15417	Hawes, Benjamin.	Pte.	
2935	Hewitt, Alfred J.	Pte.	w
2714	Hicks, George.	Pte.	
3164	Higgs, Albert E.	Pte.	
16529	Hill, Arthur.	Pte.	
2829	Hindson, Harry John.	Pte.	
15565	Hine, William.	Pte.	
3210	Hodges, Arthur.	Pte.	
2168	Holbrook, George.	Pte.	
1550	Hollingworth, John.	Pte.	
27462	Holt, Alfred E.	Pte.	
3313	Holvey, Sidney.	Pte.	*
2808	Hone, Harold.	L/Cpl.	
2780	Hopkins, Ivor.	Pte.	

2475	Hornsby, Gilbert Arthur	Pte.	
3001	Hughes, Charles William.	Pte.	
2952	Hughes, Francis.	Pte.	*
3279	Hughes, Frederick G.	Pte.	
17362	Hughes, Thomas Edwin.	Pte.	
23953	Hulme, George.	Pte.	
2781	Hutton, Sydney J.	Pte.	
887	James, James Morgan.	L/Cpl.	*
2451	James, Llewellyn.	Pte.	
2546	Jelland, William.	Pte.	
2580	Jenkins, Frank John.	L/Cpl.	
3147	Jenkins, George W.	Pte.	
2643	Jenkins, Henry.	Pte.	
2471	Jenkins, Jehoiadd.	Pte.	*
2172	Jenkins, Peter.	Pte.	
3179	Jennings, William J.	Pte.	
3137	Johns, William C.	Pte.	*
2002	Johnson, Herbert R.	Pte.	*
2848	Jones, Alfred J.	Pte.	*
2588	Jones, Benjamin	Pte.	
2395	Jones, Charles.	L/Cpl.	*
25467	Jones, Daniel.	Pte.	
2406	Jones, Edwin.	Cpl.	
2449	Jones, Elias.	Pte.	
3328	Jones, Fred.	Pte.	*
2366	Jones, Frederick.	Pte.	*
3312	Jones, George.	Pte.	*
1246	Jones, George.	Pte.	
2184	Jones, Griffiths.	Pte.	
16131	Jones, Harry.	Sgt.	
3240	Jones, Harry Leonard.	Pte.	*
2584	Jones, James.	Pte.	
1655	Jones, Richard.	Pte.	
2421	Jones, Robert Alfred	Pte.	*
2423	Jones, Seth.	Pte.	
2751	Jones, Thomas.	Pte.	
2582	Jones, Thomas John	Pte.	
1617	Jones. Walter Henry.	Pte.	
1584	Jones, William.	Pte.	
2419	Jones, William Edward	Pte.	*
2822	Jones, William Henry.	Pte.	
2902	Jones, William Henry.	Cpl.	
2622	Jones, William Thomas.	Pte.	
2982	Jordan, Melville.	Pte.	
3010	Keeling, Henry.	Pte.	
2768	Kembrey, Thomas.	Pte.	
2846	Kenealy, Thomas.Pte.	*	
2888	Kidley, William J.	Pte.	

3154	Knight, Ernest Tom.	Pte.		
2561	Knipe, George Edward	Cpl.	*	
2550	Kyte, Edward.	Pte.		
3218	Lane, Mark.	Pte.		
1730	Larder, Thomas.	Pte.		
2877	Lawler, Edwin.	Pte.		
3282	Lawrence, Edward.	Pte.		
2540	Leach, William H.	Pte.		
2649	Leddington, William G.	Pte.	*	
2548	Lee, Martin.	Pte.		
2281	Leonard, Fred.	L/Cpl.		
3323	Lewis, Edward.	Pte.		
2437	Lewis, Jack	Pte.	*	
2394	Lewis, James.	Pte.		
3178	Lewis, John G.	Pte.	*	
2512	Lewis, Nathan.	Pte.	*	
2634	Lewis, Robert Kenneth.	Cpl.	*	
2769	Lewis, William.	Pte.	w	
2994	Leyshon, William.	Pte.	*	
2915	Lilwall, Arthur E.	Pte.	*	
3091	Lloyd, William.	Pte.	*	
17410	Lovgreen, August E.	Pte.		Commission
3008	Manley, John Charles.	Pte.		
12048	Martin, Charles.	Pte.		
2962	Martin, Thomas.	Pte.	*	
2378	Mayers, William D.	Pte.		
3288	Mayo, James Eric.	Pte.		
3011	McCormick, Michael.	Pte.		
2666	McCourt, John.	Cpl.		
3213	McDonough, John.	Pte.		
2858	McNicoll, John W.	Pte.		
2909	Meech, Charles James.	Pte.		
2400	Millwater, Harold.	Pte.		
2764	Mogford, John	Pte.	*	
2864	Morgan, James.	Pte.		
1420	Morgan, John.	Pte.		
2637	Morgan, Phillip.	Pte.		
2873	Morgan, Rees.	Pte.		
2912	Morgan, Richard.	Pte.		
1178	Morgan, Samuel.	Cpl.		
2814	Morgan, Stephen.	Pte.	*	
3136	Morgan, Thomas H.	Pte.	*	
2495	Morgan, William	Pte.		
2494	Morgan, William Henry.	Pte.	*	
3081	Morris, James A.F.	Pte.		
3045	Morris, Thomas.	Pte.		
1539	Moss, Robert.	Pte.		
2347	Motley, William Charles	Pte.		

3225	Mowe, Thomas.	Pte.	
2867	Murnan, Frederick J.	Cpl.	
3305	Murphy, Richard.	Pte.	
3167	Nelmes, William.	Pte.	
3340	Newman, William.	Pte.	*
3275	Nicholls, Frank Phillip.	Pte.	*
2857	Norman, Thomas John.	Pte.	
3092	Northfield, Sydney.	Pte.	
3271	Nunnerly, Arthur.	Pte.	*
2678	Nurdin, Alfred S.	Pte.	*
10024	O'Hara, John.	Pte.	
3092	O'Neill, Albert.	Pte.	
2928	Owen, John Morris.	Pte.	
2066	Owen, Watkin.	Pte.	
2661	Palmer, Clarence H.	Pte.	
2647	Parfitt, Herbert.	C/Sgt.	
2759	Parfitt, James Henry.	Pte.	*
3293	Parkinson, William.	Pte.	
2305	Parry, Archibald.	Pte.	
3268	Parry, David.	Pte.	
3118	Parry John Henry.	Pte.	
1999	Parsons, Albert James.	Pte.	
3143	Parsons, George.	Pte.	*
2800	Pattemore, Samuel.	Pte.	*
2719	Pattimore, Alfred W.	Pte.	
2195	Payne, Clifford.	Pte.	*
1024	Payne, John.	Pte.	*
2453	Payne, Thomas A.	L/Cpl.	*
2481	Pearce, Harry R.	Pte.	
3126	Penhorwood, Percival.	Pte.	
2115	Perry, James.	Pte.	
2472	Phillips, Ernest.	Pte.	
3307	Phillips, Ernest James.	Pte.	
2493	Phillips, Ezekiel.	Pte.	
2439	Phillips, Ivor.	Pte.	
2830	Phillips, J.H.	Pte.	
2418	Phillips, Samuel, Tom.	Pte.	
3255	Phillips, Soloman.	Pte.	*
2477	Phillips, W.H.	Pte.	
3170	Phillpott, Joseph.	Pte.	
1209	Phipps, Thomas	Pte.	
3335	Phipps, William.	Pte.	*
1310	Pickford, John Henry	Pte.	*
2194	Pitt, William.	Pte.	
3011	Pitt, William, J.	Pte.	
2410	Poulson, Harold.	Pte.	
2933	Powell, Frank John	Pte.	

3171	Powell, Reginald Percy.	Pte.	
3180	Powell, Robert J.	Pte.	*
3337	Powell, Sidney.	Pte.	
2798	Powell, Walter.	Pte.	
2815	Powell, William.	Pte.	
1809	Prangley, William.	Pte.	w
2531	Preece, Edward Charles	Pte.	*
2771	Preece, Ernest.	Pte.	*
1892	Price, Arthur.	Pte.	*
2252	Price, Bert.	Pte.	*
2533	Price, David.	Pte.	
2684	Price, David Rees.	Pte.	
2159	Price, Thomas.	Pte.	
3128	Priddy, Oswald.	Pte.	
2811	Pritchard, Ernest.	Pte.	
2444	Probert, Alfred.	Pte.	
3006	Prosser, William J.	Pte.	*
2925	Prothero, Frank.	Pte.	
1876	Purcell, Ernest A.	Pte.	
2569	Read, Frederick John.	Pte.	
2374	Reardon, J.	Pte.	
2155	Redfern, William H.	Pte.	
2841	Redwood, Herbert.	Pte.	
2479	Reegan, Patrick.	Pte.	w
2636	Rees, John Ivor.	Pte.	
2454	Reynolds, David John.	Pte.	*
2443	Reynolds, Isaac.	Pte.	
1739	Roach, Michael.	Pte.	
3333	Robbins, Thomas.	Pte.	
3208	Roberts, Alfred.	Pte.	*
3199	Roberts, Charles J.	Pte.	*
2090	Roberts, Edward Ivor.	Pte.	
3270	Roberts, George.	L/Cpl.	
2797	Roberts, George Thomas.	L/Cpl.	*
3276	Roberts, David W.	Pte.	
1561	Roberts, John Owen.	Pte.	
2486	Roberts, Owen.	Pte.	
3220	Robins, George.	Pte.	
3342	Robinson, Benjamin.	Pte.	
4602	Robinson, Joseph.	Pte.	
2960	Robinson, Llewellyn.	Pte.	
2455	Rogers, Fred.	L/Cpl.	
2898	Ross, Tom.	Pte.	
2291	Rowley, John Robert.	Pte.	
2681	Ruck, Sydney Robert.	Pte.	*
2556	Salvage, Stanley.	Pte.	
2836	Saunders, Thomas G.	Pte.	*
3035	Savery, Reginald.	Pte.	*

2466	Sawyer, Archibald S.	Pte	
2301	Scott, Charles Herbert.	Pte	
1915	Seaborne, Thomas.	Pte.	
15407	Sharp, Albert E.	Pte.	
3125	Shepherd, Arthur.	Pte.	
3049	Simmonds, Idris.	Pte.	
2508	Simonds, William W.	Pte.	
19149	Singleton, William H.	Pte.	
2566	Skillern, Frederick.	Pte.	
3096	Slack, Frederick.	Pte.	
3041	Slade, James.	Pte.	
2678	Smart, Frank.	Pte.	
2978	Smart, Harold.	Pte.	
3296	Smith, Edwin.	Pte,	*
3155	Smith, Ernest Thomas.	Pte.	
3295	Smith, George.	Pte.	*
9853	Smith, George Alfred.	Pte.	
3256	Smith, Henry.	Pte.	*
2611	Smith, Thomas.	Pte.	
2866	Smith, Herbert.	Pte.	
3031	Smith, Stephen J.	Pte.	*
3025	Smith, Thomas.	Pte.	
3032	Southern, Richard.	Pte.	*
3089	Spencer, William.	Pte.	
2606	Stiff, Clarence Wilfred.	Pte.	*
13189	Stinton, James.	Pte.	
2430	Stocker, Albert.	Pte.	
17963	Stone, Alec Reginald.	Pte.	
3242	Stopgate, William.	Pte.	
2490	Stubbs, W.	L/Cpl.	
3339	Sturkey, Robert.	Pte.	
2629	Sullivan, James.	Pte.	
2359	Sulway, Stanley.	L/Cpl.	
2896	Symons, Frederick J.	Pte.	*
2715	Taylor, David.	Pte.	
2941	Thomas, Charles F.	Pte.	*
2804	Thomas, Edmund.	Pte.	*
3111	Thomas, James F.	Pte.	
2632	Thomas, John.	Pte.	
2977	Thomas, John G.	Pte.	*
1074	Thomas, William.	Pte.	
2547	Thomas, William.	Pte.	
3063	Thomas, William F.	Pte.	
18051	Thompson, Albert E.	Pte.	
2006	Thompson, Archibald.	Pte.	
3217	Tindall, George.	Pte.	*
2821	Traves, Aubrey.	Pte.	
2837	Tucker, Charles.	Pte.	

3169	Turley, Frederick.	L/Cpl.	
2000	Twilton, Henry C.	Pte.	
2364	Tyler, Valentine.	Pte.	
2412	Vernall, John.	Pte.	*
3163	Vincent, Joseph.	L/Cpl.	
2518	Waite, Albert J.	Cpl.	
2528	Wakefield, Ernest A.	Pte.	
3120	Walsh, Thomas.	Pte.	
2369	Walters, Herbert.	Cpl.	
3158	Walters, John.	Pte.	
3005	Ward, Charles.	Pte.	
2487	Warren, William J.	Pte.	*
2655	Waters, William John.	Cpl.	
2297	Waterworth, John H.	L/Cpl.	
2376	Watkins, Frederick.	Pte.	
2483	Watkins, James Henry.	Pte.	
2689	Watkins, Reginald J.H.	Pte.	
3161	Watkins, Thomas.	Pte.	
2334	Watkins, William John	L/Cpl.	
3144	Watkins, William. J.	Pte.	
2704	Watts, William	Pte.	*
3122	Weaver, George.	Pte.	
3076	Weaver, Henry.	Pte.	
3162	Werrett, William.	Pte.	
1919	West, Accluis.	Pte.	
1744	Whatley, Charles.	Pte.	*
3110	White, Frederick G.	Pte.	
3285	White, William John.	Pte.	
2914	Whitlock, Frank.	Pte.	
2100	Whitney, Worthy.	Pte.	
3188	Williams, Arthur G.	Pte.	
3044	Williams, Charles.	Pte.	
2985	Williams, Cornelius.	Pte.	
3173	Williams, Edgar.	Pte.	
2766	Williams, Francis E.	Pte.	*
2557	Williams, J.A.	Pte.	
2839	Williams, Ralph.	Pte.	*
1896	Williams, Thomas John.	Pte.	
2185	Williams, William.	Cpl.	
2424	Williams, William H.	L/Cpl	
16789	Wilson, Arthur.	Pte.	
1340	Winstone, Edwin.	Pte.	*
2365	Witcombe, Wiliam J.	Pte.	*
3191	Witherly, Thomas.	Pte.	
2828	Woods, William J.	Pte.	*
3292	Wotman, Harry.	Pte.	

Appendix 3
Honours and Awards

The Battalion was mentioned in despatches three times for meritorious and efficient service.

C.M.G.

Lieut. Col. E.B. Cuthbertson

D.S.O. and BAR

Lieut. Col. A.J.H. Bowen

D.S.O.

Lieut. Col. J. Evans
Lieut. Col. H.J. Miers
Capt. P.G. Pennymore
Capt. S.P.A. Rolls

M.C. and BAR

Major T.L. Ibbs
Capt. R.B. Comely

M.C.

2nd Lieut. C.E Birkett
Capt. C. Comely
Lieut. C.J. Crawley
2nd Lieut. H.B. Davies
Major A.H. Edwards
Capt. J.T. George
Lieut. H.J. Hopkins

Capt. W.D. Howick
Lieut. H.T. Nelmes
R.S.M. J. Noble
Lieut. & Q.M. W.M. Porter
Capt. S.P.A. Rolls
2nd Lieut. W.R. Sankey
Capt. M.F. Turner
Lieut. T.H. White.

D.C.M.

R.S.M. W.J. Bowen
L/Sgt. J. Dowding
Cpl. T.A. Drew
Sgt. C. Hayes
Pte. W.G. Hemmings
C.S.M. J.Johnson
Pte. G. Jones
Pte. J. Lewis
C.S.M. C.J. Love

Pte. J. Morgan
Sgt. A.E. Pinchin
Sgt. J. Roberts
Sgt. W. Spiers
Drmr. D. White
Sgt. W. Williams (265363)
Sgt. W. Williams (265503)
Sgt. G. Yates
Sgt. T. Yates
R.S.M. G.T. Yearsley

M.M. and Bar

Sgt. A.J. Cross

Sgt. J.M. Mc Nichol

M.M.

Pte. E. Andrews
Cpl. J.J. Bayes
Sgt. R.S. Beddin
L/Cpl. G. Bedford
Cpl. A. Belli
Pte. S.J. Burnett
Pte. W. Burnett
Sgt. D. Dallimore
L/Cpl. A. Dyke
Pte. D. Evans
Pte. T. Greenslade
Sgt. C. Griffiths
Pte. I.J. Griffiths
Sgt. J. Hale
L/Cpl. H. Hatherall
Sgt. J. Jackson
Sgt. W. Jenkins
Sgt. J. Jones
L/Sgt. W. Jones

Pte. J. Lewis
Sgt. C.H. Lock
L/Cpl. J. Phillips
L/Cpl. R.J. Powell
Cpl. S. Powell
L/Cpl. M.R. Price
CQMS C. Pritchard
L/Cpl. T. Rose
Pte. A. Schofield
Sgt. A.E. Smith
Cpl. R.Trew
Sgt. A. Turner
Sgt. E. Wagstaffe
L/Cpl. F.E. Williams
L/Cpl. J.J. Williams
Sgt. W. Williams (265363)
Pte. E. Wilson
Pte. T. Withey
L/Cpl. W. Woodland

M.S.M.

Sgt. R.A. Booth

Sgt. R. Evans

Cpl. C.H. Grey

Sgt. C. Hayes

Sgt. Hopkins

CQMS G.E. Phillips

Sgt. E.J. Pikes

Sgt. T. Priddle

Sgt. A.E. Smith

CQMS F. Wall

CROIX DE GUERRE (France)

Sgt. J. Counsell

Capt. A.L.Robertson

Capt. R.T. Saunders

Dmr. D. White DCM

Sgt. W. Williams DCM, MM

CROIX DE GUERRE (Belgium)

Capt. R.B. Comely MC

Cpl. W. Rose

Sgt. A. Watkins

Cpl. G. Whitfield

ORDER OF ST. STANISLAUS (Russian)

Lieut. Col. E.B. Cuthbertson CMG, MVO

CROSS OF ST. GEORGE (Russian)

Sgt. T. Yates DCM

MENTIONS IN DESPATCHES

Capt. H.W.E. Bailey

Lieut. Col. A.J.H. Bowen DSO
(three times)

Lieut. W.T. Charles

L/Cpl. W.H. Chick

Sgt. F. Collins

Capt. R.B. Comely MC

Sgt. J. Counsell

L/Sgt. H.C. Cox

Lieut. Col. E.B. Cuthbertson
CMG, MVO

2nd Lieut. J.E. Dunn

Major A.H. Edwards MC

Cpl. R. Emery

Lieut. Col. J. Evans DSO (twice)

Lieut. A.E. Fraser

L/Sgt. A. Hodges

Lieut. H.J. Hopkins MC

2nd Lieut. H.L. Hughes

Major T. L. Ibbs MC

Lieut. H.V. Kerr

Sgt. H.E. Mason

CSM G.S. Mellsopp

Lieut. Col. H.J. Miers DSO
(twice)

RSM J. Noble MC

Lieut. R.M. Nott

Sgt. D. O'Leary

Lieut. I.E. Owen

2nd Lieut. J.E. Paton

L/Cpl. G. Rappel

RQMS C.E. Richards

Pte. J.H. Robinson

Lieut. R.T. Saunders

Capt. F.L. Spencer

Capt. M.F. Turner MC

Cpl. S. Vaughan

Sgt. E. Wagstaffe MM

Lieut. H.J. Walters

CSM T.H. White

CSM C. Williams

Sgt. G. Wilson

CSM G.T. Yearsley DCM

Extracts from the London Gazette
DISTINGUISHED SERVICE ORDER AWARDS

Captain (Temp. Lieut. Col) Alfred John Hamilton Bowen.

On the 13th May, 1915, east of Ypres, though wounded in two places in the head before dawn, he refused to leave his company and continued to command it with conspicuous ability. After the action was over and the battalion returned to La Brique, he was found to be suffering from two other wounds in the body. He was then sent to hospital. (L.G. 3.7.15.)

For conspicuous gallantry and devotion to duty. He, with great personal gallantry, supervised the difficult task of consolidation throughout the whole night, and continually went round his working parties. He was mainly responsible for the good work carried out. (Bar to D.S.O., L.G. 12.3.17.)

Captain (Acting Major) Hanmer James Miers. (Att. East Lancs)

For conspicuous gallantry and devotion to duty during the attack on Douai Prison on 14 Oct., 1918. He personally conducted the operation under heavy machine gun and artillery fire and it was due to his quick grasp of the situation and the tactical handling of the force that this strong position was captured with comparatively few casualties. Throughout the day his exceptional coolness and disregard for personal safety had a magnificent effect on the men.

MILITARY CROSS AWARDS

Lieutenant Walter Collings
(Attached from 3rd Monmouths)

For conspicuous gallantry and devotion to duty. He displayed great courage and determination in organising and leading stretcher parties to collect wounded under heavy fire. (LG 10.1.17)

Captain John Trevor George

Who was in command of C Company on the night 27th/28th January. This officer's quickness and ability in rapidly getting the men out to work under shell fire enabled them to start immediately and dig down to such a depth that when the enemy opened an intense bombardment later his men had sufficient cover to prevent a serious number of casualties. His coolness and courage under exceptionally trying circumstances were a striking example to his officers and men, and it was largely due to his energy that the work was brought to a successful conclusion. The officer has served 16 months in France and was wounded once severely at the Second Battle of Ypres in May 1915. (Reproduced from the War Diary dated 12th February, 1917. Mentioned in Despatches 12th March, 1917)

2nd Lieut. T.H. White
(2nd/5th East Lancashire Regiment)

For conspicuous gallantry and devotion to duty. While on patrol he encountered an enemy machine gun post. With one man he immediately rushed the post capturing the gun and its crew. (L.G. 22.3.18)

DISTINGUISHED CONDUCT MEDAL AWARDS

265062 CSM W.J. Bowen

For gallantry in action and devotion to duty, particularly during the operations near Outtersteene in August, 1918. On all occasions he has displayed utter disregard for danger when working under heavy shell fire. He is most valuable and reliable as a C.S.M. and has always set a splendid example to the N.C.Os. and men in his company. He has served continuously in France since November, 1914. (L.G. 3.9.19)

265905 Cpl.(L/Sgt) J. Dowding

For conspicuous gallantry and skilful leadership during the operation east of Ledeghem on the 14th October, 1918. He was in charge of two sections detailed to secure the crossing of the Heulebeek by laying infantry footbridges. The two sections early suffered heavily through the enemy barrage, but he pluckily rallied the remainder of his men and encouraged them to complete the carrying and laying of all the bridges, thus enabling the attacking troops to continue the advance. After laying the bridges he collected his party and captured an enemy post which had held out and was hindering the advance. (L.G. 2.12.19)

2190 L/Cpl T.A.W. Drew

For conspicuous gallantry on 2nd January, 1915, at Le Touquet, in voluntarily going to the rescue of a dangerously wounded comrade in full view of the enemy, who were only a hundred yards distant. Lance-Corporal Drew brought the wounded man into cover, but was himself wounded in doing so. (L.G. 7.4.15)

265302 Sgt. C. Hayes

For marked gallantry and devotion to duty during continuous service with the battalion, particularly during the operations east of Ledeghem on the 14th October, 1918. He was in charge of two sections detailed to advance with the leading wave of infantry and secure the crossing of the Heulebeek by laying infantry foot bridges. Under very heavy shell fire he succeeded in getting to his objective. (L.G. 11.3.20)

1608 Pte. W. Hemmings

For great gallantry and devotion to duty as stretcher-bearer throughout the campaign, thereby setting an excellent example for his comrades. (L.G. 30.6.15)

290337 CSM. T. Johnson
(attached from 3rd Monmouths)

For conspicuous gallantry and devotion to duty whilst supervising working parties under continuous bombardment. His splendid courage gave the men confidence to carry on steadily with their work and contributed very largely to its successful completion. (L.G. 17.9.17)

1779 Pte. E. Jones

For gallant conduct on 15th December in rescuing a wounded comrade who was lying exposed close to the enemy's trenches, under a very heavy fire. (L.G. 16.1.15)

6458 Sgt. J. Jones

For conspicuous gallantry and devotion to duty during the period 28th September, 1918, to the cessation of hostilities, particularly in the operations to force the crossing of the Lys on the night of the 19th-20th October. He was in charge of a party of men assisting in the placing of a pontoon bridge across the river. Later he showed great coolness under heavy shell fire, and the completion of the task was due to his excellent personal example. (L.G. 11.3.20)

469 Pte. J. Lewis

For conspicuous gallantry, energy and devotion to duty near Le Touquet from 18th December, 1914, to 9th April, 1915, when engaged in working underground (continually in water) preparing a mine which was successfully exploded on the latter date. This work was very arduous and most hazardous, as the possibility of the German counter-mine being exploded at any moment was ever present. (L.G. 3.6.15)

2058 A/Sgt. C. Love

For great gallantry in going to the rescue of a wounded comrade at night under a heavy rifle and machine gun fire near Le Touquet. Also for conspicous good work since 5th November, 1914. (L.G. 30.6.16)

1420 Pte. J. Morgan

For conspicuous gallantry, energy and devotion to duty near Le Touquet from 18th December, 1914, to 9th April, 1915, when engaged in working underground (continually in water) preparing a mine which was successfully exploded on the latter date. This work was very arduous and most hazardous, as the possibility of the German counter-mine being exploded at any moment was ever present. (L.G. 3.6.15)

1599 A/Cpl. A. E. Pinchin.

For very gallant conduct in leaving his trench under heavy fire to assist a wounded comrade, and, although himself wounded, remaining with the man until he died. (L.G. 6.1.15)

1386 A/Sgt. W.H. Spears

For conspicuous gallantry on several occasions, especially on 24th February, 1915, when he went to the assistance of a wounded man and helped to bring him into cover, under heavy sniping fire. On the 5th January, near Le Bizet, Acting Sergeant Spears displayed great coolness under shell fire, showing a fine example to his men. (L.G. 3.6.15)

265006 Sgt. J Roberts

For conspicuous gallantry and devotion to duty. He has carried out his duties as battalion transport sergeant for two and a half years with the greatest courage and resource, and when in charge of a convoy has never failed to reach his destination. His utter disregard for danger was particularly noticeable on two occasions when he was bringing up stores under heavy shell fire. (L.G. 17.4.18)

450 A/Sgt. D. White

For conspicuous bravery. When in a trench in front of the moated farm, his officer and all the superior non commissioned officers were wounded. In spite of the concentrated fire of the enemy with shells and machine guns on the farm and trenches, he swam the moat to get water for his officer, and then reported the situation at Battalion Headquarters. Having done this, he returned to his trench by the same means, and by his fine example, he held it, in spite of the enemy's fire, until relieved. (L.G. 11.3.16)

265363 Sgt. W. Williams M.M.

For conspicuous gallantry and devotion to duty. During three and a half years' service at the front he has in many engagements displayed much gallantry and ability. On one occasion after his officer was wounded, he commanded his platoon with great success. (L.G. 21.10.18)

265503 Sgt. W. Williams

For conspicuous gallantry and devotion to duty. Under a heavy enemy barrage he kept his men together by his personal example and disregard for danger. Later at a critical period when the Lewis gun had been put out of action he went across a very exposed position under heavy machine-gun fire and borrowed a machine gun from a neighbouring unit, with which he inflicted heavy losses on the enemy and kept the line intact in a difficult flank position. He did very fine service. (L.G. 3.10.18)

1373 A/Sgt. G. Yates

For conspicuous gallantry and good work. On one occasion especially his bravery and determination was of the greatest assistance in keeping the men steady under heavy shell fire. He has on all occasions set a fine example to the men, and thus greatly helped his officers. (L.G. 11.3.16)

894 Sgt. T. Yates

For conspicuous gallantry, energy and devotion to duty near Le Touquet from 18th December, 1914, to 9th April, 1915, when engaged in working underground (continually in water) preparing a mine which was successfully exploded on the latter date. This work was very arduous and most hazardous, as the possibility of the German counter-mine being exploded at any moment was ever present. (L.G. 3.6.15)

255138 CSM T.G. Yearsley

For conspicuous gallantry and devotion to duty. For over two years he has served continuously with the battalion, and both as a sergeant and sergeant-major has done splendid work. He has always proved himself to be both capable and cheerful under the most trying conditions, and has done much to sustain the morale of his company. (L.G. 17.4.18)

MILITARY MEDAL AWARDS

2851 Pte. Stanley James Burnett

On the 1st July, after the attack on Beaumont, Lt. T.E.R. Williams was left severely wounded in No Man's Land. No. 2851 Pte. Stanley James Burnett crawled out under continuous machine gun fire and shell fire over 100 yards, pulled him into a shell hole and finally brought him back to our lines. He undoubtedly saved Lt. Williams life at great risk to his own. (Awarded MM. Extract from War Diary 3.7.16)

1319 Sgt. C. Griffiths

Who was acting as Platoon Commander, and by his devotion to duty and courage on the night in question kept his men in good spirits in spite of considerable casualties due to heavy shelling. He set an excellent example which was of the greatest assistance to his company commander. (Awarded MM. Extract from War Diary 4.2.17. for operations at Le Transloy 27/28 1. 17)

1316 Pte. John Lewis

Who showed great devotion to duty. During the enemy's bombardment he was wounded by a piece of shrapnel. After being bandaged up he requested permission to go on with his work, and he accordingly finished his task in spite of his wound. The loss of a man would have meant a piece of trench not being dug through, and it was due to Pte. Lewis's determination that his particular bit was completed. (Awarded MM. Extract from War Diary 4.2.17. for operations at Le Transloy 27/28 1. 17)

3180 L/Cpl. R.J. Powell

Who was working at the northern end of the left C.T. near Landsturm Trench. He worked continuously without cover on an exceptionally difficult piece of work to prevent it falling behind owing to the hard ground, in spite of heavy shelling experienced at the time. He showed particular courage on this occasion and at all times has displayed a great devotion to duty. (Awarded MM. Extract from War Diary 4.2.17. for operations at Le Transloy 27/28 1. 17)

2898 L/Cpl. T. Rose

During an intense bombardment a shell hit the trench and killed and buried his platoon sergeant and several other men. L/Cpl. Rose at once got hold of a small party and by his energy and coolness got them quickly to work and dug out two of his comrades who had been wounded and buried. Later in the evening he was particulalry conspicuous by his coolness in carrying on his work and his good example was of great assistance in keeping his comrades steady. (Awarded MM. Extract from War Diary 4.2.17. for operations at Le Transloy 27/28 1. 17)

MERITORIOUS SERVICE MEDAL

265385 Sgt. A.F. Smith

On the 5th January, 1917 during bombing practice an NCO throwing a bomb for the first time struck the back of the trench with his hand.... Sgt. Smith..... picked it up, threw it on the parapet where it immediately exploded. Sgt. Smith has served 26 months in France and has been wounded. (L.G. 17.5.17)

Appendix 4

Lieut. Col. A.J.H. Bowen's Notebooks

The following is an edited transcript of the notebooks (Army Book 153 - Field Message Book) of Lieut. Col. A.J.H. Bowen which are now held at the South Wales Borderers and Monmouthshire Regiment Museum at Brecon. Only three books now remain but it is clear that Bowen had used perhaps nine more books during his service with the Battalion. Since the notebooks are written in pencil some of the wording has faded with the passage of time. Further, some of the writing was, for obvious reasons, hurried. Where there is some doubt over the word or where it is illegible parenthesis ( ) are used to indicate this. Italics are used by the author by way of commentary. The notes give a very good indication of the work of the commanding officer and that of a pioneer battalion from 1916 to early 1917.

Book 1 - 11th April 1916 to May 1916

(At this time the Battalion was on duty on the Lines of Communication behind the Front Line.)

Lt. J.E. Dunn
Transport Officer
Please send up 2 G.S. waggons to report to CQMS Garrett at Camp Commandants office No.4 Large Rest Camp between 10.30 and 11 am this morning. They will draw furniture etc. for our Mess in the Camp.

Boulogne   A.J.H. Bowen
11.4.16

(Lieut. John Edward Dunn had been commissioned from Pte. in the Glamorgan Yeomanry and had served with the battalion since 1915)

14.4.16
Inspected detachment at DESVRES under Sergeant Wallis. Rode on horseback to SAMER then Desvres and back (42 kilometres). 4 men short of iron rations. Sentry (off duty?) sitting down away from rifle, buttons undone.

2047 L/Cpl. Butcher has been with the Bn in France since 4.11.14 and has always done his work extremely well. He has never been sick. He is an expert bomber and on many occasions has done good work in the trenches in many parts of the line. His character has always been very good and he has ( ) never been found lacking in the performance of his duty

17.4.16
Boulogne

17.4.16 Inspected MONTREUIL detachment
Exchange Kembrey for a man from HQ K now in hospital
1209 Pte. Phipps wants a pair of boots (No. 8)
2263 Pte. Francis wants another pair of trousers: at present he has only one pair of pantaloons, also wants to exchange his tunic present one too short.
Phipps claims time expired. Rooms in billet clean and tidy, latrines clean but smell in yard from old refuse pit trench. Cookhouse clean - one canteen top lying out and ( )
Washing Bills 1.10, .90, 1.40 = 3.40

(Phipps was obviously correct in his assertion since he was discharged on the 18th May 1916. Pte. Francis died of wounds on 21.7.16)

18.4.16
Gamaches
Jack is the ( ) of Sgt. Pike and also of L/Cpl. Anderson. Men Billetted in house (very) clean and tidy. A man acting as policeman by day. Guard mounts at 6.30 pm - 6 am consisting of 1 NCO and 3 men. Williams very little to do billetted in St. Pierre Hotel. Baths with A.B.C. arranged by R.T.O. Rifles clean and ammunition correct

Longpré
Sgt. Pike. Guardroom dirty and smoky arranged that hut should be provided for the guard. Billet latrines and cookhouse clean and tidy. Two men recently down with (gonorrhoea) warned men against indulgence. Turner, recently in hospital with scabies, returned. Room and blankets have been disinfected. 330 SAA deficient. Rifles clean.

Received from 3307 Pte. E.J. Phillips 2nd Monmouth Regt. CANDAS rifle and breech cover No. on bolt 23159Y for repair of back sight.

18.4.16   A.J.H. Bowen

CANDAS Sgt. Hughes and 9 men: Billet very clean and comfortable in house 5 minutes from station. Rifles clean, one rifle back sight damaged. Guard Room in Railway trench very clean. Cpl. Yorath in charge.
Dinner at MONTRELET with Col. Ogilby Administrative Commandant No. 5 Section Railheads 4th Army. Eggs poached in milk very good.

19.4.16

PUCHEVILLERS. Sgt. Jackson and 17 men (2 men on leave). Living in tents. Bath in tent quite convenient. No houses nearby. Small separate dining tent. Police work by day, sentry work by night. Equipment not in good condition - worn out.

2858 L/Cpl. McNickall enlisted 10.11.14 age 33 asks for promotion and states his pay in debit allots 6d to wife. Wants new pack of cards.

(2858 Pte. John William McNicoll had joined the battalion in France on 17th March, 1915 - there is no record of his eventual rank when he was discharged on 4th February, 1919. Sgt. Jonathan Jackson was awarded a Military Medal and was killed in action on the first day of the Somme)

BELLE EGLISE

Cpl. Brown and 8 men in tents. Pte. Burke states he is time expired, 2196 Pte. Baker has a bulged rifle seen by ordnance Sgt. who arranged to send down another.
Get baths at ACHEUX once a week 1 pair of boots required by L/Cpl. Baker. Cpl. Brown has put in an indent for all necessary clothing which is coming.
1145 Pte BURGE enlisted 10 May 1910 time expired 9 May 1914 re-engaged for 12 months extra year expires May 1916 does not wish to re-engage.
3226 Pte Bond requires his AB 64 called in for correction
Have no games would like some dominoes card etc. get cigarettes every Saturday. Rations good get plenty of potatoes.

(The number, 1145, refers to Pte. A. Burke who had already been wounded in action on at least one occasion.)

ACHEUX Sgt. Webb and 9 men living in a billet, barn, very comfortable, has new stove for cooking. Rifles clean.
Civilians not very clean: Bass bottles, empty, outside the yard. Baths in the SUCRERIE. 2nd SWB now at COLINCAMPS.

MERICOURT. 2 Lt Howick & 10 men living in tents. Guards in tent turned out smartly has a German of the 62nd Regt as a prisoner.
2879 Pte. Jones complained of not having had leave since Februaury 1915. Rifles and bayonets clean. Want some cards etc.
Pte. Butcher informed that his brother has scarlet fever in the house so could not be granted leave.

BOUQUE MAISON. Sgt. Jenkins, Sentry Box required and windows in the Guard Hut to be repaired. 2 men recently in hospital with (gonorrhoea). Sgt. Jenkins stated that an inspection of the house had been made and things all found clean.

The OC 5th Auxiliary M. Transport Coy.
I am much obliged for the use of the motorcar No. 132794 Driver Nicholls has driven the car exceedingly well and been most useful. Neither he nor the car have been found wanting at any time.

20.4.16   A.J.H. Bowen
Car M427

20.4.16

AUBIGNY: 2 Lt. SANKEY and ( ) men. Men billetted in a cottage near the Railway Line. Clean and tidy store floor. Guard on for 24 hours. Guard Room is a hut, very comfortable. Men fit, 3 cases of influenza recently all recovered. Robertson on guard. Baths in the large hospital nearby.

SAA short arrange to complete same.

rear to CARENCY: visit in three weeks time.

(Lieut. William Manderville Sankey MC was killed in action on 23rd March, 1918 while the Battalion were stationed in the Ypres Salient)

SAVY BERLETT. Sgt Walters and 15 men Postal address O.C. Train C/O F.P.O. H.17. Billetted close to station in red French huts. Comfortable wire beds each man had three blankets but only 1 tunic, 1 pr trousers and boots each. The Sgt. stated he had indented 3 days ago to complete clothing to 2 per man. Cooking and dining hut very clean and tidy. Baths in a hut nearby. Cooks provide hot water. No sick lately. Men wash their own clothes.

O.C. A Coy Monmouths DOULLENS

Bn arrives Doullens 15.30 tomorrow 28.4.16. AAA. Please arrange guides inform Transport Officer.

Cmdg Monmouths
27th   A.J.H. Bowen

O.C. Transport 1/2 Monmouth Regt.

Transport will entrain at Quai au BESTIAUX 'PETIT VITESSE' , GARE CENTRALE, Boulogne at 6.30 a.m. tomorrow 28.4.16. You should report to RTO Gare Centrale at 6.30 am tomorrow.

2 Lt. Morgan and 50 men will report to you at Transport Lines OUTREAU RD CONTROL at 5.30 am to act as leading and ordnance party. 2 three ton lorries or 5 G.S. wagons will report also to you at that hour to convey ORDNANCE stores to the train. Bn will reach DOULLENS at about 15.30 to 16.00 hrs. Train is C98 leaves Boulogne at 9.32.

You will arrange breakfast in transport lines for loading party.

27.4.16   A.J.H. Bowen

Adjutant 1/2nd Monmouth Regt.

Please instruct Lt. BADDELLEY and CQMS + 1 man of each Company and 1 man for Transport and 1 man for HQ to proceed to BEAUSSART tomorrow 29.4.16 as advance party to arrange billets etc. They will proceed by train for ACHEUX leaving DOULLENS at 7.28 am and march from ACHEUX to BEAUSSART. They will take rations up to and for the 30th inst. Bathing in the River AUTHIE is forbidden.

28.4.16   A.J.H. Bowen
DOULLENS 5.50 pm
O.C. All Coys
Major Evans
The Bn will (be) inspected on the line of March tomorrow at MARIEUX by Lieut Gen HUNTER-WESTON VII Corps Commander, at about 10.20 am. Halts on the march to BEAUSSART will be 5 minutes at 8.25 and ten minutes ending each hour. Billets must be left thoroughly clean. They will be inspected by Major Evans before moving off.

30.4.16
Doullens   A.J.H. Bowen.

2 Lt. Rutherford
i/c Lewis Guns 1/2nd Monmouths
The Bn has moved to BEAUSSART. You will follow as ordered by Administrative Commandant, DOULLENS, probably tomorrow 2nd May 1916.
Route DOULLENS, SARTON - LOUVENCOURT - ACHEUX - BERTRANCOURT - BEAUSSART 15½ miles
Your rations for 3rd will be waiting for you at BEAUSSART. Wire me probable time of arrival.

1.5.16   A.J.H. Bowen

O.C All Coys, Transport, Lewis gun
In the event of a Stand To be ordered the Bn will parade in the Street in Column of Route. Head of the column by the northern Guard Post facing BERTRANCOURT. Order of march D,C,A,B, Lewis Gun Detachments, 1st Line Transport, Ammunition and Tool Mules will accompany Companies. The Bn must be nearby to march within 15 minutes of Stand To being ordered. Dress: Full Marching Order.

1.5.16   A.J.H. Bowen
BEAUSSART

O.C. All Coys
Parades today
9.45   Close order Drill by Platoons
11.15   Rapid Firing Practice
           Extended Order Practice
11.30 - 12 Gas Helmet Inspection
Return by 3 pm of all damaged gas helmets

2.5.16   A.J.H. Bowen

FAIRWEATHER RD.
from CRE 2.5.16 we are to construct a road from ACHEUX to ENGELBELMER about 3½ miles long. Route marked out, ditching on each side to be done 9" x 12" x 10 yds to be one man's task equal to 30 cubic ft. Acheux Wood has many stumps in. Earth etc. to be thrown on the sides leaving the natural surface of the road. Road to be 20' wide

Major Evans

O.C. All Coys, Transport.

parade for works on FAIRWEATHER RD. tomorrow at 7.45 a.m. Order of companies work from left B, A, C, D.

Companies will march to the left of the Sectors with 1 pick & 1 Shovel per man and commence work as already directed.

Hours of work daily 9 - 12

Interval for dinner 12 - 13.30

Hours of work 13.30 - 16.30

Men must be started on their work by 9 am, 13.30 punctually.

Travelling kitchen will bring out dinners.

Dress; Marching order without packs. Tea on return to billets. Breakfast 6.30

2.5.16   A.J.H. Bowen.

Lt. Foster

(Tentage) Required

Strength Officers 31 OR 757

Tents Required

Tents Marquee		
QM Stores	1	
MO	1	
Officers & Sgts	1	
Mess	1	
Orderly Room	1	= 5
Tents Bell		
1 CO		
3 Field Officers	3	
27 Field Officers	14	
Guard Tents	2	
R Sgt. Major	1	
OR (10 m Tents)	76	= 97 say 100
Tent boards	420	
Latrine screens	30	
Buckets Latrine	48	

Camp in ACHEUX Wood March in 6.5.16

OC Coys warn men of necessity for absolute cleanliness, situation of latrines ( ) buckets will be put at end of lines at 8pm. Tents must be thoroughly clean and tidy before men go out in the morning. No work tomorrow.

Breakfast 7 am

Inspection of camp 8.30 am

Church Parade 11 am

Camp in N.W. Sector of ACHEUX WOOD *(Bowen's sketch)*

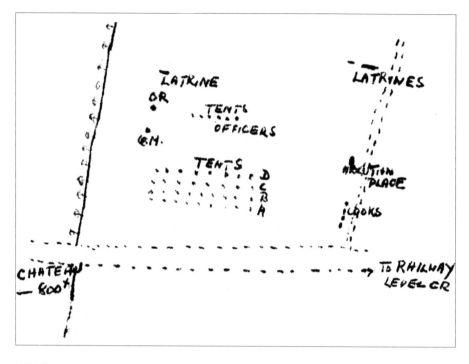

6.5.16
Transport Officer 1/2nd Monmouths
Please detail 2 G.S. Wagons - 4 men (from RSM) as bearers to fetch wood from R.E. Park ENGLEBELMER (CRE Dump) AAA. They will start at 9 am tomorrow 7.5.16 AAA. Authorities herewith to be returned to me AAA. Please use ROTTEN ROW the new road as much as possible with your transport.

6.5.16

A.J.H. Bowen
Lt. Col.
Cmdg 1/2nd Monmouth Regt.

O.C. all Coys, Transport, Lewis Guns.
While engaged in present work the Battalion will be prepared to move into action on 2 hours notice, every man fully equipped and with 1st line transport. Owing to working parties some difficulty may be experienced in getting men concentrated in Camp. Coy Cmdrs will ensure that communications with their Coys is kept open and for the rapid transmission of orders and concentration of men. As soon as a Coy is concentrated, the Commander will report position and numbers to Cmdg Officer.
Normally concentration will take place in Coy lines but if a Coy is out working an orderly should be sent out at once to report to HQ. To ensure the rapid

concentration of their Coys Commanders should warn the men what to do in case of the alarm being sounded. Rifles and equipment may be left at the place of concentration but men must always have their smoke helmets by them.

ACHEUX

A.J.H. Bowen
Lt. Col.
Cmdg 1/2nd Monmouth Regt.

O.C. C and D Coys
You will leave ACHEUX WOOD tomorrow 9.5.16 at 9am and proceed to MAILLY WOOD AAA. Capt. COMELY C. will act as guide. MAJOR E. EDWARDS will be in command AAA. The two companies will have tents struck, blankets ready to move by 8.50 am. One water cart will accompany. AAA. One Corporal and 2 O.R. per company will be at transport lines by 6 am to check tools. The Corporal should know the no. to which his company is entitled AAA. Both Coys will march to AUCHONVILLERS by 2 pm to work on the village defences. Guides and instructors will be supplied later AAA. Blanket wagons will be outside Coy lines by 7.30 am

8.5.16

A.J.H. Bowen
Lt. Col.
Cmdg 1/2nd Monmouth Regt.

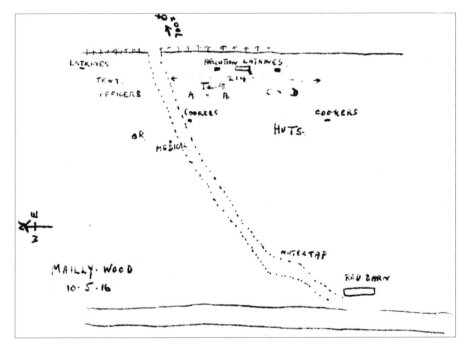

Major A.H. Edwards O.C. A Coy
Your Company will work tomorrow 11.5.16 for the Kent Field Coy R.E.
ENGLEBELMER. Work will be (a) Making tunnel dug-outs; for this work 80 men
with underground and mining experience should be detailed. (b) Sinking a well;
(c) other work as detailed by the Field Coy. (b) will require men with mining or
pit experience. Hours of work and names of officers to whom to report will be
notified later AAA.

10.5.16
MAILLY WOOD

A.J.H. Bowen
Lt. Col.
Cmdg 1/2nd Monmouth Regt.

Orders for Camp in MAILLY WOOD
(1) All ranks must keep inside the wood and not move unnecessarily beyond
the EASTERN hedge. The enemy's balloon will easily observe movement on the
E side of the hedge.
(2) Fires are to be put out by 7.45 pm and all lights kept covered.
(3) If hostile aeroplanes come over men will at once be down under cover and
remain there until the aeroplane has gone.
(4) In the event of the wood being shelled all ranks with arms and equipment will
take shelter in the trench by the hedge. O.C. Coys will practice this movement.
Platoons must keep together so that the Bn can move rapidly if ordered to do
so.
(5) All tents are to be screened with boughs, trees and brushwood
10.5.16

A.J.H. Bowen
Lt. Col.
Cmdg 1/2nd Monmouth Regt.

OC C Company
Please construct a communication trench as per sketch attached. The object is to
provide a continuous good communication trench through the Southern side of
AUCHONVILLERS to the front line from near the level crossing. Dimensions 6'
deep, 6' wide at the top 3' wide at the bottom; provide a berm and a channel on
the back side of trench 6' deep, leading to small sumps in trench. These sumps are
not to be too large, i.e. they must not exceed in width the length pieces of the
trench ladders put over them.
Provide a firing step on enemy side of the trench.
Detail Lt. FOSTER and 20 men to carry out the work. Start work today.

16.5.16

A.J.H. Bowen
Lt. Col.
Cmdg 1/2nd Monmouth Regt.

Orderly reached T.O. at Acheux 1.25 am

(The following sketches are in Bowen's hand directly from his notebook)

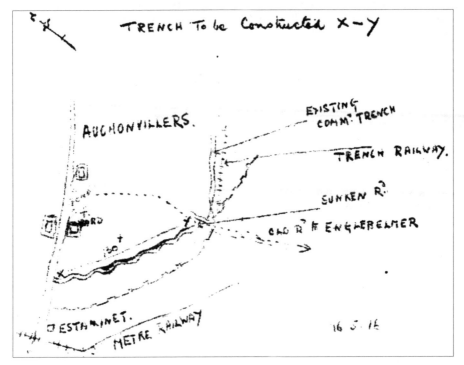

O.C. C and D Comapnies
  Section of Communication Trench

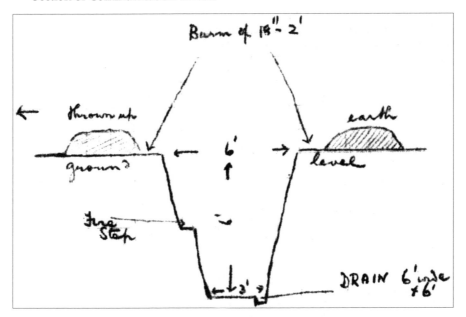

sump holes to be made in centre of trench dimensions 1' 9" wide x 3' long so that the width does not exceed width between length pieces of trench ladders.

Please see your Platoon & Section (Cmdrs) understand and follow the above directions.

16.5.16

A.J.H. Bowen
Lt. Col.
Cmdg 1/2nd Monmouth Regt.

Major Evans 1/2nd Mon Regt.
Please direct 2/Lt COPPOCK to bring his detachment to MAILLY WOOD tonight AAA. He will obtain his own transport from T.O. and report arrival in camp to Cmdg Officer. They will cease work on horse lines AAA. Please arrange to hand over your work to next senior officer. The F.A. men are going on with the work.

18.5.16

A.J.H. Bowen
Lt. Col.
4.30 pm   Cmdg 1/2nd Monmouth Regt.

Order of work tonight on YELLOW LINE 19.5.16
B Coy from 2nd AVENUE to TIPPERARY AVENUE inc. wiring a new line about 20 yards from trench between trench and preset wire. Height of wire about 3' and with trip. Remainder of men deepening fire trench and providing fire step.

A Coy (less 3 platoons) and D Coy from TIPPERARY AVENUE to bridge at FORT ANLEY. Work deepening trench making fire step out of filled sand bags (and building) traverses. Earth must not be thrown on the parapet. This now will be concealed from the enemy as fresh earth would be seen. Wiring will be done later.

C Coy (with 1 platoon from A Coy) will dig a new fire trench from end of present trench S of FORT WITHINGTON on the side of the road to GABION AV. where the trench runs on to FORT MOULIN. Depth of trench 4' 6". Bays 8 yards long traverses 3 yards deep by 4 yards wide width of trench 3' firing step to be left out of natural earth. Leave a berm for sandbag revetment AAA. Cover all work up with grass etc.

Work to be started by 8.30 am and finished by 2 pm. Haversack Ration to be taken.

A.J.H. Bowen
Lt. Col.
Cmdg 1/2nd Monmouth Regt.

Officers are reminded that they are responsible for the protection of their command against surprise.

O.C. B, C, D, Coys
The work on YELLOW LINE is proceeding satisfactorily. G.O.C. (insisits) the fire
trench to be 7 ft deep and the fire step to be 3' above the bottom of the trench.
C Coys trench should be widened to allow for extra depth. Please take necessary
action.

23.5.16

A.J.H. Bowen
Lt. Col.
Cmdg 1/2nd Monmouth Regt.

Major Evans to meet GSO2 and go up to FORT JACKSON to take over the work.

O.C. C Coy
Your section of the YELLOW LINE is extended as follows: from the Railway to
JUNCTION with GABION AV. Please arrange your work accordingly.

23.5.16

A.J.H. Bowen
Lt. Col.
Cmdg 1/2nd Monmouth Regt.

O.C. All Coys.
Sunday 4th June 2.30 pm. Parade of Platoon Sergeants CSM's and 2 Section
commanders per Platoon for instruction in Bayonet Fighting, Rapid Wiring under
Sergt. Dows, Sgt. Laws and Sgt. Stockham.

1.6.16

A.J.H. Bowen
Lt. Col.
Cmdg 1/2nd Monmouth Regt.

29th Div G.S.
The men working in Deep Dugouts BUCKINGHAM PALACE RD reported today
that they heard sounds of digging at about the same level i.e. 15' underground.
Work was stopped in both dugouts but the digging continued. It was as if a man
was working with a pick, slow strokes, and working in the German manner
according to men who have had experience of German mining in other parts of the
line. The digging was heard on the eastern side of No. 2 dugout. The Sergeant i/c
reported the matter to a Lieutenant of the 1st Inniskillings. Two men were left on
guard on the dugout.

7.6.16
8.30 pm.

Lt. Col A.J.H. Bowen
Cmdg 1/2nd Monmouth Regt.

O.C. All Companies, Transport, LMG
1. In the event of attack the Bn will assemble in MAILLY WOOD on the alarm post.
You will at once report to O.R. that your Coys are standing giving the number of
men on parade.

2. All working parties in or in front of the GREEN LINE will in case of attack come under orders of the nearest Battalion Cmdr. O.C. NCO Cmdg working parties will always ascertain the situation of the HQ nearest Bn. and as soon as work has been started should in person report to the C.O. of the Bn informing him of the strength of the working party, where they are working and for how long.

8.6.16

A.J.H. Bowen
Lt. Col.
Cmdg 1/2nd Monmouth Regt.

to Lieut. GEORGE.
Work for night 9-10th June 1916. Digging trenches (2) for B29 TMB in BLOOMFIELD AVENUE and 4 emplacements.
Tasks: Trench 50' long x 4' deep x 3' wide = 600 cft. No. of trenches 3
Task per man 5' x 4' x 3' = 60 cft
No. of men to work 20 (10 on each trench)
EMPLACEMENTS (4) two will be dug tonight. Depth 13' x 8' square = 832 cft.
1st task tonight = 2 pits of 416 cft = 832 cft = 16 men (8 on each pit) to dig 6½ deep x 8' x8'
Total number of men for work 36.
One pick and one shovel per man will be taken. Move off from O.R. 7.30 pm.

9.6.26

A.J.H. Bowen
Lt. Col.
Cmdg 1/2nd Monmouth Regt

Dear Owen,
    Will you come to dinner on Wednesday evening next 14th June 1916. Shall be glad to see your smiling countenance once more and hear how Abergavenny is looking.
    We are in MAILLY WOOD. Dine at 7.30 pm.

11.6.16

A.J.H. Bowen

2148 Sgt Davies A Coy
you with 14 OR will report to Lt WHITEFORD of RFA Trench Mortar Battery at KNIGHTSBRIDGE BARRACKS at 8.30 pm this evening AAA. Your work will be to make a Bomb Store Trench 50' long 3' wide x 4' deep and a charge store 10' long x 5' deep x 4' wide for Z29 TMB in Mary Redan. Situation of trench off Regent St.
10 men for trench 10, task per man 5' long x 4' deep x 3' wide = 60 cft
10 men for Store 4
Take one shovel per man and 1 pick between 2

10.10 am
13.6.16

A.J.H. Bowen
Lt. Col.
Cmdg 1/2nd Monmouth Regt.

2 Lt. B.D. Williams
Cable trenches to be repaired where crossing road
1. Between AUCHONVILLERS STATION & AUCHONVILLERS
2. on ENGLEBELMER - AUCHONVILLERS Road
The cable trenches have not been filled in properly, consequently lorries have stuck there.
Send party of 4 to each point carrying 4 shovels and 2 rammers to put road right as soon as possible

16.6.16
12.35 pm

A.J.H. Bowen
Lt. Col.
Cmdg 1/2nd Monmouth Regt.

(Book 1 ends here)

Book 2 - 1st July 1916 to 23rd August 1916

O.C. B Coy.
WORCESTERS will hold line tonight and carry out today's programme tomorrow. You will get men together and report to HQ situation I will try send you 10% with rations. You will carry out the same work tomorrow. You should report your situation as soon as possible. HQ remains in M Wood.

4.10 pm.
1.7.16

A.J.H. Bowen.

Get your men together, report your situation to HQ M Wood. I will try send 10% with rations this evening.

4.10 pm
per Pte. Rappell.

A.J.H. Bowen.

29th Div.

I beg to bring to your notice the gallant conduct of 2097 BURNETT G., 2nd Monmouthshire Regiment. On the 1st July (yesterday) after the attack on BEAUMONT, Lt. T.E.R. WILLIAMS was left severely wounded in NO MAN'S LAND. Pte. Burnett crawled out under continuous machine gun fire and shell fire over 100 yds, pulled him into a shell hole and finally brought him back to our line. He undoubtedly saved Lt. Williams' life.

2nd July 1916

A.J.H. Bowen.

(Pte. Burnett was awarded the MM for his gallantry and Lieut. T.E.R. Williams survived the war reaching the rank of Captain.)

Adjutant 1/2 Mons.

The battalion will move into FETHARD ST. leaving M WOOD at 9 pm tonight in Bde Reserve to 88th Brigade who attack tomorrow. I will see Platoon Commanders on my return. C Coy will move to YELLOW LINE and pick up consolidating material there and take to FETHARD ST.

Warn Company Commanders to see men have a good meal at tea time and bring plenty of water up as well as full water bottles and tomorrow's rations.

B Coy will detail 20 men to continue sap from eastern mouth of tunnel of Sap 6 starting work at 2 am (3rd) July, 1916.

We will have to consolidate a flank defence line 01-43-85 or attack Bde objective 60-89 inc.

3.50 pm
3rd July 1916

A.J.H. Bowen.

86th Bde.

2nd Lt. J. Hollywood 12th R.I.R.

I found the body of the officer and enclose herewith his identity disc and small articles which were all I could find on him. I was informed that the stretcher bearers of D Company 5th R. Sussex (Pioneers) Regt. has just previously searched his body which is now lying in a shell hole 20 yds in rear of fire trench and about 120 yds N of the junction of the fire trench and communication trench dug tonight. The badge of rank is on his shoulder straps.

12th July 1916
2.30 a.m
handed in

A.J.H. Bowen.

(2nd Lieut. James Hollywood, 18th attached 12th R.I.R., was killed in action on 1st July 1916. If his body was ever recovered following Bowen's note his burial place was not recorded since the name of the young officer can now be found on the Thiepval Memorial to the missing.)

29th Div. A.

I beg to bring to your notice the excellent work done by Captain E. EDWARDS of the battalion under my command, during 20 months in France and Belgium. He has proved himself a thoroughly reliable Company Commander under fire and has done good work in trenches at YPRES, KEMMEL, WYTSCHAETE and during the winter of 1915, opposite BEAUMONT HAMEL and SERRE. He has behaved particulary well in the recent operations opposite BEAUMONT in front of HAMEL.

14th July 1916

A.J.H Bowen.

1/2 Monmouthshire Regiment
Entraining State
28.7.16.
25 Officers
559 OR
107 Horses
13 4 wheeled vehicles
28 2 wheeled vehicles
5 handcarts.

28.7.16

A.J.H. Bowen.

29 Div A.
In reply to A 1397 I beg to recommend Capt. E. EDWARDS of the battalion under my command for appointment as commandant of a Pioneer School. He has been in France from May 1915 to the present date continuously acting as Company Commander and 2nd in Command at various times. Before the war he was a surveyor to an Urban District Council and has a thorough knowledge of civil engineering in addition to his military knowledge. He is 33 years old.

29.7.16.

A.J.H. Bowen

(Capt. Edward Edwards was killed in action on 17th August, 1916.)

Streets in YPRES 29th Div. Area.
1. SE to the Canadians.

Div. in by line from Ramparts along Rue de Jacques *(St. Jacobstraat)* to Grand Place. Along south side of Grand Place - Rue de Lille - Rue de Cassel - Rue de Scrivinaire(?) *(Seminariestraat)* - Rue de la Busche - Rue des Etudiants *(Studentenlaan)*
- also Hopital de Notre Dame on East side of Grand Place temporarily allotted to the Canadian Corps
Bn. has Bn. HQ at 25 Rue de la Bouche
Bn. HQ in Prison of 1 Coy. 1 Coy in Magasin and 1 Coy in Rue de Elverdinghe.
Coy in Edouard Francs Street and 1 Coy in Div. Switch.

1 Bn. HQ & 1 Coy at Convent des Commes
also in Rue de la Bouche
1 Coy in Boules Malon
1 Coy in Rue de la Station *(Stationstraat)*
1 Coy Rue du Temple *(Templestraat)*

RE's are all in Rue Dixmude *(Diksmuidestraat)*
12th 1st W. Rding, 1st London.
120th RE Rue du Jules Cafiron
Monmouths current Rue de Buerre. *(Boterstraat)*

Work on Road to St. Jean
2 Platoons of B will do this work tonight.

Rue de Carton *(Cartonstraat)*
> North side no cellars all houses smashed in
> In this side one small cellar accommod(ation), decayed refuse inside on other possible cellar.
> one ( ) in at SE corner of Rue de Carton and Rue de Dixmude also NE side big cellar had no roof. This could be made into a good cellar. Ditto SW corner.
> 2nd house from corner Dixmude - Carton St. good basement room - no roof
> 3rd house good cellar wants cleaning out badly No.62
> 61 Estaminet but not find cellar
> to
> 49   "   "   "   "   "

Opposite 35 small cellar wants cleaning out.

Rue de Elverdinghe 49 good cellar - accommodation 25 requires cleaning.
51 & 53 - cellar (fallen) in but could be repaired.

Rue de Fequenheerd *(Eigenheerdlaan ?)*
> 44 cellar (fallen) in - could be repaired
> 42 ditto
> 40 in fair condition basements want cleaning out.

Opposite 13 by building with vaulted hall and archways to cellar in good condition basement entirely (fallen) in

SE Corner of Malou *(Maloulaan)* and ( ) STUDTS St. 2 good cellars accommodation 20 each - entrance wants cleaning.

Malou St. Cafe Metropole No. 3
basement could be repaired and would then give accommodation for 20.
No. 5 & 7 good cellars - 20 in good condition.
No. 9 small cellar - 6 in poor condition.
No. 11 ditto 6 ditto
No. 13 cellar broken in could be repaired
No. 15 basement broken in.
Rue de la Station.
No. 44 big basement good condition accommodate 30 - house above standing
No. 42 good basement accomm(odate) 10
No. 38 good cellar accomm(odate) 20
No. 34 cellar good condition 10
No. 32 small basement wants repairing (8)
> 39 S. corner of Station Rd. - Rue St. Sabastian, basement condition fair wants strengthening.

Rue du Temple. mem. west side small (6) wants cleaning, house standing.
Rue du Beaune at NW corner with Rue du Temple. Basement wants repairing accomm(odate) 30
Church
No. 8 house next of church good cellars but 6" water and very dirty.

29th Div. G.S.

84 Sgt. Butcher C.

I beg to forward Summary of Evidence in the case of the above mentioned NCO. He was charged before me with 'Falling out without permission from a working party'. Would you please advise me to what charge he should be tried upon

11.8.16.

A.J.H. Bowen

(Sgt. C. Butcher had served with the battalion in France since November, 1914. He was transferred to W.C. Labour Centre No. 257817 (Sgt.))

O.C. B Coy 1/2 Monmouth Reg.

The 20 men working tomorrow will carry out task 2, i.e. fitting in U frames and galvanised sheets, nailing down trench boards so that they are 3" below ground level. 10 of the men will work for D Coy under Cpl. Cox. They will report to O.C. D Coy at 8.30 am tomorrow, they will take with them mauls, hammers, saws and nails. The remaining 10 will work in the trench your Coy was digging tonight. You will inspect the work early tomorrow morning and satisfy yourself that it is being correctly carried out. They will carry the same tools as above and fill in all material now in the trench. They will all take haversack rations and full water bottles.

Pte. Williams
15.8.16.
1.35 am
URGENT

A.J.H. Bowen

O.C. A, B, C, D Coys 1.2. Monmouths

The Head Censor has drawn my attention to the fact that letters censored have been received at Base which contain references to places where the Battalion is or recently has been.

This shows that there is a serious neglect of duty on the part of some officers. Please draw the attention of all your officers to the Censorship Regulations and the responsibility resting on officers to see that these regulations are strictly and loyally complied with.

15.8.16.

A.J.H. Bowen

O.C. C. Coy.

you will continue work on PARK LANE and NEW TRENCH from SUPPORT LINE to PICCADILLY tonight.

New Trench is now on average 4' wide and 3' deep. 30 men (exclusive of Sgts) will widen it to 4' 6" and deepen to 4' 6" to take U frames. The earth will be thrown on the SE side forming a parapet 3' high and leaving a berm of 2'. They will work in 10' lengths. They will place U frames in position and drive pegs for wiring.

PARK LANE

50 men (exclusive of Sgts) will continue parapet on N side leaving berm of 2'. Parapet to be 3' high.

1 Sgt and 10 men will deepen trench through Support Line ready to take U frames.

17.8.16.

A.J.H. Bowen.

O.C. A Company

You will carry up for D Company and obtain a receipt from 1914 Sgt. WILLIAMS the following goods, which are to be deposited in PARK LANE and NEW TRENCH

35 U frames PARK LANE
24 Galvanized Sheets
50 Pickets
50 Trench Boards
150 U Frames NEW TRENCH
100 Galvanized Sheets
200 Pickets
3 Coils Wire
50 Trench Boards

17.8.16

A.J.H. Bowen.

(Sgt. W. Williams had landed with the Battalion in 1914 and was to survive the war).

O.C. B Coy
PICCADILLY

The day work in this trench is not being satisfactorily carried out and it is evident that there is a lack of supervision and energy.

The trench must be finished off as it moves eastwards, at present not a yard is floored and one cannot (attack) from X line. The U frames must be picketted and wired. In future day parties will breakfast early and start work by 6 am, an NCO will remain in the trench from the night party and point out the work to be done and hand over material to the officer or NCO i/c Day Party. The day Party must be i/c of an officer or visited twice by an officer during the work.

I will inspect the trench today at about noon and will call at your HQ for an officer to accompany me.

16.8.16
2.45 am

A.J.H. Bowen.

O.C. D Coy.

You will continue work on PARK LANE and NEW TRENCH tonight.
PARK LANE

30 men (excluding NCO's) will continue revetting and making up parapet. They should carry up revetting screens and pickets.

NEW TRENCH

60 men will revet and make up the parapet in the E side by digging from borrow pits. They should carry up revetting screens and pickets. Men will work on 5' runs and should dig out and throw up earth for parapet from a trench 5' long 3' wide and 3' deep at 5 yards distance from NEW TRENCH.

5 men will work in NEW TRENCH fixing revetting screens on both sides of the trench throughout its length.

18.8.16

A.J.H. Bowen.

O.C. D Coy.

Please send an officer along POTIJZE trench to see if any new camouflage is required AAA. If there is this should be done tonight by the working party AAA. A report must be made on this work; is it finished?

18.8.16

O.C. D Coy

Please instruct the party working in PARK LANE to heighten the parapet on the Southern side AAA. Working from the support line for a distance of 40 yds towards the firing line AAA. The day party did not finish flooring PARK LANE and did not use the material sent up last night AAA. Please report the reason for this AAA.

18.8.16

A.J.H. Bowen.

O.C. D Coy

Tonight 19th you will continue work on PARK LANE and PICCADILLY.

In PICCADILLY you will deepen the existing trench from NEW TRENCH junction to where boards are now in, a distance of 88 yds so that it will take U Frames, i.e 4.0' deep and 4' 6" wide at top and 3' at bottom clearing the berm on the southern side to 2'. The earth to be put on the parapet on the southern side and camouflaged. This will take 53 men working in 5' lengths.

The remainder will be employed on revetting and heightening parapet in NEW TRENCH - PARK LANE.

Following materials will be brought up

U Frames	100
Gal Sheets	50
Revetting Screeens	50
Trench Boards	50

19.8.16
6.15 pm

A.J.H. Bowen

ADMS 29th Div.

31748 Cpl WATKINS, R.C.

With reference to the attached, I have honour to report that I have no objection to Cpl WATKINS joining the Medical Unit as I do not wish to stand in the way of his further promotion.

23.8.16

A.J.H. Bowen

O.C. B Coy

Sergt. PHILLIPS today had no definite task allotted to him and consequently was unable to say what work he had been ordered to do or whether his task was finished. The men are not to work under RE but must be given a proper task. You should see that this is done and that the task is finished, at present there seems to be no supervision of the work being done on the elephants. Please explain to your subordinate commanders that they are responsible to see that the work is properly done and finished off, and for this end definite tasks must be given. They should report to you each day the tasks allotted and you will satisfy yourself that they are carried out.

23.8.16
2.40 pm

A.J.H. Bowen

(Book Two finishes at this point)

Book 3 - 23rd January 1917 to 2nd March 1917

O.C. B Coy. 1/2 Monmouth Regt.

Please detail 2+ under Lt. Owen to carry up trench boards to and place them in the trench dug by our A Coy on the night of 21st, that is on the right of the WEST RIDINGS who were digging on your right. A guide from the KOSB's, who have relieved the Inniskillings will be at FLANK AVENUE, BULL DUMP RAILHEAD at 6.30 pm tonight to guide the party to the left (No.13) post held by the KOSB which was near where the RE on your right were digging.

23.1.17

A.J.H. Bowen.

Dear Glenister

I find the trains have been altered & shall be much obliged if I could start at 9.30 am from your office instead of the time mentioned

Yours sincerely
A.J.H. Bowen

MEAULTE
10.2.17
4.30 pm

(It would appear that Bowen was off on leave or to attend a course for the next entry is a week later)

OC 7th Bn Y & L 17 Div (Pioneer B)
The arrangements suggested in your F177 of the 17th will suit very well. My Officers & OR coming tomorrow will stay in the Company areas until the Battn arrives if you will (kindly) put them up.
My second in command is also coming over tomorrow (18th) and will return the next day. Can you let him have a trench map and statement of dispositions of companies work in hand etc.

17.2.17	A.J.H. Bowen.
MEAULTE	OCmdg/2 Monmouth Reg
1.15 pm	Pioneer 29th Div.

i/c FREGICOURT DUMP
Please issue to Monmouth Pioneers 75 Duckboards 12 lb 5" nails

21.2.17	A.J.H. Bowen
	Lt. Col

OC B Coy
Situation at present, we do not hold P(F)ALZ TRENCH from U8 D7.2 to the south. You cannot therefore dig the C Trench originally ordered.
You will report to OC 2nd Royal Fusiliers with your comp. and he will issue orders direct to you. Be prepared to hold the line reinforcing the R.F's. AAA
Guides will be at ( ) Brigade HQ to take you to Bn HQ at U14 B4.8.
Inform Bn Commander that you have two bombs per man and rations.

4.45 pm	A.J.H. Bowen
Bde HQ	
28.2.17	

O.C. C Coy Capt J.T. George
Situation at 4 pm. P(F)ALZ TR had been lost from U8 D5.3 southwards. POTSDAM TR is held by us up tp U8 D1^1/2.7
B Coy had been detailed to reinforce 2nd R.F.'s on the right.
A Coy at present under their original orders
Your Coys should be prepared to move at short notice in fighting order with 2 bombs per man and a day's ration.

28.2.17

A.J.H. Bowen

O.C. A Coy (Capt. W.D. Howick)
We have been ordered by RAKE to garrison posts U82 and U83 till tomorrow evening. You will, therefore, when the left C.T. to POTSDAM TR is complete garrison these two posts and the three bays in the left CT with 1 officer and 50 men.

28.2.17   A.J.H. Bowen
11.45 pm
handed to OC A Coy

O.C. C Coy (Capt J.T. George)
We have been ordered by RAKE to garrison the post U14.2 in the original front line of the 2nd Bn Royal Fusiliers till tomorrow evening. After the right CT is dug you will therefore leave your party of 1 officer and 31 men in the post. You must arrange with OC 2nd Royal Fusiliers for a guide and inform him of your dispositions throughout the day.

1.3.17.   A.J.H. Bowen
12.30 am

Handed to OC C Coy
at 3 am 1.3.17
U14.2 found obliterated and arranged with OC 2nd R.F's that the 1 officer and 31 (OR's) of C coy should garrison CUSHY and SAILLY STRONG POINTS.
O.C. C.Coy
Your posts in SAILLY and CUSHY STRONG POINTS will be relieved by the NEWFOUNDLAND REGT today AAA. Please inform officer in charge.

6 am
1.3.17   A.J.H. Bowen
by telegraph from
A Coy Combles

O.C. A Coy
Your posts in U8.2 and U8.3 and the left CT will be relieved tonight by NEWFOUNDLAND AAA. Please inform officer in charge

6 am   Cmdg Officer
1.3.17
by telegraph

HQ RAKE
The 50 men working on POTSDAM TR are now digging out 106 yds of flooded and derelict trenching viz: from A-B, C-D.
From A-B and C-D the trench will be cleaned and habitable with firestep by 3.15 am today.

12.50 am   A.J.H. Bowen
2.3.17

No.10 Platoon, C Company in 1917. The Officer in Charge is Lieut. H. Llewellyn Hughes.

(Photo: SWB Museum)

Sergeants of B Company photographed at Hampton Camp Bivouacs, Bleuet Farm in Belgium on 23rd September, 1917. Back: Sgt. A.J. Phelps, Sgt. C. Hayes, Sgt. Dowle, Sgt. J. Counsell. Centre: Sgt. J. Skinner CSM, C.H. Lock. Front: QMS S. Glover CSM, W.J. Bowen, Sgt. D.J. O'Leary, Sgt. A.E. Turner.

(Photo: SWB Museum)

Pte. Charles P. Heare and his trusted bicycle. Note the rifle fixed to the cross bar of the bicycle. The photograph is dated as 1916 and was taken in Poperinge.

(Photo: SWB Museum)

Pte. Charles P. Heare. This photograph was taken near the end of his service. Note the overseas service chevrons on his lower right sleeve and the divisional badge at the top of the same sleeve. It appears, also, that he is wearing the ribbon to the 1914 Star on his left breast. (Photo: SWB Museum)

Pte. John Black and the motorcycle he used for his message carrying at various stages of the war.
(Photo: SWB Museum)

Pte. John Black (right rear) and three friends of the 2nd Monmouths.
(Photo: SWB Museum)

Road repairs in the Ypres Salient near Hooge, 1st October, 1918, being carried out by the 2nd Monmouths and the Royal Engineers. Note the variety of materials being employed and the wheel of the field gun or GS waggon in the foreground.

(Photo: IWM)

Pte. Charles Alexander Williams.
(Photo: Simon Williams)

Pte. Walter Albert Williams.
(Photo: Simon Williams)

Pte. Arthur Nunnerly, seated, with Ptes. J. Higgins and K. Whilding. Nunnerly was killed in action on the first day of the Battle of the Somme.

(Photo: Rev. A. Nunnerly)

Pte. Alfred Victor Williams was killed in action on 30th January, 1917 at the age of 21.

(Photo: Simon Williams)

Lieut. Col. John Evans taking the salute at Burschied, Germany in early 1919.

(Photo: SWB Museum)

L/Cpl. Ivor Griffiths MM and his brother Albert. Note that Ivor is wearing the MM ribbon he had earned at Cambrai and the 1914 Star ribbon. (Photo: Ian Griffiths)

O.C. B Coy

1. Your company will tonight (dig) a trench from your CT at a point about 70 yds NE of the present Bn HQ in a southerly direction joining the old front line at No. 2 Post (SE of Bn HQ) U14 b2$^1/_2$ 9.

2. The trench is to face EAST and dimensions 5' deep 4' wide at the top and 3' at bottom, 4 fire bays of 8 yds each are to be firestepped facing E.

3. When the trench is dug you will lay duckboards along the bottom of the new piece. There is a dump of duckboards at Bn HQ.

4. The 6 sandbags per man are to be handed to the NFLDS at the junction of the CT with POTSDAM, receipt to be obtained. Reporting working party to Bn Comdr when work is finished.

Leave sketch of your work for me at Bde HQ.

2.3.17
7.20 pm   A.J.H. Bowen

O.C. C Coy

1. Your Coy with 15 men of B Coy will continue the work done last night on POTSDAM by digging a traverse trench NW to U8d2$^1/_2$ - 5$^1/_2$ from U8d3$^1/_2$ - 4, that is the left of A Coys work last night as shown on the attached sketch.

2. Dimensions 5' deep 4' wide at the top 3' wide at the bottom. The bays are to be fire stepped

3. Care must be taken that the enemy don't surprise the party working.

4. The sandbags carried up are to be handed to the NFLD's at the junction of the right CT with POTSDAM TR.

2.3.17   A.J.H. Bowen
7.30 pm

5. Leave (written) report and sketch of trench dug at Bde HQ for me
                          AJHB

O.C. B Coy

1. Your company will tonight (dig) a trench from your CT at a point about 70 yds NE of the present Bn HQ in a southerly direction joining the old front line at No. 2 Post (SE of Bn HQ) U14 b2$^1/_2$ 9.

2. The trench is to face EAST and dimensions 5' deep 4' wide at the top and 3' at bottom, 4 fire bays of 8 yds each are to be firestepped facing E.

3. When the trench is dug you will lay duckboards along the bottom of the new piece. There is a dump of duckboards at Bn HQ.

4. The 6 sandbags per man are to be handed to the NFLDS at the junction of the CT with POTSDAM, receipt to be obtained. Reporting working party to Bn Comdr when work is finished.

Leave sketch of your work for me at Bde HQ.

2.3.17
7.20 pm   A.J.H. Bowen

(The notebook finishes here; Bowen was killed in action a little before 8 pm that evening.)

Appendix 5

Preparations for the attack on 1st July, 1916

The following details are taken from the Battalion War Diary a copy of which is held at the South Wales Borderers and Monmouthshire Regiment Museum at Brecon.

June 29/30
Preparation for attack on July 1st.
D Co, strength 4 officers (Capt. A.C. Sale, Lt. T.E.R. Williams and 2nd Lts J.D. Simpson, H.B. Davies) 135 OR, was divided up and joined the units to which they would be attached:
No. 13 Platoon Sections 1 & 2 (Lt. T.E.R. Williams) C Co. 1st Bn. Lanc. Fus.
No. 13 Platoon Sections 3 & 4 (2012 Sergt. Jones) B Co. 16th Middlesex
No. 14 Platoon Sections 5 & 6 (Lt. J.D. Simpson) 1st Bn. Royal Fus.
No. 14 Platoon Sections 7 & 8 (Sergt. Stockham) 1st Bn. Dublin Fus.
No. 15 Platoon Capt. A.C. Sale 1st Bn. Border Regt.
No. 16 Platoon 2nd Lt. H.B. Davies. 1st Bn. K.O.S.B.

A, B, C Co's, HQ + 10% Reserve, march out of ACHEUX WOOD by platoon at 1 minute intervals. Companies to their forming up areas:
A Co. strength Officers (5) Major A.H. Edwards (Command) Lt's L.L. Williams, E.V. Hunt, 2Lt's W.W. Sankey, W.D. Howick (4th RWF) OR 140 to 86 TRENCH.
B Co. strength Officers (5) Capt. C. Comely (Command), Capt. C.W.H. Cox, Lt. A.L. Coppock (3rd Welsh) 2nd Lt's W.S. Bartlett, E.F. Lawlor. OR 138, to YELLOW LINE between FORT WITHINGTON and FORT ANLEY.
C Co. strength Officers (4) Capt. H.W.E. Bailey (Command) Lt's M.F. Turner, G.E. Foster, 2nd Lt. B.D. Williams. OR 136 to YELLOW LINE between GABION

AVENUE and FORT WITHINGTON.
HQ and 10% Reserve to MAILLY WOOD.

<u>Dress and Equipment.</u> In addition to Divisional Badge on both arms, the regimental badge will be worn viz: A band of sand bag 1 inch wide on Tunic 7 inches above each cuff. (taken from Battalion Operational Order dated 22.6.16.) Men carried equipment with 120 rounds SAA Rifle and bayonet, 2 sand bags in belt front, 2 Mills bombs (one in each bottom pocket of F.S.J.). Haversacks were carried on back and contained mess tin with iron ration inside, rations. Water bottles were carried as usual. 80% carried shovels 20% picks. These tools were carried on the back slipped under the equipment and were found to be quite comfortable as carried.

<u>Specialists.</u> Regt. and Platoon Bombers carried 50 rounds SAA and 20 bombs (these were too many for a long march), they also carried picks and shovels and were used for digging. Runners wore an armlet badge and carried 50 rounds SAA.

All ranks carried 2 PH Gas Helmets, Tear Mask, Identity Disc, Field Dressing and Groundsheet. Officers were equipped like the men except that the revolver was carried on the left side and no ammunition pouches were worn. Officers also wore men's F.S. Jacket and puttees with rank badges on the shoulders. 200 only of the men had been supplied with steel helmets. All officers and remainder OR wore service caps. Communications was arranged with the two companies digging communication trenches and with the Co. attached to the 89th Brigade by runners to HQ. The only communication arranged with D Co. (allotted to the 86th and 87th Brigades) was by checking if a man came back through the communication trenches. The reason for this was that the Co. was so split up that communication was impractical, for example, one battalion had 16 men allotted to it for carrying purposes and they were allotted one man to each section of the consolidating Co. Latrines and cooking places had previously been made (in) 86 TRENCH and YELLOW LINE and camp kettles and a supply of water taken up. C Co. had also taken up the consolidating material and left a guard over it. By the good arrangements made by Co. Commanders every man in A, B, and C Co's had hot tea, fried bacon and bread and jam for breakfast on Z morning. In addition 1/2 lb of chocolate had been brought forward for each man and issued, each man had a big bacon sandwich in his haversack.

<u>Correction</u> A Co. proceeded to TRENCH 86 less No. 2 Platoon, this platoon proceeded to Sap 7 to dig a trench from there to the SUNKEN ROAD Q4d3.6 to Q4d5.6 70 yards long. This was finished at 2.30 am on Z day and the platoon rejoined the Co. in TRENCH 86.

Appendix 6

Order of Battle
Hill 60 and the Battles of Ypres 1915

3RD DIVISION: Major-Gen. J. A. L. Haldane

7th Brigade: Br.-Gen. C. R. Ballard
    3/Worcestershire.   1/Wiltshire.   Hon.Art.Coy. (T.F.)
    2/S.Lancashire.   2/R.Irish Rifles.   4/S.Lancashire. (T.F.)

8th Brigade: Br.-Gen. Hoskins.
    2/R. Scots.   4/Middlesex.   4/Gordons (T.F.)
    2/Suffolk.   1/Gordons.

9th Brigade: Br.-Gen. W. Douglas Smith
    1/N'humberland Fus.   1/Lincolnshire.   10/King's (T.F.)
    4/Royal Fus.   1/R. Scots Fus.

R.F.A.Brigades
    XXIII.(107, 108, 109 Btys).   XLII.(29,41,45 Btys).
    XL.(6,23,49 Btys).   XXX.(How.)(128,129 Btys).

R.G.A.: 5/Mountain Battery.

Field Coys. R.E.: 56 & 1/Cheshire. (T.F.).

Mtd. Troops: C Sqdn. N.Irish Horse.   Cyclist Coy.

4TH DIVISION: Major-Gen. H. F. M. Wilson

10th Brigade: Br.-Gen. C. P. A. Hull.

1/R. Warwickshire.	1/R. Irish Fus.	7/Argyll & Suth.(T.F.)
2/Seaforths.	2/R. Dublin Fus.	

11th Brigade: Br.-Gen. J. Hasler.

1/Somerset L.I.	1/Hampshire.	London Rif. Brig.(T.F.)
1/E Lancashire.	1/Rifle Brigade.	

12th Brigade: Br.-Gen. F. G. Anley.

1/King's Own.	2/Lancashire Fus.	5/S.Lancashire.(T.F.)
2/Royal Irish.	2/Essex.	2/Monmouthshire.(T.F.)

R.F.A.Brigades.
XIV. (68,88 Btys.)   XXXII.(27,134,135 Btys.)
XXIX. (125,126,127 Btys.)

R.G.A.: 2/Mountain Battery.

Field Coys. R.E.: 9 & 1/W.Lancashire. (T.F.)

Mtd. Troops: A Sqdn. Northants Yeo.   Cyclist Coy.

5TH DIVISION: Major-Gen. T. L. N. Morland

13th Brigade: Br.-Gen. R. Wanless O'Gowan.

2/K.O.S.B.	1/R. West Kent.	9/London.(T.F.)
2/D.Wellington's.	2/K.O.Y.L.I.	

14th Brigade: Br.-Gen. G. H. Thesiger.

1/Devonshire.	1/D.C.L.I.	5/Cheshire. (T.F.)
1/E.Surrey.	2/Manchester.	

15th Brigade: Br.-Gen. E. Northey.

1/Norfolk.	1/Cheshire.	6th King's. (T.F.)
1/Bedfordshire.	1/Dorsetshire.	

R.F.A.Brigades
XV.(52,80 Btys.)   XXVIII.(122,123,124 Btys.)
XXVII.(119,120,121 Btys.)   XXX(How.) (130 Bty.)

Field Coys. R.E.: 59,2/Home Counties (T.F.) & 1/N. Midland (T.F.)

Mtd. Troops: C Sqdn. Northants Yeo.   Cyclist Coy.

27TH DIVISION: Major-Gen T.D'O. Snow

80th Brigade: Br.-Gen W.E.B. Smith.

2/K.S.L.I.	4/K.R.R.C.	P.P.C.L.I.
3/K.R.R.C.	4/Rifle Brig.	

81st Brigade: Br.-Gen. H. L. Croker.

1/R. Scots.	2/Camerons.	9/R.Scots.(T.F.)
2/Gloucestershire.	1/Argyll & Suth.	9/Argyll & Suth.(T.F.)

82nd Brigade: Br.-Gen. J. R. Longley.

1/Royal Irish.	2/R.Irish Fus.	1/Cambridgeshire.(T.F.)
2/D.C.L.I.	1/Leinster.	

R.F.A. Brigades.

I. (11,98,132,133 Btys.)   XX.(67,99,148,364 Btys.)
XIX. (39,59,96,131 Btys.) (All four gun Batteries)
VII. (How.) (61st. Bty.)

Field Coys. R.E.: 17, 1/Wessex (T.F.) & 2/Wessex (T.F.)

Mtd.Troops: A Sqdn. Surrey Yeo.   Cyclist Coy.

28TH DIVISION: Major-Gen. E. S.Bulfin

83rd Brigade: Br.-Gen. R. C. Boyle

2/King's Own.	1/K.O.Y.L.I.	5/King's Own.(T.F.)
2/E. Yorkshire.	1/York & Lancaster.	3/Monmouthshire.(T.F.)

84th Brigade: Br.-Gen. L. J. Bols

2/N'humberland Fus.	2/Cheshire.	12/London.(T.F.)
1/Suffolk.	1/Welch.	1/Monmouthshire.(T.F.)

85th Brigade: Br.-Gen. A. J. Chapman

2/Buffs.	2/E Surrey.	8/Middlesex.(T.F.)
3/Royal Fus.	3/Middlesex.	

R.F.A. Brigades

III.(18,22,62,365 Btys)   CXLVI.(75,149,366,367 Btys).
XXXI.(69,100,103,118 Btys.) (All four gun batteries)
VII.(How.)(37 & 65 Btys.)

Field Coys. R.E.: 38, 1/Northumbrian.(T.F.)

Mtd. Troops: B Sqdn. Surrey Yeo.   Cyclist Coy

50TH (1/NORTHUMBRIAN) DIVISION (T.F.): Major-Gen. Sir W. F. L. Lindsay

149th Brigade (1/Northumbrian): Br.-Gen. J. F. Riddell
    4/Northumberland Fus.   6/Northumberland Fus.
    5/Northumberland Fus.   7/Northumberland Fus.

150th Brigade (1/York & Durham): Br.-Gen. J. E. Bush
    4/E. Yorkshire.   5/Green Howards.
    4/Green Howards.   5/Durham L.I.

151st Brigade (1/Durham L.I.): Br.-Gen H. Martin
    6/Durham L.I.   8/Durham L.I.
    7/Durham L.I.   9/Durham L.I.

R.F.A. Brigades
    I. Northumbrian.   III. Northumbrian.
    II. Northumbrian. (All 15 pdr Brigades)
    IV. Northumbrian. (5" Hows)

Field Coy. R.E.: 2/Northumbrian *Mtd. Troops:* A Sqdn. Yorks. Hussars. Cyclist Coy.

1ST CANADIAN DIVISION: Lieut.-Gen. E. A. H. Alderson

1st Canadian Brigade: Br.-Gen. M. S. Mercer
    1st Bn.(Western Ontario Regt.)   3rd Bn.(Toronto Regt.)
    2nd Bn.(Western Ontario Regt.)   4th Bn.

2nd Canadian Brigade: Br.-Gen. A. W. Currie
    5th Bn.(Western Cavalry)   8th Bn.(Winnipeg Rifles)
    7th Bn.(1st Brit. Columbia Regt.)   10th Bn.(10th Canadians)

3rd Canadian Brigade: Br.-Gen. R. E. W. Turner, V.C.
    13th Bn.(R.Highlanders of Canada)   15th Bn.(48th Highlanders)
    14th Bn.(R.Montreal Regt.)   16th Bn.(Canadian Scottish)

Canadian F.A. Brigades
    I.(1,2,3,4 Btys)   II.(5,6,7,8 Btys)
    III.(9,10,11,12 Btys)(All 4 gun batteries)

R.F.A.Brigade: CXVIII.(How.) 458 & 459 Btys.

Canadian Field Coys: 1,2,3.

Mtd. Troops: Service Sqdn. 19th Alberta Dragoons. Cyclist Coy.

LAHORE DIVISION: Major-Gen. H. D'U. Keary

Ferozepore Brigade: Br.-Gen. R. G. Egerton
Connaught Rang.   57th Wilde's Rifles.   4/London.(T.F.)
9th Bhopal Inf.   129th Baluchis.

Jullundur Brigade: Br.-Gen. E. P. Strickland
1/Manchester.   47th Sikhs.   4/Suffolks.(T.F.)
40th Pathans.   59th Scinde Rifles.

Sirhind Brigade: Br.-Gen. W. G. Walker, V.C.
1/Highland L.I.   1/1st Gurkhas.   4/King's.(S.R.)
15th Sikhs.   1/4th Gurkhas.

R.F.A. Brigades
V.(64,73,81 Btys.)   XVIII.(59,93,94 Btys.)
XI.(83,84,85 Btys.)   XLIII.(How.)(40 & 57 Btys.)

Engineers: 20 & 21 Coys. 3rd Sappers & Miners

Pioneers: 34th Sikh Pioneers   *Mtd. Troops:* 15th Lancers

1st CAVALRY DIVISION: Major-Gen. H. de B. de Lisle

1st Cavalry Brigade: Br.-Gen. C. J. Briggs
Queen's Bays.   5/Dragoon Guards.   11/Hussars.

2nd Cavalry Brigade: Br.-Gen. R. L. Mullens
4/Dragoon Guards.   9/Lancers.   18 Hussars.

9th Cavalry Brigade: Br.-Gen. W. H. Greenly
15/Hussars.   19/Hussars.

R.H.A.Brigade: VII.(H.I & Warwickshire (T.F.) Btys.)

Field Sqdn. R.E.: No.1.

2nd CAVALRY DIVISION: Major-Gen. C. T. McM. Kavanagh

3rd Cavalry Brigade: Br.-Gen. J. Vaughan
4/Hussars.   5/Lancers.   16/Lancers.

4th Cavalry Brigade: Br.-Gen. Hon. C. E. Bingham
6/Dragoon Guards.   3/Hussars.   Oxfordshire Hussars.(Yeo.)

5th Cavalry Brigade: Br.-Gen. Sir P. W. Chetwode
R.Scots Greys.   12/Lancers.   20/Hussars.

R.H.A. Brigade: III.(D,E,J Btys.)   *Field Sqdn. R.E.:* No.2

3rd CAVALRY DIVISION: Major-Gen. Hon J. H. G. Byng

6th Cavalry Brigade: Br.-Gen. D. Campbell
    3/Dragoon Guards.   1/Royal Dragoons.   N.Somerset Yeo.

7th Cavalry Brigade: Br.-Gen. A. A. Kennedy
    1/Life Guards.   2/Life Guards.   Leicester Yeo.

8th Cavalry Brigade: Br.-Gen. C. B. Bulkeley-Johnson
    R/Horse Guards.   10/Hussars.   Essex Yeo.

R.H.A. Brigade: XV.(C,K,G Btys.) *Field Sqdn. R.E.:* No. 3.

Skeleton British Order Of Battle For the Battle of Cambrai 1917

Guards Division (Major-General G.P.T. Feilding)

1 Gds, 2 Gds, 3 Gds Brigade

2nd Division (Major-General C.E. Pereira)

5, 6, 99 Brigades

6th Division (Major-General T.O. Marden)

16, 18, 71 Brigades

12th (Eastern) Division (Major-General A.B. Scott)

35, 36, 37 Brigades

20th (Light) Division (Major-General W. Douglas Smith)

59, 60, 61 Brigades

29th Division (Major-General Sir B. de Lisle)

86th Brigade: (Brigadier General G.R.H. Cheape)
    2/Royal Fus.   1/Lanc. Fus   16th Middlesex.
    1/R. Guernsey L.I.   86 MGC.   86 TMB.

87 Brigade: (Brigadier General H. Nelson)
    2/South Wales Bord.   1/K. Own Scott. Bord.   1/R.Inniskil. Fus.
    1/Border.   87 MGC.   87 TMB.

88th Brigade: (Brigadier General C.H.T. Lucas)
    4/Worcesters.   2/Hants.   1/Essex.
    R. Newfoundland R.   88MGC.   88 TMB.

Field Coy R.E.: 455, 497, 510   *Pioneers:* 2/Monmouths.

RHA Brigade: XV   *RFA Brigade:* XVII

36th (Ulster) Division (Major-General O.S.W. Nugent)

107, 108, 109 Brigades

40th Division (Major-General J. Ponsonby)

119, 120, 121 Brigades

47th (2nd London) Division (Major-General Sir G.F. Gorringe)

140, 141, 142 Brigades

51st (Highland) Division (Major-General G.M. Harper)

152, 153, 154 Brigades

55th (1st West Lancashire) Division (Major-General H.S. Jeudwine)

164, 165, 166 Brigades

56th (1st London) Division (Major-General F.A. Dudgeon)

167, 168, 169 Brigades

59th (2nd North Midland) Division (Major-General C.F. Romer)

176, 177, 178 Brigades

61st (2nd South Midland) Division (Major-General C.J. Mackenzie)

182, 183, 184, Brigades

62nd (2nd West Riding) Division (Major-General W.P. Braithwaite)

185, 186, 187 Brigades

1st Cavalry Division (Major-General R.L. Mullens)

1, 2, 9 Cavalry Brigades

2nd Cavalry Division (Major-General W.H. Greenly)

3, 4, 5 Cavalry Brigades

4th Cavalry Division (Major-General A.A. Kennedy)

Sialkot, Mhow, Lucknow Brigades

5th Cavalry Division (Major-General H.J.M. Macandrew)

Secunderabad, Ambala, Canadian Brigades

Tank Corps (Brigadier-General H.J. Elles)

I, II, III Brigades

Appendix 7
Grant of Clasp

The following details are taken from the Army Order (A.F.W. 5124) published in October, 1919. It gives the qualification for the award of the *'Clasp'* to the 1914 Star.

'1914 Star' - Grant of Clasp - 1.   His Majesty the King has been graciously pleased to approve of the issue of a clasp to officers, warrant officers, non-commissioned officers and men who have been awarded the *'1914 Star'* under Army Order 350 of 1917, and who actually served under the fire of the enemy between the 5th August, 1914, and midnight 22nd/23rd November, 1914.

2.   The clasp will be in bronze and will bear the inscription *'5th Aug. - 22nd Nov., 1914.'*

3.   In undress and service uniform, when ribands are worn, the grant of the clasp will be denoted by the wearing of a small silver rose in the centre of the riband.

4.   Officers and soldiers who were actually present on duty within range of the enemy's mobile artillery and were on the strength of, or attached to the units and formations set forth in Appendix A between the above mentioned dates, will be eligible for the award.

5.   An individual who formed with a formation, otherwise than named in Appendix A, will only be granted the clasp on furnishing a certificate signed by an officer, warrant officer, or non-commissioned officer not below the rank of sergeant personally cognizant that the individual served on duty within range of the enemy's mobile artillery during the period referred to in paragraph 1.

6. Two small silver roses will be issued with the clasp to each approved individual.

7. Officers commanding units and heads of departments will forward nominal rolls of troops now serving under their command entitled to the clasp, to the Secretary, War Office, (A.G.10), 27, Pilgrim Street, E.C.4.

8. Individuals not now serving should apply on special forms (which may be obtained on application to any head or branch post office in the country districts) to the officer in charge of the record office of the corps in which they last served. If possible,the certificate which is referred to in paragraph 5 (and which will be found on the form) should be first completed and signed as directed thereon. Officers in charge of records will forward all aplications through the officer commanding the unit concerned, to the Secretary, War Office, (A.G.10), 27, Pilgrim Street, E.C.4. Applications made otherwise than on the prescribed form will be ignored.

By Command of the Army Council
R.H. BRADE

Appendix A referred to in Paragraph 4 lists all the relevant units entitled to the clasp from which the Territorial Force infantry units may be given as:

8th Battalion the Royal Scots
5th Battalion the Scottish Rifles
5th Battalion the Royal Highlanders
2nd Battalion the Monmouthshire Regiment
1st Battalion the Honourable Artillery Company
5th, 13th, 14th, and 16th Battalion the London Regiment
1st Battalion the Hertfordshire Regiment

Appendix 8

Biographies
Honours and Awards

The following notes on members of the battalion have been, for the most part, extracted from the *Roll of Honour* by the Marquis de Ruvigny which was reprinted in 1987 by the London Stamp Exchange. Other sources have been used to supplement the data contained in that work especially where it has been necessary to check the dates of death and so on. Local newspapers have been used to compile some of the notes from several reports especially the *Western Mail* and the *South Wales Argus*.

William Albert Auther. Private. 2236
William Albert Auther was the adopted son of Jane Auther of 12, Rockfield Houses, Osborne Road, Pontypool. He had enlisted in the Monmouthshire Regiment on 31st August, 1914 and had joined the battalion in the field on 17th February, 1915. He was killed in action at Ypres on 3rd May, 1915 at the age of seventeen.

Arthur Charles Baggs. Private. 265888 (2949)
Arthur Baggs was the youngest son of Mrs A. Baggs of 99, Malpas Road, Newport. He served with the Expeditionary Force from 1915 but was reported to be missing in action during the fighting of April 1918. He was eventually reported killed in action 12th April, 1918.

Arthur Birkin. L/Cpl.1288
Arthur Birkin was the son of Arthur and Fanny Elizabeth Birkin of 4, D Row, Forgeside, Blaenavon, Mon. He served with the Monmouthsire Regiment from the outbreak of the war and went overseas with the battalion in November, 1914 and was killed in action on 6th December, 1914. He was one of three brothers to serve with the battalion in 1914 the others being Pte. F. Birkin and Pte. M.E. Birkin.

Pte. F. Birkin was to comment on life at the front in a local newspaper while on leave as follows:

> Up to the time I left them about a week ago our lot had lost 37 killed and about 80 wounded. One of the men killed was my own brother, Arthur, who was only about seven yards away when he had his head blown off by a shell. That was on December 6, and I shall never forget it. I have another brother in the battalion but he was quite fit when I left the trenches.

Both brothers were wounded in action during the war and Private M.E. Birkin was made a prisoner of war during the fighting of April 1918.

Alfred John Hamilton Bowen. Lieut. Col.

Alfred John Hamilton Bowen was the son of Alfred Edward and Emily Marianne Bowen of Usk. He was trained as a solicitor and was a partner in his father's firm in Pontypool. Although he was a very capable man he was known to be modest and reticent about his own abilities. He was a keen sportsman and played in the forwards for Pontypool RFC and was a member of both Pontypool and Panteg Golf Clubs. He was an enthusiastic motorcyclist. His interest in things military began with a commission as 2nd Lieut. in the 3rd Volunteer Battalion of the South Wales Borderers in 1906. He rose to the rank of Captain in charge of C Company (Pontypool) the 2nd Battalion the Monmouthshire Regiment by 1912. He served overseas with the battalion from November, 1914 and was wounded in action at Ypres in May, 1915 the action for which he was to gain his first Distinguished Service Order. He assumed command of the battalion on the 6th September, 1915 and was to lead it, gaining further distinction and a Bar to his DSO, until his death in action on 2nd March, 1917 at the age of 31. He left a wife, Jean Gertrude Wilton but they had no children.

The following letter was written by Capt. Alfred John Hamilton Bowen, and is dated 20th December, 1914, to his parents at Castle View, Usk. The letter is held by the South Wales Borderers and Monmouthshire Regiment Museum in Brecon:

> Dear Father and Mother,
> Thank you very much for your letters but I am sorry to say the parcels never arrive. The address to my Regiment, 12th Infantry Brigade, 4th Division, 3rd Army Corps, Brit. Exped. Force. I have just received the parcels from Stevens containing the cakes and chocolate for which I am very much obliged. We are just going back to the trenches this evening for our turn which finishes on Xmas night. The last one finished on the 15th so that the...... and gift gave me a decent present by coming in. We read last night about the bombardment of Scarborough and tho' it is downright unfortunate it seems rather fitting that people at home should realise that is what we get every day in the trenches we don't look to see if a shell is coming but keep well down. I had a letter from Elliott he is with the 1st Division, 1st Divisional Ammunition Column about 20 miles away from us. He expects a lively time soon so are making preparations. I had to sit as President of a Court Martial here today. I saw Lewis day before yesterday he came over and called. I think they may have been in action since but am not sure. He had been wounded slightly on two fingers and had had an extraordinary escape his rifle getting in the way and stopping the bullet. Will write again later. Best love to all, your loving Son, John.

The following telegrams relate to the notification received by Mr. Bowen of his son's wounds in 1915 and his death in 1917. They are held by the South Wales Borderers and Monmouthshire Regiment Museum.

Telegram dated 11th May, 1915:
Record 1043. Regret to inform you that Captain Alfred John Hamilton Bowen Second Monmouthshire Regiment was wounded 8th May further particulars will be wired you as soon as received.
Officer in Charge of Territorial Force Records.

Telegram dated 17th May, 1915:
Reference my wire record 1043: Alfred John Hamilton Bowen was admitted 1 British Red Cross Hospital le Touquet eleventh May bullet wound in head.
Officer in charge of Territorial Force Records.

Telegram dated 5th March, 1917:
Regret to inform you Lieut Col Alfred John Hamilton Bowen 2nd Monmouth Regt. killed in action 2nd March Lord Derby expresses his sympathy.
Officer in charge of Territorial Force Records.

Telegram dated 17th March, 1917:
The King and Queen deeply regret the loss you and the army have sustained by the loss of your son in the service of his country their majesties truly sympathise with you in your sorrow.
Keeper of the Privy Purse.

Letter from Lieut. Gen. The Earl of Cavan K.G., C.B., M.V.O. to Lieut Col. Bowen.

Dear Col. Bowen,
I must write you a line of hearty congratulations on the splendid work of your Battalion in wiring and consolidating the position gained on the 27th inst. I much regret your losses from shell fire, but the spirit and determination shown by all ranks under the spirited leadership of yourself and your officers were worthy of the very highest traditions.
Please accept my most sincere thanks.
Yours sincerely,
Cavan, Lieut. Gen.
Jan 30th 1917 Cmdg. XIV Corps

Percy William Bridle. Private. (2205) 265518
Percy William Bridle was the son of the late William Bridle and his wife Charlotte of High Street, Winsham, Chard in Somerset. He was born in Winsham on 3rd April, 1891 and was educated there and was later employed as a gardener. He enlisted in the Monmouthshire Regiment on the 15th August, 1914 and served in France and Flanders with the 2nd Battalion from the following November. He was wounded and taken prisoner at Armentieres on 12th April, 1918 and died from the wounds on 20th May following at Stargard, Germany. He was unmarried.

Evelyn Hook Byrde. Captain.
Evelyn Hook Byrde was born on 22nd April 1884 and was educated at Cambridge University where he was a science graduate. He was a schoolmaster in Cheltenham

before the war and this was where he learned his skills as a photographer. He had served with the Territorial Force for some time from its formation in 1908 and had resigned his commission in February 1910. On the outbreak of war he sought to rejoin his unit and was granted the rank of Captain dated 16.12.14. He served with the 2nd Battalion in early 1915 and was on the Brigade Staff for part of the time he was in France. He was wounded in action at the 2nd Battle of Ypres on the 8th May 1915 receiving a bullet wound in the thigh. The wound was so severe that it resulted in the amputation of the leg. He recuperated at Roehampton where he was fitted with a false leg before returning to service as a scientist involved in the production of a more efficient gas mask. After the war he became a solicitor and, during the Second World War returned to being a schoolmaster. He retained his interest in photography throughout his life. Many of the photographs in this volume are a result of Captain Byrde's photography in the trenches of 1915.

James Percival Cater. Private. 40089
James Percival Cater was the son of John Cater of Tudorville, Ross, Herefordshire, a fitter, by his wife Catherine daughter of the late John Davies. He was born in Ross on the 14th July, 1885 and educated there. He was a Post Office Official and joined the Monmouthshire Regiment on the 3rd July, 1916 and served with the British Expeditionary Force in France and Flanders from the following October where he was attached to the 6th (Service) Battalion of the South Wales Borderers. He was killed in action at Sapignies near Bapaume on the 24th March, 1918. His company officer wrote: *'I have known your husband ever since he came to us and he always showed himself a good clean soldier, and a man who always did his duty cheerfully. We shall all miss him very much'.* His Platoon Officer wrote: *'He was loved by everyone, and his manner and behaviour was of the best. I had the greatest admiration for him, and he was a brave soldier.'* He married at Holy Trinity Church, Drybrook, Gloucestershire, on the 24th October, 1908, Mary, daughter of the late Benjamin Hope and had a son, James Albert Graham, born 26th October, 1910.

Raymond Alfred Cruickshank. 2nd Lieutenant.
Eldest son of William Henry Cruickshank A.F.I. of St. Julian's Avenue, Newport, by his wife, Martha Ann, daughter of James Parsons of Tredegar. He was born at Tredegar on the 15th March, 1893, and educated at Earl Street County School in that town and Durham Road County Council School, Newport. He was a clerk in the employ of Messrs Burton Ltd., Shippers. He then travelled to Saskatchewan, Canada, where he took up work in the Methodist Episcopal Church. He enlisted in the University Company of the 61st Battalion Canadians in July, 1915 and returned to England in 1916. He was nominated for a commission on obtaining the rank of platoon sergeant and became a cadet at Bristol obtaining a commission in October, 1916. He served with the Expeditionary Force from the 28th December, 1916 and was wounded on the 9th April, 1917, but remained on duty and was killed in action on the 23rd April, 1917, while leading his platoon. His commanding officer wrote:

> Your husband has proved himself a stout hearted good soldier, and by his devotion and always capable discharge of his duties had won for himself the respect and regard of NCO's and men under his command, and all the brother officers of the battalion who now mourn his loss. He died while leading his platoon. On the night of his death his platoon was employed

on very important work in connection with present operations; he was instantly killed by a shell, but was not disfigured, his body was brought some distance back by his men, and later was reverently buried and a cross now marks his resting place.

A brother officer wrote:

We were all very fond of him and he was very popular in the mess and we shall miss his cheery presence.

His servant wrote:

I wish to inform you how sorry all the officers and men of B Coy are at losing such a brave and gallant gentleman. All the boys were terribly cut up when they heard of his death; he was such a nice officer and a fine soldier, I am his servant and I can tell you he has been a gentleman to me and the boys.

A former comrade of his Canadian unit wrote:

Poor Ray has fallen, a noble son, a thorough gentleman and a loyal friend has gone to rest. How hard it seems that at the threshold of life, so many of our best are giving their all; yet none of us would have 'the best' act in any other way than to offer, and give if necessary, life itself for one's Empire's good, and save today a world and civilization. The year or more of friendship with Ray in our own battalion will always be a treasured memory, for I saw in him that master spirit of self sacrifice and service. The pangs of grief are somewhat allayed by the knowledge of the noble acts which have ended the mortal life; one crowned hour of glorious life is worth an age without a name.

He married at Newport on the 14th December, 1914, Gladys Maud, daughter of Frederick Green of Newport.

Ellerton Osborne Davies. 2nd Lieutenant.
Ellerton Osborne Davies was the son of Mr. and Mrs. G. Davies of Moat House, Monmouth. He was educated at the Monmouth Grammar School and before the war had been employed by the Ebbw Vale Iron and Coal Company in their offices in Abercarn. He joined the Monmouthshire Regiment in Abercarn shortly after the outbreak of the war and received a commission on 1st January, 1915 and was posted to the 1st Battalion the Herefordshire Regiment but was later posted back to his own regiment. He was killed in action on 2nd April, 1915 at the age of 22 years. His commanding officer was to write to his parents that *'He was much liked by us all and his early death is a sad loss to us all. He was a gallant officer and would be much missed by all his company.'*

Albert Dix. Lance Corporal. 266067
Lance Corporal Albert Dix was born in Fairview in Monmouth the son of Sam and Elizabeth Dix, later of 7, King Street, Cheltenham. He enlisted in Pontypool in 1914 at the age of 17 and is believed to have given a false age to achieve this. He served overseas with the 2nd Battalion the Monmouthshire Regiment from 4th September, 1915. In August 1918 he was involved in the advance in Flanders where

he was wounded in the leg and chest during the Company assault at Outersteene Ridge. He died of these wounds at the Australian casualty Clearing Station at Longuenesse on the 18th August, 1918 at the age of 20. He is buried in the military cemetery in that town.

Arthur H. Edwards. Major
Arthur Edwards was the son of Mr. Ben Edwards, JP, the Commercial Manager of Blaenavon Works. He had been granted a commission in the 4th Volunteer Battalion South Wales Borderers in 1906 and served with that battalion until the formation of the 2nd Monmouths with which he served from 1908. He was a mining engineer and used his skills during the early mining operations in France during 1914 for which he was to be awarded a Military Cross. He was wounded in action during 1918 but he survived the war.

Edward Evans. Lance Corporal, 1682.
Born 27th October, 1897 in Cardiff, elder son of Edward and Abigail Evans of 2, Gibson's Steps, High Street, Pontypool and educated at the National School there. Enlisted in Pontypool in 1912 into the 2nd Battalion the Monmouthshire Regiment where he became the servant of Captain S.P.A. Rolls. He was killed in action in Flanders on 30th December, 1914. Captain Rolls wrote: *'Your son had been my servant ever since the beginning of October when we were in Northampton, and had been with me till he met his death. I cannot tell you what a good willing lad he was in all that he did for me. He was killed like so many others - nobly doing his duty in the trenches.'*

John Evans. Lieut. Col.
John Evans was a Monmouthshire man and reputedly a descendant of Rhys Goch the Lord of Ystrad Yw. He was commissioned into the 3rd Volunteer Battalion the South Wales Borderers in 1901 serving with F Company in Newbridge and H Company in Abertillery. He was promoted to Captain in 1907 and with the reorganization of the volunteer forces in 1908 he formed a new company at Crumlin in the newly formed 2nd Battalion the Monmouthshire Regiment. In early 1914 he transferred to the Territorial Force Reserve. At the outbreak of war he offered his services to his old battalion and joined the 2/2nd Monmouths being formed at Pontypool. He served in France with the 1/2nd Battalion from April 1916 shortly before the battalion was attached to the 29th Division as Pioneers. In March 1917 he took over command of the battalion in the field following the death in action of Lieut. Col. Bowen. He served as CO for the remainder of the war and marched with the Battalion into Germany as part of the Army of Occupation. He was awarded a DSO, the TD and Mentioned in Despatches for his service. He maintained close links with the Battalion and became its Honorary Colonel and serving vice Chairman of the Regimental Association. He was made a JP in 1922 and Deputy Lieutenant for the County in 1923. In 1931 he was appointed High Sheriff of Monmouthshire. He was a prominent member of the Homfray Lodge of Freemasons at Risca. Colonel Evans was respected by his men and was known to many of those who served with him in France as a fair and just man and to have been at all times a gentleman in spite of all the pressures placed upon him by the command at a time of war. He died in October, 1942.

Thomas Henry Gwynne. Private. 1917
Thomas Henry Gwynne was the son of T. Gwynne of Greenland Farm, Abersychan, a collier, and his wife Annie the daughter of Daniel Reardon. He was

born at Abersychan in November, 1894 (1891?) and educated at Cwmffrwdoer Schools, Pontnewynydd. Later he became a collier. He joined the Territorials on 2nd June, 1914 and volunteered for foreign service on the outbreak of war. He served with the Expeditionary Force in France and Flanders from the 5th November, 1914. He was wounded in action on 2nd January, 1915. He died in Wandsworth Hospital London, SW. on 16th September, 1915 from fever contracted while on active service. He was unmarried.

Charles Parkinson Heare. Private. 1927
Charles Parkinson Heare was born on 29th December, 1891. He joined the 2nd Battalion the Monmouthshire Regiment in July, 1913 and served with the battalion in France and Flanders from November, 1914 until discharged in Germany in March 1919. During a large portion of this time he served in the orderly room. He died in January 1985.

Frederick Hillier. Private. (2134) 265476
Frederick Hillier was the fourth son of James Hillier of 3, Torlais Street, Newbridge by his wife Mary Ann, daughter of Silis Webb and brother to Private Albert Hillier (5th SWB killed in action 24th August, 1916). He was born in Newbridge on the 13 March, 1894 and educated at Tynewydd. He joined the Monmouthshire Regiment on the 16th June, 1914 and served with the Expeditionary Force in France and Flanders being killed in action on the 18th July, 1917. He was unmarried.

Percy Holland Hockaday. Captain.
Percy Holland Hockaday was born in Australia but following the death of his father some years prior to the outbreak of the war he was brought up by an uncle, Mr. F.S. Hockaday, in the Forest of Dean. He was educated at the Monmouth Grammar School and, previous to the war was working in a local bank. He was commissioned into the 2nd Battalion the Monmouthshire Regiment as a 2nd Lieut. in 1912 being promoted to Lieutenant about four months prior to the outbreak of war. He was promoted to Captain on 5th May, 1915, and transferred to the Indian Army in March, 1917, where he spent the rest of the war. He was well known in local musical circles for his ability as an organist. He was wounded on a number of occasions during the war. The following letter (published in *Western Mail* 26.3.15.) refers to the first occasion he was wounded:
Letter from Mr. F.S. Hockaday of Highbury, Lydney. Glos.

> *As the name of my nephew, Percy, Lieutenant in the 2nd Monmouthshire Regiment, appears in the list of wounded, you will be glad to hear that, so far as our information goes, the wound is not dangerous. He received a gunshot wound in his head on Wednesday morning a few hours after returning to the front trenches. He could not be removed until night, when his brother received a message from the doctor that there was no injury to the brain. A further message came on Thursday morning that he was going on all right. We now have telegram advising us that he is at Hospital 7 stationary at Boulogne and he is expected to be there about a fortnight.*

His brother, Sidney Reginald Hockaday, also served with the battalion but was killed in action in 1916. :
The following three letters relate to this and are used with the permission of Mr. C.C. Wilton-Davies, a member of the family.

287

Extract from a letter from 2nd Lieut. G.W. Greenland dated the 31st August, 1916 (accompanying note says date should be 30th):

> *I was going to write and tell you about our Coy Commander Captain S.R. Hockaday - he comes from Lydney & is very well known to Mr. Deakin. He took over 'B' Coy down South when Comley was wounded, a jollier fellow we have never had. Young, witty, happy, perfect in dress, 'Hock' as we all called him was top-hole. The mess has been such a happy family after 'Hock' joined us. This morning he was very badly wounded. Besides nightwork we always have a day party out and Hock and Lawlor had gone up to see the work this morning. A shell exploded just on the trench. Hock got two ghastly holes in the left shoulder, a Sergeant got it in the arm and a man got it in the thigh. I cycled down the shell scarred road to the dressing station - a ruined chateau - this afternoon to see him. There he lay, white as death, and still on a stretcher, covered with blankets. His hair always so immaculately parted, was ruffled and without the usual sheen. He was almost sleeping, but when I went he said in such a weak little voice 'Good-bye, Greenland'. Oh! since then I have felt so very fed up! He was wounded at 11.30 this morning but owing to that part being under observation by the boche our ambulance will not take him from the dressing station until 10.30 tonight. The doctor says he will pull through with tremendous luck, but will probably lose his arm.*

Medical Officer's letter to Percy Holland Hockaday who was also serving with the Battalion, dated 31st August, 1916:

> *Dear Hockaday,*
>
> *I'm sorry to tell you that Sydney was seriously wounded yesterday. The same horrid piece of line. He had only been just been talking to the GOC over a trench.*
>
> *HE shrapnel. It has damaged his shoulder and chest badly - but has not injured his lung I think. He could not be moved until 10.30 pm. He was wounded as about 11.30 am.*
>
> *He was seen as soon as possible by 2 MD's who gave him morphia at once. I saw him as soon as possible afterwards and went with him down to the CCS. I have been with him all day today.*
>
> *The padre asked me to write to you as I knew all about him.*
>
> *I am so very sorry as I had begun to know him so well and we always went about together.*
>
> *I shall miss him dreadfully - he was one of the best officers we had I know - and alas - one of the few originals who can never be replaced.*
>
> *He was most extraordinarily brave and devoid of nerves. He won't be wanted any more for this war which is a blessing. I will write again.*

Letter dated 3rd September, 1916 from the Chaplain 10 Casualty Clearing Station BEF.

> *Dear Sir,*
>
> *I thought perhaps you might like to hear from me. I am the C of E Chaplain at the above CCS and I have been with your brother since he was admitted early Friday morning. I have not written before as Captain Sainsbury MO has been writing and been perfectly splendid the whole time, practically never leaving your Brother.*

He no doubt has told you he died yesterday, quite peacefully and happy and is buried in the Military Cemetery in the Poperinghe-Boescheepe Road Plot 9 B8 (No. of Grave)

I need hardly add how much I liked him, he was a real brave unselfish English gentleman and died after having made his last Communion, at peace with both God and Man.

There never was a chance for him - humanly speaking, tho' while he lived there was just a slight hope. You have my deepest sympathy.

> *Yours sincerely.*
> *James R Hale*
> *Chaplain C of E*

His personal effects will be forwarded as soon as possible.

Frank James. Private. 290991
Frank James, shopkeeper of Bethcar Street, Ebbw Vale, was the nephew of Mrs. H. Scanlon of 7, 6 Row, New Town, Ebbw Vale. He had joined the 3rd Monmouths but on the disbanding of that battalion had served in France with the 2nd Battalion and was reported missing in the fighting of April 1918. He was later reported as killed in action on 12th April 1918.

John Charles Jenkins. Lieutenant Colonel.
John Charles Jenkins was born at Newbridge on 19th April, 1880. He was educated at Long Ashton School, Bristol where he played in the school rugby football team. He was commissioned into the 3rd VB SWB in March 1899 and reached the rank of Captain by December 1900. He resigned this position in 1903 and subsequently qualified as an accountant. On the formation of the Territorial Force he rejoined the army and was commissioned into the 2nd Battalion Monmouthshire Regiment reaching the rank of Major by 1911. He reached the rank of Lieut. Col. and in 1915 commanded the battalion in France briefly before being returned home sick. Thereafter he commanded the second line battalion at home. He was a keen sportsman throughout his life and played rugby at the highest level being capped by Wales against the South Africans in 1906.

Eddie Jones. Sergeant. 173
Eddie Jones was the son of Mr. W.J. Jones of Newport Road, Cwmcarn. He was an official at the Prince of Wales Colliery in Abercarn but served with the battalion from the outbreak of the war and was seriously wounded in the head during the fighting around Ypres in 1915. He survived the war.

Fred Jones. Private. 2366
Fred Jones was the son of William David Jones, a miner, and his wife Matilda. He was born at Upper Cwmbran, Monmouthshire, one of five sons and two daughters, and educated in the Board Schools in Cwmbran. He joined the 2nd Monmouthshire Regiment in September, 1914 and was killed in action near Ypres on 8th May, 1915 at the age of 21. He was unmarried.

Harry Leonard Jones. Private. 266071
Born in Canton in Cardiff on 21st January, 1896, and educated at Canton Secondary School. He lived in Treorchy with his parents, Godfrey and Matilda Jones, at 32, Clifton Street, Cwmparc where he was a grocer's assistant. He enlisted in March 1915 in Pontypool and served on the Western Front from

September 1915. He was unmarried. He died of wounds on the 3rd July 1917. One of his officers was to write: *'I greatly regret the loss of so good a soldier.'*

Rowland Samuel Jones. Private. 538

Rowland Samuel Jones was the eldest son of Thomas Hanbury Jones of 75, Monnow Street, Monmouth, Builder and Decorator and Member of the Monmouth Town Council and his wife Rachel daughter of Rowland Samuel Bevan of Penlarken Farm, Pontypool. He was born in Monmouth on the 7th December, 1883 and educated at St. Mary's National School there. By trade he was a plumber. He joined the Monmouthshire Volunteers in 1902, which became the 2nd Battalion the Monmouthshire Regiment in 1908 on the formation of the Territorial Force. On the outbreak of war he volunteered for Imperial Service and went into training with the battalion at Pontypool although barely recovered from a serious cycling accident which befell him on the day of mobilisation. He left for France with the battalion on 5th November, 1914 and served in the trenches throughout the following winter. His officers were highly complimentary of his ability as a practical plumber in keeping the pumps in working order, and was placed in charge of 18 pumps. He took part in the 2nd Battle of Ypres in which his battalion acquitted itself most gallantly and suffered severe losses. He died at the 3rd Casualty Clearing Station at Bailleul on 16th June, 1915 of wounds received while on sentry duty at 5.30 am on the 14th near Ypres. The Rev. A.T.G. Fletcher, Chaplain to the Forces (C.E.) wrote that he was admitted to the Clearing Station, unconscious with a terrible wound in the head caused by shrapnel, and died without recovering consciousness. He added *'I buried him in Bailleul Cemetery in grave No. 1313. A cross has been erected on his grave bearing his name and regimental number and giving the cause of his death. He died nobly, while bravely doing his duty.'* Private Jones had been repeatedly offered promotion to non-commissioned rank but had always refused it. He married at the Parish Church of Newland in Gloucestershire on the 31st August 1909. His wife Sarah was the daughter of Herbert Turneyhough of Highbury Farm in Newland. He had two sons and a daughter; Thomas Hanbury Herbert, born 28th May, 1910; Rowland Leonard born 17th August, 1911 and Dorothy Rachel born 26th May, 1914 died 19th March, 1915. Two of his brothers, Hanbury John Jones, Bombardier 43491 RGA (volunteered August 1914 from Bristol City Police Force) and Thomas Hanbury Jones, Sergt. 1430 The London Regt. (Auditor in the Exchequer and Audit Department, Whitehall), are now (1916), on active service in France, and another brother, Leonard Hanbury Jones, Cadet, Monmouth Grammar School Corps, has been medically rejected.

Albert King. 2nd Lieutenant.

Son of Rees King of 13, Church Street, Rhymney, Merchant by his wife, Elizabeth, daughter of Rees Davies. He was born at Rhymney on 23rd December, 1893. Educated at Pengam School, St. David's School, Lampeter and St. David's College, Lampeter where he was when war broke out. He was not married. He enlisted on the 31st December, 1914, and obtained a commission in the Monmouthshire Regiment on the 1st August, 1916. He served with the Expeditionary Force in France and Flanders from the following October and was killed in action at Monchy-le-Preux on the 31st May, 1917, and was buried there. His commanding officer wrote:

> *On the night in question he was acting as a guide to a platoon of another Company, attached for the night to his Company, for the purpose of carrying out some very important work south-east of Monchy-le-Preux; he,*

290

together with a sergeant from the attached platoon, were instantly killed by a shell. Both were reverently buried near the spot where they fell. I trust that it will be of some consolation to you to know that during the seven months he served with the battalion he proved himself a very capable officer, always reliable and conscientious in the discharge of every duty entrusted to him. He had won for himself the respect and regard of the NCO's and men under his command, and all the brother officers, who now deeply deplore his loss.

Another officer wrote:

We are all very sorry to lose him; he was such a cheery boy, full of pluck, and always ready to do anything he could to help others with the work in hand, and his men were awfully fond of him.

Yet another officer wrote:

I shall always remember your son as one of the kindest-hearted men it has been my fortune to meet, he was a splendid soldier - popular with officers and men. His memory will live with the battalion.

Herbert Lewis. Lance Corporal. 2255
Herbert Lewis was the son of F.W. and Mary Lewis of Milford House, Pontypool Road. He had joined the Territorials after the outbreak of war and had gone overseas with his battalion in November, 1914 and had served throughout the winter with his unit. He was killed in action at Ypres on the 3rd May, 1915 at the age of 23.

John Llewellyn. Private. 3816
Born in Whitchurch, Cardiff, the son of Llewellyn and Ada Llewellyn of Castell Farm, Tongwynlais where he lived with his parents until his enlistment in May 1916. He died of wounds in France on the 28th October, 1916, aged 18.

Cornelius Joseph Love. Sergeant 2058.
Cornelius Joseph Love was born in Newport on 8th May, 1878 the son of George and Ellen Love. The family moved to Pontnewydd in 1880 and in 1881 Love began his elementary education at Cwmbran Roman Catholic School. He left school in 1888, at the age of 10, to take an apprenticeship to Mr. Parfitt, boilermaker, of Merthyr. This lasted four years before hearing difficulties dictated that he must resign the apprenticeship. He was then apprenticed to John Jenkins, Mason, of Clifton Place, Newport but did not finish his time. He joined the 3rd VB SWB on 19th February, 1895 serving in C Company, at Pontnewydd then commanded by Capt Cliff Jacobs. He served until 31st March, 1908, when, with the formation of the Territorial Force he resigned and joined the National Reserve. At this time he was working as an Agent for the Pearl Assurance Company. In May 1914 he enlisted in the 2nd Battalion Monmouthshire Regiment and on the outbreak of war went overseas with the battalion and transferred to the 20th Division Reception Camp in 1917 serving until disembodied in May 1919. He was a regimental shooting champion and represented it at Bisley on three occasions. He was awarded the DCM in 1915.

Alfred Leslie Mitchell. Lieut.
Alfred Leslie Mitchell joined the 1st Battalion Monmouthshire Regiment in October 1914 as a rifleman and was commissioned into the 2nd Battalion on 20th July, 1915.

He served with the battalion overseas and was billeting officer during the time the battalion was in Germany. He remained with the battalion until 1939 reaching the rank of Major. He was the grandson of Thomas Mitchell VD.

John Mogford. Private. 2764
John Mogford was the son of Mr. and Mrs. S. Mogford of Pontnewynydd. Prior to the outbreak of the war he had been employed as a collier in the Llanerch Colliery. He served in France and Flanders from the 17th February, 1915 and had been engaged as the servant to Lieutenant W.J. Williams. Pte. Mogford had been awarded a certificate for his bravery in the field. He was killed in action on 8th May, 1915 at the age of seventeen.

Francis Walter Morgan. Private. 285024
Born in Cardiff the son of Mr. and Mrs. T. Morgan of 65, Cathays Terrace, Cardiff. He was a well-known local footballer and had worked for the Taff Vale Railway before he enlisted in Cardiff. He was killed in action on the 12th April, 1918, aged 23.

Phillip Morgan. Private. 1640
Phillip Morgan was born in Crumlin Street, Pontypool on the 13th February, 1896. He grew up in Pontypool and attended the Race Chapel regularly. He joined the 2nd Battalion Monmouthshire Regiment in 1914 and served overseas with the regiment from November of that year. He was one of the members of Captain Edwards' Mining party formed in 1914 before the British Army had developed a policy for the offensive mining of the Western Front. He was wounded in action but survived the war. He was married and for the remainder of his working life was employed at Panteg Steel Works. He died in December 1997 and was the last surviving member of the 2nd Battalion who served in the Great War.

Stephen Hubert Morgan. Private. 2814
Stephen Hubert Morgan was the son of David James and Hannah Morgan of Talywain. He joined the 2nd Battalion the Monmouthshire Regiment in November 1914 and went overseas in February, 1915. He died of wounds received in action at Ypres at the No.12 Field Ambulance Station on 4th May, 1915 at the age of eighteen.

Ernest Palfrey. Private. 2341
Born in Abersychan, son of Charles and Ann Palfrey, and lived at 10, Foundry Road, Abersychan where he was a miner. He enlisted in Pontypool and was killed on the 25th December, 1914 when returning from burying commrades during the 'Christmas Truce', at the age of 21. He is commemorated on the Whitchurch Memorial in Cardiff though his connection with the area has not been established.

John Edward Paton. 2nd Lieutenant.
John Edward Paton was the eldest son of John and Susan Paton of Waun Wern, Pontypool where he was born on the 6th September, 1895. He was educated at Copthorne school, Sussex and at Winchester College. In the spring of 1914 he passed the entry examination for Pembroke College, Cambridge, where he would have continued his studies in October, 1914, but for the outbreak of war. He had attained the rank of sergeant in the Winchester O.T.C. and had represented his school at Bisley in 1913 and 1914. With this background it is hardly surprising that he obtained a commission on 14th October, 1914. He was killed in action at Le Bizet on the 31st December, 1914 and although his military career had been brief

he was mentioned in Sir John French's dispatch of January, 1915 for gallant and distinguished conduct in the field.

Percy George Pennymore. Lieut. Col.
Percy George Pennymore was born on the 7th December, 1869 the son of Lieut. Col P.G. Pennymore JP VD and Lucy Anne Pennymore. Married Mabel, daughter of J. Fowler. He served with the 2nd Monmouths during the Great War and was promoted to temp. Lieut. Col. in the Royal Welsh Fusiliers. Served with the B.E.F. from 5.11.14 (overseas with the 2nd Mons) and was awarded the DSO for service during the 2nd Battle of Ypres. He was mentioned in despatches on two occasions. He held the Territorial Decoration and King Edward's Coronation Medal.

Albert E. Pinchin. Corporal. 1599
Albert Pinchin was a collier working at the Blaensychan Colliery near Pontypool and was living at 1, Emlyn Terrace, Talywain at the time of the Great War. His father worked as an upholsterer and French polisher whilst his grandmother was the licensee of the Winning Horse public house in Pontypool. He joined the 2nd Monmouths in 1912 and served overseas with the battalion from November 1914. He was to be awarded the DCM for his bravery under fire on 8th December, 1914 and in so doing became the first Territorial to receive a fighting decoration. He was wounded in this action. He survived the war and spent most of his life in Newport though he died in Cardiff in 1963 at the age of 66.

Henry William Terrent Reed. 2nd Lieut.
Henry William Terrent Reed was the son of George and Ellen Reed of Durham. He was educated at Durham School, Durham University and Trinity College, Cambridge becoming an assistant master at Cheltenham College in 1909 where he also took charge of the College Boat Club. He was commissioned in November 1914 and joined the 2nd Battalion in Flanders where he was killed in action during the 2nd Battle of Ypres on 2nd May, 1915 at the age of 30.

Lawrence Braham Rosenbaum. Lieutenant.
Lawrence Braham Rosenbaum was a native of Tredegar where he was born in 1893 to Mr. & Mrs. Soyomon Rosenbaum of Church Street. He joined the 3rd Battalion the Monmouthshire Regiment in August 1914 and went to France with the Battalion in February 1915 where he served in the ranks. He was wounded in the fighting of May 1915. On recovering from his wounds he was commissioned in to the regiment at the beginning of 1916 being promoted to Lieutenant in July of the same year. He was considered to be an efficient officer and appears to have earned the respect of his men. He was killed in action during the Battle of the Lys. He was one of five brothers, his eldest brother, Sgt. Monty Rosenbaum, served with the Canadians and Lionel served as a sub-lieutenant in the RNAS, whilst brothers Mostyn and Cyril were graduates engaged on war work for the government.

Sydney Robert Ruck. Sergeant. 2681
Sydney Robert Ruck was a native of Monmouth and had been associated with the Territorial Force for a number of years. He had been known as a fine shot and had won the Monmouth Corporation Cup, the trophy for which the local Territorials competed. He was also a keen rugby football player and had played as a forward in the successful Monmouth side in the years before the war. He was, by trade, a linotype operator and worked at one of Monmouth's local newspapers. At the out-

break of the war Sgt. Ruck had already left the Territorials but rejoined at once and regained his former rank and landed in France on 17th March, 1915. He was killed in action on 8th May, 1915. He was married and lived in Goodrich in Herefordshire.

William Harry Shaw. Private. 2130
Harry Shaw was the son of Mr. and Mrs. W.J. Shaw of Griffithstown, Pontypool and prior to the outbreak of war had been employed as a collier at the Varteg Tops Pits near Pontypool. He had landed in France with the battalion in November, 1914. He was killed in action on the 12th March, 1915, when he was only 16 years of age.

W.G. Sweet. Sgt. 1357
Mr. Sweet was a native of Usk and joined the 2nd Monmouths in 1912. He served with the battalion throughout the Great War and was amongst the first of the battalion to go in to the trenches in November 1914. He was with the battalion when it marched in to Germany and as part of a billeting party was amongst the first group of soldiers into that country. He has left a memoir of his experiences of that time which was published recently. He reached the rank of RQMS whilst in Germany. On his return to Usk he started his own building business and continued to live in the town until his death in 1977 at the age of 81.

William John Taylor. Lieutenant.
William John Taylor, formerly of Vronheulog, Cwmcarn was the son of the late Mr. & Mrs. John Taylor of Cwmbran. He was born in Leicester in 1883. He had been a lieutenant in the Abercarn Company of the Monmouthshire Cadets but received a commission as 2nd Lieutenant in the 2nd Battalion the Monmouthshire Regiment. Two months before the outbreak of the war he was promoted to Lieutenant and was, at the time of his death, in charge of the machine-gun section. He had been the vice chairman of the Cwmcarn Cricket Club and acted as secretary of the local football club.
In civilian life he was a schoolmaster who had begun his career at the Tredegar Schools as an assistant master. Following a short spell at Whitby Schools he returned to South Wales to take up the post of commercial master at the Pontywaun Intermediate Schools where he served for eleven years prior to the outbreak of the war. He was a deacon at the Zion Baptist Church, Cwmcarn and was secretary of the church. Lieut. Taylor had been a successful athlete and had won a considerable number of prizes for his prowess as a runner. He left a widow and two children.

Herbert James Watkins. Private. 2385
Herbert James Watkins was the son of James and Rachel Watkins of Gelly Pistill, Pontypool. Prior to the outbreak of the war he had been employed as a collier in the Tirpentwys Colliery. He joined the 2nd Monmouths shortly after the outbreak of the war and served in France and Flanders with the battalion from November, 1914. He was killed in action at Ypres in May, 1915 at the age of 21.

Illtyd Edwin Maitland Watkins. Captain.
He was the only son of John Maitland Watkins, solicitor of Usk, and was born at Usk on the 25th March, 1890. He was educated at Downside School, near Bath, between 1904 and 1908, and King's College, Cambridge where he took his degree of LL.B. and B.A. (Law Tripos) in 1911 and was articled to his father in the same year passing his solicitor's examinations in 1914.

Whilst at college he was a keen sportsman rowing each year in the Lent and May races. He was fond of all outdoor pursuits, but had special artistic and literary gifts showing great promise as a portrait painter and being well read in both French and English literature. He joined the Monmouthshire Regiment with a commission dated 29th March, 1909 reaching the rank of Captain in July, 1914. At the outbreak of war he volunteered for active service and was appointed to command the No. 4 Section Welsh Divisional Signal Company R.E. at Northampton. He rejoined his own Regiment in January, 1915 and went to France in February following. He was killed in action on the 7th May, 1915, during the 2nd Battle of Ypres. He was twenty five years of age. His commanding officer, Lieut. Col. E.G. Cuthbertson was to write as follows:

> *He was killed on the morning of the 7th just at the end of the Germans' attack, and his death was instantaneous and painless. Of his qualities as a soldier and gentleman, I cannot speak too highly: cheerful, gallant and unselfish, he died as he would have chosen to die, his face towards the enemy and in the middle of the men whom he loved and commanded so well. We buried him on the battlefield ... his loss is deeply deplored by all ranks.*

Vivian Holmes Watkins. Captain.

He was the fifth son of Thomas Watkins, solicitor of The Wern, Pontypool, and of Fanny Maria. He was born on the 25th April, 1889 at Castle Parade House, Usk. He was educated at West Monmouth School, Pontypool and afterwards at Monmouth Grammar School. On leaving school he became an articled pupil to his father and then to the Town Clerk of Cardiff. He qualified as a solicitor in November 1913 and became a member of the legal staff of Cardiff Corporation. Whilst at school he had been a sergeant in the Cadet Corps and on leaving he was given a commission in the 2nd Battalion the Monmouthshire Regiment, reaching the rank of Captain in July, 1914. On the outbreak of war his battalion was mobilized and he volunteered for overseas service and was sent to France in November, 1914.

Captain Watkins was wounded in action on the 16th January, 1915 whilst in the process of warning some of his men, who were using a pump, not to expose themselves unnecessarily. He was eventually recovered under fire after five and a half hours when it was discovered that the bullet had caused a wound to the upper right side of his head. He was immediately admitted to No.2 Casualty Clearing Station that night and thence to Boulogne and eventually England. He died on the 20th February in the Empire Hospital, Westminster. He was buried with military honours at Pontypool on the 25th February, 1915, when the route from the Drill Hall in Osborne Road to the cemetery was lined by many of the local townsfolk.

Captain Watkins had been a keen sportsman and had represented his school in cricket, Rugby football and hockey and had rowed in the school boat. After leaving school he had played hockey for the Newport team and was a member of the Newport Athletic Club. He was not married. His brother 2nd Lieut. Horace Holmes Watkins was killed in action while serving with the 1st South Wales Borderers on 21st October, 1914. His brother, Hubert Holmes Watkins, also served with the 2nd Monmouths reaching the rank of Captain while another brother, Colin Holmes Watkins, served in the ranks of the 10th Canadian Mounted Rifles.

James Robert Watts. Private. 2458

James Robert Watts was the son of Aldwyn Watts of 26 Railway Terrace, Griffithstown, Monmouthshire, a haulier in the employ of Panteg Urban District Council, and his wife Sarah the daughter of John Thornton of Gudestry, Herefordshire. He was born at Kings Pyon in Herefordshire on the 4th October, 1896 but was educated at Griffithstown Council School. After finishing school he was employed at the Panteg Steel Works. He enlisted in the Monmouthshire Regiment on the 8th September, 1914 and went to France with the Battalion on 5th November, 1914. He was killed in action at Le Bizet on the 12th March, 1915. He was unmarried. Colonel Cuthbertson, his Commanding Officer was to write; *'Your son was killed on the 12th of this month, and a more gallant soldier never lived. He is buried in a soldiers cemetery not far from the trenches where he met his death, and a careful record of his place of burial is being kept. A small cross with his name has been put up to his memory.'* One of his comrades was to write; *'We all found him a jolly and good-hearted lad, and a very brave soldier. He feared nothing, but always thought of his duty to his country, of which he carried out to the last.'*

Lionel Digby Whitehead. Captain

Lionel Digby Whitehead was born in York on the 10th August, 1877, the son of George Whitehead and Mary Jane Baines. He was educated at Charterhouse. He married Edith Marion Brown on the 15th July, 1903. He served as a 2nd Lieutenant in the 3rd Battalion the Monmouthshire Regiment from 9th September, 1914 and was promoted to Captain in May, 1915. Following the disbanding of the 3rd Battalion he was attached to the 2nd Monmouths. He was wounded in action on at least two occasions during 1915.

Appendix 9

Rules of the 2nd Monmouthshire Rifle Volunteers

1.   The Corps having been raised under the Act 44, Geo.III., cap. 54, the members are consequently subject to the provisions of that Act, and to all regulations which have been or shall be issued, under the authority of the Secretary of State for War.

2.   The Corps shall consist of two classes - (1) ENROLLED Members, consisting of EFFECTIVES, NON-EFFECTIVES, and SUPERNUMARIES, and (2) HONORARY MEMBERS, the latter contributing to the funds of the Corps, but not enrolled for service.

3.   The committee to aid the Commanding Officer in the non-military affairs of the Corps, shall consist of the Commissioned Officers, the Honorary Secretaries, and twelve members of the Corps; which twelve members shall retire at the Annual general Meeting of the Corps, but shall be eligible for re-election. Five to be a quorum; the Senior Officer to preside, and have a casting vote.

4.   All subscriptions shall be paid in advance, and shall fall due on the first day of each year. The annual Subscription of Commissioned Officers shall be not less that £2 2s per annum; and of non-commissioned Officers and privates, 12s. per annum, to meet the ordinary expenses of the Corps; but such subscription shall not be called up unless the Committee be satisfied that the funds at the disposal of the Corps render such subscription or any portion thereof necessary.

5.   The Officer in command will propose gentlemen to the Lord Lieutenant for commissions as officers, but the appointment of all officers is vested by Act of Parliament in the Lord Lieutenant, subject to the Queen's approval.

6. That Officers of the Corps, upon appointment, shall pay the following Fees of Honour, exclusive to the fee to the Clerk of the Peace; and on his promotion, the difference between his old and new rank:

	£
Captain	20
Lieutenant	10
Ensign	5

7. That every non-commissioned officer shall be appointed by the officer in command, after consultation with the members.

8. Candidates for admission to the Corps must be proposed by two members, and their names laid before the committee. The election to be by ballot, at a general meeting of the Corps. One black ball in five to exclude.

9. That no candidate for admission be qualified to act as a member before he has paid his subscription, and given his written adhesion to the rules and regulations of the Corps.

10. Each member shall provide himself with a uniform and accoutrements to which must be in accordance with the sealed patterns selected by the Corps, and approved by the Lord Lieutenant.

11. Each member shall be responsible for the due preservation of all articles issued to him, which are the property of Her Majesty's Government, or of the Corps, fair wear and tear only excepted.

12. The expression *'Property of the Corps'* shall include all articles which have been purchased out of the general funds, or have been contributed to, or hired by the Corps.

13. When the corps is not assembled for actual service, the commanding Officer is, by general provision of the Act 44 Geo III., cap.54, solely responsible for the discipline of the Corps; but it shall be lawful for him at any time to assemble a court of enquiry, consisting of two officers and two enrolled members of the Corps, to be appointed by roster, for the purpose of investigating any irregularity and assisting him in coming to a conclusion upon it; and any member who shall be proved to have done any act which may injure the harmony or reputation of the Corps shall be liable, at the discretion of the commanding officer - who shall consult the committee before giving his decision - to a fine, a reprimand, or (if not a commissioned officer) expulsion; and any member expelled shall forfeit all interest in the Corps.

14. The commanding officer shall fix the time and place for parades, drills and rifle practice.

15. That none but effective volunteers, returned as fit for the ranks, be permitted to compete for any prize open to the members of the Corps. That no member be allowed to vote at any meeting, or enter for any prize, until his subscription, and all other sums due to the Corps, have been paid in full.

16. That the Commissioned Officers shall make such arrangements, subject to the approval of the Commanding Officer, that one, at least, of each Company be present at the ordered parade, or whenever a special parade be ordered. In case this rule be broken, each officer of the company shall be subject to a fine of 5s., unless it be proved that the non-observance has been occasioned by neglect of the officer whose turn it was to be present, in which case the officer shall be fined 20s.

17. That the non-commissioned officers shall make such arrangements subject to the approval of the commanding officer, that at least two sergeants, and two corporals, shall be present with the company as often as it may assemble. In the event of this rule being broken, each non-commissioned officer of the company shall be subject to a fine of 2s 6d., unless it be proved which of them is to blame, in which case the offender will be fined 10s.

18. Standing orders are to be exhibited at head-quarters, and the senior Officer in command shall have power, subject to the approval of the Commanding Officer, to inflict fines for disobedience, not exceeding 10s., or less than 2s 6d.

19. The following fines shall also be imposed, viz:

For loading contrary to orders, or shooting out of turn.	2s 6d
For discharging the rifle accidentally, or through carelessness.	5s 0d
Drawing swords or bayonets without orders.	2s 0d
For pointing the rifle, loaded or unloaded, at any person without orders.	10s 0d
Talking, laughing, or misbehaving in the ranks.	1s 0d
Being absent from parade at the time of roll call.	0s 6d
Being absent during the whole time of parade.	1s 0d
These fines shall be doubled if it be the Commanding Officer's parade.	
Quitting parade without the leave of the superior officer present.	5s 0d
Coming to parade not properly dressed or accoutered.	2s 0d

20. All fines imposed on members of the Corps shall be entered in a book kept by the commanding officer for that purpose.

21. All fines shall be due on the first day of every month succeeding that in which they have incurred, and shall be collected by the Company's Sergeants, and paid by them to the Commanding Officer, for the general fund.

22. The property of the Corps is by 50th Section of the Act 44 Geo.III., cap.54, legally vested in the Commanding Officer; but the committee shall aid him in the management of its finances, and in such other questions as he may refer to them.

23. The Commanding Officer shall cause an abstract of the accounts to be annually prepared, for the information of every member of the Corps.

24. The expense of the ammunition furnished by Her Majesty's Government, as specified in paragraph 21 of the War Office Memorandum of July 1859, shall be defrayed out of the funds of the Corps; but the cost of any further ammunition used for purposes of practice shall be defrayed by the members or members expending it.

25. Honorary members shall severally pay a donation of £5, or an annual subscription of £1.

26. Honorary members shall not interfere in any way with the military duties of the Corps, neither shall it be obligatory on them to provide themselves with uniform.

27. The system of musketry instruction, as recommended for volunteers by the commandant of the School of Musketry at Hythe, must be adhered to.

28. Every member is expected to provide himself with the Rifle Volunteer manual, and a copy of the rules of the Corps.

29. There shall be a fund raised for giving prizes to the best marksmen in the Corps, under regulations from the Committee, subject to the approval of the Commanding Officer.

30. That no member address his Commanding Officer, except through his immediate superior officer.

31. The annual meeting of the Corps shall be held on the first Monday in June. Special meetings may be convened by the commanding officer, at his discretion; but it shall be obligatory on him to summon one, whenever he shall receive a requisition to that effect, signed by 25 members of the Corps, stating the object of the desired meeting. No business shall be discussed or transacted at any special meeting, except that for the discussion or transaction for which the meeting was convened, unless with the permission of the Commanding Officer. At all meetings of the Corps each member shall have one vote.

32. All money received for the Corps shall be paid by the treasurer, without delay, to the credit of the account at the bank.

33. That if any case arises not provided for by the preceding Regulations, or if there should be any doubt in the interpretation of them, the Commanding Officer after consultation with the Committee, shall decide the course to be adopted, and from his decision there shall be no appeal.

APPROVED BY THE SECRETARY OF STATE FOR WAR
28TH FEBRUARY 1860

The following qualifications for efficiency are those of the 3rd Volunteer Battalion The South Wales Borderers which were issued on the 20th June 1891.

Every volunteer in order to become efficient and earn the Capitation Grant must attend a certain number of drills and make a certain score at target practice during each volunteer year, ie, between the 1st November and the 31st October.

The following are the minimum requirements in each case:

RECRUITS

1st Year - 30 Squad, Company or battalion drills, 60 rounds of ball ammunition in class firing, with at least 12 direct hits.

2nd year - 30 Squad, Company or Battalion drills, or such number (not less than 9) of Company and Battalion drills, - 3 of which must be Battalion drills - as will with the number of drills attended in the first year amount to a total of 60 for two years.

A score of 45 points in the 3rd class in class firing, which must be made in twenty rounds. Three attempts are allowed.

TRAINED VOLUNTEERS .

9 Company and Battalion Drills, three of which must be Battalion Drills.
Class firing, same requirements as for (b).

INSPECTION

No volunteer must be absent from inspection without leave of the Commanding Officer (for which a written application must be made), or unless prevented by sickness, in which case a proper medical certificate must be obtained.

Any volunteer so absent must attend two drills IN ADDITION to those above-mentioned.

Appendix 10
Battle Honours Awarded to the Monmouthshire Regiment for the Great War

Ypres 1915
Gravenstafel
St. Julien
Frezenberg
Bellewaarde
Somme 1916
Albert 1916
Arras 1917
Scarpe 1917
Ypres 1917
Pilkem
Langemark 1917
Poelcappelle
Cambrai 1917
Lys
Messines 1918
Hindenburg Line
St. Quentin Canal
Beaurevoir
Cambrai 1918
Ypres 1918
Courtrai
Sambre
France and Flanders 1914 -18
Aden
(The Battle Honours shown in bold text are those that are borne on the Colours)

Appendix 11
Notes on the 2/2nd Battalion and 3/2nd Battalion
The Monmouthshire Regiment

It will have become clear throughout the discussion of the main part of the text that during the war there were many occasions when the 1/2nd Battalion of the Monmouthshire Regiment were supplied with battle replacements from home. In many cases this was the result of the work carried out at home by the reserve battalions which were known as the 2/2nd Monmouthshire and the 3/2nd Monmouthshire Regiment.

The 2/2nd Monmouths were formed as early as September, 1914 as a direct result of the enthusiasm for the war with Germany. Many men flocked to the colours and in the Territorial Force there was no difference. It was not long before the first line battalion, the 1/2nd Battalion, was up to establishment and it seemed a sensible idea to create another battalion ready for overseas service if necessary. The senior officer on formation was Major (later Lieut.Col.) J.C. Jenkins and his experience as a Territorial soldier was soon put to good use. Warrant officers and NCO's were soon found amongst those men of the first line battalion who were considered at that time to be too old for overseas service. Others were found from the men who rejoined the colours in the months immediately following the outbreak of war. This core of experienced soldiers meant that it was not long before the 2/2nd Battalion was fully equipped to commence the training of the raw recruits that were swelling the ranks of the Monmouthshire Regiment.

It is recorded that in September, 1914 the battalion was already over 800 strong. It was at this time stationed in Pontypool but with the shortages in arms and equipment being felt by those units preparing for overseas service it can be imagined that there was little to spare for the second line territorial battalions. Nevertheless the men were kept busy with various types of drill and plenty of route marches to various towns in the eastern valleys to ensure that they were at least fit when the equipment arrived. The route marches were also used to encourage recruitment in the small towns and villages through which they passed though the effect that unarmed and probably poorly equipped soldiers had on recruitment can only be imagined since it has not been recorded. There would not, however, seem to have been any problem with recruitment since during the early months of the war the 2/2nd Battalion continued to grow.

In early November, 1914 the Battalion was sent to Northampton and, effectively, replaced the 1/2nd Battalion in that town following its departure for France. The billets in the town were organised by Major (later Lieut. Col.) John Evans and a billeting party of the 1/2nd Battalion and because of their particular knowledge of the town Evans and his billeting party remained with the 2/2nd Battalion for some time. Whilst at Northampton the battalion received most of the necessary arms and equipment for it to begin training in earnest and under the leadership of the experienced officers and NCO's it was soon to become a useful unit.

Two months later the battalion was moved to Cambridge where it was billeted in any convenient place within the town. Billets varied from private homes to the colleges of the famous university and boat houses on the Cam. The men were spread out in small groups and, as can be imagined, this presented some problems in the training and administration of the battalion. Not the least of these problems was the issue of rations since it was often necessary to rely on the ability of the individual in the billets to deal with the sometimes unusual army rations. It was during this stay in Cambridge that the battalion was to receive the first casualties from the 1/2nd Battalion sent to recover from wounds before rejoining the first line battalion overseas. It can be imagined that these men were looked upon with some respect and, no doubt, envy by the enthusiastic men of the 2/2nd Battalion who were, at that time, still expecting to be posted overseas themselves. For the Monmouthshire Regiment as a whole, Cambridge seems to have been a place where the units were inspected by high ranking officers and it was to be no different for the 2/2nd Battalion, for during their stay they were inspected by General Sir Ian Hamilton and His Majesty, King George V, on separate occasions. In the absence of any information to the contrary it is assumed that these inspections found the battalion to be satisfactory.

Up to this point the battalion had been attached to the 53rd Welsh Division, a Territorial division that was destined to begin its overseas service in Gallipoli. It was hoped by the members of the battalion that when the division went overseas it would accompany it. In April, 1915, however, the division was reorganized ready for departure and it was decided that first line units would be taken where possible. Since the Monmouthshire Regiment already had three first line battalions serving in France it was decided that the second line battalion would not be included in the new organization. Thus, the 2/2nd Battalion was destined to remain in Britain for the rest of the war. Whilst this was something of a disappointment for the members of the battalion, it was recognized that many of its number would see service overseas as replacements for the 1/2nd Battalion in France. Indeed the first replacements were found as early as December, 1914 and it was probably no surprise to the officers of the 2/2nd Battalion that it was to be seen as a draft finding battalion for the one serving in the field. From that time onwards the demands for drafts were frequent and bearing in mind the involvement of the 1/2nd Battalion in the 2nd Battle of Ypres it was not to be too long before some of the men who had been disappointed at not being accepted for overseas service were in fact serving in France as replacements for the casualties at Ypres. As well as providing replacements the battalion continued to receive those men recovering from wounds and sickness before they were returned to front line duty. In this way many of the men who fought and died in France and Flanders passed through the ranks of the 2/2nd Battalion.

Even though the battalion was not to be destined for overseas service they were kept busy and moved to various stations throughout the country through the war years. In June, 1915 they were moved to Essex and spent a number of weeks preparing defences for London in the event of a German invasion. Later the battalion returned to Northampton and there the men were given the opportunity to sign for Imperial Service. Many, who had not already made the obligation, did so in Northampton and those that did not were posted to the 2/4th Battalion in Cromer to be used for coastal defence purposes.

Some time during the stay in Northampton Capt.A.J.H. Bowen joined the battalion for duty after recovering from the wounds he had received on the 8th May, 1915. During his stay the battalion were marched to Bedford on the 20th July, 1915 where it was to stay until the spring of 1916. Capt. Bowen rejoined the first line battalion in France before the end of July, 1915, where he took temporary charge of the 1/2nd Battalion. In early August Lieut. Col. Jenkins relinquished his command of the battalion so that he could be posted overseas to take command of the 1/2nd Battalion, briefly, in France. He left the 2/2nd Battalion under the command of Major Henry Charles until the arrival of Lieut. Col. G. Turner.

The Spring of 1916 saw the battalion move to Howbary Park where Lieut. Col. H.J. Miers took over the command. He was to remain with the battalion until April, 1918 when he took command of the 2nd East Lancashire Regiment in France service for which he was to gain recognition by the award of the Distinguished Service Order. Shortly after the arrival at Howbary Park the battalion was required to provide 500 men to garrison Sudbourne on the east coast and it was not until December of that year that the battalion was reunited in its winter quarters at Lowestoft. At this time the battalion was released from garrison duty and became a training battalion providing drafts for the first line battalion and many other units in many theatres of the war. Sadly, this is reflected in the number of former Monmouth men that can be found amongst the Rolls of Honour of many famous regiments. This work of providing drafts while stationed in the east of England continued in to early 1918 when the system of providing drafts was changed. At this stage the war had become an enormous drain on resources and it was considered to be more appropriate to train men on the basis of their fitness category for duty for service for home or overseas. This meant that there was no longer a requirement for a second line battalion for provision of drafts and in April, 1918, the 2/2nd Battalion the Monmouthshire Regiment ceased to exist with its personnel being posted for service as necessary. Many of these men would have seen service with the 1/2nd Battalion but in general they were sent to wherever there was a shortage of manpower.

Thus ended the service of the 2/2nd Battalion the Monmouthshire Regiment. Most of the officers of the first line battalion had served with the battalion at some time or other and a large number of all ranks who served overseas had either trained with the battalion or had recovered after wounds or sickness while with the battalion. Thus even though it had not served overseas it had played an important part in the war effort and a part which is recognized here.

The history of the 3/2nd Battalion the Monmouthshire Regiment is somewhat similar in that it was raised to provide drafts for the first line battalion in France. Initially it was commanded by Lieut. Col. H.D. Griffiths and Major Broackes and was, until early, 1915 billeted in Pontypool. Following the stay in Pontypool it was then brigaded with the 3rd line of the 1st and 3rd Battalions at Abergavenny throughout the summer of 1915 where they were given a basic training in trench warfare including the digging of a trench system in the vicinity of the castle in the town. In September, 1916 the battalion was moved to Oswestry where it remained until March, 1916 when it was moved to a camp in Whittington.

During the early part of its existence recruits flowed into the battalion and it soon had a strength of over 900 and there was talk of the possibility of forming a unit for service in France. As the casualties on the Western Front increased so did the call for drafts from the first line battalion. By September, 1916, its numbers had been so reduced that there was no further thought of going overseas independently and the battalion was merged with the third line of the other two Monmouthshire battalions under the command of Colonel Blethyn Rees. This combined unit spent a short time in Oswestry before being moved to Kinmel Park where it remained until June 1918. It was then moved to Herne, in Kent, where it remained until demobilization.

Glossary

2nd Lieut.: *2nd Lieutenant.*

AAA : *used in army orders etc. to indicate a break in the wording, like 'stop' used in dictating a sentence.*
AB64: *Army pay book.*
A.D.M.S.: *Assistant Director of Medical Services.*
Adjutant: *officer responsible for the administration of an infantry battalion.*
Anordnungen: *Declaration, the rules laid down for the behaviour of the German population during the early part of the occupation.*

Bangalore Torpedoes : *explosive tubes used to clear a way through barbed wire entanglements.*
Battalion: *unit of infantry made up of companies and usually forming part of a Regiment, during the Great War about a thousand men.*
Bdes.: *Brigades.*
berm : *flat area in trench parapet.*
Boche: *German.*

Brig. Gen.: *Brigadier General*
Brigade : *smallest tactical formation above battalion and usually four battalions.*
'buckshee': *From the Arabic meaning a gift but in this context meaning free.*

Capitation Grant: *the grant made by the government to volunteer rifle units based on the number of efficient soldiers in a unit.*
Capt. : *Captain.*
CE : *Chief Engineer, Engineer's officer at Corps level, often of Brig.Gen. rank*
'coal box': *shell burst from a heavy gun which left a black cloud of smoke.*
C.O.: *Commanding Officer.*
Col.: *Colonel.*
communication trench : *A trench linking the front line to rear areas and other trench systems*
Company: *subdivision of an infantry battalion usually four to a battalion.*
Coy. and Co.: *Terms short for 'Company'*
'comforts': *anything sent from home to the front line soldier to make his life that bit more comfortable.*

Corps: *body of men usually comprising a minimum of two divisions.*

Co. S. Maj. : *Company Sergeant Major.*

Cpl. : *Corporal.*

C.R.E.: *Officer Commanding Royal Engineers at Divisional level usually with the rank of Lieut. Col. or Col..*

C.S.M.: *Company Sergeant Major.*

C.T. : *Communication Trench.*

'cushy': *From the Hindi meaning comfortable or easy.*

DCM : *Distinguished Conduct Medal.*

départements: *Administrative district in France rather like the English county.*

Division and Div. : *large body of men often comprising three brigades and the next largest tactical grouping to a brigade.*

D.O.W.G.H.: *Died of Wounds in German Hands.*

DSO: *Distinguished Service Order*

estaminet : *A small public house or bar*

Field Coy. : *The Field Company was the unit of organisation of the Royal Engineers*

fire bay: *the most forward part of the front line trench, manned in preparation for attack.*

fire step: *the raised portion of the trench floor on which the soldiers stood to fire at the enemy*

flechettes : *from the French for dart as used in the game, in this case steel darts which were dropped from planes on to the troops below.*

F.S.J. : *Field Service Jacket. The normal jacket of the serving soldier in the trenches.*

Georgette : *Code name used by the Germans for one of their attacks which formed part of the Spring Offensive.*

GHQ : *General Headquarters.*

G.O.C. : *General Officer Commanding.*

G.S. waggon: *General Service waggon one of the main means of transport of equipment on the Western Front.*

Hants: *Hampshire Regiment.*

Hindenburg Line: *The English name for the major defensive line behind which the Germans retired in 1917.*

'Hommes 40, Chevaux 8'. : *the words carried on the side of the cattle trucks used for transporting men or horses on the Western Front (40 men, 8 Horses).*

HQ: *Headquarters.*

i/c : *in charge.*

I.G.C. : *Inspector General Lines of Communications.*

'iron ration(s)' : *rations issued to the troops comprising hard biscuits, tinned corned beef and tea and sugar which could only be used under the express direction of a senior officer.*

Kaiserschlacht : *The name by which the Germans knew the Spring Offensive (the Kaiser's Battle).*

K.O.S.B. : *King's Own Scottish Borderers.*

K.O.Y.L.I : *King's Own Yorkshire Light Infantry.*

K.R.R.C.: *King's Royal Rifle Corps.*

K.S.L.I. : *King's Shropshire Light Infantry.*

Lanc. Fus. : *Lancashire Fusiliers.*

L/Cpl. : *Lance Corporal.*

Lieut. : *Lieutenant.*

Lieut. Col. : *Lieutenant Colonel - usually the rank of officer commanding an infantry battalion.*

Lieut. Gen.: *Lieutenant General - Officer Commanding a Corps.*

LMG : *Lewis Machine Gun.*

Lt.: *Lieutenant.*

Lines of Communication: *Rear areas through which all the material for war would travel.*

MC: *Military Cross.*

MD: *Doctor of Medicine - in this case the Medical Officer.*

MM. : *Military Medal.*

MO : *Medical Officer attached to a battalion.*

MSM : *Meritorious Service Medal.*

NCO : *Non Commissioned Officer.*
NFLD(S) : *Newfoundland Regiment or members of that regiment.*

O.R. : *Other Ranks, that is, not officers.*

PH gas helmet : *helmet for protection against gas in the early part of war, an early gas mask.*
parapet: *the raised portion at the front of the trench.*
pavé: *road construction of blocks of stone, or stone setts, used in in France and Belgium at the time of the Great War.*
platoon : *a part of an infantry company, usually four to a company.*
'pledge', the : *signing up for overseas service, or Imperial Service, a requirement before a Territorial soldier could serve overseas.*
pontoon: *temporary bridge of varied construction.*
Pte. : *Private.*
puttees : *from the Hindi for bandage and meaning a long strip of cloth wound spirally around the lower leg to provide support and protection.*

QMS : *Quartermaster Sergeant.*
quartermaster: *battalion officer reponsible for quarters, rations and so on.*

RE : *Royal Engineer.*
RF : *Royal Fusiliers.*
R.I.R. : *Royal Irish Regiment.*
RQMS : *Regimental Quartermaster Sergeant.*
RSM : *Regimental Sergeant Major.*
RTO : *Rail Transport Officer.*
'Red Militia' : *An informal police service set up by the Germans in occupied Cologne.*
revetting : *support of earthworks such as trenches.*

SAA : *small arms ammunition - bullets.*
salient : *a protrusion of the line in to that of the enemy.*
S.B.'s : *stretcher bearers.*
Sgt. : *Sergeant.*

Sher. For.: *Sherwood Foresters, the Notts and Derby Regiment.*
Siegfried Stellung: *the German name for the line that the British called the Hindenburg Line.*
SMLE : *Short, Magazine Lee Enfield the standard British rifle during the Great War.*
smoke helmets : *helmets for protection against gas.*
'Stadt Koln' : *lettering carried on the armbands of the 'Red Militia' meaning City of Cologne.*
Stand To : *the time when the front line was fully manned in preparation for attack and always at dawn and dusk.*
Stokes gun: *a small calibre (3 and 4 inch) trench mortar.*
SWB : *South Wales Borderers.*

T.F. : *Territorial Force.*
Tirailleurs : *French infantry, sharpshooters or skirmishers.*
T.M.B. : *Trench Mortar Battery.*
T.O. : *Transport Officer.*
traverse : *the portion of a trench connecting fire bays.*
Turcos : *French light infantry of Algerian origin; Zouaves.*

U Frames: *support to trench to allow fixing of revetting and trench boards.*

War Diary : *the record of the events of the day maintained by all units throughout the war, in infantry battalions usually the job of the adjutant.*
Worcs : *the Worcestershire Regiment*

VC : *Victoria Cross*
Vermol : *alcohol, possibly slang for Vermouth.*

Zouaves : *French light infantry units of Algerian origin and especially known for their bright, oriental, uniforms; often known to the British troops as 'Turcos'*

Bibliography

Atkinson, C.T. (1931) The History of the South Wales Borderers 1914 - 1918. *The Medici Society.* London.

Baker, A. (1986) The Battle Honours of the British and Commonwealth Armies. *Ian Allan Ltd.* London.

Barrie, A. (1961) War Underground. *Tom Donovan.* London.

Becke, Major A.F. (1935) Order of Battle of Divisions. *HMSO*

Bond of Sacrifice, The. (1992) *Naval and Military Press.* London.

Brett, Capt. G.A. (1933) A History of the 2nd Battalion the Monmouthshire Regiment. *Hughes & Son, The Griffin Press.* Pontypool.

Brown, M. & Seaton, S. (1984) Christmas Truce. *Leo Cooper, Secker & Warburg.* London.

Dixon, J. & Dixon, J. (1990) With Rifle and Pick. *Cwm Press.* Cardiff.

Dudley Ward, C.H. (1988) History of the Welsh Guards. *The London Stamp Exchange Ltd.* London

Edmonds, Brig. Gen. Sir James E. (1987) The Occupation of the Rhineland. *HMSO.*

Falls, C. (1959) The Great War 1914 - 1918. *Longmans.* London.

Farndale, Gen. Sir Martin. (1986) History of the Royal Regiment of Artillery. Western Front 1914 - 18. *The Royal Artillery Institution.* London.

Farrar-Hockley, A.H. (1966) The Somme. *Pan Books.* London.

Gillon, Capt. S. (1925) The Story of the 29th Division. *Nelson.* London.

Grieve, Capt. W.G. & Newman, B. (1936) The Tunnellers. *Herbert Jenkins.* London.

Heare, C.P. Unpublished. The War Diary of Pte. C.P. Heare, No.1927 2nd Mons Battalion July 1913 to March 1919. Held by the South Wales Borderers and Monmouthshire Regiment Museum, Brecon.

Hughes, L.P. & Dixon, J. (1995) 'Surrender Be Damned.' A History of the 1/1st Battalion the Monmouthshire Regiment 1914-18. *Cwm Press.* Caerphilly.

Johnson, B. (Ed.) (1990) A Memoir of the Final Advance 1918. By Sgt. W.G. Sweet. *Stand To.* 30, 13-16 and *Stand To* 36 32-35

Kipling, R. (1997) The Irish Guards in the Great War. The First Battalion. *Spellmount Ltd.* Staplehurst.

Liddell-Hart, B.H. (1970) History of the First World War. *Cassell.* London.

Love, Sgt. C.J. (1933) The War Diary of CSM Cornelius Love DCM. *The Free Press of Monmouthshire.* March to September 1933.

Low, Lieut. Col. G. & Everrett, Col. H.M. (1969) The History of the Royal Monmouthshire Royal Engineers (Militia). *The Griffin Press.* Pontypool.

Magnus, P. (1958) Kitchener. *Murray.* London.

McWilliams, J. & Steel, R.J. (1985) Gas! The Battle for Ypres, 1915. *Vanwell Publishing Ltd.* Ontario.

Medal Rolls Monmouthshire Regiment 1914 Star. Unpublished. Public Records Office. WO329 2482.

Medal Rolls Monmouthshire Regiment 1914-15 Star. Unpublished. Public Records Office. WO329 2862.

Mitchell, Col. T. (1913) History of the Volunteer Movement in Monmouthshire. *Newport and Monmouthshire Newspaper Co. Ltd.* Newport.

Mitchinson, K.W. (1997) Pioneer Battalions in the Great War. Organized and Intelligent Labour. *Leo Cooper.* London

Official History of the War. 1925 Military Operations. France and Belgium. 1914 Vol II.

Official History of the War. 1927 Military Operations. France and Belgium. 1915 Vol I.

Official History of the War. 1928 Military Operations. France and Belgium. 1915 Vol II.

Official History of the War. 1932 Military Operations. France and Belgium. 1916 Vol I.

Official History of the War. 1938 Military Operations. France and Belgium. 1916 Vol II.

Official History of the War. 1940 Military Operations. France and Belgium. 1917 Vol I.

Official History of the War. 1948 Military Operations. France and Belgium. 1917 Vol II.

Official History of the War. 1948 Military Operations. France and Belgium. 1917 Vol III.

Official History of the War. 1935 Military Operations. France and Belgium. 1918 Vol I.

Official History of the War. 1937 Military Operations. France and Belgium. 1918 Vol II.

Official History of the War. 1939 Military Operations. France and Belgium. 1918 Vol III.

Official History of the War. 1947 Military Operations. France and Belgium. 1918 Vol IV.

Official History of the War. 1947 Military Operations. France and Belgium. 1918 Vol V.

Parks, Major E. (1992) Diex Aïx: God Help Us. The Guernseymen Who Marched Away 1914 -1918. *Guernsey Museums and Galleries.*

Parsons, W. D. (1994) Pilgrimage. A guide to the Royal Newfoundland Regiment in World War One. *Creative Publishers.* St. John's, Newfoundland.

Smithers, A.J. (1992) Cambrai. The First Great Tank Battle 1917. *Leo Cooper.* London.

Somerset, W.H.B., Tyler, H.G. & Whitehead, L.D. (1926) On the Western Front. *Sergeant Brothers.* Abergavenny.

Soldiers Died in the Great War 1914 - 1919. (1921) & **Officers Died in the Great War 1914 - 1919** (1919) HMSO. London. (Also CD-ROM Version (1998) by *Naval and Military Press.* London.)

Southey, S. (undated) The Roll of Honour of the Empires Heroes. *Published for private circulation.*

War Diary: 2nd Battalion the Monmouthshire Regiment. Unpublished. Public Records Office. WO 95 2295. (Copies held at the South Wales Borderers and Monmouthshire Regiment Museum, Brecon).

Watson, G. (1996) Militiamen and Sappers. *Brigadier J.H. Hooper, OBE DL, Col. E.D. Smeeden, DL. and Lt.Col. R.J. Pope MBE, TD.* Monmouth.

Westlake, R. (1986) The Territorial Battalions. *Guild Publishing.* London.

Westlake, R. (1994) British Battalions on the Somme 1916. *Leo Cooper.* London.

Westlake, R. (1997) British Battalions in France and Belgium 1914. *Leo Cooper.* London.

Index

317